10283223

Eastern Africa Series

HAWKS & DOVES
IN SUDAN'S
ARMED CONFLICT

Eastern Africa Series

Women's Land Rights & Privatization in Eastern Africa
BIRGIT ENGLERT & ELIZABETH DALEY (EDS)

War & the Politics of Identity in Ethiopia
KJETIL TRONVOLL

Moving People in Ethiopia
ALULA PANKHURST & FRANÇOIS PIGUET (EDS)

Living Terraces in Ethiopia
ELIZABETH E. WATSON

Eritrea
GAIM KIBREAB

Borders & Borderlands as Resources in the Horn of Africa
DEREJE FEYISSA & MARKUS VIRGIL HOEHNE (EDS)

After the Comprehensive Peace Agreement in Sudan
ELKE GRAWERT (ED.)

Land, Governance, Conflict & the Nuba of Sudan
GUMA KUNDA KOMEY

Ethiopia
JOHN MARKAKIS

Resurrecting Cannibals
HEIKE BEHREND

Pastoralism & Politics in Northern Kenya & Southern Ethiopia
GŨNTHER SCHLEE & ABDULLAHI A. SHONGOLO

Islam & Ethnicity in Northern Kenya & Southern Ethiopia
GŨNTHER SCHLEE with ABDULLAHI A. SHONGOLO

Foundations of an African Civilisation
DAVID W. PHILLIPSON

Regional Integration, Identity & Citizenship in the Greater Horn of Africa
KIDANE MENGISTEAB & REDIE BEREKETEAB (EDS)

Dealing with Government in South Sudan
CHERRY LEONARDI

The Quest for Socialist Utopia
BAHRU ZEWDE

Disrupting Territories
JÖRG GERTEL, RICHARD ROTTENBURG & SANDRA CALKINS (EDS)

The African Garrison State
KJETIL TRONVOLL & DANIEL R. MEKONNEN

The State of Post-conflict Reconstruction
NASEEM BADIEY

Gender, Home & Identity
KATARZYNA GRABSKA

Remaking Mutirikwi
JOOST FONTEIN

Lost Nationalism
ELENA VEZZADINI

The Oromo & the Christian Kingdom of Ethiopia
MOHAMMED HASSEN

Darfur
CHRIS VAUGHAN

The Eritrean National Service
GAIM KIBREAB

Ploughing New Ground
GETNET BEKELE

Hawks & Doves in Sudan's Armed Conflict
SUAD M. E. MUSA

Ethiopian Warriorhood
TSEHAI BERHANE-SELASSIE

Land, Migration & Belonging
JOSEPH MUJERE

Land Tenure Security
SVEIN EGE (ED.)

Tanzanian Development
DAVID POTTS (ED.)

Nairobi in the Making
CONSTANCE SMITH

The Crisis of Democratization in the Greater Horn of Africa
KIDANE MENGISTEAB (ED.)

The Mission of Apolo Kivebulaya
EMMA WILD-WOOD

Imperialism and Development
NICHOLAS WESTCOTT

The Struggle for Land and Justice in Kenya
AMBREENA MANJI

Hawks and Doves in Sudan's Armed Conflict

Al-Hakkamat Baggara Women of Darfur

SUAD M. E. MUSA

JAMES CURREY

James Currey
is an imprint of Boydell & Brewer Ltd
www.jamescurrey.com

and of

Boydell & Brewer Inc.
668 Mt Hope Avenue, Rochester, NY 14620-2731 (US)
www.boydellandbrewer.com

First published 2018
Paperback edition 2020

British Library Cataloguing in Publication Data

A catalogue record for this book is available from the British Library

ISBN 978-1-84701-175-6 (James Currey cloth)
ISBN 978-1-84701-265-4 (James Currey paperback)

Typeset in 11 on 12pt Times New Roman with Gill Sans MT display
by Avocet Typeset, Somerton, Somerset TA11 6RT

Dedication

*To my late Father and late Grandmother, Hajja Zahra,
who raised me and made me who I am today*

Contents

List of Illustrations viii
Acknowledgements ix
Glossary xi
Abbreviations xiv
Note on Transliteration xv

Introduction: Conflict in Darfur and the Role of Rural Darfuri Women 1

1 Ethnicity and Administration in Darfur 9

2 Conflict in Darfur: Causes and Implications 30

3 Al-Hakkamat Women 46

4 Local Inter-ethnic Conflicts 68

5 Government and Racial Assimilation of Ethnic Groups 96

6 Liaising with Government 115

7 New Duties and Obligations 131

8 Roles in Peace and Reconciliation 150

9 Urban Identity and Social Change 167

10 Conclusion 182

Appendix: Darfur Chronology, 1445–2017 193

Bibliography 197
Index 207

Illustrations

Map

1.1 Sudan with Darfur borders 11

Figures

0.1 Al-Hakkamat network of roles and relationships 7
5.1 The interplay of the attributes of political influence of women in conflict and peace contexts 113

Photographs

1.1 A woman preparing land for the farming season, 1995 27
3.1 Hakkamah from Rezeiqat with a stick used as a sign of her authority 53
4.1 Al-Hakkamah singing at a wedding party; Baggari men firing their rifles in merriment 73
8.1 Six Baggari Hakkamat performing at a peace festival, 2014 158

Tables

0.1 Consonants in Darfuri Baggara Arabic xv
0.2 Vowels in Darfuri Baggara Arabic xvi
1.1 Enrolment in primary and secondary education in Darfur 1999/2000 compared with Northern and Central Sudan and with Khartoum 26
1.2 Medical provision in Darfur compared with Northern and Central Sudan and with Khartoum, 2000 26
2.1 'Martyrs' during the first twelve years of the NIF's reign 43
4.1 Examples of ethnic conflicts in which al-Hakkamat were engaged 72
4.2 Examples of Hakkamat nicknames 92
5.1 Sudan ruling systems between 1821 and 2016 98
7.1 Hakkamat tried at Nyala Court, South Darfur (2002–3) 140
9.1 The effects of government liaison with al-Hakkamat 173

Acknowledgements

The primary data used for writing this book is collected from Darfur at a time fraught with risks and precarious security even though the Darfur Peace Agreement (DPA) had just been signed in Abuja. Peace dividends were not immediately forthcoming and the mere talking about the conflict was still risky. I was lucky in such a tense environment to find men and women who were so excited about my topic that they readily helped in facilitating my fieldwork in ways I could not have imagined. I am hugely indebted and thankful to those brave and generous people – family members, in-laws, colleagues, friends and formal and informal gatekeepers. I am very grateful indeed to the people who kindly volunteered time and effort, and consented to provide information in such awkward times and circumstances.

I am also most grateful to Professor Donna Pankhurst, Bradford University, for her tireless and shrewd advice, help and guidance. I am grateful, too, to Professor Abdelsalam N Hamad for his insightful comments and encouragement. I also thank the anonymous reviewers whose comments have substantially enriched the content of this book. I am grateful, too, to the Gordon Memorial College Trust Fund for their financial support that made the study possible. Special thanks are also aptly due to my publishers James Currey, led by Jaqueline Mitchell, Lynn Taylor and Belinda Cunnison who guided me through uncharted territory with the utmost patience, expertise and professionalism.

I would also like to thank Adam Abel, Kareem Daggash and Ibrahim Abbakar at the state Ministry of Culture and Information and Social Affairs and Ahmad al-Mahdi Jowah and Mohamed Salih at Nyala Radio and TV. Thanks also due to Dr Mahmoud Adam Daoud, a Lecturer at Nyala University, and to his colleague, the late Ali Noah, Chairperson of the Union of Folklore and Heritage. My appreciation extends to Abdelrahman Dabakah from the Bani Helba Nazir family and El-Nour Daud Khair Allah, a resource person in the Baggara folklore – all in South Darfur state.

There are also my lovely young female relatives in Sudan, Sujood Salih, Aasma Mustafa and Manahil Babikir, who dedicated their time to looking after my then 18-month old daughter, Hadiya Adam. My gratitude also extends to other relatives, friends and colleagues, in al-Fashir, Nyala, Khartoum and Manchester, who are far too many to name individually. I must however mention you, Abdeldin Adam Mahmoud, not just for your generous and wonderful hospitality and help during my stay in Nyala, but also for the follow up with many issues afterwards to enable me to successfully accomplish my fieldwork. Special thanks go to Imad Shutta who accompanied me during some of my information-gathering trips and followed up with further information and updates. I am hugely indebted to their families, too. I would also like to thank the late El-Sadiq Babikir for his sympathy during the fieldwork.

Last but not least, my great heart-felt appreciation and thanks to my husband and daughter whose selfless support, love and compassion have sustained my drive and patience to complete this book.

Glossary

ʾaʿrāf	Local tribal customs, regulations and conventions used in *judiyah* to settle disputes between and across tribes. ʾaʿrāf are also known as *rākūbah*, which literally means an umbrella/shelter.
Ageed (pl. Augada)	A tribal military commander, usually leading fighters from one of the clans of the tribe
Ageed al-Augada	The chief Ageed, just like a commander general in modern armies
Ageed al-Shoosha	As Ageed al-Augada
Ajaweed (sing. *Ajwadi*)	Refers to the members who form the conventional institution for conflict resolution by serving as mediators. Both words can be titles for the group and individuals. Unlike titles, such as Nazir, Omda, etc, these are temporary and not hierarchical titles.
Amir	Prince
Baggara	Cattle raisers/herders, Arab tribes of Darfur and Kordofan
Baramkah (sing. *Barmaki*)	*Baramkah* (sing. *Barmaki*) is a group of local men with expertise in folkloric arts some of whom may be poets (similar to *Hadday*, the male folk poet counterpart of Hakkamah).
Boshan	A type of chivalrous poetry focusing on horsemen
Cadal	A folk dance
Dar	Tribal homeland
Darb l-marʿūb	Footprints of the terrified
Eid	Muslim festival
Emara (pl. *emarat*)	An emirate, a small native administrative unit, encompassing or supposed to encompass a tribal *Dar*. The *emara* policy granted land in *Dar* Masalit to Chadian Arabs.
Faqir	A local Muslim scholar/teacher

Fartūk	A rope made from palm leaves, used to scare away birds
Faza'	Communal solidarity gathering, normally to recover stolen animals
Fursan (sing. *Faris*)	Horsemenfighters
Gaydoomah	A folk dance
al-Gidairee	A folk dance
al-Harimah	A folk dance
Idd al-Fursan (a new name for the town of Idd al-Ghanam)	The Wells of Horsemen
Idd al-Ghanam	The Wells of Goats
Iiya basi	Queen Mother/First Lady
Iiya kuuri	A premier's wife
Iraij	A folk dance
Jamal Ragad	A folk dance
Janjawiid	Rogue armed horsemen of predominantly Arab composition
Judiyah	Mediation of local people to solve a problem
Khalwa (pl. *khalawi*)	Local Islamic schools run by a *Faqir*
al-Katim	Folk dance
Khail	Horses
Khashum bait	A clan
Mada	An open dance courtyard
Maraheel (sing. *murhal*)	Seasonal migratory routes for nomadic pastoralists through the lands of settled farmers
Masar (pl. *masarat*)	Same as *maraheel*
Mayram (pl. *Mayarim*)	A princess
Murhakah	A flat stone used by women for grinding grains
Murhal (pl. *marahil*)	A social and administrative migratory route for the nomadic pastoralists to navigate their paths through lands of settled farmers.
Nafir	A cooperative gathering to perform voluntary work for individuals, e.g. harvesting their plot or community projects, e.g. building a school.
Nazir (pl. Nuzzar)	Title of the supreme tribal chief in the tribal administrative hierarchy of Arab tribes

Nuba	Tribes especially in southern Kordofan but used pejoratively in the context of the war in Darfur to mean a slave.
al-Nuggarah	A folk dance
Omda (pl. Omad)	The title of a tribal chief who ranks second in the tribal administration hierarchy
Omodiya (pl. *Omodiyat*)	Chieftainship (native administration)
Rākūbah	An umbrella/shelter; symbolically, a set of tribal conventions/regulations
Sheikh	The title of a tribal chief who ranks third in the tribal administration hierarchy
al-Sheikha (pl. al-Sheikhat)	The title of a woman who has the customary authority of organising women in the neighbourhood
Tobe	A saree-like Sudanese women's national dress, 4.5 metres in length
Tora Bora	A reference to militias of African tribes in Darfur, especially Fur militias
Umm Jekkay	A folk dance
Wadi	A small stream
Zihba	Horse ornaments, especially for the bridle

Abbreviations

CAP	Comprehensive Advocacy Project
CPA	Comprehensive Peace Agreement
DPA	Darfur Peace Agreement
DUP	Democratic Unionist Party
H/S	Hakkamah/Sheikha
JEM	Justice and Equality Movement
MCI	Ministry of Culture and Information
NCP	National Congress Party
NIF	National Islamic Front
PDF	Popular Defence Forces
PIM	Popular Information and Media
PPF	Popular Police Force
SLM	Sudan Liberation Movement
SPLA	Sudan People's Liberation Army
SPLM	Sudan People's Liberation Movement
SWU	Sudanese Women's Union
UAF	Union of Art and Folklore
UHS	Union of Hakkamat and Sheikhah

Note on Transliteration

The symbols used for transliteration are shown in Tables 0.1 and 0.2, the former showing consonants and the latter vowels. A notable difference in pronunciation between Darfuri Baggara Arabic and *fuṣḥa* is that the uvular *qāf* /q/ in *fuṣḥa* is invariably pronounced as a velar /g/. Where the source transliterated is spoken /g/ is used, but if written, the /q/ is used. Proper nouns are romanised and, for popular names, popular spellings are used, e.g. *Muhammad* is also written *Mohammed* and *Mohamed*, as and when the latter two spellings are preferred by the authors themselves. Also, romanisation was preferred in the text to transliteration but the latter was used for all cited poems. The definite article is always written *al* even when assimilated in pronunciation into the following letter, e.g. *al-Tiʿīshī* as opposed to *at-Tiʿīshī*. *Tā marbūṭah* is written as /h/ or /t/ depending on whether it is paused at or followed by a voiced sound.

Table 0.1 Consonants in Darfuri Baggara Arabic

	Labial	*Dental*	*Palatal*	*Velar*	*Pharyngeal*	*Glottal*
Stop	b (ب)	t (ت	ṭ (ط)	k (ك)		ʾ(أ)
		d (د)		g (ق)		
Nasal	m (م)	n (ن)				
Fricative	f (ف)	th (ث)	ẓ (ظ)	kh (خ)	ḥ (ح)	h (ه)
		dh (ذ)		gh (غ)	ʿ (ع)	
		ḍ (ض)				
Affricate			j (ج)			
Sibilant		S (س)	sh (ش)			
		ṣ (ص)				
		z (ز)				
Lateral		l (ل)				
Trill		r (ر)				
Glide	w (و)		y (ي)			

(*Sources*: Caton (1990, pp. 271–3); www.mcgill.ca/islamicstudies/students/arabic_unicode_font/; www.muslim.org/english-quran/a-translit.pdf; http://transliteration.eki.ee/pdf/Arabic_2.2.pdf.)

Table 0.2 Vowels in Darfuri Baggara Arabic

	Front	*Central*	*Back*
High	i (kasrah, as i in *pin*)		u (short ḍammah, as in *put*)
	ī (long kasrah, as ee in *deep*)		ū (long ḍammah, as oo in *moot*)
Mid	e		o
Low		a (fatḥah, as a in *tab*)	
		ā (long fatḥah, as ā in *father*)	
Diph-thongs	ey (shortened form of *ay*)	ay (fatḥah before *yā*)	oy
		aw (fatḥah before *waw*)	ow

(*Sources*: As Table 0.1) Both tables were adapted from: Caton (1990: 271–3)
http://www.mcgill.ca/islamicstudies/students/arabic_unicode_font/
http://www.muslim.org/english-quran/a-translit.pdf
http://transliteration.eki.ee/pdf/Arabic_2.2.pdf

Introduction: Conflict in Darfur and the Role of Rural Darfuri Women

Darfur is the westernmost region of Sudan and it extends over an area of approximately 500,000 square kilometres. Since the split of Sudan into two countries in 2011, Darfur remains the largest region of the Republic of Sudan. Like the seceding Southern Sudan region, it has also suffered prolonged armed conflict and bitter civil strife for decades, the most violent being the recent Darfuri insurgency against the National Congress Party government in Sudan. This insurgency started in early 2003 and has continued to date although active insurgency has subsided especially following the most recent battles in which the insurgents suffered heavy losses.[1]

Like those of their southern counterparts, Darfur insurgencies were triggered by the domestic political approach to distributing power and wealth in the country. Using this approach, the riverine ruling and governing elites pursued discriminatory policies whereby the central and northern regions were favoured, leading to their economic domination and cultural hegemony being solidified to the disadvantage and negligence of the vast majority of the peripheral regions.[2] The insurgents had seen a succession of peaceful lobbying and activism either unanswered and/or dubbed racist or subnational (geographic), which left them with no other option but to take up arms in order to seek out a just share of the wealth and power of the country, and end the patronising and discriminatory approaches and policies.

The independent Sudanese central government did not take into account the possibility that peaceful lobbying could change into boisterous and violent trends at a time when simple pre-emptive constitutionally mandated measures could have been put in place to enable justice and equality as requested by the activists (Khalid, 2009, p. 39). In fact, the current central

[1] See 'Sudanese army, SLM-MM in fierce fighting in Darfur', *Sudan Tribune*. Available at: <https://www.sudantribune.com/spip.php?iframe&page=imprimable&id_article=62509> [accessed May 2017].

[2] For instance, Arabic and Islamic programmes monopolise the national radio and television, local languages and cultural manifestations of most of the society are seldom presented. Educational, health and development programmes and projects are concentrated in the irrigated and mechanised agricultural subsectors, which are owned and managed by personnel from the riverine centre of the country (Yongo-Bure, 2009, pp. 68–71).

government rejected the activists' demands outright, and substituted condemnation for persuasion, thus refusing from the beginning to engage in dialogue and negotiation in order to redress grievances and settle differences. This approach inescapably pushed the peaceful activists to lurch further into a fully armed struggle by 2003. Systematic attacks were then launched on government strategic assets such as al-Fashir airport, which were then met with a vicious government onslaught that killed and devastated vast populations in the rural conflict zones.

In this war, more than two million persons are estimated to have ended up as internally displaced people (IDPs) and refugees across borders and the death toll reached more than 200,000. People suffered horrendous human rights abuses and gender-based violence, including mass rape. This inhumane scene in Darfur beckoned the United Nations' Humanitarian Coordinator in Sudan at the time to describe it as the 'the world's greatest humanitarian crisis' (Kapila, cited in Nolen, 2005). The situation provoked wide international condemnation and massive movements of human rights institutions to end the violence and enact justice.

Their efforts culminated in the issuance in 2009 of an arrest warrant[3] issued by the International Criminal Court (ICC) for Sudanese President al-Bashir, for the war crimes committed. In waging this war, the government used tribal and ethnic groups in Darfur, and their conventional defence institutions, which eventually pit Darfuri inhabitants against each other and shattered the social harmony and the mediation frameworks they had had for centuries. The disastrous effects of the conflict have been classified differently by different reporters, for instance, as 'ethnic cleansing', 'slaughter ... more than just a conflict' and 'genocide',[4] but their cruelty has been recognised by all (El-Battahani, 2009, p. 43).

Local, regional and international institutions such as the African Union (AU) and the United Nations (UN), as well as human rights institutions and activists, not only sought justice through the ICC but also rallied for instant negotiation and reconciliation, despite the challenges. Nevertheless, the situation deteriorated further as sporadic incidents of violent confrontation between the two parties continued relentlessly (ibid.). By this time, Darfur had become quite overwhelmed by the precarious security situation and fragile peace. Alongside this main conflict between the insurgencies and the government, other armed conflicts also erupted among the local populations of Darfuri tribes and ethnic groups. These conflicts are not new, though they were limited before Sudanese independence in 1956. But they started to develop on a dramatic scale in the aftermath of the environmental crisis of the late 1960s, and have become vigorous and widespread since the 1980s.

This has been quite noticeable from the estimates, which show that since the 1970s Darfur has witnessed more than 80 per cent of the tribal

[3] See online: International Criminal Court. Available at: <https://www.icc-cpi.int/en_menus/icc/structure>.

[4] Genocide is defined as state-organised mass murder and crimes against humanity characterised bythe intention of the rulers to exterminate individuals because they belong to a particular national, ethnic, racial or religious group (Scherrer, 1999, pp. 56–7).

and ethnic armed conflicts experienced in Sudan, in which almost all the tribes and ethnic groups in Darfur have been involved (Bashar, 2013, p. 80). The trend of these conflicts has increased every decade since the 1960s. The exact number of conflict incidents is unknown; however, the reconciliation attempts give some indication of the level of their escalation.

It has been recorded that two conferences were held between 1924 and 1969, four between 1970 and 1979, thirteen between 1980 and 1989, fourteen conferences during the period from 1990 to 1999; and from 2000 to 2002, there were eleven reconciliation conferences (Mohamed, 2003b, p. 41; Bashar, 2013, p. 81). With the starting of the second Darfuri insurgency in 2003, the escalation reached a climax when thirty-seven conferences were held during the period between 2003 and 2009 (Mohammed, 2009, pp. 82–3), which nearly equals the total number of all the conferences held in the region in the period from 1924 to 2003. These were government-sponsored conferences held to settle relatively large-scale armed conflicts, and they usually involved personnel from outside the social milieu of the tribes. The government did not organise these conferences until a series of violent incidents had taken place. Some serious incidents were resolved locally and therefore not included in the tally. This is because rural communities used to have their own mechanisms and frameworks for effective reconciliation and conflict resolution, which have been incapacitated since the dissolution of the tribal administration in Sudan in 1971 (Mohammed, 2003b, p. 40).

Simple disputes can easily transform into large-scale aggression that transcends the local management capacity of the presently handicapped frameworks. The main battlefield of these conflicts has normally been rural vicinities where tribes employ their conventional defence organisations to fight, whilst the ruling and governing elites turn a blind eye most of the time. When the elites intervene, they often side with one party against the other in a process that is usually intended to claim favours later on, when they will utilise the parties they have supported as subservient clients serving their own vested interests. The ruling elites have thus used the two forms of conflict in Darfur as a divide-and-rule tactic, or divide-and-destroy, to destabilise the insurgents (Khalid, 2009, p. 39). The latter was illustrated by the government's approach of mobilising support along 'racial' perceptions and by incorporating Arab militias, including the most notorious paramilitary forces, the Janjawiid, into a counter-insurgency strategy (El-Battahani, 2009, p. 43).

Violent armed conflict in Darfur thus appears as just another instance of the protracted brutal African wars that are often fought either between insurgencies and central governments and/or between tribes/ethnic groups – indeed, instigated, more or less, by similar structural causes and triggers. Nonetheless, the motives behind these conflicts are complicated and intertwined, and it is important to investigate and comprehend their historical roots. Most of this history concerns the relationship between the tribes and ethnic groups, and the state's political and economic approaches to administering land, land-based resources and people.

These are the main constituents of the people's power relationships, and women have been part and parcel of these relationships.

There is vast analysis in the literature on the conflict in Darfur on various stakeholders involved in these conflicts, including the perpetrators and the victims (see for instance El-Battahani, 2009, pp. 43–67; Mohamed, 1998, pp. 33–68). The portrayal of Darfuri rural women in these conflicts, however, has shown them all as mere victims. Though these accounts may be genuine and authentic, I perceive that this image as inadequate and does not reflect the whole picture. The perception of women as permanent victims also explains their persistent exclusion from reconciliation processes and equally offers a justification for the persistent inability to project sustainable peace in Darfur. In other words, the gender aspect of these conflicts has been overlooked and not fairly explored, either in conflict management or in peace resettlement. Can women be seen as aggressors as much as their male counterparts during raging conflicts, but estranged from the quest for peace on the pretext that they are vulnerable victims? The persistent failure of reconciliation initiatives in Darfur, which were mediated locally, regionally or internationally, could be attributed, by and large, to this omission of women. The intention of this work is to explore these issues with reference to al-Hakkamat women (sing. Hakkamah) of the Baggara[5] tribes in Darfur.

This book introduces al-Hakkamat and investigates and clarifies the roles they undertake in general but especially during armed conflicts. It presents al-Hakkamat women as constituting a continued legacy of those female figures who assumed powerful positions in traditional African authority and leadership systems, e.g. the female spirit mediums in Zimbabwe who appear to have been disempowered by colonial and post-colonial powers. It argues that al-Hakkamat women are a vivid manifestation of the ability of rural women to exercise agency and influence in favour of their tribes and to strike a balance in gender power relationships in favour of the female category in their social milieu. They are morally obliged to come to the rescue of their tribes and to contribute proactively to maintain their dignity and pride, especially during turbulent times, where conflict events pose the most appealing way to uphold their status. Their involvement often makes the wars between tribes in Darfur quite frequent and more devastating.

The mutual connection of al-Hakkamat with their own tribes has become subject to exploitation by the ruling NCP, formerly the National Islamic Front (NIF), when they mobilised al-Hakkamat on ethnic and racial pretensions, and threw them in the midst of violent events to fulfil sinister manifestations that could enhance the government's position in the civil wars in the country. Their engagement has exacerbated

[5] The label 'Baggara', cattle herders, is a collective word used to describe a variety of cattle-breeding tribes of mainly Arab origin who live in South Darfur and Kordofan. They are nomads and their grazing routes take them into the South Sudan province of Bahr al Ghazal; sometimes they reach as far south as the Central African Republic (Prunier, 2007, p. 166).

the deadly atrocities inflicted on rural populations in Darfur and Sudan at large. By using al-Hakkamat as a means for an immediate benefit, the government appeared to have ignored the strategic social harmony that a government should seek, reinforce and maintain among its citizens.

By performing this and similar other roles, al-Hakkamat have proved that women do not always stand out as victims of violent armed conflicts, as often portrayed, though victimisation certainly exists. Women can equally become devastating agents of aggression worthy of the description as 'hawks' of violence and aggression during armed conflict, rather than as 'doves' of peace. This is not an arbitrary portrayal, however; their unfolding manifestations and experiences in the conflict witnessed in Darfur and Sudan at large are astoundingly adequate testimony, as revealed in this book.

This position of al-Hakkamat has developed over a long period of history and many factors have contributed to their continuation and thriving. These factors include what is historically known of Darfuri rural women as economically and socially significant actors.[6] They acquired this position through the nature of the political economy and gender division of labour, which have granted women access rights to production resources and personal autonomy. They exercise these rights to contribute to the wellbeing of families and communities. Presumably, this has enabled them to exercise agency and power and to force their presence in a political domain that is conventionally recognised as belonging to men. They are not perceived as passive and/or inactive in matters of importance to their communities.

My social background as a Darfuri and my professional experience of working for over a decade in gender and development with government and international non-governmental organisations (INGOs), such as Oxfam, as well as my observations about the social and cultural context of Darfuri rural communities, suggest that this position will not only continue but will become more consolidated with the deteriorating security situation and increasingly precarious livelihoods in the areas.

But the most significant stimulus was the role the Fur sultanate (1445–1916) played with respect to women's roles and status in society. For over four centuries, the Fur sultans facilitated and cemented the position of women in the royal office and gave them titles with powerful roles, such as *iiya basi*, the queen mother (Shuqayr, 1981, p. 178). Besides, women were often consulted in matters of concern for the state. The trickle-down effects of this position of royal women, together with the general attitudes of the sultanate towards women, have resulted in a conducive position for all women in Darfur, both African and Arab, and enabled those who have power within their tribes to continue to exercise it without fear.

[6] For instance, the women of the sedentary Masalit tribe enjoy land ownership and autonomy in farm production, consumption and distribution (Kapteijns, 1985, p. 35). Al-Tunisi, who visited Darfur during 1803–11, was quite surprised by the level of women's mixing with men and that men would not do anything in the absence of women, including public activities (Al-Tunisi, 1965, p. 93).

Hence, we find that within all the tribes in Darfur, there are always women who are locally legitimised to exercise power to make their voice heard and to represent the female community. These are mainly the Sheikhat (sing. Sheikha) among the African tribes, and al-Hakkamat among the Arab tribes. Al-Hakkamat, in particular, have far-reaching abilities to influence their communities in both peaceful and turbulent times, more so than the Sheikhat have.

In the aftermath of the conquest of Darfur by the Anglo-Egyptian forces (1916), the colonial authorities estranged the titles of the royal women and their associated vested power from the native administration structure they put in place, whilst preserving the men's titles. Not being the central focus of the invaders, the title al-Hakkamat, as a powerful female title and position in their communities, has been preserved together with its associated roles in both the social and political domains of Arab societies in Darfur, particularly among the Baggara of South Darfur. With the escalation of armed conflict in Darfur since the 1970s, the reputation of al-Hakkamat rippled out quite dramatically and has become an integral part of the violence that engulfed the region till now (2017, as this research concludes). Their contribution to the violence witnessed in Darfur overrides, in the view of this study, all expectations and knowledge about women as mere victims of wars and aggression.

Al-Hakkamat work within a well specified framework of roles and a network of relationships within the local tribal setting. With the environmental, social and political changes experienced by rural communities and by al-Hakkamat per se, this network has extended to connect with forces outside the local village boundaries and tribal territories to encompass regional and national institutions of power in a more challenging urban setting. Their relationships are framed around certain duties, activities and obligations, which together constitute the main guidance for al-Hakkamat to make choices and exercise agency, as shown in the model of roles and relationships of al-Hakkamat (Figure 0.1).

In breaking a stereotyped analysis of women that presents them as mere victims of conflicts and aggression, this book explores in depth, perhaps for the first time, the political involvement of rural Darfuri al-Hakkamat women as potential or real actors, sometimes in agitating for and igniting conflict, and at other times in settling disputes. It aims to unveil the overlooked and obscured agency and political influence of this category of women, and their subtle, yet conscious, contribution to these conflicts. It also explores their positive endeavours and self-censorship in the interests of reconciliation and peace resettlement. By so doing, it proves that a contextualised gender analysis framework is essential for objective conflict resolution and sustainable reconciliation, and emphasises the need to bring women's political experience to the fore. The book tends to fill a considerable gap of knowledge on gender power relationships in Darfur and Sudan and in Africa at large, in the context of armed conflict, which may be relevant and beneficial to the debate on women in conflict and in building peace beyond Sudan.

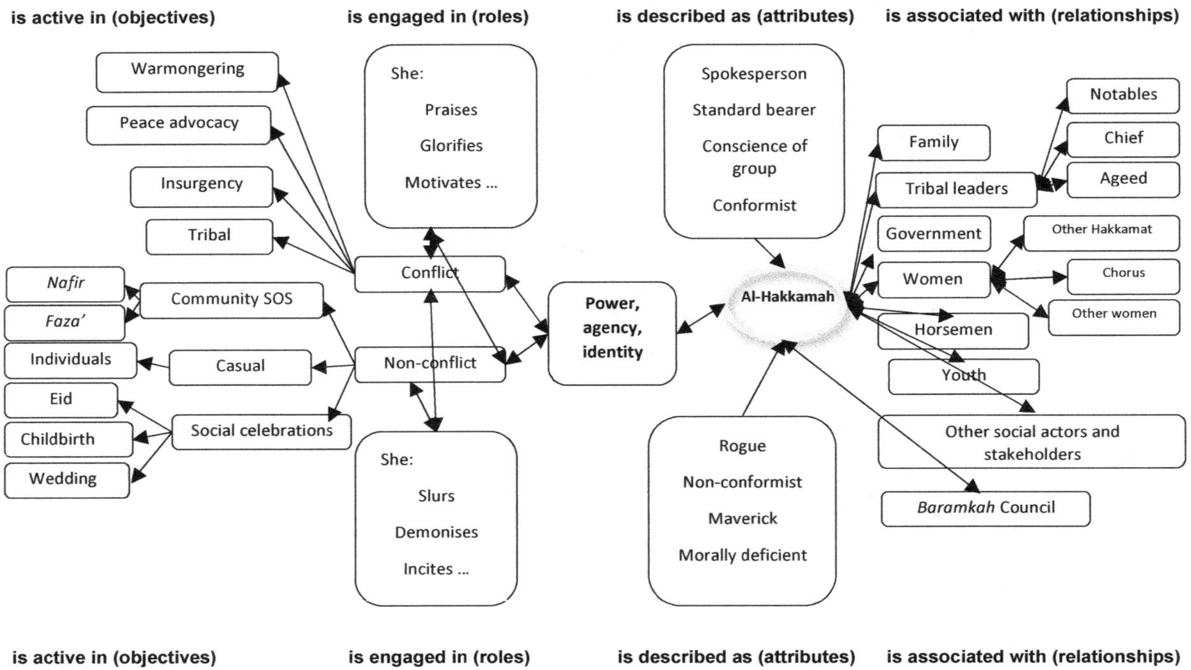

Figure 0.1 Al-Hakkamat network of roles and relationships
(*Source:* Author)

METHODOLOGY

The book is based on qualitative research conducted in 2006 in the towns of Nyala and al-Fashir, respectively the capitals of South and North Darfur regions of Sudan, and followed up until 2016. South Darfur is densely populated by Baggara and therefore most of the research period was spent in Nyala where Baggara Arabs, and their notable Hakkamat, usually congregate from various parts of the state. Seventy-two men and women of various ages participated in individual and in-depth group interviews. They were classified along seven sets of categories: al-Hakkamat, tribal leaders, politicians, government officials, academics, non-governmental organisation (NGO) workers and a loose category of social actors. However, apart from al-Hakkamat, most of the informants were found to belong to more than one category, thus making the categories more overlapping. Most of the informants were residents in rural areas who would come intermittently to Nyala town for social and economic transactions and sometimes for political purposes. There were also informants who eventually chose to settle in town but still maintained intimate connections with the village/camp contexts.

Oral and recorded recitations/performances of al-Hakkamat have been collected, documented and analysed. Live performances of al-Hakkamat were observed on different occasions. The analysis was guided by concepts of tribe, ethnicity, women's agency, power and identity and the interplay between these concepts was investigated in reference to the involvement of al-Hakkamat Baggara rural women in armed conflict in Darfur since 1970s. The study was conducted with complete observance of and compliance with the relevant research ethics of confidentiality, privacy and no harm.

1

Ethnicity and Administration in Darfur

Ethnicity and administration in Sudan are complex and interwoven issues and they form the foundations of its socio-economic and political power relationships. The ethnic composition in Sudan is mixed and diverse and its administration has been influenced by the historical approaches of various ruling systems of the kingdoms that formed Sudan and the colonial and national regimes that have ruled the country. Darfur society is representative of the wider society in Sudan, but it has unique characteristics in its ethnic composition and administrative system. The latter is an extension of the Fur sultanate's administration, in which tribes and tribal territories were significant pillars. This chapter outlines the historical complexity around identity in the country, the political approaches based on ethnic and racial discrimination that were embraced by the rulers who have governed Sudan, and how these have been manifested in the administration and ethnic relationships in Darfur since it was annexed to Sudan in 1917.

GEOGRAPHY AND POPULATION

Darfur (*Dar*Fur – the homeland of the Fur tribe) was founded as an independent Fur sultanate (1445–1916). It was annexed to Sudan in 1917 when the last sultan, Ali Dinar (1889–1916), was defeated by the Anglo-Egyptian condominium administration. The sultanate was the heir of the prior kingdoms of the Daju and Tunjur African tribes, which today represent minor ethnic groups in terms of both population and political weight. In the mid-fifteenth century, the Keira Fur sultanate was established by sultan Suleiman Solung (1445–76), purportedly born to a Fur mother and an Arab father, who came down from Jebel Marrah to extend the sultanate to the plains east of the Jebel (Shuqayr, 1981, p. 150). Darfur was also governed respectively by the Turco-Egyptian invaders (1874–81) and the Mahdiyya (1881–98), led by the Sudanese cleric, Mohamed Ahmad al-Mahdi.

Modern Sudan is thus an amalgamation of several adjacent, often warring kingdoms that existed in Sudan in the precolonial period, e.g. the Fung in the centre, Darfur in the west and other numerous kingdoms and sultanates in the east and the south. For more than a century, until 2011, Sudan remained the largest country in Africa and the Middle East, with a total area estimated at 2,505,813 square kilometres. Following the choice made by the overwhelming majority of the south Sudanese in a referendum held on 9–15 January 2011 (UNDP, 2017), the country split into two states: North Sudan, now known as the Republic of Sudan, and South Sudan, the world's one hundred and ninety-third country, referred to as the State of South Sudan. The Republic of Sudan is now located in the Horn of Africa and occupies an area of 1,882,000 square kilometres, which still makes it Africa's third largest country.

The Republic of Sudan is currently organised federally into eighteen administrative states. Greater Darfur (made up of five states) is the westernmost and the biggest region, and extends over an area of approximately 500,000 square kilometres (Burr and Collins, 2008, p. 227). Whilst the country shares international borders with seven countries, Darfur neighbours five of these – Egypt in the north, until recent stealth border changes, Libya in the northwest, Chad in the west, the Central African Republic in the southwest and the Republic of South Sudan in the southeast (see Map 1.1). Inside Sudan, Darfur neighbours Kordofan region in the east and the northern region in the northeast. It is separated from the Nile Valley by the region of Kordofan.

These borders break through tribes and ethnic groups. For instance, both the Zaghawa and Arabs of Darfur have affiliates in Chad; the Beja of Eastern Sudan has tribal links with Ethiopia and Eritrea, whereas the Nubians in the north have affiliates in south Egypt. It follows that people from neighbouring countries often cross the borders in times of crisis, into the adjacent regions of Sudan to take refuge among Sudanese relatives and affiliated groups. This is evident in the unimpeded entry of refugees into Sudan from Ethiopia, Eritrea, the Democratic Republic of Congo and Chad, as well as reverse movements by Sudanese refugees fleeing their country for similar reasons, particularly from and into Darfur.

Sudan displays a wide range of climatic conditions, and although it lies entirely within the Savannah belt, most of its areas are characterised by low rainfall. The amount and distribution of rainfall decreases as we move from south to north, where a semi-desert climate extends towards the borders with Egypt and Libya. At the centre, the River Nile runs across the country from south to north and provides a rich source of economic activities at the centre of Sudan, whereas the Red Sea extends over around 550 miles of the eastern coast, a position electing Sudan as a bridge between Africa and the Arabian Peninsula (UNDP, 2017). These climatic variations are reflected in the social and livelihood systems of people, most being farmers who follow either pastoral or agro-pastoral forms of socio-economic activity.

Darfur region, on the other hand, is climatically divided into three main zones based on the amount of rainfall and soil type. The dry zone in the north (semi-desert), where the annual rainfall reaches 300 millimetres, is populated by Abbala groups, and nomadic Zaghawa who raise camels as a method of livelihood. The central zone (Savannah) is

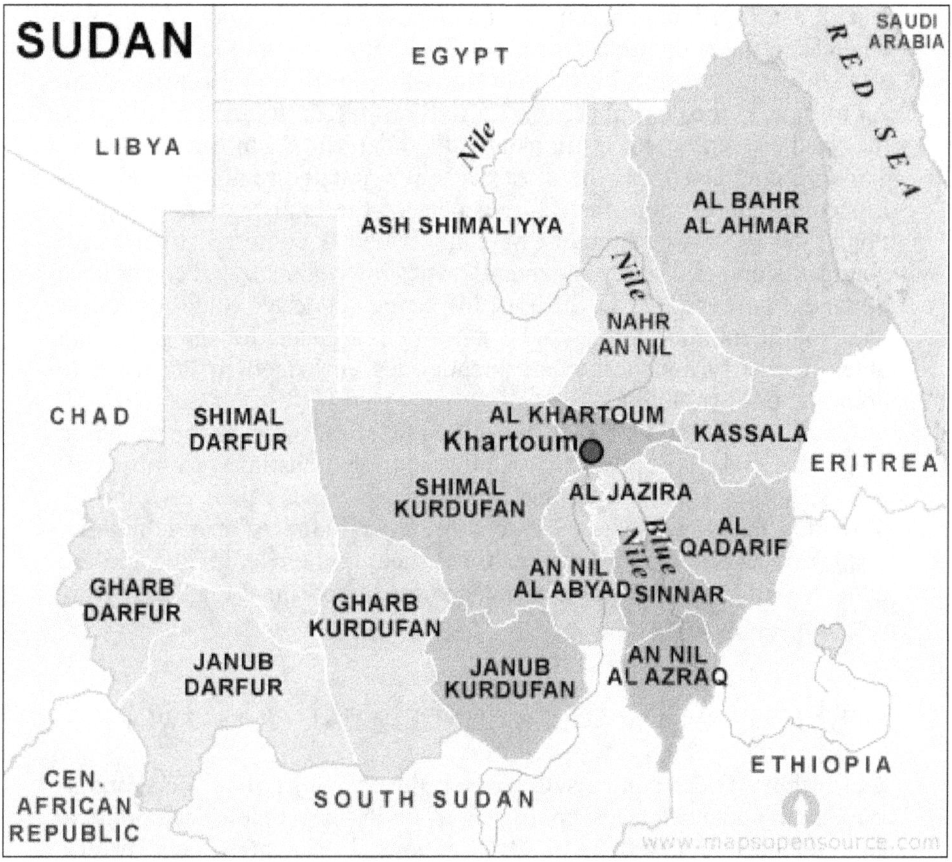

Map 1.1 Sudan with Darfur borders
(*Source:* www.mapsopensource.com/sudan-map-black-and-white.html)

semi-fertile sandy land (*goz*), where the average annual rainfall reaches about 500 millimetres and therefore farming productivity is low. It is populated by agro-pastoralists who farm and practise animal husbandry. The semi-humid zone (rich Savannah) extends in the south and south-west areas, where the soil is more fertile and the average annual rainfall reaches between 800 and 900 millimetres – a quantity quite adequate for farming and cattle herding (Prunier, 2007, pp. 2–3). At its centre stretch the series of Jebel Marrah (the Hills of Marrah), a mountainous area that was the seat of the early Fur kingdom, the most fertile land in Darfur in both soil and rainfall (Mohamed, 1998, pp. 33–69).

Even though agricultural activity and vegetation cover are usually largely affected by variations in rainfall, agriculture constituted the backbone of Sudan's economy for a long period of time, before Sudan became an oil exporter in 1999. But the split of Sudan into two states has significantly reduced oil revenues to the North, as more than 80 per cent of Sudan's oil reserves are located in the new State of South Sudan (UNDP, 2017).

The estimated population of Sudan post-secession was 42,181,593,[1] whereas in the population census estimate before the split in 2009, it was 39.15 million; notably 5.7 million in Kordofan, 4 million in Eastern Sudan, 7.5 million in the central region, 1.5 million in Khartoum, 3.1 million in the Northern region, 8.4 million in South Sudan and 8.5 million in Darfur. This presents Darfur as the most densely populated region in Sudan as it accommodates more than 20 per cent of the total Sudanese population. These census estimates were nevertheless contested by Darfuri insurgents and the South Sudan authorities, as well as by other northern Sudanese parties (DRCD, 2010, p. 14). Some suggested that the process was fraudulent and that it was no more than a means for the governing elites to justify and perpetuate inequalities enshrined in the trend to domestic politics (ibid.).

There are more than 597 tribes in Sudan, speaking over four hundred languages and dialects. All are almost entirely Muslim with most citizens speaking Sudanese Arabic but many also speak their own mostly unwritten languages. The tribes comprise Arab and African ethnicities displaying a society of diverse historical backgrounds,[2] ethnicities, tribes, cultures, languages and ways of life, and livelihoods, making Sudan truly a microcosm of Africa.

ETHNICITY AND RACE: A CONCEPTUAL FRAMEWORK

As in other African contexts, the tribe is the primary unit of social organisation in Sudan and has continued to underlie people's sociopolitical and economic interactions and transactions. In Sudan's recent history, belonging and loyalty to tribes, i.e. tribalism, have evolved and become a political strategy in the state's domestic politics and a markedly embedded feature of its officialdom and bureaucracy.[3] The characteristics of tribes in Sudan are compatible with those commonly perceived by anthropologists as sharing a name, a language, a belief in a common ancestor, and a common feeling of solidarity. They are organised along inherited social hierarchies and live independently of each other in demarcated geographical territories where each has its own administrative system (Manzool, 1998, p. 79; Berghe, 1975, p. xi).

These characteristics apply more to those who still live in rural areas and have ample reasons to maintain their ancestral qualities; and less to those living in or around urban centres, even though they are still identified by their tribes. The status of a tribe in Sudan, as manifested in

[1] 'Sudan Population, 2017': available at: <http://worldpopulationreview.com/countries/sudan-population> [accessed 31 July 2017].

[2] The people are of diverse origins and historical backgrounds: the Kushite kingdoms, in 2500 BC, were succeeded by Christian Nubian kingdoms on the Nile in AD 543; the Islamic Fung sultanate in 1504; parallel to this in the west of the country is the Keira sultanate in Darfur, and Arab infiltration from the north and west in the thirteenth and fourteenth centuries. O'Neill and O'Brien, 1988.

[3] In today's Sudan, tribes pledge their political loyalty, as one polity, to the government and the ruling party.

the social and political domains, disproves the stereotypical sociological depictions of a tribe as 'primitive' and 'backward' organisations of people in Africa that were constructed and propagated by colonials and colonial anthropologists (Firth, 1958, p. 6). Given its unique position in African politics, the tribe can be a useful unit of analysis in studying African societies, as it can help deconstruct several dimensions and ambiguities in the social development of communities and societies and their current bearing on events. The tribe has therefore been used since the 1980s as an analytical framework in population censuses in Sudan (Hassan and Ray, 2006, p. 17).

On a related but different note, a tribe is also conceived as an 'ethnic group' (Appiah, 1999, p. 703), which is widely perceived (Scherrer, 1999) as a human collectivity that is organised along a shared belief in real or imagined common origin or descent, or historical background and cultural[4] attributes, such as language, values, customs, social and economic activities, etc. Ethnicity is therefore about ethnic differentiation and consciousness of the 'we' that a group shares, as opposed to the 'they' (Fukui, 1994, p. 33). The concepts of 'we' and 'they' are usually ingrained in people's consciousness through the socialisation processes that build strong bonds among people of a particular ethnic group and exclude those who are not part of the group or, at worst, create feelings inimical to them. Ethnicity is thus not about the factors that people set to differentiate between 'us' and 'them', rather, it is about the social organisation of cultural differences embodied in the socialisation of individuals (Barth, 1998, p. 6). In other words, it is the deliberate social demarcation to maintain differences and boundaries, as elaborated below:

> An ethnic group is not one because of the degree of measurable or observable differences from other groups; it is an ethnic group, on the contrary, because the people in it and the people out of it know that it is one; because both the 'ins' and the 'outs' talk, feel, and act as if it were a separate group. This is possible only if there are ways of telling who belongs to the group and who does not, and if a person learns early, deeply, and usually irrevocably to what group he belongs. (Hughes, 1984, p. 91)

Since the early twentieth century, concepts of ethnicity and ethnic groups have dominated the politics of group differentiation all over the world. A general belief that every person has an ethnic identity has become the norm, and ethnic terms are now used to label a variety of situations where people live and act together. When describing African communities, the terms 'tribe' and 'ethnic group' are often used interchangeably for the similarity of meanings they embrace (Fukui and Markakis, 1994; Vail, 1989).

On the other hand, a belief in 'race' is usually associated with an ideology of racism, which implies that the genealogically based physical differences between human groups are essentially connected with the

[4] The term 'culture' is defined as a system of shared meanings developed in a social and economic context that has a particular historical and political background. It is a group's distinctive 'design for living', the sum total of its rules and guides for shaping and patterning its way of life (Khan, cited in Richardson and Lambert, 1985, p. 53).

presence or absence of specific socially relevant features. Racism based on racial differentiation therefore exists as a forceful element that gives social prominence to physical characteristics, especially among societies that are racially identified (Berghe, 1967, pp. x–xi). Racial categories are therefore often used to intensify ethnic tensions and justify unequal treatment and the exploitation of one group by another (Rex, 1986).

ETHNIC AND RACIAL DISCRIMINATION IN SUDAN

In Sudan in general, there is a clear demarcation between a tribe and an ethnic group. The tribe is a single unit that is founded on a blood-based relationship and networks of clans (*khashum bait*). It has its own norms and rules that identify and regulate the power relations between its affiliates, as well as with other tribes (Fruzzetti and Ostor, 1990). Tribalism is thus the bond that connects the tribe's affiliates and fosters their loyalty, cooperation and solidarity. People can therefore easily and clearly identify their tribes, but identifying their ethnicity is a complex process, as it occupies a more public domain and politically comprehensive dimension. It follows that a tribe is a private entity that grants people social identification, more than their ethnicity can. However, the significance of their conscious belonging to a certain tribe and subscribing to its rules (Manzool, 1998, pp. 78–80) varies across individuals, as it is determined by local, regional and national socio-cultural, economic and political contexts.

An ethnic group, on the other hand, is an aggregation of tribes that are connected through a common belief in being of a similar race and shared ancestor. Other ethnic traits used to identify people include religion and geographical location, as well as livelihood style. Various dichotomous identities have therefore evolved in Sudan, such as Arab/African (Zurga), Muslim/animist, Muslim/Christian, northern/southern, northern/western (*gharaabah*), farmers/pastoralists, Baggara/Abbala, etc. (Deng, 1987, p. 63). Yet ethnic labels may not always be harmful and may be used by individuals and groups in their daily and routine activities and interactions without repulsive meanings attached to them. They can only acquire the more powerful and politically significant connotations of negativity when the state uses them to justify discriminatory policies or to drive a wedge between otherwise well-meaning groups of citizens (Nagel, 1998).

Arguably, belonging privately to a tribe explains people's frequent engagement in violent conflict more than belonging publicly to an ethnic group. Nonetheless, there are times when counting on ethnicity, especially based on race, location and religion, outweighs tribalism. This normally occurs in situations where a higher alliance order is required, at which point ethnicity will come into play much more forcefully. In addition to the various significant triggers for wars fought in Sudan, there was also a sinister manipulation of tribalism and ethnicity by the ruling and governing elites.

It should be noted though that most Sudanese people still perceive race as an attribute that differentiates between indigenous Africans and claimants of Arab ethnicity, the two main ethnic groups in the country (Morton, 2011, p. 2). This is the only perception that brings the term 'ethnicity' to the fore as a divisive cultural attribute within the society. Indeed, ethnicity in Sudan is about racial differentiation, rather than cultural identification, as manifested by the many armed conflicts experienced in the country in which the ruling and governing elites in Sudan have wilfully emphasised ethnic differentiation based on race.

The origin of this dilemma of race-based ethnicity in Sudan dates back to decades before independence in 1956, and seems to be rooted in the legacy of the slave trade in the northern region, where Islam and Arabic dominate, long before the Anglo-Egyptian condominium rule started in 1898. The historical enslavement of some African Sudanese citizens has created a perception that detracts from the humanity of all African Sudanese people who do not belong to Arab ethnicity and/or Islam in the independent Sudan. The term slave (ʿabid, pl. ʿabīd, in Arabic) often denotes a black person and the term 'al-Sudan' means 'the land of black people'. In the collective psyche of most northerners, the term 'Sudanese' is associated with slaves and people of low social status and is therefore stigmatising (Sharkey, 2003, p. 19).

Thus it is not just the description of colour that is disliked by those who perceive themselves as Arabs, but also the 'Sudanese' label itself, which lumps them together with those whose ancestors belong to non-Islamic and non-Arab ethnicity, mainly in Southern Sudan and the Nuba Mountains, i.e. the Africans. This is despite most of those northern Sudanese 'Arabs' being essentially undifferentiated from the African Sudanese, both in colour and in physical features (Morton, 1992, p. 28). But the perception was sustained until the late 1920s when some educated northerners, despite their aversion to the term 'Sudanese', began using it to identify nationals, including themselves, of the country known as Sudan.

Over time, colonial policies of privilege based on education have also inadvertently sustained northern elites' sense of ethnic and religious superiority over the rest of the Sudanese people, despite the abolition of slavery in 1924. Access to education was determined by gender, social status, region and religion. Meanwhile, higher education, such as admission to Gordon Memorial College, favoured males, Muslims, Arabic-speaking people and 'Arabs' of high social status. Education in general was exclusive to the riverine central and northern regions of Sudan until the 1930s, when occasional elementary schools were established in some rural areas, including in Darfur (Sharkey, 2003, p. 21). Thus the seeds of inequality were sown by the rulers' domestic politics on the basis of culture, religion, race, gender, social status and/or geographical location.

The educated northerners who benefited from the favouritism policy of the colonials, most of whom attended Gordon Memorial College (Natsios, 2012, p. 30), cooperated with the colonials and served in their administration. Later, as the independent rulers of their country, these elites laid down a quasi-national political foundation for the country's ruling system, and presided over the government, security and military offices, as well as the economy. The ruling system they have adopted ended up reproducing ruling elites who have set their own social background as the cornerstone of the nationalist movement, and therefore Arab(ic) culture and Islam as the main organisational principles for justifying the granting or denial of rights and obligations of citizenship (ibid., p. 21).

It was no surprise therefore that the elites have pursued domestic policies that are deemed primarily to favour the (Arabised) northern and central regions whilst neglecting the other regions. Mechanisms and structures of exclusion based on tribe, ethnicity, race and region have been covertly mainstreamed, especially in employment, but overt social behaviour based on the same elements are also manifested by the public. The term 'slave', which was explicitly used to describe people from South Sudan and Nuba Mountains (ibid., pp. 17–19), has also been extended to Darfuri people, despite historical variations in the power relationships between Darfur and Northern Sudan.[5] Racism has thus continued to grow and infiltrate almost all social domains and political structures, i.e. it has become a subtly built institution in Sudanese society.

Ethnic identification as 'Arab' and 'black' (or 'African') has been translated to represent the power relationships between these two main ethnic groups, as it influences their access to the state's political office and to leadership positions. It has therefore acquired more importance for northerners as an indication of status, not just as a sheer statement of ethnicity or skin colour. More importantly, the term Arab has increasingly denoted a distinguished ancestral background (Sharkey, 2003, p. 20), and hence, a more privileged status today. Whilst Arabism is seen commonly as a cultural rather than a racial determinant in Sudan, Sudanese claimants of Arab origin usually vindicate their claim to a higher status on imagined racial eminence, which they see as sufficient justification for discriminating against others (Deng, 1993, p. 213).

Imagined and real Arab and African ethnicities appear to be two different, irreconcilable races in Sudan; as for many in the country, ethnic identity is more a judgemental designation than a real fact (Deng, 1987, p. 61). These ethnic dichotomies would not have constituted a threat to peaceful coexistence and/or posed as a source of violent disputes had they not been manipulated in discriminating ways to the disadvantage of the vast majority of the Sudanese.

Early signs of imbalanced power relationships between ethnic groups have shown up since independence, when the riverine governing elites appeared to line up with the Arab world. Pan-Arabism and Islamism were consistently emphasised as organising principles in a country where ethnic and religious diversity should not have been in doubt. Arabic became the formal language and Islam the main religion – measures that eventually formally shaped the identity of the country as attached to the Arab world. This *ethnicisation* of the sociopolitical environment underlies the misgivings associated with the 'christening' of Sudan as an Arab state, despite the fact that most of the country's population is African (Prunier, 2007). No surprise therefore that the elites employed ethnicity based on race

[5] The sultanate of Darfur historically extended to Shendi in North Sudan.

and religion in mobilising the 'the state' against the southern (and other) insurgencies.

Ethnicity based on racial differentiation and tribalism have thus engulfed the social and political contexts in Sudan, especially under the current NIF regime. Undertones of political rhetoric have robustly mushroomed and infiltrated most aspects of domestic politics to the extent that the government now demands, and gets, tribal loyalty rather than the loyalty of its citizens. Tribalism and ethnicity have therefore always been the most significant determiner in most of the political turmoil experienced in the country since independence, and particularly with the current regime led by the National Islamic Front (NIF).[6]

ETHNICITY IN DARFUR

Like other regions in Sudan, Darfuri society consists of tribes that are organised along two main ethnic groups: indigenous Africans and claimants of Arab descent. Generally, both groups have shades of black skin colour, even though they perceive themselves as distinct races. Yet many of the Arabs see themselves as more privileged and look down upon the Africans, the indigenous land owners, and pejoratively call them Zurga (literally, the blues, a euphemism for black, and hence, slaves). But whilst most Africans are certainly indigenous, most of the Arabs could also be labelled indigenous because of the length of their settlement in the region, which extends to centuries.

On the other hand, these two ethnicities are socially quite intermixed and there are no observable physical differences between them; and they are all Muslims. Among the indigenous Africans, the Fur constitutes the largest tribe, and cohabits with other indigenous tribes, such as Masalit, Zaghawa, Gimir, Berti, Daju and Tunjur. There are also tribes of West African origin, such as the Fellata and Borno. The Arabs include tribes such as Rezeiqat, Bani Helba and Ta'aisha.

Most of the population live in rural areas and only 17.7 per cent in the urban areas. The majority therefore pursue either pastoral or agro-pastoral livelihoods. There are also a few who venture into commerce and the making of traditional handicrafts (Abdel-Jaleel, 2003, p. 170); meanwhile, government employment constitutes the main source of income for most of the educated persons in urban areas. Hence, estimates of Darfur contributions to the country's GDP amount to 80 per cent of Sudanese meat exports and 26 per cent of livestock exports (Bilal, 2003, p. 146).

The tribes of both ethnicities are categorised according to socio-economic livelihood systems, as Baggara (cattle herders) and Abbala (camel herders), who are mainly nomadic pastoralists, and sedentary farmers or agro-pastoralists, who are mostly indigenous Africans. They are geographically distributed more or less according to the

[6] The NIF has now, eventually, been rebranded as the National Congress Party (NCP) but its core membership still remains members of the Muslim Brotherhood, even when they seem to be sidelined.

climatic zones that foster their livelihood patterns: the nomadic Abbala inhabit the dry north, the Baggara pastoralists in the south and southwest, whereas the agro-pastoral sedentary farmers are found in the soil-rich centre (Haaland, 1972, p. 150). Most of the Baggara and Abbala groups are claimants of Arab ethnicity, whereas sedentary farmers who practise farming and animal husbandry belong mainly to African ethnicity (Takana 1998).

The two ethnic groups have different social organisations and structures of traditional authority; for instance, the Dimingawi and Shartai[7] are supreme chiefs among the indigenous farming groups but the Baggara and Abbala have the Nazir and Omda instead. Each group has distinct cultural characteristics, especially with regard to ceremonies, rituals and traditional weapons.[8] Language[9] may be the only marked indicator of cultural difference – the mother tongue of the Baggara and Abbala is Arabic, whereas the indigenous groups have their own languages, which are referred to locally, perhaps contemptuously, as vernaculars (Morton, 1992, p. 28).

These tribes and ethnic groups do not live in isolation from one another; rather, they have flexible administrative and socio-economic boundaries that allow individuals and groups to interact. They often cross these boundaries to establish themselves among other host groups and adopt their ethnic cultures and symptomatic labels. It was observed in the past that individuals from the Fur tribe could be assimilated economically in the Bani Helba Baggara Arab society to become Baggara (Haaland, 1972, p. 164). Whilst some ethnic labels based on livelihood styles are flexible and accommodating, by virtue of their fundamental association with blood relationship, the tribe is nonetheless a comparatively fixed construction that is rarely, if ever, open to outsiders (or aliens). It follows that the people of Darfur can be re-ethnicised when the ethnic determinant is economic and/or cultural, but may not be retribalised.

On the other hand, the social change processes witnessed by Darfuri society during the last four decades through education, migration and socio-economic interactions, as well as conflict, have steadily eroded most of what was recognised in the past as the distinguishing cultural traits of these rural communities. Some of the newer generations have already lost contact with their mother tongues and now only speak Arabic. The characteristic styles of houses that were quite noticeable in rural areas four decades ago[10] have altered. Currently, most houses

[7] *Shartai* (pl. *Sharati*) is the title of the supreme tribal chief in the tribal administration hierarchy of indigenous Darfuri African tribes. *Dimingawi* is the title of the *first* supreme tribal chief below the sultan, and he is in charge of the *Sharati* in the administration hierarchy of Darfur Sultanate.

[8] The indigenous farmers possess throwing-spears, as against the lance of the Baggara.

[9] The Baggara speak only Arabic, whereas the Fur and other African tribes speak not only their own native languages but most speak Arabic as well.

[10] The old style was mainly a cylindrical construction of interwinned branches fastened to one-and-a-half metre poles arranged in a circle, whereas the Baggara use a tent, a hemispherical construction of straw mats on a frame of branches. The dwellings of the Zaghawa consist of a square structure within which a straw fence demarcates a smaller room containing a bed (Haaland, 1972, p. 165).

are imitations of the prevalent designs in urban areas. In the face of the availability of modern weapons, the traditional ones have virtually disappeared or become just historical relics. Perhaps the only traits that have survived are some ceremonial procedures and rituals of joy and sorrow. Long years of intermixing between these groups appear to have moderated the physical and cultural differences that may have been apparent in the past. Therefore, it is no wonder that outside observers find it difficult to distinguish between people based on locally constructed perceptions and conceptions.

Nonetheless, people still believe in racial differentiation, which they justify on what they tend to believe as their racial backgrounds. This seems to inform the proposition that the features that count the most are those that the actors themselves perceive and cherish as signs of differentiation, not necessarily the objectively perceivable differences that outsiders may be able to detect (Barth, 1969, p. 14). Thus, in Darfur, as elsewhere in Sudan, 'race' appears to be just a belief rather than an objective reality. Arguably, exploiting belief in an imagined race as the most significant cultural attribute in identifying people is indeed a reproduction of the domestic political approaches that are inclined to transform people's normal identity labels into divisive ideological tools. The ultimate aim of the ruling and governing elites is to manipulate these tools to preserve a status quo that perpetuates their privilege.

ADMINISTRATION AND ETHNICITY IN DARFUR: THE PRECOLONIAL ERA

As in most African countries, the recent administration in Darfur would likely be well comprehended if compared to ruling structures that existed in the periods before colonialisation and the engagement of national governments. These administrative structures were kingdoms that existed for centuries, until the Darfur sultanate became part of Anglo-Egyptian Sudan in 1917. During this period Darfur's administration peaked into a well-established centralised authority, where the state was organised into four main centralised provinces called *Dars*, each divided into a number of district chiefdoms or *shartayas*.[11]

The provinces were complemented by another level of administration, based on the organisation of tribal constituencies along specific land areas, also called *Dars*. Within the *Dar* territories, tribes were somewhat autonomous in administering their own affairs, and the peoples were free to disperse within areas governed centrally. Apparently, the system was built on a fundamental principle of power devolution to a hierarchical structure of leaders – chiefs and Sheikhs, who were granted significant authority to oversee land and people on behalf of the central figure, the sultan.

[11] Dar aba diima, in the southwest; Dar abbo uumo in the southeast; Dar Daali (or Dar al-Sabah) in the east, and Dar al-Takanawi (or Dar al-Rih) in the north (O'Fahey, 2008, p. 164).

Within this system, most tribes inhabiting Darfur acquired territories or *Dars*, often in their own names. These *Dars* bestowed on the respective folks a private, or sovereign, space that was characteristically theirs, whereby both people and land were administered through their own chiefs (O'Fahey, 1980, p. 70), thus developing a form of local sovereignty that proved to have serious implications. The majority of these *Dars* were granted by Fur sultans, whereas others were granted later by the Anglo-Egyptian condominium authorities (1917–55). At the village level, the Sheikhs were often in charge of land distribution and the settlement of land disputes, a practice that has continued in rural areas to the present day, although less authoritatively.

The tribal organisation and the *Dar* appeared to have been an effectual administrative tool during the sultanate, and therefore, when Sultan Ali Dinar (1898–1916) revived the sultanate after the Turco-Egyptian conquest (1874–81) and the Mahdiyya (1881–98), he preserved the old rights over land as granted by previous sultans, together with the authority of the *Dar* and the associated administrative tools (O'Fahey and Abu Salim, 1983, p. 158). Later on, this *Dar* system was also used, with minor adjustments, by the colonial and national administrations (Morton, 2011, p. 5).

A similar practice involving private land was widespread in Africa, where tribes or ethnic groups would become strongly attached to specific land boundaries that would then serve as homelands for the tribespeople, wherein they would exercise and preserve their own socio-cultural attributes and foster solidarity among their affiliates (Ali, 1996). This homeland has been given different names by different people. For instance, whilst it is called *Dar* in Darfur, it is known as *Nyika* by the Shona tribe in South Africa. The homeland territories are also often associated with spiritual powers. For instance, *Nyika* represents both the land and the society of Shona, but it also embraces mythical linkages with the spirits of their ancestors. Shona people believe that these spiritual forces monitor their interactions, and guide them through local leaders who were believed to have divine authority to manage the land and its resources (Butcher, 1980, p. 31). In Darfur, the *Dar* has no similar spiritual aspects, even though it was recorded that at times during the Fur reign, some Fur women exercised spiritual powers to protect the harvest.[12]

In addition, the land, which in this case was called *hawakir* (sing. *hakura*, an estate landholding), was also offered to males or females, individuals or groups. The *hawakir* might be land tracts or nomad communities administered by the recipient, who would collect taxes and fines and control access to grazing and farming plots, labour, etc. In particular, *hawakir al-jah*, i.e. estates of privilege, were usually granted to the

[12] It was suggested that in order to get sufficient rain, the old women used to gather under a special tree where they presumed a sacred snake lived in a hole. They sprinkled a mixture of flour and water on the tree to prevent the snake from coming out and to stop the rain from falling (Shuqayr, 1981, p. 178). Today these rituals have vanished and the only one left is usually performed by a special locust magician called dambare, who performs magic rites to drive the locust away from the crops (Haaland, 1972, pp. 153–54).

sultans' close relatives, particularly females, and to Muslim holy men, the *fuqara*, who usually came from West and North Africa, but also from the Nile Valley. These men were usually exempted from paying taxes to the sultan.[13] Land in Darfur has therefore, for centuries, constituted the main pillar of social, political and economic power for the sultans, as also for 'privileged' inhabitants.

On the other hand, whilst most tribes have acquired lands in their names, some tribal groups, such as the camel-herding Abbala in North Darfur, have no specified land. This was attributed to the nature of the nomadic style of their livelihoods: they needed not a sedentary residence but only safe passage throughout the year, which was adequately secured through administrative arrangements and local conventions among the *Dars*' owners (Salih, 1998, p. 113).

That arrangement was indeed facilitated primarily by the availability of abundant land and common resources, the relatively small population[14] and hence, the lack of competition. But it was facilitated even more by the respect of all beneficiaries for local conventions and the tribal leaders who oversaw them. When conflict, which was sporadic at the time, erupted over these resources, tribal leaders were often able to resolve the disputes through local resolution mechanisms (Morton, 1992, pp. 27–9). Should these mechanisms fail, the central authority of the sultan would always intervene and resolve the situation.

Despite this clear organisation, tribespeople were not isolated from one another. Mutual economic livelihoods and social relationships often connected and integrated them seamlessly. Baggara and Abbala pastoralists often interacted with sedentary agro-pastoralists through the exchange of livestock and other farm produce that was connected to their different, yet complementary, livelihoods. The *Dar* system facilitated and regulated this socio-economic reciprocation, through agreed and respected rules and norms within and across tribes (or tribes' *Dars*).

These conventions maintained cooperation, regulated and administered people's movement and conduct across the *Dars*, and cemented security and unity among the tribe's members (Mohamed, 1998, pp. 33–69). The economic and social boundaries between the Baggara and Fur tribes, for instance, were therefore flexible and open in ways that usually preserved access to productive resources for everyone involved. Thus, a person from the Fur could give their cattle to someone from the Baggara Arabs to look after; or they could conveniently join the Baggara livelihood style and become a nomadic pastoralist (Haaland, 1972).

[13] Hakura is 'an estate, comprising usually a number of villages, less often a group of nomads, granted by the sultan to a member of his family, a title-holder or a faqih' (O'Fahey and Spaulding, 1974, p. 157).

[14] The 1955/6 First Census estimated Sudan's total population at 10.25 million; 8 per cent were urban and 92 per cent lived in rural areas; the population density was less than 30 persons per square kilometre (Davies, 2007, pp. 32–4). The Darfur population was estimated at: 750,000 in 1911; 1,328,000 in 1955/56; 1,869,000 in 1973; 3,093,700 in 1983; and 5,352,000 in 1993 (Darfur Information Centre, 2015).

ADMINISTRATION AND ETHNICITY IN DARFUR: THE COLONIAL ERA

In the aftermath of the conquest of the Darfur sultanate in 1916, the condominium rulers in 1917 transformed Darfur into a province. They used the 'indirect rule' framework previously adopted by the Turco-Egyptians (1821–81) as a blueprint for ruling Darfur. Subsequently, they maintained and mainstreamed the sultanate administrative legacy of the tribe-based *Dar* system to rule the vast areas of rural Darfur. Apparently, there were no expectations of developing, or, indeed, any intention to develop a more cohesive system for social integration lest it might pose a threat to their authority in the future. They thus removed the top two levels of the previous administration, the sultan and the authorities, from the four provinces, but they all kept the other junior levels.

Both tribes and *Dars* were maintained, but with less integral connection to the authorities in Darfur than they had before. Within Darfur, the tribes and *Dars* became detached and alienated units lacking a reliable patron to attend to their needs in normal times or restrain them and compel them to comply when necessary. The *Dar* system, which was used to keep the sultanate united, had now become manipulated into keeping society divided. To address these shortcomings, the condominium rulers backed up the native administration with limited executive, financial and judicial powers by a series of ordinances, especially between 1919 and 1931. Furthermore, a new system of local government was introduced as an institutional reform (1937–8) in village and town councils, aiming at stimulating public participation beyond the authority of tribes and traditional leaders (Kurita, 1994, p. 205; Morton, 1992, p. 30). Paradoxically, the two systems contradicted each other; for whilst the native administration instituted and consolidated tribes' boundaries and authority as private and personal, the newly established councils made the areas outside these boundaries public and common. This was particularly threatening to the people and tribes that have had no *Dar* in their own names; ironically, the Fur people, the founders of the sultanate, counted among them.

ADMINISTRATION AND ETHNICITY IN DARFUR: THE POSTCOLONIAL ERA

In the early postcolonial era, Darfur remained, as it was during the condominium rule, a province of the then Sudan. The tribal-based authority and administration also continued, together with the legacy of the *Dar* and the historical rights of title holders, now known as the 'native administration'. Drastic changes in the administration, however, started in early 1970 with the introduction of the Unregistered Lands Act (ULA), which stipulates that all unregistered lands are deemed government property. This legislation theoretically transforms the land used by ordinary citizens in rural areas for subsistence agriculture into government ownership, including the *Dars*. It ignored the fact that *most* of the land in Darfur, including the specified *Dars*, was unregistered. This was because formal registration was not a familiar practice among rural people, and for centuries they considered the land as indisputably theirs.

This perception of the locals is compatible with what has always prevailed in Africa, where land is a public resource, and activities such as hunting, grazing, watering and collecting firewood, etc., are regulated by customary law and practice. The system usually gives usufructuary rights to every individual in need, but strictly prohibits individual users from pursuing methods detrimental to the community, such as selling land or allocating it to strangers or others not domiciled in the village (Runger, 1987, p. 53). Further, apart from sultanic charters that have confirmed stable legal title to the land in Darfur, i.e. the *hakura* system (Hamza, 1986: 43), land transactions are usually made verbally in the presence of a witness, and no written documents are ever required (ibid.). Recent observations suggest that these communal laws and practices have hitherto continued in most rural areas of Darfur, particularly those areas of no interest to the government.

The ULA was soon followed, in 1971, by the abolition of the native administration system along with the authority and influence of tribal leaders over land distribution (Mohamed, 1998; Prunier, 2007). Arguably, these domestic policies could only pose a threat to individuals and tribes in rural areas, especially in Darfur, where for decades people perceived the right to their land, materially, morally and administratively, as a sacrosanct heritage from their ancestors. Following their failure to justify their actions and/or consult with the respective people, the government has come to be seen by the people as an adversary, rather than their reliable protector.

The native administration was replaced by a system of local elected administrative councils. However, this newly introduced local government administration appeared to have failed to address people's mounting needs, especially with regard to their security and livelihoods. The revoked traditional authority was often trusted to address people's needs and resolve their problems. The worth of traditional leaders in most African countries is not questioned in their communities who see in their wisdom and leadership effective tools that are relevant to the issues surrounding the community. Unlike government personnel, these leaders continue to readily earn the trust of their own people (Dodo, 2013, p. 33). In Darfur, tribal communities continue to consider their tribal authority as a primary source of help when the need arises.[15] Traditional leaders have therefore been able to restore and further strengthen their informal power.

Resorting to traditional leaders has often become the main choice for rural people when faced with personal ordeals, e.g. the theft of animals or other assets. The leaders would call for *Faza'*, a communal mobilisa-

[15] Group interviews, Nyala, May 2006.

tion of solidarity, to track down robbers and recover stolen assets. During the famine and environmental crises that struck Africa and Sudan in the 1960s and 1970s, traditional leaders accommodated in their *Dars* groups of affected migrants from Zaghawa, Gimir, Fur and other tribes, who left their homelands when governmental support was either quite minimal, or non-existent (ibid.).

The native administration continued to function informally in rural areas throughout the 1970s and 1980s. In 1974, Darfur was split into two provinces, North Darfur and South Darfur, allegedly to enable its effective administration. Then Darfur was reassembled as a single region following the introduction of the Regional Government Act in 1980 (Mohamed, 2003b, p. 26). No significant change was made to the operational capacity of the new administration, however, as the regional government lacked adequate resources (human and financial) to effectively deliver services and/or maintain law and order (Harir, 1994; Daly, 2007).

This was evident in the administration's inability to control the overwhelming violent conflicts taking place between tribes as well as the banditry that beset the region in the 1980s and early 1990s. For instance, regional police forces often commandeered vehicles and fuel from the humanitarian aid agencies working in the region, such as Oxfam UK and Save the Children, in order to track down robbers.[16] It was inevitable, with such an incapacitated government, that tribes would become entirely reliant on the dynamic of their traditional institutions and use their tribal support systems to further their tribal objectives, regardless of the outcome.

From 1986 onward, the influence of the tribal leaders, especially as manifested during the democratic elections of 1986, was undeniable, and so was the importance of the native administration. Khartoum governments then started to revive the native administration but noticeably with limited capacity. They reduced the power of the recognised chiefs by creating new leaders and giving preference to landless Arabs. New Nuzzar were appointed and many were given the title Amir (a prince), even for the Fur leaders and the Janjawiid. The title Amir was indeed historically exclusive to sultans' family members, Fur and Masalit sultans, for instance. After overcoming the Darfur sultanate, the British gave the title Amir to the descendants of sultans who were perceived as rivals to the deposed sultan in an attempt to protect their rule from possible uprisings by the deposed sultan's family (Tubiana, 2007, pp. 81–2).

In 1994, the NIF regime redivided Sudan into twenty-six states (*wilayat* in Arabic). Darfur was divided into three states: North, South and West Darfur and their regional capitals were al-Fashir, Nyala and al-Geneina, respectively. Undoubtedly, this redivision would affect the *Dars'* boundaries. For instance, part of *Dar* Zaghawa in the northwest of Darfur has become located in West Darfur, a region recognised for decades as the homeland of the Masalit tribe, that is, *Dar* Masalit,[17] whereas previously the whole of *Dar* Zaghawa was located in North Darfur.

[16] My personal experience in Darfur, during the period from 1992 to 1996.
[17] Dar Masalit, the homeland of the Masalit African ethnic group, was the most recent sultanate to be annexed to Sudan (1870–1930) (Kapteijns, 1985).

This policy seemed to have been set to serve multiple objectives for the NIF. Historically, traditional parties have sizeable loyal followings among these communities. The Umma Party, for instance, enjoys massive support from Ansar (partisans) in Darfur and was therefore able to win almost all the constituencies in the 1986 elections and lead the government of the third democratic rule (1986–9). It was therefore of strategic importance to re-establish a new patron–client relationship with these communities whereby the NIF would take on the position as new patron. This was apparently thought of as possibly paving the way for the eventual transfer of the people's allegiance to the NIF and its alleged Civilisation Project.

On the other hand, most Fur, who constitute the largest tribe in Darfur, were loyal to the sectarian Democratic Unionist Party (DUP). The Fur were able to win the 1981 regional governorship election in Darfur when Ahmad Diraige, a Fur candidate running against Ali al-Haj, the NIF candidate, was elected regional governor (Flint and de Waal, 2005, p. 21). Subsequently, when Elhaj became the minster for local governance during the early years of the NIF regime, he planned and executed the division of Darfur society across *Dars*, presumably to weaken their loyalty to the sectarian parties, but also to retaliate for his earlier defeat (Burr and Collins, 2008).

The NIF regime also introduced a new tribal administrative framework in order to extend and solidify its influence over tribes and ethnic groups. It ordered tribal leaders to be elected, a deceptively democratic measure that was actually intended to manipulate tribal constituencies and structures (Haggar, 2003, p. 222). Similarly, the title Amir was soon supplemented by a new land distribution policy known as *emirates* (*emarat*, sing. *emara*, an estate),[18] in March 1995. Noticeably, this policy was enacted only in *Dar* Masalit under the command of Governor Mohamed al-Fadl (Haggar, 2003, pp. 222–3).

It worth noting that the abolition of the native administration in 1971 was not applied to *Dar* Masalit (ibid., p. 219), perhaps for reasons related to the relatively late annexation of the *Dar* to Sudan in 1932. In addition, its very remote location may have discouraged Khartoum from actively realigning its administration to that of the central authority, and Khartourm may therefore have preferred to keep its historical administration intact. *Dar* Masalit continued for decades as a distant province deprived of an integrated relationship with the centre: the ruling and governing elites could not see the importance of forming such a relationship until the 1980s. This was when Chadian Arab groups started to infiltrate the land, either as ordinary immigrants fleeing drought and conflict in their own country, and/or as politicians in search of political refuge and a rear base for their armed struggle against Chadian governments. This movement into Darfur was, however, sanctioned and overseen by the state government and the ruling elites, and later in 1995, influenced the division of *Dar* Masalit into *emarat* to accommodate those Chadian Arabs (ibid.).

[18] The estate constitutes a patch of land granted and administered along ethnic lines; the name emara is reminiscent of the Arab and Islamic system of governance.

The *emara* policy is an obvious system of clientalism and patronage that was carefully planned and was meant to reinforce the presence of the Arabs, no matter where from and no matter at what cost, to serve the pan-Arabist orientation that the ruling elites strive to accomplish. This policy could only prove to be disastrous as it fomented resentment among ethnic and tribal groups, especially in *Dar* Masalit, West Darfur. It eventually led to the outbreak of aggression and violent ethnic conflict between the dispossessed indigenous land owners, the Masalit, and the beneficiaries, the newly settled Arab groups (ibid., pp. 227–9).

ADMINISTRATION AND SERVICE DEVELOPMENT

The central ruling elites paid great attention to the management of Darfur, particularly in rural areas, without attempting a parallel intervention to improve the social services or facilitate people's sustainable livelihoods through development initiatives. The combination of incompetent management, scarcity and the degradation of infrastructure has shown a level of systematic neglect that is all too often regarded as deliberate, as indicated by the state of services in Darfur compared to those in the riverine regions, as shown in Tables 1.1 and 1.2.

Table 1.1 Enrolment in primary and secondary education in Darfur 1999/2000 compared with Northern and Central Sudan and with Khartoum

Region	*Primary and secondary education*	
	Enrolment in primary education, 1999/2000 (%)	*Enrolment in secondary education, 1999/2000 (%)*
Darfur	30.63	11.9
Central Sudan	54.72	16
Northern Sudan	87.8	36
Khartoum	86.4	35.1

(*Source*: Adapted from Sudanese Strategic Report (2000, p. 288))

Table 1.2 Medical provision in Darfur compared with Northern and Central Sudan and with Khartoum, 2000

Region	*Population estimate*	*Number of Medical Doctors per 1000 Persons*	*Number of beds persons per 100,000 persons*
Darfur	4,740,000	1.6	23.8
Central	6,659,000	5.52	78
Northern	3,655,000	10.5	192
Khartoum	4,740,000	35	111

(*Source*:Adapted from Sudanese Strategic Report (2000, p.288))

Photo I.1 A woman preparing land for the farming season, 1995
(*Source*: The author took this photo in the summer of 1995 in a Kebkabiya rural area in North Darfur, a mountainous area where women lack the appropriate technology to help reduce their strenuous efforts in farming.)

As shown quantitatively in these tables, the evidence of imbalanced distribution of power and wealth in the country cannot be missed. It substantiates the claim of Darfuris that Darfur receives the lowest share in services relative to other regions; whereas the northern and central regions, the homeland of the riverine ruling elites, receive the lion's share of services and investment.[19] Nevertheless, these facts were ridiculed and contested by the ruling elite. The persistent denial of the substantiated allegations by the riverine ruling elites may have justified the subsequent armed struggle that has swept the region since 2003.

It has to be stated that the general social and economic context of Darfur has been exacerbated by drought, famine and poverty. Estimates of poverty in 1997 were at 97 per cent and 98.1 per cent in rural and urban areas, respectively (Sudanese Strategic Report, 1998, p. 98). The combination of these three pillars of suffering in Darfur has created the indelible legacy of a lack of basic human needs and humanitarian crises in the recent past. Rural communities have lost their herds and endured successive dry seasons since the 1960s. Reviving the degraded livelihoods

[19] A statistical overview of services and budgets allocated to different regions was outlined in *The Black Book* (Seekers of Truth and Justice, 2000), which was authored and published by the so-called Seekers of Truth and Justice. The book's full title is *The Black Book: The Imbalance of Power and Wealth in Sudan.* It outlines and illustrates the pattern of inequalities in the distribution of resources across Sudan, the political control by the riverine elites and marginalisation of the rest of the country. It was published in two parts: in May 2000 and in August 2002. The book appears to provide the concrete grievance statement that may have underlain the emergence of insurgencies since early 2003 to date (2017) in Darfur.

cannot be expected to stop the migration of massive flow quickly enough, especially of young people in search of jobs into the riverine areas, where they have found poorly paid menial jobs and are exploited and demeaned.

Whether by design or indifference, a combination of the administrative policies pursued in Darfur and the attitudes of the riverine ruling and governing elites towards the region has kept Darfur as a reservoir for cheap labour, primarily in the irrigated mechanised enterprises. For instance, the 1993 population census shows that 506,473 young persons born in Darfur emigrated either to Khartoum, Aljazeera, Gadarif, Kassala or the White Nile regions, where they formed a massive labour force in the public and private mechanised agricultural enterprises established in these regions (Abdel-Jaleel, 2003, p. 184). Besides, the youth in rural areas have also constituted the main source of combatants, whether in the regular armed forces or in pro-government militias fighting in the government's unwarranted civil wars, as has been the case recently, especially since 1992.

Obviously, the policies that the riverine ruling and governing elites have pursued in keeping Darfur vulnerable to the uncertainty of livelihoods have paid off quite convincingly. The elites have reaped (un)expected dividends in sustaining and cementing their position in authority, and hence securing the effective manipulation of Darfuri people, who, because of the policies that these elites have enacted, appear to be fighting each other without realising that the intention of the elites was for the status quo to be perpetuated.

CONCLUSION

Darfuri society mirrors the general characteristics of Sudanese society, which is ethnically diverse and generally organised into tribes that make up two main ethnic groups: indigenous Africans and claimants of Arab descent. But Darfuri society is further organised on a social and economic basis according to the means of livelihood, where the indigenous Africans are mostly sedentary agro-pastoralists and the Arabs are mainly Baggara and Abbala pastoralists. Yet it is often quite difficult to distinguish between who belongs to what race because of intermixing between the ethnic groups. But the riverine ruling and governing elites who claim Arab ethnicity, and who have been at the helm of Sudan governance since independence, have followed similar social and political approaches to the colonials. They have tended to emphasise the racial differences between people, building into the governance of the country some racially discriminatory policies and trends.

Despite this ethnic organisation in Darfur, it was not an ethnic group but the tribe, together with the *Dar* system, that served as the main administration mechanism during the Fur sultanate. Since Darfur's annexation to Sudan in 1917, the administration of its tribes has suffered confusion and decay, which have generated serious implications for the social and political settings in Darfur. The new rulers created a power vacuum for the tribes by destroying or weakening senior levels of the organisation and management of the sultanate and their provincial authorities who were closely administering and overseeing the *Dars*. Meanwhile, they maintained and consolidated the tribes and the *Dars* as individual and isolated entities through the newly introduced native administration system, which allowed the concealed notion of tribal 'sovereignty' to emerge and flourish. This has effectively marked the beginning of transforming the tribes and the *Dars* from being effective administrative mechanisms into 'micro-states' and Darfur into a 'multi-nation' society.

National governments thereafter could not make, and indeed were indifferent to making, any reforms to alter this situation; instead, Darfur witnessed inconsistency and confusion in the administrative policies pursued by various national regimes, which included the dissolution of the native administration in 1971 along with the tribal authority for over fifteen years. Later, the NIF regime revived the native administration and tribal authority especially for the Arab tribes, conforming to the ideology of pan-Arabism, but only as a means to serve socially divisive ends. Their approach included discriminatory policies in favour of Arabs and to the disadvantage of Africans, as manifested in the *emara* policy in *Dar* Masalit in March 1995. This policy was nothing more than a manipulation of tribes, especially Arab tribes.

While the ruling elites have paid considerable attention to the administration of the tribes, the region, especially the rural areas where these tribes live, was denied access to sustainable livelihoods and social services. Ironically, it has been transformed into a reservoir for cheap recruits to strengthen the economic and political status of the ruling elites, either by serving their economic projects along the Nile, or by joining civil wars as fighters against the uprising and armed struggle of disaffected citizens suffering such discriminatory policies and whose claims to fairness and justice have been ignored. Various causes have ignited and exacerbated these wars, as will be discussed in the following chapter.

2

Conflict in Darfur: Causes and Implications

Violent conflict in Darfur is not a new or a sudden phenomenon; tribes of the same or different ethnic groups have engaged in sporadic disputes and deadly clashes in the past. Since the 1970s, however, these clashes have become more recurrent and have often involved groups of pastoralists of the Baggara and Abbala Arab tribes. The situation has further been compounded by the emergence of politically motivated Darfuri-armed movements and insurgencies since 1991/2. Many causes could be cited for the eruption of these conflicts and their escalation into fatal violence beyond the local capacity to resolve them, as discussed below.

A HISTORY OF CONFLICT IN DARFUR

During the Fur sultanate (1445–1916), most of the conflicts between Darfuri tribes were disputes either over the use of common resources or over authority and administration. The former often ensued from pastoralists breaching local conventions on common resource management and causing damage to farmers' crops by allowing their herds to encroach into the farms of sedentary communities, whereas the second usually erupted when the authority of tribes over their *Dars* was challenged or threatened.

Tribal authorities were often able to resolve the disputes over resources through their own local resolution mechanisms, which people usually respected and abided by. But sometimes a group would attempt to grab the lands of other tribespeople by force and use it for their own settlement. Since the reign of Sultan Tayrab (1768–87), the Fur sultans intervened to force the invaders off the lands they had seized and to maintain law and order. For instance, Sultan Abd al-Rahman (1787–1801) intervened, with a force of sixty horsemen, to terminate the conflict between the Mahriyah and the Mahamid Abbala Arabs, confiscating half of their camels in retribution.[1] The pattern of conflicts caused by the encroachment of pastoralists' herds on the farms, and the subsequent interventions of the sultans to restore law and order, continued up until the era of Ali Dinar (1898–1916), who forced large groups of pastoral communities to leave the lands

[1] This happened during Browne's visit to Darfur (1793–96) (Browne, 1806, p. 345).

they seized from sedentary communities during the Turco-Egyptian rule (1874–81) (O'Fahey and Spaulding, 1974).

Nor was the state free of political opponents against the sultans. Both the Baggara in South Darfur and the Abbala in North Darfur had revolted against the sultanate several times. In the 1780s, Sultan Abdul Rahman (1787–1801) forced the Baggara to pay the due tax in addition to a fine for a two-year default.[2] The Baggara were reportedly not in a good relationship with the Fur community either (O'Fahey, 1980, p. 89). Moreover, under the Fur sultanate, the slave trade constituted a substantial source of income. The Rezeiqat Baggara of South Darfur used to raid and enslave people from South Sudan and they posed a mounting threat to the sultanate by blocking the missions of the sultan into those enslaving areas. Therefore Sultan Tayrab (1768–87) led a punitive campaign against them. The Rezeiqat also rebelled, together with the Bani Helba and other Arab tribes, against Sultan Muhammad al-Fadl (1801–39) (O'Fahey, 1980; Shuqayr, 1981). Conflict between the Rezeiqat and the sultanate intensified during the 1840s and 1850s, eventually paving the way for a third party, the riverine elite slave traders, locally called Jallaba, to dominate these trade routes and outflank the Rezeiqat (Shuqayr, 1981).

The occurrence of conflicts in Darfur continued after its annexation to Sudan in 1917, though on a much lower scale compared to the sultanate period (Morton, 1992, p. 27). They were often primarily triggered by reasons related to access to common resources. Since the 1970s, the conflicts have become more recurrent and have resulted in devastating the societal conventions and moral principles of peaceful coexistence and social integration (Mohamed, 2003b, pp. 44–50). Violence, aggression and a precarious security situation have overwhelmed the region to the extent that state intervention has appeared inadequate and unable to maintain law and order. These circumstances have cumulatively led to the emergence of Darfuri insurgencies in 1991/2 and since March 2003, the opening of a new chapter in the history of violent armed conflict and humanitarian crisis in Darfur. The structural reasons for these conflicts are arguably associated with the principles underlying the power relationships in Sudan, which are substantially promoted by discriminatory, often racist, policies, as will be discussed below.

THE ROOT CAUSES OF CONFLICT

There is a range of root causes to these conflicts that either collectively or singly trigger the conflicts in contemporary Darfur. These will be outlined below under the following subheadings: 'Drought, emigration and power relations', 'The *Dars* and land legislation', 'Regional geopolitics', 'Land policies and peace agreements', 'Elections and ethnic mobilisation' and 'The militarisation of society'.

[2] This amounted to 12,000 animals, instead of the annual 4,000 heads of cattle (O'Fahey, 1980, p. 89).

Drought, emigration and power relations

The Sahelian drought of the late 1960s and in the 1970s and 1980s, struck the region of Darfur, especially the northern part, and compelled large populations, pastoralists in particular, e.g. Zaghawa, northern Rezeiqat, Zayadiyya, Gimir and Meidob, to migrate with their remaining herds from the severely affected north to the still environmentally hospitable areas of South and West Darfur. This development coincided with the abolition of the native administration system, a measure that adversely affected the local capacity for natural resource management and dispute management and resolution. Nonetheless, the traditional leaders, who continued to exercise their extant authority informally, took the initiative to allow migrants to settle in their *Dars* (Haggar, 2003, pp. 173–81), based on local conventions that urged tribes to stand with one another in times of adversity.

In addition to the need for resettlement and access to natural resources, it was inevitable that the emigrants would also share the existing social services, such as education and healthcare, which were often inadequate for the hosting populations, let alone for thousands of new arrivals.[3] The available economic activity must also have suffered similar competition. Nevertheless, the newly introduced local government administration seemed to be indifferent and/or incapable of improving the increasingly dwindling services and organising the power relations between the *Dars'* owners and the emigrants. Conflicts between the two groups over these resources were therefore inevitable.

Before environmental degradation occurred in the late 1960s, the government launched mechanised agricultural enterprises in South Darfur. This led to a narrowing of the recognised seasonal migration routes (the *maraheel* or *masarat* in Arabic; sing. *murhal*) for nomadic pastoralists, and a shrinking of the available grazing land. The encroachment of animals on farms seemed to be inescapable, and was damaging the farmers' sustainable livelihoods.[4] To protect their farms, Fur and their neighbours, e.g. Bani Helba, built air enclosures (*Zarā'ib al-Hawā* in Arabic), a measure that in turn further reduced the pasture areas available to seasonally migrating pastoralists (Harir, 1994, pp. 179–80; Salih, 1998, p. 107).

Local leaders were unable to enforce compliance with what were effective traditional arrangements as pastoralists always tended to disregard customary laws that set the passage routes during their seasonal

[3] This is an estimate drawn from the case of the Zaghawa tribe who emigrated from the dry North Darfur into areas in South and Central Darfur. Before emigrating in 1970 their number is estimated at 255,000 and after the drought, the population in Dar Zaghawa was reduced to only 40,000, i.e. 16 per cent of their total number before the drought and their migration (Takana, 1997b, p. 15).

[4] The Baggara customarily adopt north–south seasonal movement between the wet and the dry seasons, using specific routes (maraheel), as a coping strategy for grazing and watering and against environmental and ecological hazards, e.g. insects. With the capitalists' private schemes set up on these lands, these routes and the herds' space and scope of movement were narrowed leading to unfavourable readjustments for pastoralists (Salih, 1998, pp. 99–105).

movements. Setting up air enclosures therefore became a fairly common strategy that sedentary communities used to block the pastoralists. However, this troubled situation and the expectation of attacks also prompted nomadic pastoralists to move in groups of extended families or clans to enhance their capacity against adversaries. This measure has increased the numbers of the herds using the *murhal* at any one time, which made it difficult to control, especially given the expansion of farming enterprises. The width of the *murhal* therefore increased from between two and eight miles to almost twenty miles, which was sufficient reason to ignite conflicts with farmers (Salih, 1998, p. 103).

Some pastoralists also demanded non-negotiable equal access and rights to land use against the will of the hosting communities (Mohamed, 1998, pp. 33–68). For the latter, these were over-ambitious and unacceptable demands that imply an explicit abuse of their hospitality; nevertheless, they could not challenge the complicity of the government in this dilemma. Other pastoralist groups also invaded wide areas around Jebel Marrah (the principal Fur homeland) in Central Darfur and al-Geneina (*Dar* Masalit) in West Darfur, areas recognised for their rich grazing and water sources (ibid.). The resulting conflict around these areas encouraged large groups of Baggara and Abbala to form an Arab alliance to fight against the Fur in a clear pursuit of land grabbing and 'settlement by confiscation'.

The ministries of agriculture and natural resources in Darfur are responsible for the annual demarcation of the *maraheel* to ensure smooth mobility for the herds without causing damage to the farms. But their capacity, both in finance and human resources, failed to meet the requirements for the task, and in most cases, their involvement started after many clashes had already taken place.[5] Since the late 1990s, the increasing incidents of conflict between nomadic pastoralists and farmers during the seasonal migration has drawn the attention of local and international peace NGOs to the importance of the *maraheel* in reducing conflict between these groups. The *maraheel* has therefore become one of the main intervention areas for the World Bank and United Nations agencies (e.g. USAID, UNDP, IFAD) and INGOs, particularly SOS Sahel UK and CONCORDIS, and many others involved in peacebuilding efforts. Nevertheless, the issue of land rights, whether by law or by historical legacy, and the erosion of the tribal institutions have been major challenges in managing the migration process and securing the routes (Sharawi and Gaiballa, cited in Egemi, 2012, p. 21).

Obviously, the major controversy in the conflicts between the pastoralists and sedentary communities in Darfur lies within the triangle of the historical legacy to the *Dar*, the rights of migrants as equal citizens, and the duty of the state to manage both claims fairly. When the government demonstrates inability, and/or indifference and unwillingness, to mediate and resolve such explosive matters, people can often take the law into their hands and pursue their own objectives with their own means.

[5] My personal observation when I was working with the MANR in Greater Darfur (1988–91).

Such a stalemate is behind the many conflicts experienced in Darfur within (intra-ethnic) and across (inter-ethnic) ethnic groups: for instance, the atrocious conflicts experienced amongst Arab tribes, such as the one between the Bani Helba and Mahriyah in 1976 and 1978, and between Ta'aisha and Salamat in 1979 and the 2000s; and also across tribes of different ethnicities such as that of the northern Rezeiqat and Mahriyah against Zaghawa in Kutum province in 1994. Yet the inter-ethnic conflicts between the Arab and the Fur, and between the Arab and the Masalit, were more vicious; as they were not fought only to settle tribal disputes but also essentially to grab land and emphasise racial supremacy. Indigenous Africans also engaged in fierce conflict, for more or less similar reasons, as in the conflict between the immigrant Zaghawa and the hosting Symiayat community, and between Zaghawa and Marareet in North Darfur in the 1980s and 1990s. Since the late 1980s, the inter-ethnic conflict has generally become more recurrent than intra-ethnic tribal conflict. With these conflicts becoming more racialised, al-Hakkamat have taken a more proactive role in transforming tense situations into violent confrontations, as will later become clear.

The *Dars* and land legislation

Land laws and policies that tend to limit historical property rights, on the one hand, and encourage non-owners who wish to see these rights abolished, on the other hand, have become active agents in inciting conflicts and wars between groups. For instance, the Unregistered Lands Act (ULA), introduced in 1970, declared the state to be the sole owner of all unregistered land and abolished customary land use rights. It overruled historical tribal land ownership rights, making it possible to appropriate land for public or private redistribution (El Hassan, 2008). As a consequence, even the land granted and/or reconfirmed by Ali Dinar, the last Sultan of Darfur, as *hawakir* to groups and individuals became subject to the discretion of government authorities. Tribes in rural Darfur interpreted these developments as motivated by a deliberate intention by the state to dispossess them of their *Dars*. This would certainly affect their tribal identity and culture, which rested primarily on the preservation of the *Dars*.

This policy could only generate serious blowback on the social relationships between the migrants and the *Dars'* owners, and between the latter and the state authority. The government seemed to have, deliberately or otherwise, failed to consult with land owners who had held the land for centuries and have a strong belief that it was a legacy from ancestors to cherish and protect. Meanwhile, new entrants into the *Dars* inevitably felt gratified that the policy entitled them to the same democratic rights and resources as other citizens. Subsequently, each party galvanised ethnic support to vigorously defend its position.

As a result of such unilaterally imposed policies, we saw violent conflict erupting in *Dar* Rezeiqat in 1987 and 1996, when the Rezeiqat were bitterly disappointed to see a Zaghawi candidate winning the seat of councillor for Ed Diein, the centre of their *Dar*, as indicated by the preliminary election results (El Hassan, 2008). Similarly, violent incidents broke out between Ta'aisha and Salamat in 1979/80 and 1982/3, when the Ta'aisha rejected the election result that brought a Salami man (Salamat are hosted by Ta'aisha) to the position of councillor, and murdered him (Ahmed, 1998, p. 147; Mohamed, 2003b, p. 45). Other similarly instigated incidents include the wars between Gimir and Fellata[6] in 1984, in South Darfur; between Rezeiqat and Ma'aliya, intermittently since 1968; between Hubbania and Abu-Darag, and between the Fur and Tergam in 1990 (Ahmed, 1998, p. 145; Bashar, 2013, p. 273), to mention just a few.

Conflicts with similar motives have also occurred in other parts of Sudan. For instance, in Eastern Sudan, the Bija and Rashaiyda tribes have often engaged in conflict over native administration, as the Rashaiyda have been keen to establish their own administration in the areas of Gadarif, Atbara River and Kassala. But the Bija, who have historical ownership over these areas, rejected and resisted the attempt on the pretext that the Rashaiyda were a relatively small group that had settled in the country quite recently, in 1874. In addition, they simply claimed that the Rashaiyda possessed no *hakura* to warrant exercising authority (Ahmed, 1998, pp. 143–4). The government has been unable to resolve the dispute. In southern Kordofan, the Dinka Ngok and the Misseriya Baggara Arabs both claimed Abei area to be their *Dar* even though the area was thought to be historically owned by the former. The two tribes had lived peacefully and in agreement for a long time. In the 1970s, however, some Dinka affiliates demanded separate administration, otherwise they threatened to join the Southern Sudan region. The dispute was eventually settled locally between the conflicting parties in 1977, but only for a while (ibid., pp. 145–6).

Regional geopolitics

The geopolitics played out by the riverine ruling elites in Darfur has transformed Darfur into a rear base for both the Chadian and the Libyan opposition groups, during the war between Chad and Libya in the 1980s, 1990s and 2000s, when they were hosted on Darfur soil and allowed to exercise political (and insurgency) activity. In addition to these groups, the wars and political turmoil in these countries forced over 37,000 Chadian refugees, mainly Arab pastoralists, to immigrate and settle in Darfur. The Darfuri tribes that shared the same ethnic group, i.e. their kinsfolk, such as Salamat, Mahamid, Um Jalul and Bani Helba Baggara and Abbala, were quite sympathetic toward those Arab groups and assisted in their settlement in Darfur. The land of the sedentary communities, especially around Jebel Marrah, the homeland of Fur, and around al-Geneina, the homeland of the Masalit in West Darfur, have been the main target for

[6] The Gimir hosted large groups of the Fellata and provided them with land for farming/grazing. When the rural council system was introduced, it appeared to be unclear to the Fellata where to vote, i.e. at the Gimir council in Katila where they were hosted, or at the Fellata's in Tulus. The confusion and grievances led to a vicious conflict that destroyed long-term peaceful and cooperative relations between the conflicting parties, as it compelled the Gimir to sell their herds and the Fellata to follow a longer route in their seasonal movement (Haggar, 2003).

those Arab groups (Harir, 1994, p. 169; Haggar, 2003, pp. 186–92; Flint and de Waal, 2005, pp. 54–5; Mohamed, 2003b, pp. 38–9). The estimates of those who have settled within *Dar* Masalit amount to twenty-seven Chadian Arab tribes (Mohamed, 2003b, p. 51).

The tension between the immigrants and the sedentary communities escalated to boiling point in mid-1987, when the immigrant Chadians formed a coalition of twenty-seven local Arab tribes, spearheaded by the Bani Helba, the Fur's traditionally peaceful neighbours, and the Um Jalul, led by Musa Hilal, who later became the notorious Janjawiid leader. They carried out a systematic and devastating ethnic war against the Fur. The Fur responded by burning the pasture to force the immigrants to leave, and also formed their own defence militias (Harir, 1994, p. 174; Prunier, 2007; Musa, 2009). The war continued for over two years up until May 1989 and resulted in thousands of casualties and appalling carnage. This was also a war that manifested the ambivalence of the government's judgement with regard to the inherited rights and the new legislation. At the reconciliation conference held in al-Fashir, the Arab delegates justified their aggression on the Fur and referenced their rights of land grabbing to legislation and Islamic guidance.[7]

It is indeed baffling that the national government jeopardises the safety and security of its citizens and fails abysmally to protect them, to the advantage of the Chadian Arab immigrants. It remains a mystery only until we realise that the government has already planned to settle these migrants permanently either in these areas or somewhere else. This became obvious when the NIF government introduced the *emara* policy in 1995, which legalised the settlement of these groups in *Dar* Masalit. Accordingly, *Dar* Masalit was divided into thirteen *emarat*; eight were offered to the immigrant Abbala Arab pastoralists, most were Chadians, and the remaining five *emarat* were allocated to the Masalit, the indigenous holders of the land.

It was not surprising that these steps were taken without consultation with the indigenous land owners, either whilst setting up the policy or during its execution. The Masalit's sultan, who according to historical legacy was still supposedly in charge of land distribution in his *Dar*, was disrespectfully overlooked (Ahmed, 1998, p. 152; Fadul, 1998, pp. 230–1; Haggar, 2003, p. 223). Most of these Arab groups later became regularised by the government into the so-called Border Guards (*ḥaras al-ḥudūd*) (Musa, 2009), the successor to the brutal Janjawiid militia.

The *emara* policy, along with the regulation of these Arab tribes into several regular and irregular allied government forces, such as the Popular Defence Forces (PDF), the Janjawiid militias and the peace forces (*quwaat al-salaam*),[8] could only be interpreted by the Masalit as an exis-

[7] At the conference, their delegation argued that the LRA entitles them to land access, and the shari'a states that 'land is for whoever tills it' (al-'arḍ li-man yaflahuhā).

[8] These are part of the Janjawiid forces who were brought to the area in 1999 by Mohamed Ahmad al Dabi, a Shagiyya military intelligence army general who was appointed as personal representative of President al-Bashir to deal with the situation (Flint and de Waal, 2005, p. 59).

tential threat, which made the 1996–8 armed conflict deadly and quite vicious. On the other hand, the Arabs might gleefully have thought that this was their 'holy grail'. This appeasement policy that the government pursued in the interests of these Arab groups has even tempted them to call for the name Darfur to be repealed, as it literally means 'the homeland of the Fur', something they do not agree with now. This was undoubtedly linked to the repercussions on land tenure, which is rooted in the system of the Fur sultanate. Such hostility to the old system of land tenure and its founders was clearly attested to by Mohamed al Amin Salih Baraka, a Sudanised Chadian Arab politician, who has become a member of the Sudanese national parliament, in his comments:

> The government owns all the land ... much of it is empty and not used, and things have changed since the hakura system was set up. The hakura is not a Bible, and it should be replaced by a new law to organise the land. (Cited in Flint and de Waal, 2005, p. 59)

On the other hand, the government has adopted an inconsistent, obviously discriminatory, approach in handling similar situations elsewhere in Darfur. Whereas the ruling elites enacted the Citizenship Law, which purportedly calls for the equal rights and duties of citizens, and hence legalised the presence of the Arabs and granted them more than 60 per cent of the Masalit land, they did the opposite in Ed Diein, for instance. Large groups of Zaghawa migrants (indigenous Africans) had settled since the 1970s in the town of Ed Diein, the centre of the *Dar* Rezeiqat Baggara Arabs. Contrary to the approach they followed in *Dar* Masalit, in *Dar* Rezeiqat, in the southeast of Darfur, the government failed even to legalise the presence of the Zaghawa, let alone to acknowledge their equal right to assume sovereign political office (Haggar, 2003, p. 226).

It was therefore evidently discriminatory that the ruling elites accorded discretionary powers to the Rezeiqat native authority to choose whether or not to allow 'outsiders' access to the *Dar* land and authority as equal citizens, the powers that had been denied to the Masalit.[9] For the tribes, the *Dar* is not merely a sentimental entity, it is also an existential and livelihood resource. The spiritual and material worth of the *Dar* drives communities in Darfur to construct merits compatible with the internal social and cultural contexts that heighten their belief in and value of their *Dar*. The government's partial domestic policies and approaches have therefore been at the heart of the political discord and dissent.[10] Very

[9] See detailed information in Bashar (2013, pp. 204–7) and Haggar (2003, pp. 222–4). The reconciliation agreement in 1996 provided that Arab and Masalit have equal rights and duties as equal citizens in Dar Masalit; whereas the reconciliation between Rezeiqat and Zaghawa in 1997 affirmed the sole right of Rezeiqat over Dar Rezeiqat, i.e. a restatement of the old *hakura* system.

[10] Similar cases were also evident in other parts of Sudan; for instance, tribal conflict was experienced in the 1980s between the Abd Ad-Dayyem faction of the Nawaahya clan of Dar Hamid in North Kordofan and another tribe. The reason was that in the 1980s this faction claimed that their own *Omodiya* (small administrative district) was taken from them and they themselves were made subordinate to an Omda who was not from their tribe. Therefore, they claimed their *Omodiya* back as a historical right even though they had no documents to verify such a right (El Zain, 1996). In the Nuba Mountains,

often, those casual decisions, which affect the socially recognised boundaries of administrative units, bring about unsolicited violence and tribal or ethnic polarisation, which could be avoided if a little more deliberation and consultation was used. But the practices of the ruling elites suggest that they have no sympathy toward the social harmony in Darfur and are unwilling to help prevent this happening.

Land policies and peace agreements

Attempts to settle armed conflicts have been pursued using two main mechanisms: internal conferences, locally or nationally mediated, which might involve government personnel, and peace agreements that have been pursued, mostly with the involvement of external partners, namely, to settle the conflict between the government and Darfuri insurgents. As for the first type, it is noticeable that the conflicts experienced are mostly related to the dispute over land rights between the historical land owners and those who do not have such a privilege. The reconciliation conferences held to resolve these disputes have often recommended as a starting point the preservation of the owners' rights. Government representatives have never contested the recommendations and/or suggested reforming the system, and even when government policies were sought, it was made without consulting with those affected.

These conferences are no longer effective in ending tribal conflict in Darfur. They have been manipulated politically to ensure tribal support for the ruling elites, rather than used genuinely to induce the conflicting parties to reconcile. For instance, the conference to settle violent conflict between the Arabs and the Masalit in *Dar* Masalit, held in 1996, stipulated that both the Masalit and the Arabs are equal citizens with equal rights and duties, and overlooked the *hakura* issue, the main cause of the problem. Meanwhile, the conference held in 1997 to settle the dispute between the Rezeiqat and Zaghawa in Ed Diein, as noted earlier, acknowledged the *hakura* as an exclusive right for the Rezeiqat, thus securing their right to manage their own *Dar* (Haggar, 2003, p. 224).

Also, the traditional role of the Ajaweed in dispute settlement has been changed to serve the interests of the ruling authority. The *judiyah* has therefore lost its value and status, and its moral authority to invite people to abide voluntarily by its guidance and resolutions. In addition, by virtue of their casual nature, these conferences are not decisive mechanisms for resolving controversial issues over land tenure, for they merely tend to make compromise solutions that may 'lull' the fighting without eliminating its causes. Furthermore, the ruling authority usually uses clan and tribal leaders as trustworthy spokespersons for the tribespeople, forget-

(contd) the Birgid Awlad Hilal were hosted by the *Omodiya* of Dar Bakhota for more than thirty years but when their population increased, they attempted to form their own *Omodiya* in Dar Bakhota. This was strongly resisted by Dar Bakhota on the grounds that the Dar belongs to them, and consequently bloody conflicts ensued between the two groups. When the government interfered, they approved an *Omodiya* for the Birgid in Dar Ajanj, which has created yet another conflict (Rahama and Elhussein, 2005, pp. 87–8).

ting that through hostile policies against the native administration, the ruling authorities have corroded the natives' confidence in their local leaders (Takana, 1998, p. 63).

The dynamic of change, especially in education and urbanisation, as well as the development of social and political events, has influenced the problem solving methods and the division of roles among rural communities. Tribal influence has now shifted to tribal elites and leaders of tribal militias who do not always submit to the orders of traditional authority leaders. Yet there is a crack in the relationship between the central ruling authorities and the tribal elites in Darfur, but it would always be better to win them over in order to achieve lasting peace between tribal and ethnic groups in the region (ibid.).

With regard to regionally and internationally mediated reconciliation, we have seen the Comprehensive Peace Agreement (CPA), also known as the Nefasha Agreement[11] between the SPLA/SPLM and the government, signed on 9 January 2005, enshrining the right of the southern nationals to self-determination. It also identified the dispute over land as significant in peace and reconciliation in Sudan, and hence, recommended the establishment of a National Land Commission for the whole country, and separate commissions for the Blue Nile and Southern Kordofan regions, to address similar disputes between pastoralists and farmers (Egemi, 2012, p. 25).

The Darfur Peace Agreement (DPA), signed in 2006 in Abuja to settle the conflict in Darfur, and the Eastern Sudan Peace Agreement have also stipulated the establishment of land commissions; as also did the Darfur Peace Agreement in Doha in 2011. The land commissions of Darfur were established on the principle of the recognising the historical rights of owners and the preservation of these rights. Along with this, they were tasked with designing and planning a policy for the effective utilisation and management of natural resources, including arbitration in cases of disputes.

However, these commissions have often been casual rather than permanent institutions, and therefore they have been unable to resolve the persistent dispute over land, which requires long-term operation and commitment. Yet whether or not citizens have sovereign rights over a territory they claim to have resided in for centuries, and whether migrants and displaced people should have equal rights on these lands as equal citizens, will remain constitutionally contentious issues in Sudan. The remedy inevitably entails designing a comprehensive land reform policy within just and fair governance in order to earn people's trust, respect and approval.

Elections and ethnic mobilisation

Ethnic competition over regional administrative and political authority goes back to the time when the Regional Government Act was introduced

[11] The agreement that was signed to settle the civil war in Southern Sudan, which eventually led to the separation of the Southern Sudan region into the independent state of South Sudan in 2011.

in 1980, suggesting that the region should be governed by a person native to it. The first governor appointee was the Fur Ahmed Ibrahim Diraige whose appointment received wide acclaim, even though there were no elections held. When the elections were launched after the first term, people competed for the governorship position on the basis of ethnicity. Arab tribes accused the incumbent governor of favouring his kin, the Fur, with administrative powers and gerrymandering constituencies to ensure that the Fur won subsequent elections (Harir, 1994, p. 174; also see Takana, 1998, and Musa, 2009). This accusation, along with other factors, have led to an ethnicising of subsequent elections and competition over the public office, which also, indirectly, adds up to the politics of armed conflict generally.

The ethnicisation of the process for appointing the Darfur governor has provoked ethnic division and polarisation in the social and political domains in Darfur. The situation became quite tense, to the extent that during the third democracy, 1986–9, the Baggara and Abbala Arabs of Darfur publicly demanded that Premier Sadiq al-Mahdi, the patron of the Arabs in Darfur, guarantee them their due share of power in the region. They asked for a 50 per cent share in all of the public offices in Darfur to be allocated to the Arabs in recognition of their demographic weight, their significant contribution to the wealth of the country, and their being the sole 'civilisation bearers' in the region. They presented their claims through the so-called *al-tajamu'* al-'arabi, the Arab Congregation, which boasts a mix of Arab intellectuals, tribal notables and prominent officials (El-Battahani, 2009, pp. 60–1). This bold statement of intent by the Arabs signalled the public polarisation of Darfuri society along Arab and African ethnic and racial lines. It eventually resulted in tensions being stoked incessantly, leading to violent confrontations throughout the 1980s and 1990s, as well as armed conflict in 1990 and for much of the time since 2003 (see Flint and de Waal, 2005).

Since 1989, the NIF government has reinforced these rising ethnic and racial perceptions among the Arabs in Darfur by incorporating ethnic discourse in state political rhetoric and public mobilisation for war in the south of (then still united) Sudan. It also co-opted and incorporated traditional institutions of the Arabs, such as al-Hakkamat and armed militias, in the state's war machinery. The loyalty and commitment demonstrated by these informal institutions in serving the interests of the ruling elites have driven the elites to robustly exploit them in the civil wars they waged in the country. This apparent alliance between riverine ruling and governing elites and Darfuri Arabs appears to reflect the domestic politics of favouritism and drastically reduced the prospect of ethnic rapprochement in Darfur.

Ethnic mobilisation and competition for senior public posts were not merely confined to the regional posts in Darfur, however. With the inception of the democratic era of 1986–9, national political parties were involved in a frenzied competition to lead the country by pursuing 'divide-and-rule' politics[12] in Darfur, in order to secure electoral support

[12] 'Divide and rule' is defined in the Oxford Dictionary as '(t)he policy of maintaining control over one's subordinates or opponents by encouraging dissent between them, thereby preventing them from uniting in opposition'.

from the locals. These elections were therefore open to manipulation by political party leaders. In line with this, the competing sectarian political parties formed alliances with their traditional clients: the Umma Party, which was elected into office in 1986, with the Arabs, and their partner in the coalition government, the Democratic Unionist Party (DUP), with the Fur (Harir, 1994). Following the elections, both parties continued their support for the polarised groups in Darfur by monopolising and exploiting the state's office and resources.

The leading political parties in the democratic government thus promoted tribalism and ethnicity as political tools for obtaining 'ethnic voices'. When tribes and ethnic groups realised their political significance, they began to negotiate for mutual political patronage and 'communalism' (Smith, 1981), i.e. trade their voices and political support in return for favouritism and political power, both locally and nationally. Ironically, neither party in the coalition government was able to restrain its alliance partner when the two ethnic groups were at war during the period between 1987 and 1989. Hence, tension and belligerency between the Arabs and Africans intensified unabatedly.

This form of patronage is not dissimilar to the political practice in most sub-Saharan African states where the allocation of resources and office are often decided on an ethnic basis (Smith, 1981, p. 16). Thus the partiality of the government for the Rezeiqat native authority, discussed earlier, seems to be a reward for the Rezeiqat's efforts in protecting the borders of their *Dar*, which they transformed into a buffer zone with Sothern Sudan. Arguably, although the Rezeiqat were holding back the Sudan People's Liberation Army (SPLA) from expanding into the north, they were not motivated by the desire to support the government – rather, they were principally defending their own territory from being invaded and ransacked, as has often happened in their conflict with the tribes of Southern Sudan.

As the general scene suggests, the ethnically oriented domestic politics pursued in Darfur by the riverine governing elites in the last two decades has created appalling ethnic and racial differentiation. Tribal leaders, particularly of large tribes, have become burdened with the need to establish close relationships with the governing authorities in order to avoid being removed from post. Tribal leaders and dignitories therefore often visit Khartoum to pledge their personal commitment and the loyalty of their tribes to prominent ruling elites, including the president.[13]

The militarisation of society

Since the late 1980s, several social, economic, environmental and political crises have beset the Darfur region. These include, but are not limited to, the abolition of the native administration in 1971, the economic crisis of the 1970s, drought, desertification and the severe famine that struck Darfur in the 1980s. Extreme poverty led to the raiding and looting of vulnerable villages. Banditry and retaliations

13 News bulletins on Sudanese television often contain items about tribal leaders visiting Khartoum pledging full support for the president (my personal observation).

among clans have become rife, all too often exacerbated by the state's inability to catch the criminals and their tendency instead to accuse entire tribes of banditry.[14]

Darfur has become completely besieged by such circumstances, generating a precarious security situation that has made people's internal movement quite limited. This disarray was further aggravated by the availability of illicit arms smuggled from politically unstable neighbouring states, such as Chad. With the state failing to maintain law and order, tribes robustly lobbied for the right to carry weapons and took their own initiative in forming militias and (ethnic) alliances when violent confrontation ensued. The militias came to the fore for the first time during Nimeiri's regime when they were recruited and sponsored to fight in the civil war in South Sudan, which restarted in 1983. They included the *Murahaliin* militias of the Rezeiqat and the Misseriya of Kordofan. Since then, the use of tribal militias in the civil war has been a strategy for the military establishment in Sudan, which in turn has encouraged the tribes to strengthen and rely on them as a substitute for the role of the state in providing protection (Mohamed Salih and Harir, 1994, pp. 196–7).

Thereafter, tribal militias were promoted further when the central government, facing the inadequate state of the military forces, incorporated the tribal militias as paramilitary forces in the civil wars, ignoring the negative impact this approach might have on the ground. When Nimeiri's regime was overthrown in 1985, through public uprising, the Transitional Military Council, which took over after the uprising, formalised and promoted the status of these militias (de Waal, 1993, p. 147; Flint and de Waal, 2005, p. 24). The coalition government of the Umma and NIF parties later used them extensively and eventually rebranded them as the Popular Defence Forces (PDF), under the command of the regular army. Throughout the 1990s, the NIF government continued recruiting more Arab militias from Kordofan, South Darfur and the White Nile and used them as an indispensable paramilitary force in the fight against the SPLM (Mohamed Salih and Harir, 1994, pp. 197; Haggar, 2007, p. 127).

Since then, ethnic and tribal militias have become integral to the state's military apparatus and strategies, a trend that has also been reinforced by government doubts about the effectiveness of the military. The need to recruit loyal client forces outside the regular military therefore increased and it seems that the cost was not a big concern for the ruling elites. The NIF/NCP[15] government surpassed its predecessors by actually issuing

[14] Haggar, 2003, p. 202. Haggar argues that many of those who are accused, tortured and exposed to the media as armed bandits, are not convicted for lack of evidence and therefore released. Those so treated often end up becoming armed bandits. They also often lure and entrap the regular forces in acts of revenge for the torture that they were subjected to by these forces (ibid.).

[15] The National Islamic Front (NIF) has metamorphed into a new party: the ruling National Congress Party (NCP). The core ideology and membership have remained the same, however. Reference to either of these indicates the core Sudanese Muslim Brotherhood.

the Popular Defence Act of 1989, which legitimises these militias. The notoriety of these militias became known in 1987 when the Rezeiqat militias, in retaliation for their defeat by the SPLA, attacked thousands of innocent Dinka who had taken refuge in Ed Diein, the capital of *Dar* Rezeiqat, shooting and burning them alive (Harir, 1994, p. 15; Verney *et al.*, 1995, p. 16).

The NCP government also resorted to the PDF forces along with the Arab horsemen militias of the Bani Helba tribe in 1991/2, to hold back the SPLA incursion into South Darfur led by Daud Bolad, a prominent former NIF activist who belonged to the Fur. The victory of the militias over Bolad reinforced the government's trend of using tribal militias as a counter-insurgency strategy. Ever since, the militias have become central to the government's wars, including confronting the current insurgencies in Darfur (Flint and de Waal, 2005, p. 24). The most recent form of these forces has been the Janjawiid militias, which have been catapulted into the spotlight since 2003 to become known globally as the most brutal paramilitary force operating under the Sudanese government command. It has now been renamed the Rapid Defence Forces (RDF) (Haggar, 2007, pp. 113–39).

Deteriorating services and diminishing work opportunities in Darfur, coupled with the mounting wars and the needs of the military for more soldiers, have positioned the army as an available source of unskilled labour to easily accommodate young Darfuris, without complicated procedures, as required when hiring for the civil service. The Darfuri youth, mostly from rural areas, have subsequently constituted a large proportion of the army troops. When the insurgency broke out in 2003, the government started bombing rural areas wherein they suspected rebels have sheltered. They also reactivated their mobilisation campaign to enlist more young people from rural Darfur but encountered absolute rejection from those who belonged to the rebels' tribes and who chose not to join the forces that targeted their own people. The huge numbers of the deceased and injured fighters in the civil war in South Sudan was a warning to the fighters of the fate awaiting them. Apparently, their fear, or reservation, was fully justified given the number of the Darfuri combatants who were 'martyred' in the battles, as shown in Table 2.1:

Table 2.1 'Martyrs' during the first twelve years of the NIF's reign (1989–2000)

Area/state	*Number of martyrs*	*Percentage*
South Darfur	1,923	32.31
North Darfur	1,212	20.37
West Darfur	713	11.98
Northern	111	1.87
River Nile	196	3.29
Western Kordofan	1,796	30.18

(*Source*: Seekers of Truth and Justice (2000: 33))

With the continuation of the war, the high cost incurred in the military confrontations invited the government to search for a cheap and more effective alternative. Darfuri tribal militias were then brought in. Nevertheless, it must be said that many Arab tribes, for social reasons or otherwise, seemed to have had their reservations about engaging in this conflict. The government then opted for what they belatedly discovered as a potential substitute – the horsemen combatants, who were not affiliated with specific tribes, and hence, the Janjawiid appeared in the war arena. The term 'Janjawiid' in Baggara slang simply means an unruly, rowdy group, often of youth, who care less for decorum and courtesy than for (criminal) adventure. Their name, however, acquired more fanciful and sinister meanings when the atrocities they perpetrated became well known globally.[16] Ever since, the government has given this group a robust role and granted them full impunity, especially so that they could perpetrate acts of violence that the regular army might find reprehensible and unethical.

CONCLUSION

From the previous discussion, it is plausible to deduce that ethnic differences between tribes in Darfur, whether perceived or otherwise, constitute no differentiation between these polar groups that justifies their waging war on one another. Rather, people tend to identify with tribal spirit and ethnic consciousness only to support or withstand aggression induced by reasons other than ethnic or tribal affiliation.

The pervasive armed conflicts in Darfur were caused by a complex web of structural causes and triggering factors but are principally associated with the approach to domestic politics pursued by the central riverine ruling elites towards Darfur. During the sultanate, the administration was based on the *Dars* and tribal authorities that were strongly connected to the sultan, and other provincial authorities. This form of administration, which kept Darfur efficiently united for centuries, has been broken, as the *Dars* and tribal authorities have become disconnected entities lacking the governance thread that used to link them up with close supervision and support.

Thereafter, the economic, environmental, political and social crises experienced in Sudan since the 1960s, particularly on the structures and society of Darfur, have necessitated changes in policy and approaches to cope with the impacts, especially with regard to power relationships and access to the then diminishing resources. Nevertheless, with their focus geared on the centre, the national government has overlooked these challenges, and the policies enacted at the time, for instance, the ULA in 1970 and the abolition of the native administration in 1971, have only exacerbated the problems. Darfur has subsequently been turned into a place where the people become trapped in deprivation, hostility and a violent race to secure livelihoods and authority.

[16] The reputation of the Janjawiid has rippled globally since 2003 following the inhumane atrocities they committed against villagers in Darfur.

Turning a blind eye to the urgent needs of the Darfuris, the leaders of the sectarian political parties, the core of the riverine elites, have used Darfur, especially during the democratic period (1986–9), as a race track to win the elections. They have pursued the divide-and-rule political approach through the racial polarisation of the society, as Arabs *vis-à-vis* Africans. In addition, the riverine ruling elites have made Darfur into a scapegoat to serve their pan-Arabist drive through the game of geopolitics played out for the advantage of Chadian and Libyan Arab opposition groups and immigrants. The process of absorbing these groups into Darfur has turned it into a marketplace for illicit ammunition. The resulting circumstances[17] have compelled people to get armed, as individuals and as tribal militias. Simple tribal disputes have therefore often been easily transformed into violent armed confrontations.

Amid these calamities and inappropriate policies, the welfare of the Darfur society has never been addressed, especially as far as the security and livelihoods are concerned. The state's inability to maintain law and order has generated vicious outcomes that have overshadowed the peaceful coexistence that once prevailed among Darfuri inhabitants. Moreover, since the 1990s to the time of writing (2017), Darfur soil has been transformed into military barracks and graves for Darfuri combatants. Such social destruction has been furthered by the emergence of the Janjawiid militias, since 2003, to serve up the civil wars that the ruling elites have waged in order to silence the rising voices of rights groups and justice advocates in the country. In Darfur, these militias have opened up an unprecedented chapter of brutality against the local populations.

For most of the Darfuri tribes, tribal militias constitute the basic component of the defence system, especially for the Baggara and Abbala Arab tribes, who are often the main partners in the conflict experienced in Darfur. Al-Hakkamat Arab women constitute a genuine part of this defence system where they act as ethnic zealots for maintaining the spirit of the horsemen and the militias, in defending the tribe, and, since the 1990s, in fighting for the interests of the government. The next chapter explores the character of al-Hakkamat in more detail and establishes the processes of their emergence and development and their effect.

[17] During 1994–2000 Darfur police records showed that 9,444 pieces of illicit small arms were collected, out of a total projected number of 132,174. There were 856 incidents of armed robberies, 736 incidents of drug trafficking and 972 lives lost in armed tribal conflict. The total number of crimes reported during this period was 197,568 and small arms were used in 51.4 per cent of them. Women committed 13,981 crimes involving the use of arms, which constitutes 23.5 per cent (El Obeid, 2000).

3

Al-Hakkamat Women

This chapter investigates and analyses al-Hakkamat women, as individuals, and as a traditional institution of authority within Darfuri Arab society, specifically the Baggara agro-pastoralists. It argues that the attendant uncertainties surrounding the pastoralists' livelihood patterns have dictated the creation and development of al-Hakkamat using well-established procedures that usually start at a quite young age for females who aspire to be Hakkamat. The dynamism of circumstances within the tribal boundaries have enabled and reinforced al-Hakkamat's agency and power as the successor to a rich history of women and gender power relations in Darfur. This chapter clarifies and discusses the trajectory of the emergence and development of al-Hakkamat.

AL-HAKKAMAT: MEANING AND SIGNIFICANCE

Many Darfuris think that the term *al-Hakkamah* (pl. *al-Hakkamat*: *al* is the definite article in Arabic) is the feminine form derived from the Arabic meanings of the word 'hukm', a semantic field that ranges from 'judgement', 'ruling', 'governing' or 'condemnation', to *hākim* or *hakkam*, meaning a male arbiter.[1] This is reminiscent of the common vernacular term that the Darfuris often use to describe themselves as *hukkām* (sing. *hākim*), meaning 'people with a sense of ruling canon and etiquette' (Kamal El-Din, 2007, p. 93). The senses of these male-oriented descriptions are feminised in a single word: 'Hakkamah', denoting a female who possesses a raft of special qualities: a poet, a performer and a singer. Her verse focuses on the words of wisdom, and she can exercise judgements and arbitration. These are the qualities that the respective society distinguishes as the basis for individual female's excellence.

Baggara society thus generally agrees that 'Hakkamah means *hukum* – ruling; if she orders you to offer help, you should obey, otherwise, she would dub you a coward'.[2] 'She is a person of wisdom and has the ability

[1] See *A Dictionary of Modern Written Arabic* (Hans, 1961).

[2] Interview with Ahmed Jowa (R14), radio and TV presenter from Ta'aisha, Nyala, 2006.

to judge others',[3] and she is 'one of the women in the village or the camp who have a specific form of authority of arbitration. It is her power to exercise authority that qualifies her to be Hakkamah.'[4]

However a retired Baggari teacher who is well versed in Baggara culture argues that the term *Hakkamah* is definitely not the feminine form in the Arabic language; rather, it is the neutral form of exaggeration (having more of a something) derived from *hukm*, just like the Arabic words *allāmah*, meaning a knowledgeable person, from *ilm* (knowledge), and *fahhāmah* (a very perceptive person) from the word *fahm* (comprehension/understanding).[5]

In general, al-Hakkamat is a local term that refers to Darfuri Arab females who are gifted with poetic skills and are therefore recognised as folk poets, who have normally received very little or no education (girl's education was limited in rural areas). These women possess other unique characteristics. Aided and motivated by ethnic identity consciousness, they develop a tremendous agency that enables them to exercise authority and influence in order to fulfil social and political obligations compatible with the welfare of their tribes. They can pass rulings and arbitrations that are convenient for preserving the sovereignty and sanctity of the tribal territories. Their roles are therefore legitimised, honoured and upheld by their communities.

The historical background of the development of al-Hakkamat is not, however, well recorded in literature, but the Baggara have never questioned their origin or history. The same is true of many 'icons' or phenomena of social and cultural heritage that have not been researched in Darfur, especially as far as women and gender power relationships are concerned.

Some opinions are inclined to establish a link between al-Hakkamat and the immigration of Arab groups into Darfur centuries ago. They hold that before then the so-called Hakkamah was unknown in the social organisation of groups inhabiting Darfur. She has only appeared on the scene with the settlement of Arab groups in Darfur to mark out a unique characteristic of their culture. There are female poets and singers within African groups who sing songs of chivalry and love but have not been classified as Hakkamat in the explicit sense and meanings contained among the Arab groups.[6]

Belief in al-Hakkamah as a culturally distinctive feature of the Arab groups invites objective thinking about the culture of other Arab groups in Sudan that claim the same Arab origin. Outside Darfur, al-Hakkamah, in the sense suggested above, exists only among the Baggara groups of the neighbouring Kordofan region. Most of these Kordofan Baggara are, however, an extension of those in Darfur, and have common historical, social and ethnic denominators. Al-Hakkamah does not exist among the vast majority of the claimants of Arab descent in Sudan, be they nomadic

3 Interview with government employee from Fur, Nyala (R28), 2006.

4 Interview with a politician and affiliate to PDF from Bani Helba (R48), Nyala, 2006.

5 Interviews with E. D. Khair Allah (R22), a retired teacher and researcher from Bani Helba, Nyala, 2006.

6 Group and individual interviews, Nyala, 2006.

or sedentary communities, nor does it exist in the Arab countries where these groups claim to have come from. These limited social boundaries of the culture of al-Hakkamah suggest that it might have fundamentally germinated in these two regions as an instinctual reaction and a gendered strategy against overwhelming threats surrounding the livelihoods of these nomadic groups – men move with the herds and become subject to adversity, and women stay behind to care for the village or the camp and may become vulnerable to attacks, both from man and nature. It thus appears to be a gendered resilient mechanism for dealing with hazards and uncertainties.

THE EMERGENCE OF AL-HAKKAMAH

The projection of al-Hakkamah is predicated on what she shows as indicative of talent and ability to master composing, reciting, singing and performing from an early age. At the outset, she is usually noticed by female relatives and peers in her clan in the village/camp. These peers encourage and support her to develop her skills. They do so by listening to her songs and recitations, and by accompanying her as a chorus, correcting her compositions, if necessary, and cheering her up. This process continues until her performance becomes applauded and admired by a wide audience before she becomes recognised as a prospective Hakkamah in the village.[7]

Several Hakkamat described the process of their emergence and publicity. For instance, one of them highlighted her experience by saying, 'I started singing when I was a child grazing the goats in the fields. I was singing at the *Harrim* dance, and finally, I developed myself into *Khail*-Hakkamah.'[8] Another Hakkamah explained that it all began for her when she started performing at the casual dance parties that are customarily organised in the village in the evenings when young girls and boys would make their own separate groups of three to seven persons and have fun singing and dancing. They continue to practise singing at such gatherings and build their confidence until their peers approve of them. Later, they become publicly recognised as renowned Hakkamat when they are invited to perform before large audiences, normally on social occasions.[9]

Singing and dancing parties in the evening are common in rural Darfur, and apart from the elderly, almost all of the village community take part in it. They are more often than not organised for fun and entertainment and not necessarily associated with specific social occasions. But during family celebrations and social events, e.g. weddings or Eid, these gatherings become more intensive and normally last for over a week. Adults and children may gather around the same *mada*, but age groups often opt for their own peer fun. These parties also serve as a platform for social accul-

7 Group interview with Hakkamat (G4), Nyala, 2006.

8 Accounts of Hubbania Hakkamah (R58) at group interview with Hakkamat (G4); Nyala, 2006.

9 Interview with Hakkamah from Rezeiqat Mahriyah Hemdaniya (R31), Nyala, 2006.

turation and indoctrination, where rules of conduct and moral behaviour are passed to the younger generations.

In addition to these routine nocturnal sociable gatherings, al-Hakkamat, young and old, also participate in celebrating social events, such as weddings, circumcision, arrival from travel or farewell, as well as the communal events experienced by the community, for instance, the *Faza'*. On these occasions, seasoned Hakkamat customarily nurture the budding skills of the new aspirants by allowing them to display their composing and reciting talents. Thereafter, the developing Hakkamat may take advantage of similar occasions for testing their abilities and showcasing their performances, which might endear them to the wider community.[10]

On the other hand, ordinary women and girls in the community also make significant contributions in publicising the songs of the developing Hakkamah, by singing them until they spread out and become known to all. The signs of admiration from women and their encouraging comments, together with the spread of the songs, foster the identification of the budding singer as a potential Hakkamah. The composing and performing skills of al-Hakkamat are therefore crucial in gaining the community's endorsement and support. Confidence, charisma, social relationships and the acquisition of sound local knowledge and cultural insight, are all requisite attributes for addressing community-centred moral values and the ethics of bravery, generosity, good behaviour, solidarity and philanthropy. The woman who chooses to establish herself as Hakkamah must indeed demonstrate these necessary talents and coveted qualities.

As the practice shows, many of the wannabe female singers who compete in singing and perform in accordance with the parameters set for excellence are likely to be identified as Hakkamat. That said, there is no restriction on the number of Hakkamat in the village and there could be as many as the number of the clans (*khashum bait* in Arabic) in the tribe, and sometimes more. In a village of two hundred households, for instance, there is usually at least one Hakkamah, but there could be many more Hakkamat depending on the local talent and aspirations. This open access for rural women to aspire and nurture their talents as powerful figures contrasts sharply with the position generally prevailing in other rural communities in Sudan, especially north Sudan, where rural women are still confined to indoor household activities.

The ranking of al-Hakkamah's excellence is usually determined by the quality of the expressions used and their succinct brevity, the number of stanzas, the musical tone and the coordination and performance among the chorus. This must be integrated with the ability to react spontaneously and poetically to instant occasions or incidents and to compose on the spur of the moment, for instance, describing an elegant man on a handsome horse, a courageous stance, an instance of munificence, etc. These are crucial qualities for keeping her agency thriving throughout her career.[11]

Al-Hakkamat therefore compete for the best performance during the various social occasions that inspire them to compose, recite and perform,

[10] Group and individual interviews, Nyala, 2006.

[11] Group and individual interviews with Hakkamat and others, Nyala, 2006.

and where people appraise and identify their favourite Hakkamah. Following her public recognition, al-Hakkamah's prestige becomes significantly enhanced by receiving financial rewards especially during singing and dancing shows,[12] as an expression of admiration, mainly from men, but occasionally from women too. The amount of money al-Hakkamat earn by this method boosts the stature of their social recognition and also comprises a substantial part of their income, especially when these instant contributions come from prominent figures in the community.

MODELS OF AL-HAKKAMAT

All Hakkamat start as singers but not all aspirant females who try to be Hakkamah succeed; though their skills and abilities may still qualify them for some roles and obligations short of those of the fully recognised Hakkamat. They go through the same process to gain public recognition until they eventually fit into one of two main categories: Hakkamat *al-khail* (Arabic for horses), who are also known as *al-Soja* or *al-Boshan* Hakkamat,[13] and *al-mada* (public dance yard) Hakkamat, who primarily perform in chorus in open dance yards. The former is loftier in performance and singing, and higher in stature and influence.[14]

Usually at the outset, al-Hakkamah emerges as a skilful woman performing specific folk dances at the *mada*, e.g. *Sanjak*, *Gaydoomah*, *Iraij*, etc. After these dances, they come quite naturally through the ranks to be recognised as *al-Sanjak* Hakkamat, *al-Gaydoomah* Hakkamat, *al-Iraij* Hakkamat, *al-Katim* Hakkamat, etc., before they develop into *al-khail* Hakkamat (horse Hakkamat), who do not sing at the *mada*, but extol the outstanding qualities of people and horses in solo performances.[15]

Al-mada Hakkamat are reputed to perform enthralling dancing, such as the *Jamal Ragad* dance (meaning 'a camel lay down'), *Umm Jekkay*, *al-Harimah* (a Hubbania folk dance); *al-Iraij*, *al-Murhakah*[16] (the grinding

[12] When the singing brings the admirers to an ecstatic state, a man comes forward, raises his hand saying '*abshuree*' (literally, 'cheer up!'), and then puts some money on the head of the performing or singing woman. This money is called *tangeet* or *showbash* (ibid.).

[13] *Boshan* and *Soja* are the poetry (along with reciting) that is locally recognised as focusing exclusively on describing horses and horsemen, which is otherwise performed by a single male performer, the *Hadday*, the male counterpart of al-Hakkamah who nonetheless lacks her influence. Group and individual interviews, Nyala, 2006.

[14] Group and individual interviews with Hakkamat and others, Nyala, 2006.

[15] Ibid.

[16] *Al-Murhakah* is solo indoor singing by al-Hakkamah when grinding grain on a *murhakah* (a flat stone used by women for grinding/milling grains). It has all but disappeared, however, because of the introduction of mechanical grinding mills to rural areas. The songs of *al-Murhakah* are very important and influential in mobilising people to join the fighting. They are usually sung by al-Hakkamah when a woman in the community experiences events that touch her or her family deeply, e.g. when she is humiliated and is therefore seeking protection, sympathy and/or support as well as revenge. The dancers of *al-Gidairee* are usually young people and the songs and recitations are often emotional, romantic and about the future dreams of the young, as in *al-Gaydoomah*. Interview with E. D. Khair Allah, Nyala, 2006.

stone), *al-Gidairee*, etc. They perform these dances whilst singing the songs of *al-Katim*, *al-Nuggarah* (the drum), etc. The latter embraces a dance called *Cadal*, and songs such as the one recited below:

English
The drum cried at the wedding parade.[17]
She who does not beget a boy has an unfair deal.

Transliteration
al-nuggārah bakat gaydūmah
al-mā jābat walad maẓlūmah

This Hakkamah implicitly encourages young girls to marry and have children. The importance they attach to having boys reflects the classical thinking, which presumes that in an environment often fraught with tension and fighting, male births tend to be more hoped-for in order to have the right male population defending the tribe. The stereotyped assumption always suggests that women are vulnerable to vindictive acts of tribal and family humiliation. Therefore, the more sons they have, the more powerful they will be and their womenfolk protected.

Whilst all dance types are performed to the tune of romantic, passionate and emotional songs, the songs sung at *al-Katim* dance are often provocative and rousing and frequently performed by the most skilful and prestigious Hakkamat, such as the popular verse of al-Hakkamah describing a man, as:[18]

English
The broad-shouldered five-year-old[19]
He who doesn't sit indolently, exchanging gossip,
He who always carries a Kalashnikov, marching.[20]

Transliteration
al-marbūʿ al-khumāsī
al-mā gawāl, jalāsī
shāyyil l-kilāsh, māshī

In this song, al-Hakkamah draws attention to the manifestation of valour, even before it is called for by adversity. She paints a figuratively expressive model to follow: a fully fledged male (a camel or an ox at its prime maturity), always holding onto his AK47 ready to fend off danger rather than sitting idly and exchanging gossip, unable to defend the tribe when the need arises. She meant to encourage her folks to remain vigilant and to stand by fully armed so as to square up to any eventualities. Not only do her vivid lyrics emphasise the worth of solidarity, they also reflect al-Hakkamah's sound knowledge of the desired values inculcated.

As mentioned, the highest position and prestige any Hakkamah aspires to achieve is to assume the title of '*Khail*-Hakkamah', a pinnacle that

17 i.e. the marching of a bridegroom to his bride's house.
18 Interview with E. D. Khair Allah, Nyala, 2006.
19 i.e. a bull at its prime age and power.
20 i.e. to answer a call for help.

requires outstanding poetic and other skills, experience and dedication.[21] One of the *Khail*-Hakkamat described her journey, which was typical of that of many *Khail*-Hakkamat, saying, 'at the outset, I was singing *al-Itaireenah, al-Jilaihah, al-Dabe, um-Piteete*;[22] then I gave up singing and became a chief Hakkamah'.[23] Another Hakkamah said that she initially became a singer of *Hussain*, then *Sanjak*, then *al-Katim*, before qualifying as *Boshan* Hakkamah, i.e. *Khail*-Hakkamah, performing the *borday* (extolling the qualities of horses and horsemen).[24]

Some women became *Khail*-Hakkamat for purely family reasons; as transpires from the experience of an elderly Hakkamah who started singing in 1955, praising good men and soon became *al-Katim*-Hakkamah. She excelled in composing and has been repeatedly invited over and over again to perform in many places. This Hakkamah's father and uncles were owners of cattle herds and were philanthropic horsemen. She has transformed into *Khail*-Hakkamah primarily to extol their virtues and good deeds. She also performs solo, praising the brave men who hunt elephants (elephant hunting is a dangerous activity and proof of bravery) and the wise and devoted men who could mediate and reconcile community disputes.[25]

Assuming the position of *Khail*-Hakkamah is a complicated process, which is customarily overseen by the Ageed al-Augada,[26] the supreme war leader of the tribe, and the head of its defence institution. The involvement of this Ageed is paramount, as the role of the respective Hakkamah is integral to that of the Ageed. At the beginning, the *Khail*-Hakkamah must be selected from among the recognised *al-mada* Hakkamat, especially *al-Katim* Hakkamat. Her nomination must, however, primarily be endorsed by notable village women, and generally by other community members, based on her skills and qualities of agency, personality, experience, knowledge, and outgoing and outspoken character.

The Ageed offers her the tribe's flag, but sometimes she holds the flag of Sudan. If a woman is seen dressed modishly or wearing the flag of Sudan, especially at social and public occasions, she would almost certainly be a *Khail*-Hakkamah. She usually carries a (staff-like) stick made of giraffe tail, adorned by shimmering beads and golden pieces of ornaments, as a sign of authority. The horsemen entourage must stop if she waves it at them and heed her commands; if she wishes to host them, they must follow her. It worth noting that in the past, the selection of the *Khail*-Hakkamah was habitually celebrated in a huge, lavish ceremony, attended by tribal leaders and elites. Recently however, public celebrations have received less attention than they had in the past.[27]

[21] Group and individual interviews, Nyala, 2006.
[22] These are the names of folk dances.
[23] Interview with Hubbania Hakkamah (R32), Nyala, 2006.
[24] Accounts of Ta'aishi Hakkamah (R30) at group interview (G4), Nyala, 2006.
[25] Accounts of Hubbania Hakkamah (R20) at group interview (G4), Nyala, 2006.
[26] Group interview with Hakkamat (G4), Nyala, 2006. Augada is plural (sing. Ageed). It stands for the tribe's military commander. Ageed is also the Arabic word for the army rank of colonel (also see Takana, 1998, pp. 216–17).
[27] Group interview with Hakkamat (G4), Nyala, 2006.

Photo 3.1 Hakkamah from Rezeiqat with a stick used as a sign of her authority (*Source*: Ministry of Culture and Information, al-Fashir. Photograph taken at a folkloric music festival in al-Fashir, North Darfur, 23 December 2014)

Having been selected, the *Khail*-Hakkamah is required to undertake massive social responsibilities, along with helping the Ageed and his horsemen to undertake security missions, which may involve fighting. Other social duties relevant to the Ageed that involve the *Khail*-Hakkamat include the tribal *Zaffa*[28] (parade), which is often organised on happy occasions, e.g. weddings, circumcision[29] ceremonies, etc., to showcase the wealth and power of their tribes. More crucially though, the horsemen make no move on tribal affairs unless this Hakkamah is informed.

The *Khail*-Hakkamat are therefore of vital importance during conflict. Their added responsibilities require in-depth cultural awareness and

[28] A memorable tribal parade known as Zaffat Sibdo, was organised in 1960 in a place called Sibdo in *Dar* Rezeiqat. It was attended by the Egyptian president, Nasir, together with the Sudanese president. Other parades have also been held in the recent history of Darfur. Interviews, Nyala, May 2006; also see Masajid, 1995, pp. 9–19.

[29] Male circumcision is recommended by the Shari'a and is practised all over Sudan. The notorious female genital mutilation (FGM), however, is controversial. The British attempted to ban it in 1946 but were confronted with Sudanese protests on the pretext that FGM is a cultural matter and it should not be addressed by colonials (Althaus, 1997). Yet there are many tribes in rural Darfur, e.g. Fur, who have not traditionally carried out FGM but have picked up the practice recently as a result of urban influence. This was reported by the Sudan Household Health Survey (Economic Research Forum Central Bureau of Statistics, 2006), which reveals that FGM is practised on 75 to 80 per cent of females in northern parts of the country, whereas in Darfur, 40 to 60 per cent are affected and it is more prevalent among educated and wealthy families.

broad knowledge and understanding about their tribe and the surrounding tribes, as well as the skills of mobilisation and organisation. For instance, they must know how to describe and praise the horses artfully, and how to tack them up. Among the Baggara, a horse usually constitutes not just a valuable asset, but also a source of power, wealth and prestige. Al-Hakkamat are seen by many tribal members as experts in making handcrafted horse equipment, e.g. leather water containers, sword sheaths, bridles, etc. They also make beautiful horse ornaments especially for the bridle, locally called the *zihba*, which are valued and quite in demand by the tribe's horsemen. Besides, they must be aware of and ready to feed the horses, together with their masters, when required. These obligations require al-Hakkamat to be of an age that can keep them energetic and responsive to the developing events in their society.

By undertaking these responsibilities, the *Khail*-Hakkamat have turned out to be persons who enjoy pre-eminence, as they occupy the most prestigious position and become the most feared. Nonetheless, both the *Khail*-Hakkamat and the *mada*-Hakkamat hold the same right to rule, but to a degree that differs depending on their individual charismatic power and agency to see their commands and arbitrations heeded and enforced.

By the very characteristics outlined above, al-Hakkamat represent a form of 'ethnic institution' that serves to maintain the morally differentiating boundaries between the 'we' and the 'they'. Al-Hakkamat therefore strive to sway the balance of power and enhance the recognition of uniqueness in their favour – they are the best and most powerful; others are not, or less so. This rooted ideology of identity differentiation is the force that accounts for the persistent advocacy for conflict in the discourse of al-Hakkamat, and the popularity of enlisting and celebrating the fighting spirit among the youngsters. Praising the tribes and indulging in heightening their pride are but manifestations of this commitment of al-Hakkamat to this ideology, as reverberates quite sensationally in the following recitation from a Salami Hakkamah:[30]

English
Oh, my Salamat people, the seas of religion.
Our camp has the Quran; our camp has religious disciples,
Has enormous dishes offered and sheep slaughtered,
Unless be it from Allah, Oh, nothing dares come near us!

Transliteration
yā ʾakhwānī l-salāmāt, buḥūr l-diyyāhah.
farīgnā bay qūrʾānah, farīgnā bay-ḥīrānah.
al-kubār gudḥānah, al-muḍabaḥāt khurfānah.
bala ʾallah dā, way, māfī shī bidnāna.
(H. R58, G4, Nyala, 2006).

Echoing similar sentiments, one Hakkamah from the Hubbania praises her tribe:[31]

[30] Accounts of Salami Hakkamah at group interview (G4), Nyala, 2006.
[31] Accounts of Hubbania Hakkamah (R20) at group interview with Hakkamat (G4), Nyala 2006.

English
Hubbania are people of pride whose seas aren't dark,
Their strength is divine; their business is perfect.
It is not a rope of authority, those pull (this way), and others pull (the other way).
They are slaughterers of bulls and owners of good horses,
They are pegs, the men for the whole country.
If the enemy said, 'look, there they are',
They would chase those close to al-Jurra,[32] and those far away, to al-Kurra.[33]
If he jumped over the (fence of) thorns, and met face to face.
With three thousand pounds' worth of ammunition,
How hard would be his day!

Transliteration
al-habbāniyya al-ʿuzāz, humm buḥūrhum *mā* ḍullumah.
gudrat-hum ʾilāhiyyah wa shughlut-hum ḥurrah.
mā ḥabil ḥukum, da bajurra wa da bajurra.
ḍabāḥīn abū kurjummah, siyyād l-khaṣī abu juljummah.
masāmīr l-rujjāl humma, li-balad ṣurrah.
kan al-ʿadāwah gālat daylāk, humma.
al-garīb bi-llaḥigū al-Jurrah, wa-l-baʿīd bi-waṣṣilū l-kurrah.
kan naṭṭa barrah l-shawk, wa ʾitgābalan ghurrah.
al-dhakhīrah talattālāf, gāsī lay yawmah.
(H. R20, G4, Nyala, 2006).

These two Hakkamat celebrated the power, wealth and generosity of their tribes, boasting of their bravery and the strength that frighten their foes, and also boasting that their tribes can defend the whole country with their advanced ammunition. The language of the songs is charged with cultural attributes and comes loaded with symbols that emphatically captivate the local audience. Amid their battle to hoist their tribes to such heights, al-Hakkamat also sense the importance of drawing attention to their own identity and their significance, as in the recitation below:[34]

English
I speak out, lifting my head up; I know how to extol their virtues.
Their guests are hundreds on the chairs.
You've troubled the shepherds with your abundant cattle.
Your weapons are heaped up ready for the miserable days
If ever our *Dar* experienced troubles!

Transliteration
bal-kallam rāfʿa rāsī.
baʿarf al-gawl, fīhum bawāsī.
ḍīfānhum miyyah fawg al-karāsī.
ghallabtu al-rawāʿiyya bey-kutr l-mawāshī.
silāḥku mardūm lay yawm l-maʾāsī.
kān al-dār biga layha l-gāsī
(H. R20, G4, Nyala, 2006).

[32] A village in South Darfur.
[33] A village in South Darfur.
[34] Accounts of Hubbania Hakkamah (R2) at group interview with Hakkamat (G4); Nyala, 2006.

AL-HAKKAMAT AND SOCIALISATION

Al-Hakkamat seize every opportunity to inculcate a sense of moral responsibility in the community, and to emphasise adherence to social values and customs, especially courage, generosity, solidarity, chivalry, gallantry and 'good behaviour', and to forsake otherwise. Their praise is therefore not always addressed at a specific person; rather, it might symbolically reference an *unknown* person as the recommended model for others to aspire to and to embrace, as indicated in this recitation by a prestigious Helbawiyah[35] Hakkamah:

English
Oh, the people named you Gasim, I call you the talented.
You who every morning rides in the saddle.
The generosity of Gasim has extended over the whole tribe.
Oh, you are so prominent in the crowds of heaven, from where you contribute.
If I couldn't praise you, Gasim, I must be a loser!
The Sheikhat[36] named [their sons] after you, in hope, not in despair.
And al-Hakkamat sang for him.
Our God offered you a smart look and good morals.
The provider of dinner for the guests in hard times.
The resolver of men's problems, when the dining councils are divided.
If '*aak*'[37] is shouted, you are the saddle's rider.
You are the six-year-old bull,[38] the fence breaker.
I hope your days last long with joy.

Transliteration
gāl al-nās sammawk Gāsim, sammaytak al-fāhim.
yal-kulla ṣabāḥ jadīd fawg l-lubad bitzāḥim.
Gāsim jūdah ʿamma fawg l-gabīlah.
ẓāhir fawg l-jinān fawg bitsāhim.
kin mā shakkartak yā Gāsim ma ʾana shughlī khaybah.
al-shaykhāt bisamman layk min munyāt mi-khaybah.
wa ghannan ʿalay al-ḥakkāmāt.
ʾintā rabbana ʾadāk al-khilga wa l-ʾakhlāg.
ʿashshā l-ḍayfān yawm l-sinīn shaynāt.
ḥalāl mashākil l-rijāl yawm il-gassaman l-ḍiryāt.
kan gāl ʾāk ʾintā li-l-sirūg rakāb.
al-sadīs l-kassar l-ʿarāḍ.
wa bi-l-hannā ʾayyāmak zāydāt.
(H. R20, G4, Nyala, 2006).

Gasim has thus become the idealised person, the powerful, the generous, the elegant and the good man; other men aspire to replicate his example. Generosity, 'the virtue of giving good things to others, freely and abundantly' (Smith, 2014), is one of the social attributes that

[35] Ibid.
[36] The title Sheikha (pl. Sheikhat) designates a popular and position for women among African tribes during the Fur sultanate. A woman is influential in social matters, as she represents the women in the neighbourhood. She undertakes responsibility for female initiation and domestic activities. This title was traditionally uncommon among Baggara rural communities, but has recently been adopted with similar roles. Group interview (G2) with three people from African tribes, Nyala, 2006.
[37] 'Aak' is like SOS: a cry for help.
[38] i.e. at the height of its strength.

al-Hakkamat celebrate and emphasise, for it can make a significant demarcation in the personal and social life on both sides of those engaged: for those who give and those who take. It is a trait that is learned by practice. It is not a random act, but a well-ingrained behaviour and orientation. Al-Hakkamat therefore take on the responsibility of drawing the moral compass whereby good behaviours are measured. This is explicitly recited by al-Hakkamah:[39]

English
Oh! The greedy, the mean.
When the guests came to you.
And the men called for you.
You said, 'I am in a bad mood and upset'.[40]

Transliteration
al-bakhīl l-hawān.
lamma jawk l-ḍīfān.
Wa 'ayyatū layk l-rujāl.
gultaā 'anā za'lān.
(H/S, R71, Nyala, 2006).

Al-Hakkamat themselves are recognised as generous and welcoming even though they may not always be ready to afford the expenses involved, but people are generally munificent to them to enable them to exercise this virtue. They often invite the notables and the public to banquets, where they slaughter bulls and come out afterwards to sing and commend men.[41] These invitations are often made during public occasions, such as the Eid, and also when they receive gifts, e.g. a bull, from the Nazir for example. In addition to serving the best interest of others, these occasions also constitute an opportunity to learn and develop (Smith, 2014).

Such gatherings are often intended to serve as a method of social and political networking, building institutional alliances and bridging gaps between the leaders and ordinary people, as much as a sheer act of generosity or an expression of loyalty. Al-Hakkamat have also extended their geniality to the office of the Nazir and the visiting officials by serving food and meals, as expressions of courtesy and reciprocal gratuity. The celebration by al-Hakkamat of the men's open-handedness is an ancient practice, as explained by a Ta'aishi Hakkamah, who recites her mother's poem:[42]

English
He[43] who has sugar stored in *al-Suwaybah.*[44]
He who has honey that runs as the stream of *ardaybah.*[45]
A liar who would say he didn't taste it,
And a liar, too, who would say he left him disgraced.

[39] Interview with Misseriya Hakkamah (71), Nyala, 2006.
[40] i.e. I am failing to host guests.
[41] Group interview with Hakkamat (G4), Nyala, June 2006.
[42] Interviews with Ta'aishi Hakkamah (R50), Nyala, 2006.
[43] i.e. the generous man.
[44] A container made locally from clay to store grains, sugar, etc.
[45] The name of a village in South Darfur, famous for a large stream called al-Rahad 'ardaybah.

Transliteration
ʾabb sukkran fī l-suwaybah.
ʾabb ʿaslan fī l-rahad ʿardaybah
kaḍḍāb al-bigūl mā ḍāgah.
wa kaḍḍāb l-bigūl masha bay ʿaybah.
(H/S. R50, Nyala, May 2006).

Sometimes, they direct the attention of the community to a specific person whose behaviour they admire and advocate:

English
I got men, indeed brave men.
The one who says to all, 'Hello, welcome inside'.
Whilst shaking hands[46] your mat is rolled out.[47]

Transliteration
ʾanā ʾindī laya rijāl, ʾindī lay jussār.
sīd ʾitfaḍalū, wa sīd taʿālū jāyy.
ʾīdak fī l-salām, wa burshak wagiʿ gudām.
(H. R37, G4, Nyala, June 2006).

The roles that al-Hakkamat undertake in the socialisation of younger generations and in cultural education are critical in maintaining the cultural characteristics, norms and values of tribes. Socialisation in the context of this study indicates the process through which individuals become identified as members of a society on the basis of their attitudes, beliefs and the way they behave, which reflect the cultural characteristics of that society (Schwartz, 1976, p. ix).

Certain occasions in early childhood constitute important platforms for the socialisation process. For instance, circumcision of boys and girls is a crucial occasion in the social family life, which is usually celebrated with generous ceremonies. The ceremony and the associated rituals are critical events as a *rite de passage* for both boys and girls entering the stage of gender recognition as men and women, no matter at what age this is carried out. It is indeed a physically and emotionally painful operation, especially for girls. It is used to test the courage of quite young children and their ability to control their emotions. Boys in particular are required, by virtue of the nature of the Baggara's livelihood, to grow up able to endure pain. Al-Hakkamat will always be there to sing in the voice of a female peer, reminding them of the role of al-Hakkamah in making or breaking their reputation, even at a very young age, as the song tells:[48]

English
Oh, look brother, if you cry,
I won't greet you.[49]

46 i.e. with your guests.
47 i.e. for them to sit on.
48 Interview with Ahmed Jowa (R14), radio and TV presenter from Ta'aisha, Nyala, 2006.
49 i.e. I wouldn't kiss you.

Transliteration
khayyanā hey, kam bakayt,
mā basallim ʿalayk.

Owing to its serious implications, female circumcision, and its more intrusive and painful form, female genital mutilation (FGM), are classified by the UN as violence against women, and a violation of human rights and child rights. Efforts against FGM started with the British rule in Sudan when they banned it in the Penal Code in 1946, which specified imprisonment for up to five years and/or a fine for the offenders. This law was ratified in the independence period in 1957 and was maintained until 1983, but it was repealed with the enactment of the 1983 Islamic Shari'a Penal Code. The 1991 Penal Code drafted by the current NCP/NIF regime, which is currently in operation, also contains no reference to FGM (cited in Toubia and Rahman, 2000, p. 216).

Nonetheless, since early 2000 many civil society organisations have been campaigning against the practice, in coordination with some INGOs such as Save the Children Sweden (SC-SW) and United Nations agencies, such as the United Nations International Children's Emergency Fund (UNICEF) and the United Nations International Fund for Population Activities (UNIFPA). In 2002, led by SC-SW, they formed a national anti-FGM network of more than forty women's organisations and gender-sensitive agencies. Its work, however, has been obstructed by religious institutions such as the Sudan Religious Scholars Corporation, and has not been able to reach out into all rural and remote areas.[50]

FGM therefore continues in rural Darfur, and al-Hakkamat have become oblivious to anti-FGM campaigning in Sudan. From their position as guardians of tribal culture and norms, they have continued to celebrate this practice and beautify its allegedly religious and social image. In the song below, al-Hakkamah encourages little girls to endure pain and not to cry, while reminding them of the prestige of their fathers who are robust and valiant horsemen.[51] Neither the cruelty of the practice nor its violations of women's and child rights have been matters of concern for al-Hakkamat, given where they stand as guardians of communities: this practice remains at the heart of their cultural rituals and as a rite of passage for preparing young girls for womanhood and marriage:

English
Oh, little girl, don't fear the sparks of the blade.
Your father is the bull of a buffalo![52]

Transliteration
yā binayyah, ma takhāfī min sharār l-mūs.
ʾabūkī faḥal l-jāmūs!

[50] My personal experience of working with Save the Children Sweden in Khartoum, Sudan, 2000–2.
[51] Interview with Ahmed Jowa (R14), radio and TV presenter from Ta'aisha, Nyala, 2006.
[52] i.e. as brave as a buffalo.

Wedding ceremonies also constitute an important platform for al-Hakkamat to address the groom, newly introduced to family life:[53]

English
Oh, lion, the rib breaker,[54]
A calf is nothing for you.[55]
Offering sheep is just a hen for you.[56]

Transliteration
dārjī kasār l-ṣufūf.
wald al-bār mā ḥājah layk.
Gawlat kharūf, jidādah layk.

She describes him as being as strong as a lion that kills its victims by breaking their ribs, and as wealthy and generous, since he slaughters and offers calves and sheep in hospitality. She urges and reminds the young man of the social responsibilities he must undertake, as he has now assumed the dual obligations of a family man and a community man – to be brave, wealthy and generous. He ought to observe this conduct to avoid becoming vilified.

Obviously, the examples presented above point to critical occasions and moments in the life cycle of the social upbringing of children as responsible adults and the role of al-Hakkamat in setting out the behavioural framework. Clearly, emphasis on strength and fighting always receives the greatest focus in the rhetoric of al-Hakkamat. Regardless of the nature of the occasion, most if not all of their expressions come out draped in the images and symbols of the harsh realities of their livelihood styles. Power and bravery are therefore noble attributes that al-Hakkamat strive for and are committed to inculcate in their young who constitute the bastion of the tribes' future.

AL-HAKKAMAT AND AUTHORITY OF ARBITRATION

Al-Hakkamat are equally required to oversee and monitor the behaviour of community members, the horsemen in particular, and to set disciplinary measures against the violators of the social norms and values of society. According to the Baggara socio-cultural context, these violations are regarded as cowardice and they include greediness, sitting indolently to exchange gossip, obstructing and/or boycotting philanthropic communal activities that require participation and solidarity of all men in the village (e.g. school building). The acts of avoiding fighting and confrontation, not answering the call for *Faza'*, not having proper equipment for the required missions, and actually running away from the battlefield are all ostracised by the community. Such behaviours represent legitimate objects for ridi-

[53] Interview with Ahmed Jowa (R14), radio and TV presenter, Nyala, 2006.
[54] i.e. the strong and brave.
[55] i.e. you are rich.
[56] i.e. you are very generous.

cule by al-Hakkamat and their outright rejection by every accessible means.[57]

On the other hand, different tribes have different frameworks for al-Hakkamat to legitimately exercise the authority of arbitration. Among the Bani Helba, for instance, al-Hakkamat are usually assisted by an arbitration council of around five selected women and four men. Yet in general, the arbitrations of al-Hakkamat include, but are not limited to, warning, fining, mocking and ridiculing, isolating or imposing a social boycott. Deterrents may include forced hospitality for women, buying new dresses for some of the women and/or all al-Hakkamat, and offering fodder to the horses of the horsemen. These are locally deemed demeaning punishments, and the menfolk, including the Nazir, are therefore very keen to comply with the expectations of them set out by al-Hakkamat.[58]

These punitive measures might lead to breaking the reputation of the offender, especially if they were dubbed cowards. In some instances, the Ageed might set arbitrations against the offending horsemen. A famous Hubbania Hakkamah stated that within the Hubbania, the Ageed must initially seek the consent of al-Hakkamat, and if the offender admits the transgression, al-Hakkamat may then reduce the fine established by the Ageed, but if not al-Hakkamat can force him to pay the full fine, or even more.[59] This is because cowardice is perceived by Baggara society as a major shame; therefore, al-Hakkamat pledge to publicly defame those who are identified as cowards. The recitation below ridicules a man who has failed to respond to a tribal SOS call:[60]

English
An SOS was heard; the brave horseman promptly responded.
But the coward was still wearing his charm papers.
Until the crisis was over!

Transliteration
al-karawrāk ḍarab, al-fāris marag.
wa l-khawwāf ga'ad li libs al-waraq.
lamma l-ḥāl 'inbarad.

By choosing to defame individual offenders, al-Hakkamat primarily intend to draw up a moral roadmap for the community at large. Nevertheless, a Baggari man claimed that al-Hakkamat are always wary of slandering their men and/or publicising their imperfections, lest this might, adversely, be used against them by al-Hakkamat of rival tribes. Notwithstanding, al-Hakkamat might use less self-censorship when it becomes utterly necessary to teach offenders unforgettable lessons; their fate would impel adventurers to observe the norms and principles of the tribe.[61]

Alternatively, when al-Hakkamat are unable to use poetry and songs, they may resort to symbolic behaviours and figurative expressions to convey

57 Group and individual interviews, Nyala, 2006.
58 Interviews, Nyala, 2006.
59 Group interview with Hakkamat (G4), Nyala, 2006.
60 Interviews with E. D. Khair Allah (R22), Nyala 2006.
61 Group and individual interviews, Nyala, 2006.

important messages that might, perhaps, be less susceptible to the ridicule of their opponent Hakkamat. These acts involve things such as al-Hakkamah showing up wearing a *markoob*[62] to signify that a man ran away in fear, leaving his shoes behind. If a man in the village is accused of stealing grain or groundnuts from somebody else's farm, al-Hakkamah may collect a bundle of grain heads, or groundnuts and tie it to the edge of her *tobe* and then go wandering in public places to publicise the incident. The public will immediately identify the culprit and the crime committed.[63]

Al-Hakkamat might also utilise the symbolic *darb l-marʿūb*[64], by instructing young girls to make a couple of braids in two rows in the middle of their heads, and to unveil their heads in public so as to indicate the hurried escape of a perpetrator. The meanings attached to these symbols are well grasped by the locals as indicative of somebody who has run off after committing anti-social behaviour that cannot be condoned. Everyone will then know the culprit and his shame without necessarily uttering his name.[65]

Sometimes offenders tend to challenge the arbitration of al-Hakkamat, because they may not be able to afford the resulting social and financial cost and hence would take legal steps against al-Hakkamah. A striking example was recounted by two Baggara men, as was experienced in 2005 in Idd al-Fursan Rural Council, the headquarters of the Bani Helba. Following a *Faza'* call to bring back a stolen cattle herd, all men joined in except one who failed to come out for no legitimate reason. When the *Faza'* came back, al-Hakkamat and some women, led by the *Khail*-Hakkamah, ridiculed him and organised a compulsory dinner in his house. Driven by grievance, shame and financial loss, the man lodged a complaint against the *Khail*-Hakkamah at Nyala District Court, accusing her of causing him social and financial losses. He emphasised that he had had nothing stolen and therefore he did not feel obliged to enlist in the *Faza'*.

Al-Hakkamah reported to the court escorted by more than fifty of the tribe's people, led by the Ageed, and admitted her acts, pointing to the man as 'no man'. She defended herself and explained that she was simply performing her duties in preserving the values set out by their society. She paid the imposed fine, then addressed the judge saying, '*Mawlana*,[66] if this man dies, you must come and bury him'. This implied that he would be an outcast in the village. When he heard the prospect of his destiny as resounded within the condemning expression of al-Hakkamah, the offender begged the jdge to drop the charges. Furthermore, al-Hakkamah stipulated that as a condition for accepting his repentance, he must pay her and her entourage the travel expenses they incurred. The culprit had to accept these arbitrations and succumb to the demands of the Hakkamah.

62 A pair of men's shoes made locally from animal hide
63 Interviews with Rezeiqi government employee (R5), Nyala, May 2006. A *tobe* is a Sudanese women's national dress that looks similar to the Indian sari; it is normally 4.5 metres long and is folded around the body in a particular way.
64 This means 'footprints of the terrified'.
65 Interviews with Rezeiqi government employee (R5), Nyala, May 2006.
66 Honorific title of a judge in Sudan.

A person who claimed to have been damaged by an event, demanded compensation and won his case in court had to withdraw his claim instantly after al-Hakkamah's announcement that there would no longer be a place for him in the community. Also, not only did he have to forfeit the compensation he was due but he also had to pay the expenses incurred by the entourage of al-Hakkamah. In individual cases, there could really be no better example of traditional authority and influence than that exercised by this Hakkamah. Court judgements could be done away with, whereas the judgement of al-Hakkamat could cost the offender their place and position in society permanently, whether they stayed or left.[67]

The use of ridicule by women as a cultural method of censorship and discipline was also exercised in the precolonial era in some African societies, where women were organised in powerful groups and had considerable autonomy in economic and social activity, in the marketplace and in farming and trading activities. For instance, among the Igbo women of Nigeria and the Kom of Cameroon, women wielded power that they exercised to make rules, and enforced regulations to safeguard their social and economic interests. Despite the regression influenced by colonials on the general status of African women, some of these groups have continued to operate, albeit at quite a low profile.

In Igbo society the *mikiri* or *mitiri*[68] was the most powerful group, and it had a legitimate right to exercise arbitration against offenders who violated women's rights in the market. Their arbitrations included warnings, requests for behaviour redressing, boycotts and 'making war'.[69] Making war, also called 'sitting on a man', was the ultimate punishment of violators. It was a dancing strike against the culprit, which involved singing in mockery of him and finished by destroying his hut. Demeaning acts against the offender would continue until he showed penitence. It was upheld by the society, as it was deemed the most terrifying and powerful procedure that the women could use to maintain respect and order (Wipper, 1984, pp. 70–1).

Similarly, Kom women of Cameroon also had similar arbitration to that of 'sitting on a man': the Anlu, which was designed to punish men who violated women's rights by beating, abusing and insulting them, committing incest, etc., or breaking the fighting rules (ibid., p. 91). It was often applied to recurrent offenders who had previously been fined by the women but failed to redress their behaviours. The Anlu was a long-lasting dancing strike of huge numbers of women who would parade at 5 a.m. to the culprit's compound, singing in ridicule of him and committing demeaning acts. Sometimes, they might enforce a

[67] Group and individual interviews, Nyala, 2006.

[68] For more details, see Allen (1976, pp. 68–70).

[69] 'Making war' was carried out in 1929 by Igbo women in protest against the colonials who attempted to apply taxes to women's property and economic resources. Thousands of women marched and performed 'sitting on a man' on the officer, as a punishment for threatening women's rights. The strike was interpreted by the colonial authority as a riot and was terminated violently, causing fifty women to be shot dead and many to be seriously injured. This incident was later publicised by the colonialists as the Aba Riot (ibid., pp. 69–74).

boycott on the offender, as everywhere he went, the Anlu would accompany him (ibid., pp. 71–2).

It was a quite stressful process for the offender to endure for more than a couple of months, and therefore he would appeal to the women for forgiveness. If his appeal was accepted, he would be subject to certain rituals to set him free and it would be forbidden to mention the incident thereafter. But if his appeal was rejected, he would have to leave the place. The rulings of the Anlu were binding and incontestable, and it was therefore feared as a powerful institution (ibid.).

Kom women deployed the Anlu tradition in 1957 to fend for the political rights of the whole community. Their dissatisfaction with land reform plans of the colonial government, which included the intention to sell their land, drove them to organise a mass public march and they took over the representative councils. They received the premier according to the Anlu tradition in mid-1958, and were able to secure a reassurance from him that nothing detrimental would happen to them (O'Barr, 1984, pp. 146–7). It was the women's agency, power and resolve that were behind the transformation of the Anlu into a political means for mobilising the community and enabling the maintenance of the interests of families.

Al-Hakkamat, the 'sitting on a man' punishment, and the Anlu all served as sources of power for African rural women to exercise and enforce judgements and collective action. They reveal the powerful traditional authority of African women and their means to protect the social and economic rights of their communities and families, especially when they feared a grave threat to their social values and livelihoods.

The Anlu and 'sitting on a man' have been weakened by the colonial and postcolonial forces, and almost disappeared after the events that demonstrated their spectacular sociopolitical power and influence. Meanwhile, al-Hakkamat's authority started to flourish in Darfur in the 1970s, two decades after independence. They have been able to continue and thrive with no local or national impediments, paradoxically with the government's full endorsement and support.

COMMUNITY APPRAISAL OF AL-HAKKAMAT

The social and political value of al-Hakkamat in their own societies is almost unquestioned, although their behaviour has been criticised. An influential Omda conceded that al-Hakkamat command respect and appreciation for their significant impact, not only in preserving the virtues of the tribe but also in instilling them in the first place; there seems to be no better communicators of these virtues, as he emphasised. Admittedly, they can also push the button so hard that a tribe can sometimes make avoidable decisions and take unnecessary actions.[70] Nonetheless, they serve as a resource for the tribes, documenting their history through songs and memorable speeches and actions. In addition, they are

[70] Group interviews (1), Nyala, 2006.

the informal spokespersons of the tribes and their media folk, but their messages are always taken for granted as formally representing the spirit of their community.[71]

A striking testimony to this is an incident that took place in 2004 in the Kutum vicinity of North Darfur, following the military attacks that Darfuri rebels, locally nicknamed the Tora Bora, launched against the central state government in early 2003. Their military activities included raiding al-Fashir airport, where they burned military aircraft and seized government weapons and vehicles. At a social occasion for the Rezeiqat Abbala, their Hakkamah described the Tora Bora as brave, because, when they go raiding, they often bring back valuables, such as cars and heavy arms. In the meantime she expressed disdain for her menfolk, who were Janjawiid militias, for the kind of spoils they often brought – goats and hens. She implied that her menfolk were just armed cowards. Immediately, from among the crowd, a tribal leader sprang out and shot al-Hakkamah dead. A close relative of al-Hakkamah reacted instantly and shot the killer dead. The men swiftly contained the matter, lest it might escalate into more deadly outcomes.[72]

This incident suggests that al-Hakkamah was obviously displeased with her tribesmen, the Janjawiid, who were raiding villages and perpetrating killing, burning huts and looting trivial spoils that, in her opinion, did not justify the atrocities committed. She might have meant to influence a change in the destiny of her tribe and restore its prestige by provoking the men to aspire for more valuable, rather than trivial, rewards. Her message was politically obvious: she condoned the raids but could not admire the reward, thereby she was encouraging her people, next time around, to be greedier and more lethal.

On the other hand, having a prominent tribal leader murdering one of their own renowned Hakkamat in cold blood suggests that he might have feared that the opinion of al-Hakkamah might create a serious rift within the tribe and pivot it towards brutal internal violence. Moreover, the retaliatory shooting also reveals that the influence of al-Hakkamat effectively rests on the inner circle of supporters and relatives who could rise to her defence, or revenge, when required. This and similar incidents further confirm the powerful agency of al-Hakkamat and their unrivalled influence in these communities (now the Abbala communities).

This fear on the part of tribespeople of al-Hakkamat's conventional power and influence tends to exceed their awe of the Nazir's, even though the Nazir's formal power and authority are formally beyond the reach of al-Hakkamat. This proposition could be justified on the premise that if a person misbehaved, the authorities would normally exercise a time-bound prosecution on him. In contrast, a punishment meted out by al-Hakkamat, such as ridicule, could accompany the culprit like a shadow for a long time, if not beyond their lifetime. Indeed, the whole tribe might be punished or debased by just a couple of words from al-Hakkamat.[73]

71 Ibid.; also Al-Asbat, 2014.
72 Interview with Oxfam Coordinator, from Tunjur (R70), Nyala 2006.
73 Group and individual interviews, Nyala, 2006.

It is not off the mark to interpret al-Hakkamat's authority as a mechanism for challenging the gender-subordinating practices that typically obstruct females from thriving and prospering in the public domain. As has been shown, their methods and practices bring public opinion perceptibly into alignment with the courses of action that their tribes follow. For instance, unless al-Hakkamat sharpened the men, as you sharpen a blunt piece of metal, and heartened them to act according to the tribe's conventional sets of rules, and the values embraced in the concept of manhood, men might be defeated and women become victims. For fear of this potentially atrocious consequence, al-Hakkamat often push their men extremely hard to win, and so spare their womenfolk from vulnerable situations.[74]

Their capacity for enthusing tribesmen and transforming the community into a constantly ready platform for fighting is but a moral duty and an exercise of a genuine obligation to connect and integrate with the defensive organisation of the tribe, the Ageed. The latter is the most powerful and formidable of the traditional authority and leadership institutions among the Baggara society in Darfur.

CONCLUSION

Al-Hakkamat is a title used to denote a category of women actors, who are often illiterate, in the social organisation of Darfuri Arab pastoralists, mainly in rural areas. They exercise a tremendous agency, which together with their demonstrated natural talents, elected them to this position. They are nominated through a complicated process that starts in the early days of their trajectory to recognition. The position is open to any aspirant woman who shows the requisite qualities and gains communal acceptance to undertake the associated roles and obligations.

Their creation is presumably dictated by the nomadic pattern of their livelihoods, wherein women are often left to care for families and whole villages/camps, whilst the men travel far away with the herds. Flexible gender power relationships are inevitably significant in fostering this style of living and in generating new engagements for women to adapt to such precarious situations. Their obligations therefore embrace the social and political duties that are geared towards maintaining the social and physical boundaries of the tribes. Through the socialisation of youngsters and monitoring the behaviours of the adults, they strive to ensure a dynamic ingraining of tribe-specific virtues, values and norms, which are centred on the values of bravery, heroism and generosity, and to reject unworthy conduct and qualities. They have a legitimate right to undertake any course of action they think might contribute to enhancing the welfare of the community, but generally, their poetic diction, singing, speeches and symbolic acts are the most common and significant.

[74] Interviews with E. D. Khair Allah (R22), Nyala, 2006.

The obligations of al-Hakkamat and their practical manifestations have paved the way for them to be accredited with the authority of arbitration, which they exercise to nurture compliance with the society's rules and to bring any errant behaviours under control. Their most striking role is their association with the task of preserving the social and territorial boundaries of their tribes. This strategic role of al-Hakkamat necessitates the engagement of all sectors of the community in the process of their identification. Their pledge to reinforce the maintenance of tribes' boundaries brings them into close association with the military organisation of the tribes, where they undertake significant assignments, especially during times of war.

They are therefore cherished by those loyal to the social norms but feared and abhorred by the violators of these norms. It follows that in all the choices they opt for, they are supported unequivocally by their society even though some see them as immoral and vicious. By the very nature of their characters, roles and obligations, they stand as a socio-cultural and political institution of women firmly embedded in the conventional leadership and authority system of the pastoralist communities of Darfur.

4

Local Inter-ethnic Conflicts

It has been established already that al-Hakkamat have significant power and agency, which they use to influence the social and political conduct of men, despite being excluded from the decision-making frameworks and initiatives within their tribes. Their influence, more often than not, has surfaced quite intensely as they have turned simple disputes among tribes and ethnic groups into events with disastrous outcomes. Since the 1970s, their destructive influence has featured quite remarkably in most of the conflicts experienced in Darfur. This is certainly not accidental, or a revelation of merely personal interests and attitudes. Indeed, it is the result of an authentic adherence to the ethical responsibilities and obligations towards the defence ideals of the tribe and the Ageed organisation. In the following pages, we explore the relationship between al-Hakkamat and the Ageed, and how it has unfolded in the context of conflict in Darfur since the 1970s.

AGEED MILITARY ORGANISATION

The complexity of nomadic life has compelled the Baggara communities in Darfur, since time immemorial, to frame their own arrangements in order to be able to protect their communities and herds from various adversaries. These arrangements have taken the form of a military organisation that has progressively acquired substantial importance, especially with the recent deterioration of social and economic resources and the mounting insecurity in Darfur, not least the absence of reliable governance to maintain law and order. This organisation operates quite independently of the native administration: the authority that should be responsible for administering people's affairs within the tribes' land boundaries. This military organisation is called the Ageed.[1]

The Ageed (sing. Ageed; pl. Augada)[2] organisation usually consists of a group of Augada and horsemen (combatants on horses). Each Ageed represents a clan and he often commands about one hundred horsemen. The size of the Augada therefore depends on the number of clans (*khashum bait*) affiliated to the tribe. The tribal supreme military chief

[1] Interviews, Nyala, 2006.

[2] The war leader of a tribe, like the commander-in-chief in a state's army.

referred to as Ageed *al-Shoosha*[3], also called Ageed al-Augada, is just like a commander general in modern armies, and commands a group of Augada. The Augada constitute the military council of the Ageed organisation, whereas select horsemen would up make the executive body. It is a framework for unity and solidarity that responds to calls for help, especially in times of extreme need.

Incidents such as disputes, the theft of animals, raiding and looting often overwhelm the social setting of Baggara society. Native administration chiefs are responsible for calming down these inter- and intra-tribal tensions and facilitating resolutions and reconciliation. But it is the tribe's military organisation, the Ageed, that usually takes full responsibility for handling the unfolding military situation. Traditional authorities in African local communities, for instance in Zimbabwe, also have their own defence armies as a symbol of unity to protect people against external aggression, maintain order and facilitate effective development (Dodo, 2013, p. 32).

An influential Ta'aishi man has illustrated the Ta'aisha military structure as follows:

> When conflict erupts, there is the so-called Augada who are in charge of the *fursan*.[4] Each Ageed is responsible for one hundred *fursan* and each of the Ageed *al*-Augada commands ten Augada. In Rihaid al-Birdi,[5] we have three Ageed *al*-Augada, which means we have three thousand horsemen in the district, well organised, well armed and on standby. This is a traditional tribal organisation, which is not only used to deal with disputes, but also to safeguard and defend the Ta'aisha *Dar* and its pride from savage adversaries. It is also utilised for *Faza'* purposes.[6]

The traditional Ageed organisation thus appears to be responsible for a number of ordinary, local tribe-centred activities, such as tribal parades, wars, etc. Furthermore, it undertakes the management of the seasonal movement of the tribe by locating available and accessible grazing sites, water resources, and the whereabouts to camp safely at a distance from harm's way. These tasks are underpinned by a sentimental drive to secure the tribe's land and community.

The Augada are generally knowledgeable, veteran, courageous and skilful horsemen. Ageed al-Augada, in particular, is usually chosen based on singularly significant criteria that qualify him for the responsibility of a war leader. These include criteria such as talent, insightfulness, nego-

[3] *Shoosha* in Sudanese colloqial Arabic is the forefront hair of the crown of the head. The legend of Ageed al-Shoosha among the Bani Helba suggests that some three hundred years ago, the *nahas* (a huge drum made from copper and a symbol of power associated with the ruling families within tribes) was seen in the stream, about to sink. A man called Zantoot jumped into the water and kept the drum afloat. Later, some tribesmen came, and together they pulled out the drum. Thereafter, Zantoot was appointed with honour as the top Ageed *al-Shoosha* of the tribe; since then this position has been inherited by Zantoot's family and even those who have obtained higher education in military studies are not entitled to assume it unless they come from Zantoot's family. Women are not represented in the Ageed system. Interviews, Nyala, 2006.

[4] i.e. fighting horsemen (sing. *faris*).

[5] A town in South Darfur and the main centre of *Dar* Ta'aisha.

[6] Interviews with a politician (R55), who was a member of the regional National Congress Council, Nyala, 2006.

tiation kills and persuasiveness, planning ability and charisma. Besides, he must own pedigree horses and personal wealth in order to be able to afford the financial demands of his obligations, even though help from the tribe is often at hand.

The Ageed and Ageed al-Augada are usually selected by consultation, but may also be inherited positions. Initially, each clan in the *Omodiya*[7] would choose its Ageed, and the group of Augada in the *Omodiya* would meet and choose from among themselves the Ageed al-Augada, also called Ageed *al-Shoosha*. The more *Omodiyat* there were in the district, the more Ageed al-Augada there would be. Under the command of one of them, who would then become the supreme security and war leader for the whole tribe, the group of Ageed al-Augada would work jointly to discharge the tasks of the Ageed organisation. The instructions of Ageed al-Shoosha, especially during wartime, would simply over-rule those of the Nazir, the supreme tribal chief.

The Ageed therefore constitutes a powerfully prestigious position of leadership and responsibility. In al-Hakkamat's perception, he embodies the tribe's legacy of virtue, values and good conduct. When invited to any social occasion, al-Hakkamat often sing and praise the host and include him among the community leaders – the Ageed, the generous, the horsemen and the tribe's supreme head – who symbolise the power and prestige of the tribe. An example of how al-Hakkamat praise the Ageed as the most courageous and generous horseman in the clan is shown in the recitation below: [8]

English
Many greetings to you, Oh, the Ageed of the horses.
Day and night, on the horses' backs, off you ride.
The Ageed sang that he craves for horses and aspires to ride off.
Also to see smart youth on the saddles, singing.

Transliteration
salām ʿalayk yā ʿagīd l-khayl katīr.
fī laylak wa nahārak, fī ḍuhūr al-khayl bitsīr.
al-ʿagīd ghannā, gāl al-khayl layhin ḥannā, wa layhin rannā.
wa layhin ṣubyān zayn, fawg l-surūj ghanna.
(H/S, R4, G4, Nyala, 2006).

AL-HAKKAMAT AND THE AGEED ORGANISATION

Al-Hakkamat's political significance is embodied in their structural involvement in the political activities that the tribe pursues in order to secure its *Dar* boundaries. These activities might involve attacks or counterattacks, which are usually undertaken and managed by the Ageed military organisation of the tribe, and in which all the tribe members are

[7] Pl. *Omodiyat*, sub-district and district, or tribal administrative units in the native administration system.

[8] Narratives of Salami Hakkamah (R4) at the group interview with Hakkamat (G4), Nyala, 2006.

required to join. By virtue of their authority and influence, the institution of al-Hakkamat assumes major prominence in these activities.

Like the Ageed organisation, the institution of al-Hakkamah functions independently of the native administration. However, al-Hakkamat and the Ageed are closely connected in a collaborative relationship to serve the interests of their tribe. The Ageed institution is assigned responsibility for maintaining the security of the tribe and its *Dar* boundaries against the backdrop of the state's failure to undertake its obligation to maintain law and order. Al-Hakkamat are required to ensure an efficient execution of this assignment. In attending to this objective, al-Hakkamat undertake specific activities, especially during wartime, to ensure the readiness of the Ageed and his horsemen. Hence, when a tribe military mission is imminent, they inspect the weapons, the horses and the horsemen's equipment to ensure that nothing important is missing. Al-Hakkamat must also be ready to replace equipment that is in poor condition.[9]

Despite this working relationship with the Ageed, al-Hakkamat do not attend the meetings and discussions of the Augada council, nor are they involved in the decision making. However, the *Khail*-Hakkamat, in particular, have the leverage and authority to invoke and incite the Ageed and the horsemen to execute wars. On the other hand, the horsemen and al-Hakkamat somehow share a common language for understanding and interpreting suspicious events.[10] Their physical absence from the decision making of the Augada therefore does not affect their tremendous influence on events and their outcomes, as their rhetoric usually hovers over the decision-making mechanisms of the Augada, even when it is not expressed publicly.

Apparently, the inability of the tribal administrative leaders in Darfur to influence and/or negotiate effective and sustainable resettlement and peace have usually resulted from a presumption that in wartime, people's loyalty rests with the Ageed and al-Hakkamat, the institutions on the ground that are in actual charge of managing wars between tribes.

It must be noted though that al-Hakkamah is an institution that is independent of the Ageed, whereas the Ageed institution is hugely influenced by al-Hakkamat. As such, al-Hakkamat could exercise judgement on the Augada, who might be subject to their scorn and arbitration if they violated the norms of society and behaved unacceptably. Al-Hakkamat have the right to investigate transgressions and to hold offenders to account for their behaviour. Their disciplinary actions include warnings and fines, but they might also seek to revoke their confidence in the Ageed and urge the nomination of a new Ageed.[11]

According to the arbitration framework for the Bani Helba, if the Ageed is condemned but resists the judgement of al-Hakkamat Council, the council can refer the matter to the Ageed al-Augada. The latter would invite al-Hakkamat Council (ten persons), and another five men to make a council of fifteen, to review the case; otherwise, the

[9] Group interview with Hakkamat and Sheikhat (G3), Nyala, 2006.
[10] Interviews with Rezeiqi government employee (R5), Nyala, May 2006.
[11] Group interview with Hakkamat (G4), Nyala, 2006.

offending Ageed would be deposed.[12] Obviously, there are no exceptions in the mores of al-Hakkamat, and this authority indeed significantly enhances their position and makes them feared by all, including the Ageed.

AL-HAKKAMAT AND INTER-ETHNIC CONFLICT

Since the 1970s, ethnic conflict has become phenomenal in Darfur, as it has taken place among tribes of the same ethnicity, i.e. Arab *vis-à-vis* Arab, or Africans *vis-à-vis* Africans, as well as between tribes of different ethnic groups, i.e. Arabs *vis-à-vis* Africans. Since 1987 however, ethnic conflicts between individual Arab and African tribes, and/or involving congregations of ethnic groups, have become widespread. The Baggara have often been partners in these inter-tribal and inter-ethnic conflicts. This calamitous environment has summoned the agency of al-Hakkamat, who is best known in Baggara society, to cheer the fighters on, only to result in escalating conflict situations and perpetuating the aggression (see Table 4.1):

Table 4.1 Examples of ethnic conflicts in which al-Hakkamat were engaged

Tribes involved	*Year*
Ma'aliya and Rezeiqat	1968
Rezeiqat and Dinka	1975, 1981 to 2011
Bani Helba and Mahriyah	1976, 1982
Salamat and Ta'aisha	1978/80, 1983 to 2013
Fellata and Gimir	1987
Fur and Arab	1987 to 1989
Fur and Tergam	1991
Zaghawa and Northern Rezeiqat	1994, 1997
Arab and Masalit	1996, 1997
Hubbania and Abu Darag and Hubbania and Darfur insurgency	2005
Bani Helba and Terjam	2006

(*Source*: Interviews, 2006; Bashar, 2013, pp. 140–46, 165–81)

Al-Hakkamat have therefore become widely recognised as women who often seek to fuel simple disputes and turn them into flaming situations. Al-Hakkamat's belief in enthusing the belligerence of tribesmen resonates quite dramatically in a provocative and arousing song, which is one of their most popular compositions, as recited below:[13]

[12] Ibid.
[13] Interview with a government employee from Fur (41), Nyala, 2006.

Photo 4.1 Al-Hakkamah singing at a wedding party in the suburbs of South Darfur; Baggari men firing their rifles in merriment
(*Source*: Photograph by and © Imad Mahmoud, Nyala, 18 August 2017)

English
He who has death,
I will buy it from them for a lactating cow.[14]

Transliteration
al-ʿindah mawt.
bay bagarah shāylay babīʿah lay.

[14] A lactating cow is generally too valuable for the Baggara to sell off, but in this case, she will be sold.

This boldness in articulating the quest for aggression is characteristic of al-Hakkamat's poetic diction, which they harness to emphasise that even times of relative tranquillity and peace must not pass without the excitement of always being ready to fight. It is a concerted determination that serves as a conclusive motive for the horsemen, in particular, to be 'on form', and ready to come when signalled. This manifestation may envisage al-Hakkamat as evil incarnate, but it may also reflect their integrity in fulfilling their role to agitate and inspire. Besides, this spirit tends to also reflect their trust in the strength of their tribes and their steady readiness for fierce confrontations.

This charismatic authority of al-Hakkamat seems to be instrumental in turning petty disputes into dreadful cycles of vicious retaliation. As such, there is no moral posturing against al-Hakkamat, as they are morally obliged to pursue actions that are compatible with their social obligations and norms, and to side with their folks, right or wrong. Their customary perception is underpinned by an absolute belief that infringement against you, your family, kin or tribe should not go unpunished. Thus, there are no qualms about turning simple disputes into brutal violence.

It could hardly be described as ethical for al-Hakkamat to get involved in fights between tribes in Darfur during the late 1970s throughout the 1980s, 1990s and 2000s, when they played a negative role in most of them. Yet though their support was often solicited, they were plainly described as a source of trouble and distress, and have been a curse to their communities and to those who get in conflict with them. On the other hand, they are described by a large spectrum of tribesmen as trustworthy members of their community, diligently undertaking their responsibilities with total commitment and supporting their tribe at times of need. The four instances below demonstrate some examples of al-Hakkamat's involvement in conflicts in Darfur during these four decades.

The conflict of Bani Helba and Mahriyah, 1975/6

The conflict between the Baggara Bani Helba and the Abbala Rezeiqat Mahriyah tribes in 1975/6 constitutes the most violent conflict thus far between two parties of the same Arab ethnicity. It marks the inception of al-Hakkamat's fame for exercising agency and influence in the recent history of tragic conflict in Darfur. Many interlocutors recounted that the Bani Helba would willingly host within their *Dar* the nomadic groups of immigrant Abbala Mahriyah (affiliated to the Rezeiqat Shamaliya) with their camels, and allow them to share the available natural resources. Apparently, following the drought and desertification of the late 1960s and early 1970s the Mahriyah stayed longer than the usual short seasonal period. Notwithstanding, the *Dar* owners agreed to continue to harbour them as relatives, and the relationship between the two tribes was subsequently consolidated by intermarriages.

A teacher from Bani Helba (a Hilbawi) narrated that violent clashes erupted between groups from the two tribes over a water well on 15 April 1975. The dispute soon escalated into severe violence when the Rezeiqat used small arms, such as G3 rifles, whereas the Bani Helba relied on traditional weapons, e.g. swords, spears, etc. Inevitably, the balance tipped in favour of the advanced weapons.

In order to end the violence, the government ordered the Rezeiqat nomads to move off the Bani Helba's land until the matter was resolved. Neither side was satisfied with the government arbitration; al-Hakkamat, in particular, protested heartily. They rallied against each other's tribes, insulted their partners in the dispute and agitated their folks to acts of aggression by singing. Soon, the dispute developed into large-scale armed violence that lasted for months and resulted in dozens of casualties.[15] Hakkamah from Mahriyah admitted that she was quite enraged by the government's instructions for her tribe to leave the *Dar* of Bani Helba, and thus she composed and recited poems inciting her tribesmen to lead their camels forcibly to graze in the prohibited meadows of Bani Helba:

English
Where are the compassionate broad-chested cows?[16]
Alas, they are denied their grazing land.
I am appealing to whoever could fight for them.
Before the reconciliation was accomplished!

Transliteration
al-ḥanānah ʾumm zawr, waynah.
al-ʾimanaʿan marāʿīha.
ʾanā dāyrah al-yabāriz fīha.
gabal l-ṣuluḥ mā yajīha!
(H. R31, Nyala, 2006).

Whilst the Mariyah Hakkamah was singing, Hakkamah from Bani Helba (Hilbawiyah), married to a Mahri and residing with the Mahriyah community, was grinding, using *Murhakah*, in her dwelling house. In order to intentionally provoke and disturb the Hilbawiyah Hakkamah, another Mahriyah Hakkamah led her camel nearby and loudly sang mocking songs:

English
Graze freely, you whose tooth clefts are just like routes.
The *Helbawi* does not repent![17]
This year you will graze by gunpowder.

Transliteration
ʾartaʿī yā ʾumm filaygan durūb.
al-hilbāwī mā bitūb.
al-sanah tartaʿī bi-l-barūd.

This Hakkamah exclaimed that, against the Bani Helba's will and the government's instructions, the Mahriyah were grazing their camels on the land and would subdue the Bani Helba with armed force. The Helbawiyah Hakkamah hit back instantly:

[15] Interviews with E. D. Khair Allah (R22), Nyala, 2006.
[16] Female camels are called cows.
[17] i.e. it does not learn the lessons of previous encounters.

English
They are the riders on the backs of horses.
They are the ones who make a young woman grieve.
The camels have certainly gone thirsty, since early afternoon!

Transliteration
rakkābīn l-dābbah.
wa ḥazzānīn l-shābbah.
'umm guggah min l-'iṣayr ṭala'at ghābbah.

She boasted that the horsemen of her tribe were famous for their courage and ferocious in the saddle. She portrayed them as fearless fighters, who would kill the Mahri men and turn their young women into grieving widows. The Mahri camels, too, would flee the land, suffering from thirst, as their owners, the Mahri men, would not be able to withstand the fight.

Having interpreted Helbawiyah Hakkamah's words as mocking poetry and demeaning to their tribe and their men, some Mahri men determined to kill al-Hakkamah, for it was bitter to let go without taking revenge. To ensure her safety, her five sons escorted their mother back to her own tribe, the Bani Helba. This incident and other similar ones demonstrate that whilst they owe their husbands full deference, al-Hakkamat do not adopt their husbands' identities and usually keep their own tribal identity, especially in times of conflict. The tribal identity is therefore inalienable for al-Hakkamat, and their inflamed passion seems to be fuelled by this resident ethnic consciousness.

Another Mahriyah Hakkamah also shared similar feelings of anger and resentment. She emphasised the might of her tribe in fighting and warned the Bani Helba of the destiny that would befall them:

English
Oh, Bani Helba!
You are, but dancers of *'umm Digaynah*[18] and gum arabic[19] collectors!
If 'Abu Tamūnga[20] sets his eyes on the rifle sight point,[21]
You will all die like *simmayn*.[22]

Transliteration
daggāgīn 'umm digaynah, Taggāgīn l-jinaynah.
Abū Tamūnga kān ṣarra 'aynah,
tamūtū mawt l-simmaynah.

This revelation generally echoes the scorn that the Abbala reserve for settled farmers, no matter what ethnicity they belong to. As both tribes share Arab ethnicity, the Abbala found it expedient to look down on the Bani Helba, who were no longer pastoralists. She therefore referred to Bani Helba as settled agro-pastoralists tending gum arabic fields, who have lost the strength and skills associated with their previous status

18 A folk dance (Bani Helba are among the tribes who are famous for it).
19 A natural product from the acacia tree that is used in several industrial products.
20 A famous Mahri militia leader.
21 i.e. takes aim.
22 Ant-like flying insects that die in hordes when they grow wings.

as nomadic pastoralists and stringent horsemen. Tit for tat, Hilbawiyah Hakkamah responded wrathfully:

English
Oh yes, these dancers of *'umm Digaynah* are my right hand.
When their Ageed raided with his jagged spear,
The camel herder saw him, why did he throw his automatic rifle?

Transliteration
daggāgīn 'umm digaynah, humma 'īdī l-zaynah.
'agīd-hum marag bay ḥiraybtah l-khishaynah,
al-'abālī shāfah, mālā zagal biraynah.

Meaning the Mahri were scared of the Bani Helba, even though they used more advanced weapons – guns rather than spears.

Whilst al-Hakkamat of the tribes were trading insults and agitating their tribes, a Mahriyah Hakkamah called Zarga showed aggressive discontent with the government's decision to expel her tribe from Bani Helba land, and with the consent of some Mahri men who wanted to comply. She turned to her brother, and in the following song invited him to disobey the order:[23]

English
Saying 'get up, pack up and leave', upsets me.
Oh, you, the solid armour.
The spoon of poison.
How many of these pests would you kill for me?

Transliteration
gawlat gūmū wa sīrū sawwat lay hamm.
yā l-dir' l-'aṣamm.
mal'aqta l-samm.
min al-ḥasharāt dayl bitaktul lay kam.

Authentically responding to his sister's ordeal and her appeal, the brother swore the oath of divorce[24] that he would not let anyone approach his sister's house to his last breath. He then armed himself, and true to his oath, he attacked and fought the Bani Helba until he was killed.

The culture to which al-Hakkamat subscribe expects a person who is killed in such circumstances to be avenged by the death of someone of no less value and status than him. Following the death of her brother, and driven by grief, rage and the desire for revenge, Zarga demanded the beheading of each of Issa Dabaka, the Nazir of Bani Helba, Hawwa Tummah, his beloved daughter, and his cousin Ahmed Ismael. She proclaimed that she would use the heads of the three to make *ladaya*.[25] She perceived that the loss of her beloved and courageous brother could only be compensated for by the killing of these prominent characters.

[23] Interviews with E. D. Khair Allah (R22), Nyala, 2006.
[24] If a man swears the 'oath of divorce', his wife is automatically divorced from him unless he commits himself to whatever he has sworn. It is a man-specific oath and while it is used in prattle in North Sudan, it is serious and binding in Darfur.
[25] A *ladayab* is a fire-pit that is made locally from three pieces of stone.

Her demands escalated the conflict gravely, for her tribe's horsemen sincerely wanted both to appease her and avenge the killing of their tribesman.

Though events might be long forgotten, forgetting the bitterness of defeat may not be easy for al-Hakkamat. A Hilbawi teacher told us that in 2005, years after the conflict with the Mahriyah, some affiliates of both tribes attempted to build up the bridges of brotherly relations once again, and ease inter-communal tensions, by getting together on social occasions. To pursue this objective, a Mahri man invited a Hilbawi friend, together with a group of his tribesmen, to a wedding occasion in a Mahriyah camp. They were well received, and soon joined the dancing party where al-Hakkamah was singing. Some Mahri men were shooting their G3 and Mengistu assault rifles, in joy and merriment, as a habitual expression among village communities. Soon, some of the Helbawi invitees, all carrying Kalashnikovs, entered the *mada* and fired in the air too, which was also a normal courtesy gesture to their hosts on such a jovial occasion. When they entered the *mada* and fired for the second time, the Mahriyah Hakkamah was enraged and displeased; she started composing and singing in what could only be interpreted as a rebuke to the guests:[26]

English
The AK47[27] is just a *Fartūk*,[28] don't annoy me with its damned sound!
The perfect weapon is a Mengistu, which the men hung on the side of the camel.

Transliteration
al-kilāsh Fartūk mā takattir lay ḥissū.
al-shughul Mangistū, al-dār'a fī jalīstū.[29]

The description of al-Hakkamah of the weapons of the guests as *Fartūk*, was indeed degrading, and also implied that their presence was no longer desirable or welcome. The guests left the place hastily to avoid the possibly imminent confrontation that al-Hakkamah's songs might arouse. They realised quite well that their presence had revived the memory of the grief and anger induced by the conflicts of the 1970s and 1980s, which largely escalated following al-Hakkamat's intervention, especially al-Hakkamah who sang on that occasion.

The conflict of Ta'aisha and Salamat, 1979/80

As discussed earlier, the native administration operated in parallel with local administrative councils until the Nimeiri regime (1969–85) enacted the People's Local Government Act in 1971 in the north of the country and abolished the native administration system. A system of elected administrative councils was put in place at village, rural and provincial levels.

[26] Interview with a Bani Helba teacher (R29), Nyala, 2006.

[27] A Kalashnikov assault rifle.

[28] *Fartūk* is a rope made from palm leaves and is used to scare away birds that come to eat grains during the harvest season. When twisted and then stretched out, it makes noises like guns that scare away birds.

[29] *Jalīstū* is a leather container used for carrying guns on camels.

The drought of the late 1960s, 1970s and 1980s have resulted in the immigration of huge groups of rural populations. The traditional authorities of many tribes received those immigrants and voluntarily hosted most of them within their *Dars*.

The stability of the immigrant groups within their new locations inevitably necessitated new administrative measures to manage the relationship between them and their hosts, the indigenous land owners. In order to establish harmony and avoid conflicts between the host and the hosted, the required arrangements should have taken into account the local belief in the historical rights and legacy of ownership. These rights have been a matter of great dispute and conflict between the owners and those who referred to the ULA to justify and demand the rights access to the land equal to that of the owners. On the contrary, the government carried on enacting policies that undermined these rights and overlooked the old frameworks. This was exemplified by the situation that developed in the 1980s when some immigrant groups, supported by the new administration system, started to demand equal participation with the landowners in the local authority.

This attempt was quite out of keeping with the concept of the *Dar*, which presumes that authority must remain in the hands of the *Dar* owners. Indeed, it implies that new settlers could participate fully in every aspect of the society's life except running for and/or assuming political office, which were generally viewed as exceptional prerogative for the *Dar* owners. This state of affairs has generated much conflict that has beset Darfur since the 1980s. The conflict between Ta'aisha and Salamat tribes is live testimony to this administrative malfunctioning.

The Ta'aisha have hosted the Salamat within their *Dar* in South Darfur for a long period of time. Under the auspices of the Ta'aisha, the Salamat lived peacefully with no confrontations that might jeopardise the relationship between them and their hosts. Following the enactment of the election-based administrative system, it was possible for the hosted groups, including the Salamat, to express their ambitions for political office. This policy posed a great threat to the stable relationship between the two societies, which in turn has started to deteriorate. The deterioration has unfolded significantly during the process of electing a councillor for one of the village councils, the lower local government office. At this point, the issue of tribal sovereignty over the *Dar* was brought into the political consciousness of the *Dar* owners. Al-Hakkamat, who serve as 'territorial agents', came forward voluntarily to fulfil an uncompromising role.

It really started in 1979 when Hassan, from the Salamat tribe, won the election for the councillor of Id al-Goor village council in Rihaid al-Birdi, the main centre of the Ta'aisha *Dar*. Most of the Ta'aishi people rejected the election result outright, on the pretext that this position should only be assumed by Ta'aishi men. Subsequently, four Ta'aishi men colluded in murdering Hassan. One of the killers confessed to the murder and was sentenced to death. Whilst awaiting the execution, a famous *Khail*-Hakkamah from Wolad Kawoon, a clan (*khashum bait*) of the Ta'aisha, was much upset by the turn of the events and expressed her feelings in songs that portrayed the

Ta'aishi murderer as a hero, and lamented that he would be punished just for killing a 'puppy', i.e. Hassan, the Salami:[30]

English
Alas! The blooming flower
Is imprisoned just for killing a puppy!

Transliteration
khasārah, al-zihūr al-mashtūl.
masjūn ʿashān al-kilayb l-maktūl.

Describing the victim as a 'dog' demonstrates not only lack of respect for the deceased but also shows al-Hakkamah's sinister intention of humiliating the Salamat. Such a degrading symbol could only evoke comparable reactions to fend off the insult.

Al-Hakkamah went on advocating for sympathy and support for the killer. These events coincided with the gum arabic harvesting season and the government instructed that the gum arabic field of the prisoner should not be approached. But in protesting the instruction, al-Hakkamah encouraged the tribesmen to harvest the prisoner's field, aiming to use the money earned from selling the produce to hire a lawyer for his defence. Fifteen Ta'aishi men volunteered to carry out the task and also, with many Hakkamat, organised a dancing party to celebrate the anticipated harvest and release of the prisoner.

The Salami Hakkamat were quite overwhelmed and found it just and obligatory to respond to this provocation, as well as to the failure of their people to avenge their relative's murder. Two months later, at *al-Katim* dance party during the Eid festival, the Salami Hakkamat made a move: they instructed young girls to dance with men from other tribes and to ignore their Salami men, whom they deemed cowards for not taking revenge against the Ta'aisha. When the dancing finished, prompted by feelings of embarrassment and humiliation, a group of Salami men attacked a group of Ta'aishi men in a gum arabic field and killed eleven of them.

The Ta'aisha responded still more brutally, when one of their Augada, called Ab-Karank, ambushed some Salami men near a small stream and killed over thirty. The Ta'aishi *Khail*-Hakkamah was pleased and thrilled, and so she pushed for more misery to pile on the Salamat. She described them as cowards who ran away like ostriches, in fear of confrontation, and challenged their ability to confront Ab-Karank:

English
Ab-Karank is really tough; he cannot be tracked down.[31]
The ostrich flew by his wings.[32]

[30] Many people, including Hakkamat, who were key witnesses, alleged that it was the songs and recitations of al-Hakkamat that fuelled the dispute between Salamat and Ta'aisha, which developed into a large-scale violent conflict in 1979/80 and 1982/3. Group and individual interviews, Nyala, 2006.
[31] i.e. for fear of death by his hands.
[32] i.e the Salamat fled, running as fast as ostriches.

Transliteration
Ab-Karank shayn, darbah mā binshāl.
al-naʿām bay janāḥā ṭār.

She understood quite well that her words would provide sufficient motivation to intensify aggression against the Salamat, a situation she most heartedly desired:

English
The Salamat have become rats and hid in holes.
The sons of *kāwūn* have orphaned the children.
Oh, nobody is there to take revenge!

Transliteration
al-salāmāt bigaw fār, wa khashū fī l-nuggār.
wulād kāwūn, ʾattamū l-ʿiyāl.
māfī zawl bishīl l-tār.

The Ta'aisha Hakkamat engagement in this ordeal also involved escorting their Augada in raiding Salamat villages, where their presence increased the cycle of violence and aggression to an unprecedented level. The elders and the leaders of both tribes, whether or not they desired these events to spiral out in the direction al-Hakkamat had provoked, encountered a situation in which they wielded little influence on the course of its escalation and/or the management of its direction.[33] The tension between the two tribes thus persisted for more than a year before a fragile deal was reached.

Most of the inciting songs and poetic recitations were thought to be performed by the now deceased Ta'aisha Hakkamah, Bit Hassaan, the most astounding Hakkamah in the recent history of ethnic and tribal conflicts in Darfur. She was renowned for her strong charisma and authority, and was popular and beloved. Her abilities, qualities and performances elicited the respect and appreciation of the whole Ta'aisha society. In the latter days of her life, she moved to Nyala town. When she was visiting the Ta'aisha *Dar*, the people would usually welcome her in the way they would receive senior government officials, and publicly celebrate her visits. Now Bit Hassaan has passed away, but her legacy seems to have thrived among the vast majority of al-Hakkamat. She became a model and a symbol of ethnic zealotry and passion that al-Hakkamat strive to follow and replicate, as was noticeable in their conduct during the conflicts that engulfed the whole society of South Darfur.

The conflict of Masalit and Arabs, 1996

Once again, the conflict between the Masalit of West Darfur and the immigrant Abbala Rezeiqat in 1996/7 recalls the complexities of the notion of the *Dar* for the Ta'aisha and Salamat tribes. Trouble erupted in 1996, following the introduction of the *emara* system in March 1995, when *Dar* Masalit was divided into thirteen *emara*: eight were granted to the newcomer Abbala (the Masalit claim most are Chadians), and only five

[33] Group interview with some Baggara men (G5), Nyala, 2006.

emarat allocated to the Masalit, the indigenous residents and the masters of the *Dar* where the sultan was still nominally in charge. This policy deliberately meant to undermine the social and political organisation and customs of the Masalit, which presume that the sultan, and not any other entity, must preside over land distribution in their *Dar*.

The Masalit interpreted this policy and the pattern of its execution, as motivated by racial prejudice, and the government's intention to disempower their society and displace them from their homeland in favour of the Arab ethnicity. The stubborn resistance of the Masalit to such a population replacement policy led to a devastating war from 1996 to 1998, which resulted in hundreds of civilian casualties, thousands of internally displaced, and refugees across the borders, especially in Chad. Local Arab tribes joined in support of their Darfuri relatives and the Chadians. The Sudanese government took part in the war alongside the Arabs using official and unofficial forces, such as the PDF (Popular Defence Forces), al-Salaam Forces (*quwaat al-salaam*) and Janjawiid militias.[34]

The conflict started as sporadic clashes, but soon escalated into large-scale, violent confrontations. This development was thought to have been triggered by the killing of a group of Abbala Omad, who were invited by a group of Masalit notables for peace negotiations. The Abbala Omad, however, were all burned to death in the Kirainik mosque, the meeting venue (Haggar, 2003, p. 223; Ahmed, 1998, p. 152). The incident unleashed a spiral of violence and retaliatory aggression.

It was obvious that the conflict was carried out along ethnic lines, Africans *vis-à-vis* Arabs, a fault line that brought al-Hakkamat to the battlefield in support of their ethnic groups. The Arab Hakkamat, in particular, celebrated the triumph of their folks in taking over the Masalit homeland. They were in the forefront, as usual, honing ethnic consciousness and documenting the course of violence. One Hakkamah from the Mahriyah described the Masalit, in a lyric poem, as *abeed*,[35] the label that Darfuri Arabs often use for Africans, and urged her tribesmen to humiliate and exterminate them, by reciting:

English
Oh, my tribesmen! Hit hard the slave who misbehaves in this place.
His women are but slaves, busy with their Jangal dancing.
I want him here to cut firewood for me.
And I want his sister to wash my clothes!

An Arab tribal chief, firing his gun in the air, responded gleefully to her imperious appeal emphasising that the Masalit were there just to serve the needs of the Arabs:

[34] These forces were recruited and brought to the area in 1999 by Mohamed Ahmad al Dabi, a Shagiyya general in the military intelligence. Al Dabi was acting as the personal representative of President al-Bashir to manage the conflict in the way the government preferred (Flint and de Waal 2005: 60). Also see Haggar (2007, pp. 113–39).

[35] *Abeed* in Arabic corresponds to slaves (sing. *Abid*, and *ibaid* is diminutive); Darfur Arabs usually use these terms to insult and denigrate the Africans.

Oh! Hakkamah, feel good.
What is wrong with the Nuba?[36]
Regarding their wealth, they accumulate it for us to take away.
Regarding their crops, they plant them for us to take by force and eat.
Oh! Hakkama, feel good.
There is nothing wrong with the Nuba.[37]

Another Hakkamah from Rezeiqat also celebrated the victory over tribes in South Sudan and the grabbing of their land. Her supremacist tone similarly reflects the tendency to take the land of others and transform the owners into slaves and (tied) farmers:[38]

English
The slave is stupid, he wouldn't have rest
As we farmed his land.[39]

Transliteration
al-ʾibayd balīd, mā jātā rāḥa.
baladah ḥashaynah zirāʿah.

Calling indigenous Africans *abeed* is not only a racist attitude, but indeed an instrument of subjugation and dominance. For instance, Amnesty International reported that the Janjawiid said to the residents of Deisa, a Masalit village, '(t)he blood of the Blacks runs like water, we take their goods and we chase them from our area and our cattle will be in their land. The power of al-Bashir belongs to the Arabs and we will kill you until the end' (Amnesty International, 2004a, p. 22). This proclamation of the Janjawiid is, indeed, resonant of the racial discrimination entrenched in the culture of Arab groups in Darfur against indigenous Africans, and is reinforced by the state's apathy in safeguarding the dignity of those indigenous citizens.

Hence, the implications of the domestic policies pursued by the government could not be more disastrous to the security and coexistence of communities in Darfur. In *Dar* Masalit, the situation continues to reproduce alienation and social fragmentation, which has transformed West Darfur into a major site of human rights violations. As for al-Hakkamat, who are essentially a social construct for supporting their own groups, they have earned an extra licence to nurture the norms of their society and cement efforts to fortify their social boundaries against concern toward human rights violations. Apparently, within this complex sociopolitical context, the fully pledged loyalty by al-Hakkamat is not subject to arbitration according to considerations of right and wrong.

Observably, however, especially in the last three decades, rural communities have undergone tremendous change as a result of more exposure to schooling and urbanisation, as well as the availability of telecommu-

[36] Baggara used to call the Africans 'Nuba', a word they sometimes substitute for *abeed*, or slaves.
[37] i.e. 'They are our slaves.' Recited by Hilbawi, a retired teacher and folk researcher (R22), Nyala, 2006. Also cited in Mohamed, 2003a, pp. 2–3, 480–81.
[38] Interview with a Rezeiqi government employee (R5), Nyala, 2006.
[39] i.e. as we took it over and forced the owners to farm it for us.

nications media, such as television and telephones. These media often show the physical and psychological effects of war on societies across the world, and call for people to stand against war and violence. Presumably, the evidence of this suffering might induce al-Hakkamat to begin a retrospective journey for reviewing the past miserable events and their conduct, which contributed to similar suffering in Darfur. But it is quite comprehensible that dissociating from familiar and enduring projections may not be easy for al-Hakkamat, especially when those projections are pivotal in their roles. Nevertheless, it would still be interesting to see how new attitudes and responses developing within al-Hakkamat, could place them as peace actors heading towards positive change.

The conflict of Ma'aliya and Rezeiqat, 2006

The conflict between the Baggara Ma'aliya and Rezeiqat Arab tribes also bears further evidence of al-Hakkamat's authority and influence, and time and again reveals the non-negotiable loyalty people pledge to their Hakkamat.

In early 2006, a commissioner in South Darfur organised formal religious sermons in a Ma'aliya village, and assigned a *Faqir* (a *khalwa*[40] teacher) to deliver preaching sessions to the village community, who were accused of involvement in frequent violent disputes. The sessions emphasised the need to forsake homicide and the raiding, looting and burning of people's assets as unlawful and sinful. Large numbers of people were present when a group of Rezeiqat horsemen attacked the tribe and many people were killed.

Some horsemen of the Ma'aliya who were attending the session quickly left to prepare a counter-attack. Having learned about the incident, the commissioner swiftly arrived at the scene in an attempt to prevent an escalation into further violence. He requested the horsemen to listen to the counselling teacher, and out of courtesy they obeyed instantly. At the end the Ageed al-Augada asked the *Faqir* to confirm that he had finished his preaching. As soon the teacher had done so, the Ageed addressed the horsemen: 'Did you hear what the *Faqir* said?' They answered, 'Yes.' 'And do you remember what al-Hakkamah said?' They answered, 'Yes, certainly.' He promptly instructed them: '*Akufru*' (which literally means to disbelieve, or to renounce your religion). They all said: 'We have.' Then he commanded them: 'Let's go and fight,' and off they went.[41]

Apparently, al-Hakkamat's authority and influence, as seen in this incident, emanate from a well-entrenched societal belief in their role as an integral part of the security system – the Ageed and his horsemen, to whom the tribe people owe reverence and gratuity. It is this belief that has blocked any ideological intervention from outside the social and cultural setting of al-Hakkamat from having an effect. The possibility that al-Hakkamat could endeavour to turn their influence towards peace advocacy, remains a prospect to be reckoned with. This is despite the

40 A religious school (pl. *khalawi*)

41 Interview with the chief of Ta'alba (R10), Nyala, 2006.

fact that for the power brokers, al-Hakkamat are not counted as potential contributors to conflict resolution.

These instances show how al-Hakkamat's influence on youth reaches its zenith and reinforces a strong mutual relationship between them – al-Hakkamat go on praising and enthusing the youth, and the youth show loyalty by responding positively to al-Hakkamat's expectations of them. Yet these experiences also show that the cost incurred is often high and bitter, especially when the youth are pushed to engage in armed conflict – from which more often than not they return only as corpses.

WOMEN AND MOBILISATION IN SUDAN

Narratives about Hakkamat's power to steer events towards devastating outcomes are but testimony to the traditional engagement of women in the history of relationships between tribes and ethnic groups in Darfur, as well as other parts of Sudan. Al-Hakkamat's distinction in this experience is their poetic ability to construct mocking and inciting diction, which has become a characteristic feature of their mobilisation methods.

Slatin Pasha[42] recounted an incident that happened when he was Darfur commissioner. It involved an attack on Sheikh Ali Wad Hegeir of the Ma'aliya tribe accompanied by his father-in-law and a group of men, by a group of Ma'aliya and Rezeiqat, led by Sheikh Belal Nagur. Hegeir and his companions escaped, and when he arrived at his home, his wife received them by singing in ridicule:

English
My husband is but a male ostrich.
My father a female ostrich.
A two-day journey, they made it in just a moment!

Transliteration
rājlī ḥiḍlīm wa 'aboy rabdāh.
safar yawmayn sawwuhum fi jabdāh.

They were further chased by the attackers but, this time, smarting under his wife's mocking diction, Hegeir determined to fight, saying, 'I shall never fly to save my life. Better is it to fall under the sword than to be laughed at by a woman.' True to his words, he defended himself until he was killed and his father-in-law, too (Slatin Pasha, 1930: 72–3). Obviously, the voice of the wife, who was presumably Hakkamah, was the main force behind the killing of her beloved, as the men were unable to endure her demeaning expressions and tried to salvage their reputation, only to be killed for their trouble.

The demeaning expressions of women towards men could thus be unchallenged and therefore disastrous. On the other hand, al-Hakkamat are not the only female characters who tend to employ such expressions

[42] Slatin Pasha was the governor of Darfur during the Turco-Egyptian rule (1881–3), and ended up as a prisoner of the Khalifa during the Mahdiyya rule.

to stir their people. Similar expressions were also used at the royal household in the very last days of the Darfur sultanate, when the Condominium troops were approaching Darfur but Sultan Ali Dinar[43] seemed unready for confrontation. His sister Taja, an *iiya basi*, incited her reluctant brother to fight the British: 'If you don't fight, give me your trousers and take my *kanfus*.[44] You are no man' (cited in O'Fahey, 2008, p. 116). Thus egged on, the sultan fought the invader's army unprepared, only to witness his ultimate destiny and ensure the downfall of his sultanate in 1916.

The news about the Condominium army invading Darfur was indeed communicated to Sultan Ali Dinar by a royal court Hakkamah called Safiyaat. It was reported that Safiyaat was roaming with some royal women around the area of Saylay, in the northern outskirts of al-Fashir, the seat of the sultan's court, when she noticed the presence of a massive gathering of strangers marching towards al-Fashir. The women hurried to al-Fashir over night and arrived early in the morning. Safiyaat hastily came into the Sultan's palace and passed on to him what they had seen. She communicated this in the following recitation:[45]

English
Good morning, My Lord, I have come to you with news.
If you allow me to talk, My Lord, I will come forward.
May God make you victorious, My Lord!
My Lord, yesterday, as we were coming off the north of Saylay,
We saw a gathering of people there, not Bertie, nor were they Mellay.[46]
May God make you victorious, My Lord!
They were Christians and Turks, evil whisperers along with mischievers;[47]
Riding automobiles, seemingly coming to fight.
May God make you victorious, My Lord!
Salim, the father of Hawwa, come forward along with Ramadan,[48]
Come on inside (to defend), may peace be upon the kings of Turrah[49]
May God make you victorious, My Lord!
I have no more to say, as Evil has now gathered pace,
The army is ready, nothing else but to uphold your resolve,
May God make you victorious, My Lord!
The time for speeches is now over; we are smelling war.
The honour of Taja must be protected, and may you be safe too, the saviour of Nammah.[50]
May God make you victorious, My Lord.

Transliteration
ʾaṣbaḥta yā sīdī, jītak maʿnyei kalām.
kam gultā lay kallimī, sīdī ʾānī gudām.
sīdī ʾallā yanṣurak.

43 The first downfall of the Sultanate was in 1874 when it was invaded by the Turki-Egyptians. Sultan Ali Dinar then restored the Sultanate in 1898, after the demise of the Mahdiya. In 1916, Darfur had fallen for the last time to the condominium authority in Sudan.
44 A *kanfus* is a type of women's skirt.
45 Follow-up interview with Mohamed Salih, Radio Dabanga, France, October 2015.
46 Bertie and Mellay are tribes living north of al-Fashir, i.e. the gathering must be invading enemies as they do not look like local people.
47 Reference to chapter 114, verse 4, of the Quran, *Surat An-Nas*.
48 Salim and Ramadan are courageous notables who would help during times of adversity.
49 Turrah was the original capital of the Sultanate before al-Fashir became the capital.
50 Taja was the influential sister of the Sultan, Nammah was his wife.

sīdī ʾamis jāyyīn min rīḥ, gabul Saylay.
shufnā nās lāmīn, lā Bartī, lā Melī.
sīdī ʾallā yanṣurak.
sīdī naṣārā Turuk jaw, waswās maʿa khannās.
rākbīn ʾutūmbīlāt, shītan budūrū duwās.
sīdī ʾallā yanṣurak.
Sālim ʾabū Hawā, taʿālū maʿa Ramadān.
ʾabgū lay juwā, yaslam mulūk Ṭurrāh.
sīdī ʾallā yanṣurak.
mā ʿindī shayʾ bitgāl, wā sh-sharr khalāṣ lammā.
ʾajaysh mā dām jāhiz, bas ʾarfaʿū ʾal-himmah.
sīdī ʾallā yanṣurak.
waqt-al kalām tammā, ḥarāba binshammā.
yaslam sharaf Tājā, wa yaslam faddāy Nammah.
sīdī ʾallā yanṣurak.

The news was also taken seriously by the sultan and the royal family. Mayram Taja, the most influential woman in the sultan's court, therefore urged him to behave as a courageous man. The sultan's acquiescence to his sister's provocation was not an overnight development in the relationship between the two characters. Rather, it was a manifestation of well-established gender power relationships within the Darfur sultanate, which enabled women to exercise their own choices and influence. Women had formal titles, which included *iiya kuuri* (the Queen Mother, for the sultan's wife, akin to the First Lady), *iiya basi* (the Royal Mother, for the sultan's favourite sister), *Habboba* (grandmother), and *Mayram* (princess, pl. *Mayarim*).[51] These women were characteristically among the group of notables and officials running the sultanate and they were usually mentioned in the sultans' charters and statements. Women's representation at the highest echelon of the state's political hierarchy thus stands as a substantial challenge to the attitudes and the ideology of gender discrimination, i.e. male public domination and female subordination. It is a testimony of the role of sultans and the sultanate ruling system in empowering women and strengthening their position as part of the ruling elite. Inevitably, this context has promoted the position of women generally and paved the way for favourable gender power relationships as the mainstream.

Moreover, women were generally recognised to have wisdom and insightful opinions and were therefore often involved in public political matters and decision making. When they were absent, their views were often consulted and men do not take decisions that might, otherwise, contradict those views (Al-Tunisi, 1965, p. 93). During the sultanate, wars were frequently fought within and outside Darfur boundaries, and they constituted a domain for serious political engagement and action. The significance of women was often manifested through their engagement in the

[51] *Iiya Kuuri* was the First Lady or the Queen Mother, and the most powerful position given to women in the royal palace. She would be the Sultan's favourite and could be his eldest sister or the widow of the deceased sultan. She had the privilege of owning large *hawakir* from which she would collect taxes, and which she would manage through powerful men who were loyal and submissive to her. Among those who assumed such a powerful stature was *iiya Kuuri Kinanah* who was famous for her wisdom and was very close to Sultan Mohamed Tairab (1768–87) (al-Tunisi, 1965, p. 93).

proceedings of these wars. Royal women were consulted and their views respected.[52] In most of the tribes inhabiting Darfur, ordinary women also traditionally had influence over warfare decisions, especially when their own communities were engaged (See Cunnison, 1966, p. 117). Women of Darfur, both royal and ordinary, had the power and agency to make their voice heard and to direct events in the way they perceived to be the best, using the means accessible and authorised to them, e.g. singing and speech.

On the other hand, the use of songs and poems to secure desired initiatives in the tribesmen is arguably not a characteristic exclusive to al-Hakkamat in the recent history of conflict in Darfur, but a general practice among Baggara women outside the Darfur boundaries, for instance, the Baggara Humur of Kordofan (ibid. pp. 117–18). It is also a cultural feature of the Nuer of South Sudan to sing war songs – *Diid koor* – that are insulting, arousing and explicit, and a woman could be divorced if she expressed the abuse she suffered at the hands of her husband by well-articulated singing (Svoboda, 1985, p. 79).

When the NIF seized power in 1989, they launched an extensive mobilisation campaign for the war in South Sudan, which they interpreted as a Jihadi war against Christians. Women in the north took an extensive and proactive part in the campaign, by contributing gold, money and food and by encouraging their young sons to enlist as Jihadists. Similarly, the women in the south, the Nuba Mountains and the southern Blue Nile encouraged their sons to join the SPLA to fight against the inequality and tyranny adopted by the central government to govern the citizens (Itto, 2006, pp. 56–7; Mathiang, 2008, p. 17).

Al-Hakkamat thus appear as just an antecedent manifestation to a precedent history of women in Darfur. They are not royal: they are ordinary women who are able to craft their way and establish themselves in the inner circle of elites in society, and to force their recognition as indispensible to the organisational structure of the leadership and authority of their society.

CONFLICT AND AL-HAKKAMAT INTER-RELATIONSHIPS

The conflicts between tribes also often cast a gloomy shadow on the relationships between al-Hakkamat themselves, and induced them to trade insults against one another at dancing and singing events. For instance, a Salami Hakkamah[53] claimed that the late Ta'aisha Hakkamah Bit Hassaan exchanged insults with the Salami Hakkamah, A'aiyasha al-Austowania.

This happened at a wedding occasion where women, including Hakkamat from both tribes were invited. These women were organised

[52] It is recounted that Sultan Tairab (1768–87) consulted his wife on whether to choose her son (Ahmad) or her stepson (Ishaq) for the position of the sultan upon his retirement. The sultan put their abilities to the test in her presence. Ishaq proved that he was the one who suited the position of sultan, but the sultan was still waiting for the approval of his wife. She said: 'No, your son Ishaq is a man; as for my son, I am ashamed.' Shuqayr, 1981, p. 156.

[53] Interviews with Salami Hakkamah (R51), Nyala, 2006.

as contesting groups and were named, perhaps in humour, after the two most popular and rival football teams in Sudan: *al-Mareekh* (Mars) for the Ta'aisha women, and *al-Hilal* (the Crescent) for the Salamat women. During the party, Hakkamah Bit Hassaan, by then advanced in age, seemingly was annoyed by something, she took the opportunity and started degrading the Salamat women (*al-Hilal*), by singing on the spur of the moment:

English
Oh, my girls are calves!
Women of *al-Hilal* do not shave their legs.
You bring the trail.[54]
Vaccinate them with penicillin, before their infection can spread.

Transliteration
banātī ʾanā ʿujūl.
ʿawīn a-l-Hilāl, mā bit-ḥifan a-l-rijūl.
tajīban a-l-ʾattar.
ʾattʿanhum banadawr, gabl al-bajar ma-ʾintashar.

Proud of the integrity and cleanliness of the young and pretty girls of Ta'aisha, she loathes what she sees as the filth of the Salamat women and the sexually transmitted diseases they carried. The words suggest that an illicit sexual relationship has been committed with these infected women as could be inferred from the stench on the men that cannot be hidden. Therefore, she stresses that Salamat women should be vaccinated to prevent the spread of the infection to Ta'aishi women (in case their men get engaged in sexual affairs with the Salamat women).

Boiling with anger, A'aiyasha al-Austowania hit back:

English:
Oh, you, the bitter, as the grasshopper[55] of calotropis.
I found the shallow *barnoog*[56] but couldn't find its roots!
I've strongly rejected intermarrying with you, as you are of unknown parentage.
You are just brought by the headmost flood of Wad Birli[57] with the froth.
I have reported to the Water and Sanitation Department to come and clean the nasty rubbish.

Transliteration:
al-murrah jarātt l-ʿushar.
ʾana ligīt al-barnūg wa ma ligīt layya gaʿar.
ʾabayt nisbitkū katīr, wa mā ʿindukū ʾahal.
al-jābkū Wadi Birlī fī ʾawāl l-ḥashar.
balāghī fawq al-sāhah, yajī yashīl al-zafar.

[54] i.e. the bad smell of the disease.
[55] This is an insect called Grasshopper Poecilocerus Pictus F., which feeds on the poisonous milkweed Calotropis Gigantea. For more information, see Pugalenthi and Livingstone, 1995.
[56] There is a local proverb, '*Barnoog* without root', which is used to insult those who have no recognised tribes or identified fathers.
[57] Wad Birli is a small but strong-current seasonal valley, which divides Nyala town into two.

In an equally venomous response, the Salami Hakkamah slaps Bit Hassaan, and describes her tongue as nasty and bitter, like the calotropis locust. She despises the menfolk of Bit Hassaan, portraying them as the most abhorred men, just like the *barnoog* (mushroom), which has no roots and is known locally as a food source for foul-smelling insects. Al-Hakkamah refuses to intermarry with them because they are aliens and dirt, washed up by the first flood of the *wadi*. She urges the Health Department to come to rescue them from such a sickening and annoying presence.

Here we see multiple examples of women's affairs and relationships being iconised in a poetic exchange of al-Hakkamat that exudes defending the self and detracting from the other. The verses of both women were designed to earn the sympathy and pride of their respective tribes. This manifestation also demonstrates that al-Hakkamat have no taboo issues in their poetic language – whereas other women might choose more semantic and/or symbolic means of expression to avoid what may be seen as unethical expressions in public. This is one of the strengths of al-Hakkamah: the all-around woman, the woman for all occasions.

It is because of the freedom of speech that al-Hakkamat enjoy that they are figuratively described as *kasrat-qaid*, a term that literally means a 'shackle breaker'. It is also a label that implies their emancipation from the gender constraints that usually block women from speaking up on issues that concern them. I perceive this boldness in exercising personal choices as embodying the very essence of the concept of human agency that identifies individuals 'as autonomous, purposive actors, capable of choice' (Lister, 1997, p. 36). It is this agency of al-Hakkamat that forces the tribesmen, especially prominent notables, to abide by societal regulations in fear of their reputation becoming broken by the articulations of al-Hakkamat should they violate these rules.

Al-Hakkamat are consistently described as constituting a model of moral behaviour within the Darfuri Arab society, a position that earns them people's respect and tightens their confidence in exercising agency. Yet perhaps a contradictory image that is drawn by some of their kin in evaluating them could be attributed to this freedom of speech and action:

> She is a woman who has no values and no ethics, [and is an] uncontrollable person and morally deficient; she only composes for money, like a beggar, begging officials for tea and sugar.[58]

> The majority, I would say up to 99.9 per cent of rural women, seldom aspire to be Hakkamat; only the remaining few may aspire to become Hakkamat as a result of certain circumstances. Consequently, the incentives, the obscurities, the conducts, the surrounding media and the environment, are the main stimuli that create al-Hakkamah. You would never find a Hakkamah, with all respect, from respected and powerful families – for instance the Nazir's.[59]

Indeed, denying al-Hakkamat any virtuous background, decency or moral rectitude is a perception mainly based on an evaluation of the

[58] Interview with a Masalit government employee who was the NCP affiliate, Nyala, 2006.
[59] Interview with a retired soldier for Fur (R72), Nyala, 2006.

arrogated Hakkamat in Nyala town and their actions, which obscure and stand at odds with al-Hakkamat's recognised moral commitment. It is the decency they observe that reinforces and solidifies the public acceptance and respect that they attract from their communities, in both towns and villages. Besides, the Islamic project that was launched and advocated by the NIF government was intended mainly to reconstruct Sudanese citizens to fit an Islamic ideological model. In this political ideology, women are more focused on as a site of identity politics than men; and most shari'a law targets women's dress, movements, etc.; i.e. women's decency.

Certainly, the regime would not risk their central political project and social campaign by incorporating al-Hakkamat if they were perceived to be morally deficient. Moreover, most of al-Hakkamat belonged to prestigious families that were famous for power and horsemanship. Apparently, the attitudes toward al-Hakkamat are based on value judgements on ideologically divisive issues, rather than on their actual social value and the effects they have in their own societies.

AL-HAKKAMAT AND REWARDS FROM THE COMMUNITY

It has been established so far that al-Hakkamat's contribution and efforts are well acknowledged and consolidated by their communities. Since the early days of their emergence up until the very last minute of their active life, individuals, especially prestigious people and horsemen, are keen to offer them moral support and pay them gratuity to enable them to undertake their obligations effectively.[60] Wealthy people offer them material gifts, which might include a rewarding prize, such as a camel, and/or anything that an excited youth could readily offer. Some notables were seen to have left all the cash they owned in the hands of al-Hakkamah.[61] Nonetheless, whilst wealth has no bearing on the emergence of a woman as Hakkamah, most al-Hakkamat after being publicly recognised, have possessed considerable wealth in the form of farms and herds of animals that they accrued from the gifts they received.[62]

Although the rewards offered to al-Hakkamat have varied with time and circumstances, their symbolic value has never changed. Before the 1980s, for instance, hunting horsemen usually brought tusks of elephants to al-Hakkamat. Women's accessories made of elephant tusks were a familiar spectacle on al-Hakkamat, and reflect the hunters' appreciation for them.[63] These gifts were also a form of public celebration of the eminent courage and gallantry needed for hunting, which was always hazardous and demanded outstanding skills.

Before Sudan split into two states in 2011, horsemen from Rezeiqat brought captives/abductees from the battlefield and from their raids on villages in South Sudan. These abductees were usually used in domestic,

[60] Interview with a retired soldier from Fur (R72), Nyala, 2006.
[61] Group interview with seven tribal chiefs (G1), al-Fashir, 2006.
[62] Group and individual interviews, Nyala, 2006.
[63] Ibid.

chores and economic activities and kept in captivity until a deal was reached, when they would be returned to their tribes. The horsemen would usually offer al-Hakkamat strong and young abductees to serve their domestic and farming needs.[64] Alongside these donations, al-Hakkamat might also receive other material rewards, especially from the horsemen, as presented in the following recitation:[65]

English
Oh, Hakkamah.
She who has waist-long hair,
She would not shuttle in public transport,
Nor would she throng with passengers.

Transliteration
al-ḥakkāmā
'umm sha'aran li-l-ḥazzāmā
mā rikbat 'umm dawarwar wa mā zaḥamat rukābā

Al-Hakkamah is praised as a beautiful, comforted and privileged woman (she has waist-long hair, does not travel on public transport like ordinary villagers, etc.). These descriptions suggest that al-Hakkamat are persons well taken care of.

The community also rewarded their Hakkamat by labels and nicknames with actual and/or symbolic meanings that glorify them by recognising their duties and the traits they nurture in carrying them out. Such nicknames would remain lifelong, as an honourable identification and recognition (for some examples, see Table 4.2).

Table 4.2 Examples of Hakkamat nicknames

Hakkamat nicknames	*Remarks*
Dahab al-Madīnāh	Gold of the town
Kassū	Literally, means 'they stayed away', i.e. whenever she showed up, others would give way
Maryam Zakhīrah	Woman of ammunition
al-Rājma	The bomber

(*Source*: Generated by author using data from interviews, Nyala and al-Fashir, March–June 2006)

In fact, most Hakkamat who I met have nicknames and four of them proclaimed that all prestigious Hakkamat have held nicknames indicative of their character and level of influence.

A typical reaction of the horsemen to al-Hakkamat's influence is to attract their attention and win their praise, sometimes by committing cruel acts. Some horsemen cut the ears off those they have killed on the battlefield, and present them to al-Hakkamat on their return as evidence

64 Interviews with two Rezeiqi men, Nyala, 2006; also see Masajid, 1995.
65 Interviews with a retired teacher and folk researcher E. D. Khair Allah from Bani Helba (R22), Nyala, 2006.

of their bravery and heroism. I was told that 'Whenever you found a [live] man whose ear was cut off, know for sure that it was brought to some Hakkamat'.[66] One Hakkamah who was still residing in the village, and witnessed the government campaign against the Bolad insurgency in the early 1990s, attested to this by saying:

> Yes, to tell the truth we saw with our own eyes men's organs brought by horsemen. They brought ears for us to see ... Anyone who saw them would cry. I myself saw many of them; as every horseman brought as much as he could from the bodies of those he claimed to have killed, as evidence of his bravery ... I just saw them and left them to their owners ... In this case we praise all the men collectively, not merely the ones who brought [the trophies]. But in fighting elephants, we only identify the brave man and praise him alone.[67]

Nonetheless, it was generally agreed that although al-Hakkamat do not normally demand fighters to perpetrate such atrocities, some of them do to satisfy their own sense of triumphalism. A prominent Baggara chief explained that even though al-Hakkamat usually stay close to the battlefield to watch the fighting performance of the horsemen, and are certainly in a position to see at first hand the cutting off of ears, none of them has ever admitted seeing it happening. He pointed out that tribal leaders often advise against this practice, but many do not heed the advice.[68]

On the other hand, cutting off victims' organs and presenting them to al-Hakkamat is deemed an old and well-known practice.[69] It has been carried out during the conflicts between tribes in Darfur, especially under the current regime, as well as in most recent fights between government-sponsored Janjawiid and Darfuri insurgents since 2003. It always implies an intolerable humiliation and a sedition, more than if a homicide was committed. This alone could lead to a resumption of the aggression in which revenge of a similar kind will be sought.[70]

Some accounts have tried to cast an ethnic dimension to the practice, in the sense that it is perpetrated, especially during the current conflict, by Arabs against Africans. There have, however, been alternative accounts suggesting that the practice is common among all warring tribes, and that they have used it against one another irrespective of their ethnic background. Notwithstanding, it might have been practised

[66] Interview with Ahmed Jowa (R14), radio and TV presenter from Ta'aisha, Nyala, 2006.

[67] Interview with Hubbania Hakkamah (R19), Nyala, 2006.

[68] Interview with the chief of Ta'alba (R10), Nyala, 2006.

[69] Sultan Husain, who ruled Darfur between 1839 and 1874, offered his daughter Mayram Arafa a clan of Ta'aisha called Um Ribda as *hakura*, with a large population. She would go and collect taxes by herself and the people used to welcome her by organising big dancing ceremonies in appreciation of her gentle treatment of them. On one of her visits, however, the people refused to pay the taxes and instead killed her, cut off her hands and used them to play the *Nuggara* while dancing. The Hadaleel clan of the Ta'aisha rejected this inhumane conduct of killing a woman and mutilating her body, and subsequently cooperated with the sultan and defeated Um Ribda in a fight. Their remaining men were divided into three groups: two of the groups were killed and the third was allowed to live (Mohamed 1982:40-41; narrative of an old sheikh, Mohamed Awad, an informant in the interview (tape number mdaa/1971, diary number 2, pp. 83–4).

[70] Group interviews (G2, G3, G4), Nyala, 2006.

in a more demeaning and vicious manner against tribes of a different ethnicity.

For instance, in 2004, a group of men from an Arab tribe attacked a camp of the Bani Helba tribe. They stole their herds, killed four men, cut an ear off one of them and took it to their Hakkamat. As an unforgettable and unforgivable humiliation, this atrocity led to a vicious cycle of violent conflict between the two Arab tribes.[71] Similarly, conflict also erupted some years ago between the northern Rezeiqat and Fur, in Tuwal village, South Darfur. In retaliation for the killing of two Fur men by the Rezeiqat, the Fur killed a Rezeiqi man and cut off his ears. Persistent hostilities between the two tribes continued and resulted in the destruction of Tuwal village several times by northern Rezeiqat militias.[72]

Even though al-Hakkamat's association with such violations reflects their powerful impact on the perceived evils of ethnicity and racial hatred among their people, it also paradoxically embodies the respect and veneration that are felt for them and for their roles in the village/camp.[73] On the other hand, the persistence of this violent practice could be explained by the failure of al-Hakkamat to combat it or to invite people to relinquish it as an inhumane demeanour. Rather, al-Hakkamat have continued to celebrate the heroism associated with killing people and seeing their bodies mutilated. This practice seems to add an aura of importance and singularity around al-Hakkamat, which instigates them not to act against the ambitions of their tribesmen, but rather to bolster them to the full, no matter how macabre their conduct. They are therefore described by their societies as a double-edged sword that can drive people to good or evil conduct. Obviously, al-Hakkamat are rewarded by their communities for the harmful dimension of their role and conduct – the part that ties them strongly to the Ageed organisation and the horsemen.

CONCLUSION

It has become abundantly clear that al-Hakkamat are an integral part of the Ageed organisation and that their coordination usually gains strength during conflicts with other tribes. During the Ageed's military missions, al-Hakkamat usually carry out several military activities, enthusing the horsemen who often respond with great pleasure anticipating al-Hakkamat's praise. Al-Hakkamat's military engagement has been revealed in many incidents in Darfur in the last four decades in which their pre-emptive participation turned minor skirmishes between tribes and ethnic groups into full-scale wars. Even though they are not involved in the Ageed organisation's decision making, and do not serve as the main instigators, they have proved to be agents of fierce attack and retaliation. Their poetic attacks at social events, especially against each

[71] Group interview (G3), Nyala, 2006.
[72] Interview with a poet from Bani Helba (R45), Nyala, 2006.
[73] Group and individual interviews, Nyala, 2006.

other's conflicting groups, may become the most likely of their strategies to escalate events.

On the other hand, even though al-Hakkamat's intervention has generated disastrous outcomes, including the deterioration of peaceful coexistence between tribes, the tribal native authorities that often seek to end these conflicts have seldom attempted to apply restrictive measures on al-Hakkamat's pursuits. The attitude, of these authorities in turning a blind eye on al-Hakkamat's deeds also suggests that they implicitly encourage al-Hakkamat to continue with their conduct, no matter how aggressive. The belligerent voice of al-Hakkamat has therefore incurred a high cost in human resources, as huge numbers of Baggara combatants either return handicapped or end up dead.

Al-Hakkamat are highly valued and the choices they make are usually seconded by their communities. They are generously rewarded by and gain huge recognition from their tribespeople, especially the prominent, and combatants who aspire to be in al-Hakkamat's good books. Presenting to al-Hakkamat the ears from the dead bodies of combatants as a proof of heroism and in the hope of getting praise, constitutes the most provocative effect of al-Hakkamat's engagement in conflict. No Hakkamah has been found to have shown any sign of remorse about the mutilations, or have endeavoured to advise perpetrators to forsake them. Rather, they continue to praise the perpetrators and thus perpetuate the practice and the animosity. The manifestation of this conduct also confirms the description of al-Hakkamat as representing 'a shadow of a big tree for their tribes', by accommodating both the evil and the good, and also as a 'double-edged sword', of unpredictable swing; for it can both cause pain and provide relief.

5

Government and Racial Assimilation of Ethnic Groups

Since independence, the government office of Sudan has been dominated by people who are affiliated to the northern part of the country. Those elites served as the right hand of the condominium rulers and then took over when the colonials left the country. They then established themselves as the ruling elites. In order to maintain power and serve their own vested interests, their political approach to ruling the country has become characterised by a system of governance and domestic politics based on racial discrimination: the assimilation of some and dissimilation of others.

This attitude has influenced polarisation among tribes and ethnic groups and created dire situations, especially in peripheral regions where tribes and ethnic groups have been transformed into vehicles for cementing the elites' power and cultural hegemony. Conflicts have therefore erupted between tribes and ethnic groups, and the government has used this as an opportunity to further polarise people by interpreting these conflicts in ethnic and racial terms. This biased intervention by the government seems to have fuelled the zealous spirit of al-Hakkamat and heightened their ethnic consciousness, which has surpassed all considerations.

THE NATIONAL RULING ELITES

Following independence in 1956, national governments became dominated by the political elites who belonged to northern riverine Sudan and tended to share similar interests and attitudes towards other people in the country. The origination of these elites dates back to the colonial era when they cooperated, as individuals and as families, with the rulers and were able to reap the advantage of the privileged educational and training provisions that the colonial authority offered. Access to these opportunities, however, was not offered equally to all people and sections of society, but to certain people, regions, tribes and ethnic groups, in order to create a loyal clientele class, as well as an efficient clerical elite who could manage the administration office upon the colonials' withdrawal. Subsequently, they dominated employment and acquired firm control of the economic resources. When they took over from the colonials, they continued with very much the same politics and policies as the colonials.

Thereafter, those elites came together through what could be described as the 'reciprocal assimilation'[1] of elites, and firmly entrenched their position as a privileged class in the independent Sudan. They have become a powerful allied force that dominates the economic, political (both government and political parties in whatever colour or form) and social domains of activity, using, at different times, every manipulative means to protect their personal interests.

The political history of independent Sudan has therefore been dominated by the social groupings of those who were spoiled by the favouritism of the colonials, and who continued afterwards with the same political approaches and policies, whilst showing deficiency in the goodwill needed to pursue justice and improve the socio-economic performance of the country at large (Niblock, 1987, p. 204). Given that the Sudanese state was amalgamated from different and often warring kingdoms, it is unsurprising that no belief in public interest among the riverine ruling and governing elites could be envisaged in the first place, let alone be expected to materialise.

Broadly speaking, the social and political forces in Sudan assemble under the auspices of two main family-based sectarian parties that dominated the political scene early on: the Umma Party, which affiliates to al-Mahdi family, and the Ansar (Partisans)[2] sect, and the Democratic Unionist Party (DUP), which affiliates to al-Marghani family and al-Khatmiyya sect (Sikainga, 1993, pp. 79–80). The two families have actually combined the traditional religious influence and the leverage of state office that they appropriated in order to forge strong patron–client relationships, especially among rural communities.[3] The vast majority of the urban elites have also eventually come under the umbrella of these two families. Through these networks, they have consolidated their political and economic powers, as their political parties proved to be the most popular and hard to beat in the democratic elections held during Sudanese democratic parliamentary periods (Daly, 1993, p. 7; Sikainga, 1993, pp. 79–80).

The political conduct of these family-based political parties reveals that they were never nationally oriented in policy, nor did they represent the geographical and cultural diversity of Sudan. Besides, judging by the very nature of their sectarian and religious power bases, they appeared to be undemocratic in both theory and practice, as the religious and sectarian leaders normally manipulated authority over the party organisation, management and decision making. The elites who faithfully abided by party values and were loyal to the party's leaders were often blessed and rewarded by assuming the senior ranks, and control over the executive, legislative and judicial organs of any government party that assumed leadership.

Alongside these two sectarian parties, there are also other left-leaning parties, such as the Socialist Party, which have not gained wide political

[1] This term was coined by Bayart, 1993, p. 150.

[2] The Ansar (Partisans) are the followers of the Mahdist religious revolution that overthrew the Turco-Egyptian colonial rule (1881–98); most come from Darfur, Kordofan and the White Nile areas.

[3] The vast majority of the urban elites have also eventually come under the umbrella of these two families.

Table 5.1 Sudan ruling systems between 1821 and 2016

Years	*Regime*	*Remarks*
1821–81	Turco-Egyptian rule	The first colonial period
1881–98	Mahdist national revolution	A religiously oriented rule
1898–1955	Anglo-Egyptian condominium rule	The second colonial period
1956–8	First parliamentary democracy	The first national multi-party regime after independence
November 1958–October 1964	General Abboud's military regime	The shortest military regime in the country's history
October 1964–May 1969	Second parliamentary democracy	An outcome of October mass revolution against General Abboud's military regime
May 1969–April 1985	Military regime led by Nimeiri	Continued for 16 years until it was overthrown by mass revolution in April 1985
1985–6	Transitional government	Formed following the overthrow of the Nimeiri regime and served to hand over the state administration to an elected parliamentary government
1986–9	Third parliamentary democracy	Coalition government led by Sadiq Al-Mahdi's Umma Party
June 1989–present (2016)	NIF military regime	An Islamist regime led by the NIF party that assumed power through a military coup

(*Sources*: Compiled by author from multiple sources, including Shuqayr, 1981; Hassan and Ray (eds) 2006)

support as they are perceived as founded on anti-Islamic ideology, calling for infidelity and atheism, and felt to be unaccceptable. Belatedly though, the National Islamic Front (NIF) emerged on the scene in the 1980s and earned a relatively solid base among the urban middle and working classes. In the parliamentary government of 1985–9, the NIF became a vocal partner before they took full control of the government by overthrowing the democratic regime in a military *coup d'état* in June 1989.

The NIF soon laid an iron grip on the country, and determined to transform the secular state into an Islamic one. Such a strategic intent certainly requires time and resources, and therefore remaining in power, by whatever appealing or forcible means they could muster and exploit, constitutes a divine objective. It drove them to form opportunistic alliances and to adopt a violent approach to suppressing dissent. They even shed off some parts of the country when this suited their coveted Islamic hegemony over Sudan.[4] Their discriminatory, racial and unjust policies have inflicted untold suffering upon peripheral regions and widened social and political polarisation among tribes and ethnic groups, leading thus to unwarranted violence and oppression.

Within such a tense situation, it was inevitable for regionally felt grievances to be expressed loudly, and for these voices to organise, as they have since the 1960s, along the lines of regional political parties, groups and movements. These opponents included the Beja Congress (from the Red Sea area), the Darfur Development Front, the General Union of Nuba Mountains and various southern Sudanese parties, e.g. the Sudan African National Union (SANU) (Niblock, 1987, p. 204).

The emergence of the most recent political insurgencies in Darfur, the Sudan Liberation Movement (SLM) and the Justice and Equality Movement (JEM) and others in the Blue Nile, Nuba Mountains and Eastern Sudan, constitute compelling evidence of resistance to the national rulers and their unbalanced approaches to domestic politics. The leaders of these political resistance movements have been mostly educated people from the remotest, most marginalised and least developed regions of the country. Their cause, as they claimed, was to roll back the taken-for-granted, unfair distribution of power and wealth in the country and to challenge the socio-cultural domination and hegemony of the riverine ruling elites (Shaddaad, 1987; Kurita 1994, p. 214; Seekers of Truth and Justice, 2000). Alternatively, they have advocated equality and equity for all Sudanese and for plurality in power sharing.

Their concerns and peaceful struggle have nevertheless been belittled and often ignored, as the riverine governing elites have adopted an approach to ruling, to use Alex Thomson's phrase, 'by confiscation rather than conciliation' (Thomson, 2004, p. 118). Peaceful means of activism seem not to be tolerated by the governing elites, leaving the option of armed struggle as the only means for opponents to attempt to redress historical and current injustices. The attitude of the ruling and governing elites raises many questions about the state's perception and vision for development and prosperity for all the citizens. The ambiguity of this vision could be comprehensible if we analysed and developed an insight into the underlying politics of the state's approaches to domestic politics.

NEOPATRIMONIALISM AND DOMESTIC POLITICS IN SUDAN

Postcolonial national governments have adopted the policies and attitudes of elite domination and marginalised a large proportion of people, especially those in peripheral regions, from decision making. They have perpetuated regional inequalities in resource allocation, especially

[4] Sudan split in 2011 into two states after a long civil war that started in 1972. In 1991 the NIF portrayed the war as ethnic and religious, i.e. Arab against Africans and Muslims against Christians. The outcome of the war was the secession of south into the independent state of South Sudan.

between the north and the south, by consolidating a monopoly of political power through a pattern of domestic politics that embodies institutional exploitation of the state's material resources, human resources and office, and serves their own vested interests. This has included securing long-lasting and unimpeded *personal* power – an approach that is recognised sociologically as the 'neopatrimonial order to domestic politics'.

Patrimonialism and neopatrimonialism[5] are part of the new political economics that emerged in the 1980s to explain the social, economic and political dilemmas and crises of the civil wars and armed conflicts in contemporary Africa. They meant to examine the 'inner workings of power politics within Africa', and how small ruling and governing elites have exercised personal rule, by retaining a monopoly over public resources (patrimony) and political activity, and transformed the state and its institutions into a subservient tool to further their private interests, rather than fulfilling public interest and reform. They are political approaches that are deemed an extension of the politics of patron–clientelism and political patronage. They constitute an instrumental political contract of trading mutual benefits between patrons and their clients, but the patron retains the entire authority, i.e. support is exchanged for loyalty (Francis, 2008, pp. 9–12; Medard, 1982, pp. 181–2).

Neopatrimonialism politics and its embodiment in Sudan, i.e. the elite's dominant ruling and the clientelism and political patronage, have virtually infiltrated the political contexts of the country since the colonial era when the rulers co-opted and mainstreamed the tribal authority as a cost-effective mechanism for ruling Sudan's vast areas. With no clear perception on governing the country, counting on tribes and tribal institutions became an entrenched political approach in the periods that followed. The modern clientelism attitude of the elites is but an echo of what was embraced under the colonial administration. For instance, most of the educated elites tend to associate with sectarian powers to promote their own personal interests, but they often claim that they actually mean to promote the national interest. The sectarian powers are doubtless quite delighted to receive frequently into their clubs loyal members who can be counted on to bolster their positions as patrons.

Following independence, the governing elites appeared to have adopted what Medard (1982, p. 180) describes as colonial 'suppression and exploitation', by continuing to be more devoted to reinforcing their own positions of power and wealth than to creating a national society and/or bothering about the people's welfare. This approach did not go unnoticed and/or submissively accepted by the citizens, however, as the democratic principles adopted at independence alluded to the possible emergence of rivals who might threaten those elites' status and ethos. Using strategies such as forging alliances and expanding and reinforcing the existing patron–client reciprocal networks, the ruling elites blocked such a threat from occurring and harnessed their legal authority to maintain and strengthen their sectarian monopoly over human resources.

[5] For more on neopatrimonialism, see Thomson, 2004, pp. 107–28 and Francis, 2008, pp. 3–16).

The network of the elites' private interests has encompassed the co-option of traditional authority leaders, grassroots structures and conventional institutions, such as tribal militias and al-Hakkamat. Using the neopatrimonial strategies mentioned, the elites have succeeded in reinforcing their political position, ironically at the expense of achieving national unity, and by generating a socially and politically confrontational environment that has eroded the social fabric of Sudanese society, most sorely in Darfur.

DARFURIS AGAINST DOMESTIC POLITICS (1991–2016)

The case of Daud Yahya Ibrahim Bolad, a Fur from Darfur, stands as a true testimony to the exclusion by the alliance of the riverine ruling and governing elites of those who come from remote regions of Sudan. Neither Bolad's competence nor his faithfulness to the ideology and literary aspirations of the elites persuaded them to accept him within their mainstream. He was a prominent leader and a dedicated Islamist who, in the 1970s, became the first president of the then powerful Khartoum University Student Union (KUSU) who did not originate from the riverine elites (Flint, 2007, p. 142; Burr and Collins, 2008, p. 281).

Bolad was a key witness of the systematic targeting of his tribe, the Fur, by an alliance of Baggara Arab militias in South Darfur in the late 1980s. He was also well placed to see not only the other main traditional parties but also the Islamist party to which he belonged appearing to condone the horridness committed against his own tribe. His attempts to draw the attention of his party colleagues to this dire situation, and to seek political reform, were all overlooked and he received no sympathy or commiseration. He was identified as troublesome and eventually found himself estranged from the riverine elites' Islamist bloc. Frustrated and disillusioned, he decided to turn to arms against his colleagues, the ruling and governing elites.

In November 1991, supported by the SPLA, which had he stood against in the past, Bolad led a military expedition despatched from South Sudan to Darfur. The expedition was however aborted by the NIF regime, supported by an alliance of militias of some Arab tribes in South Darfur. He was arrested and killed in January 1992. The militias retaliated extremely brutally, burning of dozens of Fur villages and killing hundreds of Fur people (Flint and de Waal, 2005, p. 21).

Bolad's unsuccessful campaign fomented more frustration among many Darfuris, but it took more than a decade for successor insurgencies to revive in February 2003. These were the Sudan Liberation Army (SLA), led by a Fur lawyer, Abd al-Wahid Muhammad al-Nur, followed soon afterwards by Justice and Equality Movement (JEM). By then, mobilising Arab militias for counter-insurgency has become a central strategy of the government in its civil wars. Subsequently they unleashed the notorious Janjawiid militias and allowed them to perpetrate atrocities that wrecked the region almost irreparably.

The feeling of discontent with domestic politics and geopolitics based on neopatrimonialism and divide-and-rule approaches appeared to have motivated these movements, as stated in their manifestos. For instance, the demands, interests and the main cause of the SLA were indicated in their Political Declaration, which provides the following statement:

> Since Khartoum government systematically adhered to the policies of marginalisation, racial discrimination, exclusion, exploitation, and divisiveness the SLA opposes the policies of Arabization, political and economic marginalisation, and the 'brutal oppression, ethnic cleansing, and genocide sponsored by the Khartoum government'. (Burr and Collins, 2008, p. 289)

Driven by this resolve, SLA and JEM began their armed struggle to end the political, economic and cultural domination of the riverine elites, and to seek an equitable settlement against marginalisation and racial discrimination. These two movements succeeded in launching several attacks on government positions and installations in Darfur, especially police stations.[6] As signified earlier, the government reacted viciously and transformed the conflict into a state of full-blown war, especially after the insurgents' bold raid on al-Fashir airport on 25 April 2003. In the attack, they destroyed helicopters and bomber aircraft, seized weapons and vehicles and captured prominent commanders in the army forces.[7] During these violent confrontations, from their position as part of the Baggara institutions, al-Hakkamat rose to support the government by playing a dual role that included promoting and mobilising the youth and horsemen for fighting, and advocating for peace when dictated by the authorities.

Government interpretations of armed struggle in Sudan

The discriminatory domestic politics pursued by the riverine ruling and governing elites, which allow some sections of the populace access to the honey pot whilst depriving others, have generated regional grievances and popular discontent. Peaceful political activism therefore started emerging from the 1960s, in the regions of Darfur, the Blue Nile, East Sudan and the Nuba Mountains, adding to the already active insurgencies in Southern Sudan. Over the years, peaceful activism gradually gave way to armed struggle in South Sudan first and, later, in other marginalised regions of the country.

In confronting these movements since 1983, the government (both military and democratic regimes) has used ethnicity, based either on religion and/or on race as appropriate. Hence, anti-insurgency strategies pursued in the civil war in South Sudan included forming and arming Baggara Arab tribal militias in Kordofan and the Blue Nile provinces. The *Murahaliin* of the Misseriya and the Rezeiqat of Darfur were among the first tribes to be used in this domain.[8] They were mobilised on the

[6] Police stations and posts being used for military purposes, as well as police taking an active part in the hostilities, are valid military targets under international humanitarian law and may be attacked (though armed rebel attacks remain violations of Sudanese law). See: <www.hrw.org/backgrounder/africa/darfur1104/7.htm> [accessed 17 April 2007].

[7] Among the detainees was air force Major General Ibrahim Bushara (Burr and Collins, 2008, p. 291–92).

[8] The government endorsed some of these militias following the Gardud massacre in 1985 in the southern Kordofan region. The second episode was in the Ed Diein massacre (in South

basis of Arabism to fight those other Sudanese, the Negroid, the black Africans, i.e. the *abeed* (slaves). When the NIF seized power in 1989, they instantly declared the war as a holy war in 1990 and called for Jihad (the war of Muslims against non-Muslims). The Islamists thus added a religious dimension by fighting not only non-Arabs but also non-Muslims, dubbed *Kuffaar* (atheists) by Muslims.

The neopatrimonial approach of the riverine ruling elites to domestic politics and policies was doubtless behind the rise of armed struggle that has unfolded since the 1990s in Darfur. Bolad's origin in the Fur tribe and his connection with the SPLA were of significant help to the elites' political mind in interpreting and publicising the movement as an anti-Arab and anti-Islamic attack on Arabs (Baggara and Abbala) by the African Fur tribe. Convincing Darfuri Arabs that they were targeted for extermination (e.g. Ibrahim, 2007; Haggar, 2003; Prunier, 2007; Tanner 2005) was a sufficient drive to win their support, especially the Bani Helba, and to fight alongside the government.

In recognition of the significant contribution of the Bani Helba horsemen in defeating Bolad insurgence, and to honour them, the centre of Bani Helba, Idd al-Ghanam (the Wells of Goats), was renamed by the government Idd al-Fursan (the Wells of Horsemen) (Flint and de Waal, 2005, p. 25). These *fursan* were largely mobilised and then glorified by their Hakkamat. This legacy however, might constantly stir up ethnic emotions and create a permanent schism in tribal relations, but ironically, this latter outcome was not a big deal for the ruling elites once their vested interests had been served.

By the time the armed struggle against the Sudanese government was launched in 2003, a decade after Bolad, by the Sudan Liberation Army/Movement (SLA/M) and JEM, the riverine elites were already well versed in perturbing and demoralising political movements. Instead of addressing the expressed demands rationally, they invoked that same divide-and-rule strategy that they used against the first Darfuri insurgency in 1991, to deter and terminate them.

Yet whilst the elites flatly dismissed the validity of the causes and the triggers, they were unable to use religion against these insurgents, for the insurgents were presumed to be all Muslims and the Darfuris were one of the largest bases of the call for the application of shari'a law (Ibrahim, 2007, p. 11); however, they still tried to paint Bolad as regressed from Islam, as his forces had burned and desecrated mosques. Hence, ethnicity based on race was at the top of the agenda for providing propaganda and motivation – otherwise, religion would have provided in abundance. But to add insult to injury they blamed the insurgents for the troubles, describing them as 'gangs' and 'highwaymen', and then outlawed outsiders (Burr and Collins, 2008, p. 291). They ordered them to lay down arms and surrender, or the army would 'solve the situation within twenty-four hours' (cited in Daly, 2007, p. 281).

(contd) Darfur) committed by armed Baggara, the Rezeiqat, on 27–8 March 1987, where hundreds of Dinka were burnt to death and others abducted into captivity. In 1989, 214 Shilluk from the south were massacred and 2,000 displaced by Rufa'a militias in Al-Jabalein, in the Blue Nile region, at the borders of the White Nile and the Upper Nile regions. Many other atrocities were not recorded (Mohamed Salih and Harir, 1994, pp. 186–7).

Moreover, the struggle was stripped of any legitimate basis for representating the Darfuri society and was interpreted as primarily racial, in the sense that African tribes were targeting Arabs, again by extermination. This approach echoes the elites' interpretation of the armed conflict between tribes and ethnic groups in Darfur, which they attributed mainly to their belonging to different racial backgrounds. Ironically, those who took up arms to eliminate the sources of injustice that have been manifested in tribalism, ethnicity and the neopatrimonial approaches to domestic politics found themselves accused of the same approaches the elites have designed and executed. The rebels responded by attacking al-Fashir, the historical capital city of Darfur, including the airport, where they seized weapons and captured Major General Ibrahim Bushara, the military commander, proving that they were rebels, not thugs (Burr and Collins, 2008, p. 292).

This was a painful strike for the government, and prompted an immediate return to the old methodology of counter-insurgency by proxy, turning a blind eye to the damage this would inflict on coexistence in the region. The riverine governing elites understood quite well that the Darfuri Arabs are loyal allies, at least by virtue of sharing Arab ethnicity. Subsequently, propaganda about an expected attack by 'Africans' against 'Arabs' was employed to alert Arabs and stir their fury against the rebel movements. This was followed by extensive mobilisation and recruitment, and the arming of Arab militias. But the steadfastness of the movements in their confrontation with the government forced the latter to mobilise and unleash the so-called Janjawiid militias, who were granted full impunity. The Janjawiid were allowed to perpetrate inhumane atrocities: looting and raiding; they burned hundreds of villages. Thousands of people were killed and thousands more were forced to flee their homes, ending up as internally displaced, as refugees over the border, especially in Chad, or as abductees into slavery (Amnesty International, 2004b). Mass rape constitutes the clearest gender-based violence committed against women and girls by these terrifying militias (ibid.; UN Report, 2004).

The atrocities committed by the Janjawiid in Darfur received strong international condemnation. Human rights activists and institutions, such as Amnesty International and Human Rights Watch, have subsequently campaigned for the dismantling of these unscrupulous forces. In negotiating the ceasefire and peace resettlement, the Darfur insurgents consistently demanded the disbandment of the Janjawiid, but the government often stipulated the disarming of the rebels as a condition (Darfur Peace Agreement (DPA, 2006). In this conflict, al-Hakkamat stepped onto the scene performing the dual role of inciting fighting and encouraging reconciliation. Disturbingly, there have been those who tended to glorify the Janjawiid's conduct, seeing no wrong in such behaviour, including the violence perpetrated against the females.

The ethnic fervour and the fighting spirit of the Baggara horsemen in these violent upheavals convinced the government that the horsemen are efficient warriors, and cheap, especially when aroused by al-Hakkamat. Al-Hakkamat, in turn, proved their readiness to participate in the field of aggression in order to promote the objectives of their sponsorship and to affirm their loyalty. The government has therefore carried on incorporating the ethnic perspective in interpretating and disseminating all wars in Darfur, whether between tribes or between Darfur rebels and the government, as driven by race hatred, i.e. of Africans against Arabs. Thus, al-Hakkamat have found no incentive that can pull them away from indulging and participating in these wars, and they have continued to play provocative and enthusing roles.

Al-Hakkamat and Bolad's movement, 1991/2

Following their *coup d'état* in 1989, the NIF government initially appointed a riverine army commander, Lieutenant Colonel Abuelgasim Ibrahim, as the governor of Darfur region, but replaced him in 1991 by the fundamentalist Islamist, al-Tayeb Ibrahim Mohamed Khair (1991–5), nicknamed 'al-Tayeb Sikhah' (the Iron Bar), a medical doctor and also a military and security professional. Sikhah is notoriously reported to have attacked student demonstrators habitually with an iron bar during his university days (Flint and de Waal, 2005, p. 21). At the time of his appointment, the security situation in Darfur was precarious and the whole region was overwhelmed by armed banditry. This state of insecurity actually started in the 1980s and was exacerbated by the availability of illicit weapons flooding the region from neighbouring Chad, which was already in political turmoil at the time.

Sikhah put considerable efforts into ending the armed robberies without apparent success. Eventually, he was advised by some local intellectuals to try using indigenous means, such as local folklore, to communicate governmental messages, as it was thought that this might appeal to the hearts and minds of rural people, particularly the Baggara. He took the advice seriously, calling for those associated with folklore from all over rural Darfur and inviting them to a festival in al-Fashir – the Creative Popular Arts Festival (CPAF)[9] – in early 1991. This event marked the inception of the engagement of al-Hakkamat by the government.[10]

The CPAF was followed soon after, in October 1991, by a further assembly whereby all folklore performers (including rural poets and al-Hakkamat) were registered as members of a newly formed institution called Popular Information and Media (PIM), *al-ʾiʿlām al-shaʿbī*. Four offices of the PIM were established in each of the four main towns in Darfur, Nyala, al-Geneina, Zalingei and al-Fashir. The PIM was affiliated to the governor's office and was directly overseen by the governor himself. Furthermore, it was blessed by President al-Bashir and his vice president, the now deceased General al-Zubair Mohamed Salih.[11] This co-option, however, was viewed suspiciously by some employees at the Culture and Information Unit,[12] whose fears appear to have been borne out by subsequent events.

Through the PIM, the folklore practitioners were guided to support the government's campaign against armed robbery (*al-nahb al-musallah*) and

9 In Arabic, *mahrajān al-ʾibdāʿ al-shaʿbī.*

10 Group (G5) and individual interviews, Nyala, 2006.

11 Ibid.

12 Ibid.

in favour of the Arms Repossession and Confiscation Campaign (ARCC), *ḥamlat jamʿ l-silāḥ*. They used songs and slogans such as 'sallim nārak, taḥmī diyārak' ('Hand over your weapons, so you can protect your homeland') to encourage rural people to voluntarily hand over their privately owned illicit small arms to the government. This was followed by an Adult Literacy Campaign (ALC), which led to a celebration of the district of Um Keddada in North Darfur as a purportedly illiteracy-free district. In these campaigns, especially the ARCC, al-Hakkamat's performance and impact appear to have outweighed that of the rest of all other folkloric campaigners.[13]

For the governor, the impact on weapons' recovery was miraculous compared to his previous faltering approach, which entirely relied on military force and the police. The recitations that al-Hakkamat contributed to this campaign have included:[14]

English
Oh brothers, war is evil, give it up!
He who surrenders his weapons is noble and great.

Transliteration
al-ḥarb al-laʿīnah sībūhah yā ʾakhwān.
a-bijmaʿ silāhū zawlan ʿaẓīm al-shān.

Arguably, such a simple verse might not be seen as communicating an astounding meaning in other contexts, but when delivered by al-Hakkamat to an audience who usually personalise the meaning of the songs for their own dignity, it touches their passion and stimulates their conviction. Both the positive response to al-Hakkamat's appeal and the outcome of the campaign inspired the riverine governor to use al-Hakkamat to promote the regime's formative advocacy and propaganda, which they launched under the Comprehensive Advocacy Project (CAP), *mashrūʿ al-daʿwah al-shāmlah*. This project constituted a crucial blueprint pursued by the NIF to transform the Sudanese people into advocates of their Islamist ideology, and particularly, into supporters of the government's civil war against the *Christian* SPLA/SPLM in the south.

Since then, it has become routine for the government to employ al-Hakkamat in their sociopolitical schemes. The most notable among these, as mentioned above, was the mobilisation and recruitment of Darfuri youth as soldiers and paramilitary combatants to fight government wars. This was initially experimented when the government took al-Hakkamat on an extensive tour around all Darfur provinces and rural areas to solicit support for their recruitment projects.[15] The campaign generated huge success by virtue of the unprecedented numbers of youngsters who joined the Jihad campaign that the government launched against Bolad and his companion, the SPLM/A military commander,

[13] Group interviews (G1, G3, G4) and individual interviews in al-Fashir and Nyala, 2006.
[14] Recited by Fawziya Abbas, then Advisor of the Governor on Women and Children's Affairs in North Darfur (2005–2012).
[15] Group (G1, G2, G3, G4 and G5) and individual interviews, al-Fashir and Nyala, 2006.

Abdel Aziz Adam al-Hilu,[16] in December 1991. Al-Hakkamat proudly confirmed their contribution, and admitted mobilising the youth and secondary school students to join the army against Bolad's insurgents, whom they dubbed the *Khawarig*.[17]

A prominent Hubbani social actor who participated in the militia forces that fought Bolad explained that when they were marching out of Buram (the main town centre of *Dar* Hubbania) to the battlefield, the now deceased Hakkamah Azzah Gaidoom composed the song below and recited it in encouragement (Ali Noah, Nyala, 2006):

English
My horsemen marched away, never fear death.
They left the coward behind to guard the houses.
Die for your dignity, brave sons will be born after you.
Capture Bolad and make him your goats' shepherd.
The young set out and spared the elderly.
Oh, share the death on your horsebacks.
The gun hit and by the spear they stab.
Oh, don't come back in disgrace, as tribes would gloat at your misdeed.
No one dies but on their day!
Dignity is precious and doesn't have limits.
Bolad is a non-believer who defied [the legacy of] ancestors.
Buram is beloved; we die for it.

Transliteration
fursānī ʾitḥaraku, wa-l-mawt mā bakhāfaw.
al-khawwāf lil-bayt ḥarrasaw.
mūtū fī sharafku, warāku al-fāris baldaw.
Bawlād ʾamisku, bay ghanamku sarriḥu
al-ṣibyān ʾitḥarku, wa-l-kabīr rajjū.
al-mawt fī ḍuhūr khiyūlku ʾittgasamū.
al-bundigiyyah ḍarabat wa bi-l-ḥarbā ṭaʿinnū.
mā tarjaʿū, ʿalaykū al-gabāyyil yashshamatū.
al-zawl balā yawmā ma bimūt.
al-sharaf ghālī mā baʾrif ḥidūd.
Bawlād kāfir nakar al-jidūd.
Burām ghāliyyā fīhā nimūt.

Another prominent Hakkamah also declared that when the army were leaving to fight Bolad, she composed in anticipation of the government's guaranteed victory, and recited, on the departure of the army to the battlefield, as follows:[18]

English
I've got some speech to deliver!
The men of the army and the police are lions and tigers.
I would like to deliver a speech on them.
You held off and repelled Abdel Aziz and Bolad.
You laid down in trenches to ensure victory.
Bolad and Abdel Aziz should know what does 'we're winners' means
When you hoist the flag!

[16] Abdel Aziz Adam al-Hilu survived this fateful incursion into Darfur and went on to become a top SPLM/A commander and political leader.
[17] Outlaws in Arabic, but the term also has religious overtones of 'non-conformist Muslims'.
[18] Interview with Hubbania Hakkamah (R32), Nyala, 7 May 2006.

Transliteration
ʾanā ʿindī layyā kilmah ʾagūlhā.
rijāl al-daysh wa rijāl al-shurṭā dīdān wa nimūrā.
ḥadīthan fawg-hum ʾanā dāyrā ʾagūlā.
waggaftū ʿabdalʾaziz wa bawlad ʾalā ṭūlah.
ragdtū fawg al-khandag jibtū al-naṣur maḍmūnā.
Bawlād wa ʿabdalʾaziz, gawlat fāyzīn yamsik qānūnhā
waggaftū al-ʿalamʿalā ṭūlāh.
(H. R32, Nyala, 2006).

When the government won the fight, al-Hakkamat composed and recited in celebration of the victory, and ridiculed Bolad and his colleagues:[19]

English
Would you like to be told the truth?
Omer Hassan al-Bashir either writes with his pen, or directs with his hands.
Whoever antagonises Omer al-Bashir, they get themselves in trouble.
Al-Zubair Mohamed Salih, you whose brain is full and whose speech is useful.
Whoever opposes him, the governor of Darfur will ruin their livelihoods.
Bolad left this world; John Garang would like to shake hands.
And Abdel Aziz was just sitting over there, we couldn't define his destiny.
I said to him 'come on Abdel Aziz, let me console you'.
If you don't fend off the furious billy goat, it will castrate you.

Transliteration
dāyyir yawarrūka al-ḥagīgāh.
ʿUmar Ḥasan al-Bashīr, walla katab bi-galamah walla ʾashshar bey-ʾīdā.
al-baʿadi ʿumar al-bashīr wagaʿ layya fī muṣībāh.
al-Zibayr Muhammad Ṣāliḥ, yā ʾabū rāsan malyān, ʾabū kilimtan mufīdāh.
ḥākim wilāyat dārfawr, gawlta al-biʿādi kan gaṭṭaʿata ʿalayyā al-ʿīshāh.
Bawlād tarak al-dinyā, John Garang dāyyir yasallim bi-ʾīdā
wa ʿabdalʾaziz gaʿad daykan mā ʿirifnā layya jīha.
gulit lu taʿāl ʿabdalʾaziz, khalīnī ʾawaṣṣīka.
ʾinta tays al-ghanam mā dagaytā bakhaṣṣīkā.
(H. R32, Nyala, 2006).

She praises the ruling elites by name, and brags that Bolad would be unable to withstand the deadly confrontation; Bolad passed away leaving John Garang, the SPLA/SPLM leader, begging for peace and reconciliation.

Upon the arrival of the army troops and the militias from the battlefield, al-Hakkamat gathered to receive them at Nyala airport. One Hakkamah recited the following poem:[20]

English
The judgement of Allah is accepted; the human submits to it.
Our Popular Defence Forces shouted, 'God is great!'
Our armed forces swore the oath, 'We will fight till we perish.'
Our students ripped up their notebooks, threw their pens away.
They said to al-Hakkamah, 'Oh, your ears would hear the news.'
From hand to hand, we receive the shroud.
In order to liberate the country.

19 Ibid.
20 Interview with Salami Hakkamah (R51), Nyala, 2006.

Transliteration
ḥukm ʾallāh rāḍī, al-makhlūg bayya yagbal.
difāʿ shaʿbīnā, gāl ʾallāhu ʾakbar.
wa quwātnā al-musallaḥa ḥalafat al-qasam gālat namūt naʿdam.
ṭalabānā sharrāṭū al-kurrās, zagalū al-galam.
gālū lil-ḥakkāmā ʾadānik tasmaʿ al-khabar.
min ʾīd ʾalā ʾīd nastalmū al-kafan
ʾashān naḥarrirū al-waṭan
(H/F. R51, Nyala, 2006).

Al-Hakkamat's involvement in this instance, and their pride and exuberant confidence in describing and articulating their contributions, proved their position and capacity as genuine social actors who have the power and leverage to sway conflict processes and outcomes. One was indeed amazed at the excitement and reverence with which people were talking about their Hakkamat, especially when they recited their poetry and songs, in particular those of the deceased ones.

Some other Hakkamat who still reside in the conflict zone took part on their own volition, mobilising their tribes to join the fight; according to Hakkamah who still lived in a rural area. She admitted that when she witnessed the fight, she instantly composed and recited to enthuse her tribesmen to fight furiously. From revelations at interviews, it was quite evident that al-Hakkamat from almost all Baggara tribes in South Darfur participated in mobilising Arab tribes, but as the Bani Helba militias were the government's main target of the mobilisation, they were the most furiously engaged. Nevertheless, apart from minor gifts that could not have cost more than a few Sudanese pounds, al-Hakkamat received nothing in recognition of the role they played, even though they served as the main stimulus behind the horsemen's fighting spirit.

Al-Hakkamat and the Darfur insurgency, 2003 to 2016

The role al-Hakkamat have played in mobilising Baggara horsemen against insurgents since 2003 has indeed been powerful and game-changing, although overlooked in the scholarship describing and documenting those turbulent events. Al-Hakkamat often reported that their influence often weighs the balance of events. For instance, a group of rebels reportedly attacked the police headquarters and the post office in Buram – the main centre of *Dar* Hubbania – in South Darfur state, in 2004.[21]

In the aftermath of the attack, and in order to subside the anger of the Hubbania tribe, the rebels met with the Nazir of Hubbania, and explained to him and to the residents of the town in a public meeting that their motives and actions in Hubbania were not meant against the tribe and/or its authorities. They assured then that their war was against the government and their objectives were political, not banditry as the government has propagated. Even though their explanation does not justify the destruction of public facilities, especially in rural areas that have already suffered severe deterioration of such resources, the rebels therewith left the area after winning a verbal confirmation from the Hubbania native

[21] Group (G2, G4) and individual interviews, Nyala, 2006.

authorities that the tribe would not seek to hunt them down and/or to get engaged in the war alongside the government.

However, the incident only served to provoke al-Hakkamah and summoned her to interfere by stimulating some Hubbani horsemen to disrespect the verbal assurance their Nazir had given to the insurgents. Upon learning of the incident, immediately after the rebels left Buram, al-Hakkamah Kaltoum Bit Gawindah came right away to the Nazir's meeting place. She came full of resentment and anger, induced by what she judged as an offence against her tribe. Wearing a mismatched pair of shoes – a black shoe on her left foot and a white shoe on her right foot and, dressed in *arāgī*[22] with a bedsheet folded around her,[23] she represented the utmost grievance and scorn.

Her bizarre appearance was indeed provocative and symbolic. The six men who were congregating in the place asked her why on earth she should appear in that manner. She explained that the Tora Bora, i.e. the insurgents, took the right shoe from her black pair of shoes and left her with the left shoe. Therefore, she put the white shoe from another pair of shoes on her right foot. She added that she would like to seek refuge with Rezeiqat to escape the fear of a further possible attack by the same rebel group. Besides, the Rezeiqat might be able to bring back her stolen pair of shoes.

Both verbal and symbolic manifestations of wearing a white right shoe indicated that the Hubbania, her tribe, were cowardly and unable to confront the rebels who committed an assault right in the heart of *Dar* Hubbania, and in the very presence of the Nazir, the Ageed and the horsemen. She insinuated and lamented that had the attack been committed in *Dar* Rezeiqat, the Rezeiqat would have reacted differently and destroyed the rebels.

This insult from al-Hakkamah was too much to bear. A brother of the Nazir, who was a university graduate, a politician and an Attorney General resident in Nyala, was among the six men sitting at the Nazir's place. Like the other men, he felt offended by what al-Hakkamah indicated, as a violation of the tribe's honour and dignity. In spite of the Nazir's undertaking, the strong feelings that al-Hakkamah aroused drove the men to a deadly action: they quickly rode their horses, together with others who joined in, and pursued the rebel group. The rebels were moving cautiously and were always ready to attack; so the horsemen lost the ensuing battle. Sadly, they endured the loss, among many others, of fifteen members of the Nazir's family, including the Attorney General, together with many Omad, Sheikhs and horsemen.[24]

Another famous Hakkamah condemned the killing episode and the actions and speech of the respective Hakkamah, saying: 'Indeed, it was al-Hakkamah herself who killed these men; as had she not uttered those expressions and shown up looking like that, the horsemen would not have chased the rebels and died.'[25] Nevertheless, to give her the benefit of

[22] Arāgī is a man's local dress.

[23] Ibid. In the local culture of Baggara the black colour symbolises bravery and the white colour symbolises cowardice.

[24] Ibid.

[25] Interview with Hubbania Hakkamah (32), Nyala, 2006.

the doubt, al-Hakkamah was following her obligation to ensure that her tribesmen behaved in the manner expected of them and defended the tribe's privacy. Albeit the attack on the tribe was unintended, it was nevertheless committed within the tribe's territory, and therefore, in al-Hakkamah's perspective, the rebels' attack constituted an unpalatable breach of the tribe's sovereignty – a humiliation that should not be condoned.

The culture of al-Hakkamat in Darfur is shared by the Baggara pastoralists of Kordofan, the region that neighbours Darfur from the east and southeast. There were many wide-scale disputes among the Baggara of Kordofan in which al-Hakkamat were involved, and their interventions brought about similar deadly outcomes. One of these disputes occurred between the Misseriya Humur and Zurug[26] in 1991, when a man from the Zurug proposed to marry a woman from the Humur, but her family refused his request.

The couple defied the refusal, and fled the village to Khartoum where they got married through the court. After being blessed by two or three children, they returned to the village, but the woman's cousins killed the husband in an honour reprisal. Incited by their Hakkamat, the husband's relatives avenged the killing by murdering eight men from the Humur. Al-Hakkamat of both tribes went on provoking a vicious cycle of revenge, until the death toll reached over sixty in three days. The disputing parties were eventually brought to a negotiated settlement through the mediation of the Rezeiqat of South Darfur, who are their neighbours.[27] It is worth noting that al-Hakkamat did not practise composing and/or recitation in this case, but used rousing speeches for ethnic mobilisation.

It was also revealed that despite the devastating impact of al-Hakkamat's role in these conflicts, al-Hakkamat were not the direct cause, but acted far more as a provoking trigger to transform simmering causes into deadly outcomes. Whether this view could be seen as chauvinistic might not be of much concern to al-Hakkamat: their concern was to ensure respect and protection for their socio-cultural norms. This is the basis of the unimpeded flow of their agency, which came in handy, especially given the conclusive endorsement that their communities have granted them. A Baggari from Buram also underlined these conclusions. He asserted that al-Hakkamat have both the power and the duty to express tribes' collective wisdom openly and to enforce it in a way that other tribal institutions could not or might not do. Where pacification undertaken by other such institutions appears to jeopardise the tribe's dignity, it is al-Hakkamat's moral obligation to step in to restore that violated dignity, no matter what price this may incur.[28]

In meeting the expectations of their communities, al-Hakkamat's rallies involved representations that many people identified as malicious, as they tended to heighten ethnic tensions among tribal groups and over-

[26] The Misseriya is a Baggara tribe residing mainly in Kordofan. It consists of two sections that are believed to be cousins, Humur and Zurug (literally Red and Blue i.e. light-coloured and blacks, respectively).

[27] Interview with a Rezeiqi government employee (R5), Nyala, 2006.

[28] Interview with the chief of Ta'alba (R10), Nyala, 2006.

step their tribal mandate. Some argued that al-Hakkamat have currently become more powerful and have developed stronger agency and influence than they had before the 1980s, as in this account of a teacher, who was also a prominent Nazir:

> At the moment they have direct influence on events, even though they are not considered in discussions and decision making … Since the eruption of the conflict of 2003, al-Hakkamat have become like a horse without a bridle; now they are adding more fuel to the fire. I hope that the state, the native administration and/or any relevant institution will interfere to reduce their influence, especially on the youth, and stop them from inciting the youth to conflict, as they have done recently.[29]

Although this appeal of the Nazir seems appropriate for use in public, apparently he was not keen to see it happening on the ground. It was more a replication of government propaganda about the need to control the belligerent voice of al-Hakkamat. This could partially be inferred on the premise that the supreme leader of the tribe did nothing to restrain al-Hakkamat and debilitate the fighting tendency of the youth. Most Baggara and Abbala people tend to see these deeds of al-Hakkamat as justified and requisite given the harsh realities, insecurity and uncertainties that engulf and characterise the livelihood of pastoralists in general.

A member of a Nazir's family suggested that al-Hakkamah does not choose to promote fighting unless situations become untenable and resolution by means of war becomes inevitable. She will in turn, dedicate her agency and influence to addressing the need to fight and to win the fight. He added that women generally should not be censured and/or rebuked for this spirit, let alone al-Hakkamat, as unless they encouraged their men to strike first they would be the ones to face the direst consequences.[30]

Al-Hakkamat must therefore push their men to stay put and fight hard, even though they are quite sure that in wartime they may lose a loved one – a son, husband, brother or father. Five Hakkamat claimed to have lost at least one family member in the conflict and/or have family members permanently maimed or disabled.[31] This fear of loss felt by al-Hakkamat has featured in their composing and recitations, as admitted by Hubbania Hakkamah, who had witnessed the fight between the government and the Bolad insurgents in 1991/2 and could still hear the noise of guns. Her fear of the enemy approaching prompted her to encourage her men to be courageous, as expressed in her recitation below:[32]

English
Those are the sons of Hubban[33] who confront the flaming fight head on.
Our Popular Defence Forces fastened their belts, our soldiers' skin scratched.
Oh, Bishari, hurry up with your your G3 and AK47 rifles.
I can see a non-believer enemy desecrating my land.
I'm scared, the consequences might separate me from my children.
Oh, brave men, hit them hard with your rifles!

29 Pastoralists' accounts of the Nazir at group interview (G1), al-Fashir, 2006.
30 Interview with a poet from the Nazir of Bani Helba's family (R45), Nyala, 2006.
31 Group interview with Hakkamat (G4), Nyala, 2006.
32 Interview with Hubbania Hakkamah (R19), Nyala, 2006.
33 Affiliates to the Hubbania tribe.

Transliteration
dawl ʿiyyāl habbān al-mitlagiyyīn al-ḥāmi.
shaʿbīnā ʾil-karrab, jundīnā jildā musharraṭ.
shāyill al-jīm wa al-kilāshinkūv ʾalḥag yā bishārī.
ʾanā shāyyfā kāfir ʿadū bi-l-jammad li dāri.
khāyyfā lil-ʿugbal yafrugnī min ʿiyyālī.
bi-raynjāh ya-l-ʿushārī.
(H. R19, Nyala, 2006).

She warned of the dreadful consequences that women and children would face if their men lost the fight, and urged the men to defeat their fear and bring her good news. Concern for women and children is of paramount importance for al-Hakkamat; they often speak up about issues that affect women.

A typical testimony to this was recounted by a Baggara man, who said that some women were abducted during the armed conflict between tribes in 2003, and their men were reluctant to go to their rescue. Al-Hakkamat of the abductees' tribe took the lead and incited lactating women not to breast-feed their male babies. They also instructed all women to refuse marital contact (sexual) with their husbands, and to abstain from the domestic obligations. They got armed and rode on horses to pursue the rescue by themselves. Alarmed and also humiliated by the organised women's protest and the movement of al-Hakkamat, the men eventually submitted to the women's demands and carried out a counter-attack, which led to the abductees being freed.[34] Had al-Hakkamat not exercised such pressure on men, effected here via symbolic acts, the kidnapped women could not have been rescued and might have been slaves throughout their lives, marring the tribe with lasting shame. This interplay of the agency identity, power and political influence of al-Hakkamat is shown in Figure 5.1.

The testimonies presented suggest that by embracing multiple personal and social identities, al-Hakkamat faithfully nurtured and translated their

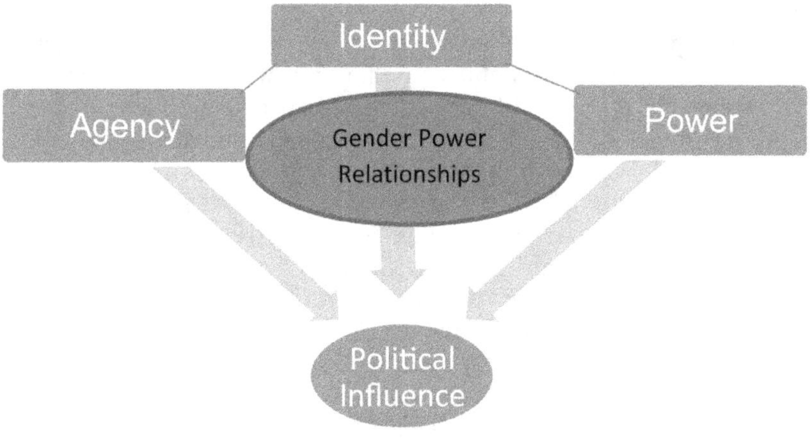

Figure 5.1 The interplay of the attributes of political influence of women in conflict and peace contexts.
(Source: *Author*)

[34] Interview with the Chief of Ta'alba (R10), Nyala, 2006.

agency into actual power and influence, particularly in the domain of armed conflict. Their representation was influential enough to merit the recognition of local and regional power brokers and later paved their way to be incorporated in the state institutions of power.

CONCLUSION

The riverine political elites in Sudan have produced, reproduced and consolidated a characteristic approach to domestic politics in power sharing and allocation of public resources. Using this approach they have instituted the marginalisation of peripheral regions, structural and cultural inequalities and deprivation, particularly in the South Sudan and Darfur regions. The resulting dismal situation has generated wide resentment in many of these peripheral regions, and resulted in the political instability and civil wars that led in 2011 to the split of Sudan into two countries.

In Darfur, since the 1990s the situation has prompted some resentful Darfuris to take up arms, in an attempt to realise the political demands that their peaceful activism had failed to secure. Like the approach the governing elites had followed previously with the southern insurgencies, the governing elites interpreted the Darfuri insurgents entirely in ethnic and racial terms. These interpretations helped to justify appeals to Arab ethnic groups, particularly the Baggara, who have well-organised combatants to help with the defeat of the insurgent movements.

When the ruling elites realised al-Hakkamat's significance to the military organisation of their tribes, and to the mobilisation of horsemen and other combatants, they used them exploitatively, on racial grounds, in the campaign against Bolad. Through the remarkable role they played in the mobilisation of the Baggara combats, al-Hakkamat reaffirmed their status as the hawks of armed conflict in Sudan. Following Bolad's defeat by Baggara horsemen, al-Hakkamat have embraced the government's racial interpretation of political movements in Darfur and voluntarily become a voice of ethnic mobilisation for violence and aggression, which has incurred huge loss of life and demoralised social harmony in Darfur.

Al-Hakkamat's engagement in mobilising Arab combatants was facilitated primarily by the neopatrimonialist approach to domestic politics adopted by the riverine ruling and governing elites, where ethnic discrimination based on race ranked the highest. Using tribes, ethnic groups and their conventional organisations is therefore integral to this approach, which serves the interests of the ruling elites.

Al-Hakkamat's significant impact in mobilising Arab militias has paved the way for their being a strong ally of the government, and an integral part of its military campaign and strategy against its rivals in Darfur and elsewhere in Sudan. This alliance has been formed through a complex series of procedures and events that has allowed al-Hakkamat to continue to exercise and consolidate their agency and power from within the state's defence establishments, as explained in the following chapters.

6

Liaising with Government

We understand that the governments' attention was initially drawn to al-Hakkamat by their performance in the arms confiscation campaign in the early 1990s. Their subsequent contribution to the mobilisation of combatants during the Bolad campaign in 1991/2 has further proved their potential as one of the most effective conventional rural and tribal institutions that could further the neopatrimonial approach of the riverine ruling and governing elites to domestic politics. This has coincided with the elites' approach of interpreting all wars in Sudan as primarily racial and religious conflicts. By virtue of their ethnic foundation and political identity, al-Hakkamat have been brought to the fore of the politics of war and ethnic polarisation, which has now become the mainstay and the mainstream politics in Darfur and across Sudan.

The government deployed several measures for co-opting al-Hakkamat and manipulating their power and influence. These measures were meant equally to solicit the Baggara's sympathy for the government in wars that they interpreted on racial and religious terms, and to ensure endorsement of their political approach. They included exposure to the media, assembly and organisation, remodelling the conventional framework of al-Hakkamat, Islamic reorientation and military training, as discussed below.

AL-HAKKAMAT AND THE MEDIA

TV and radio are the state's media outlets and therefore represent the voice of the government and their means to manipulate information and to influence opinion. For rural people, radio constitutes the most available and accessible information device, and it is therefore used intensively by the governing elites to address the rural population. Nyala radio and TV stations were used to broadcast extensively specific programmes that featured and glorified al-Hakkamat and publicised their songs and performances.[1] These programmes included, for example, *jalsat inbisatah* ('a sitting for entertainment/cheerfulness'), *Murhakt al-gol* ('a grinder of

[1] Group and individual interviews, Nyala, 2006.

speech') and *al-mughrāfah* (the ladle/scoop, i.e. the scoop of wise and nice utterance).

Through these programmes, al-Hakkamat demonstrated beyond doubt that they are the right people to communicate effectively with people in rural areas, the Baggara audience in particular. They appeared to be speaking in tune with the government's politics, i.e. if the government call was Jihad, they would call for Jihad, and similarly if the government called for peace.[2] Hearing the voice of their Hakkamat on the radio would presumably inspire delight in tribespeople, particularly the horsemen, with both their Hakkamat and the government. Their Hakkamat would be elevated to even higher esteem, a matter of importance for tribes that cannot be overstated.

The voice of al-Hakkamat was also used to address national political issues, especially where the government needed a show of public support. For instance, when the economic embargo was imposed on Sudan by the United Nations Security Council in 1994, the government organised public singing parties and used al-Hakkamat to mobilise the public in order to mitigate possible public discontent, and to earn support against these American-led sanctions.[3] One Hakkamah recited the following:[4]

English
At early dawn, I was hearing heavy guns roaring.
Oh, horsemen, my kinfolks, I advise you.
Unite together; don't let America colonise you!

Transliteration
maʿa shagat al-sharḥān basmaʿ ḥisays al-birayn rannā.
Bawaṣṣīku yā al-fursān ʾawlād ʾahalnā.
limmū baʿaḍkū, mā takhallū ʾamrīca tastaʿmarkū!
(H. R58, G4, Nyala, 2006).

Al-Hakkamah appeals to her tribesmen to stand firm with the government in disproving and challenging these American-led sanctions. She urges the armed horsemen to join in to prevent America from 'colonising' the country, as propagandised by the government.

The most crucial dimension of the alliance forged between al-Hakkamat and the governing elites was to ensure the loyalty and publicly announced corroboration of al-Hakkamat, and on the other hand to dissuade them from opposing and/or slandering the regime. The riverine governing elites equally realised not only the Nazir, but also al-Hakkamat, are the key powers in the tribal administration and the entry points for obtaining the tribes' endorsement.[5] This was clearly articulated by a journalist:

2 Interviews with two radio and TV presenters (R12, R14), Nyala, 2006.
3 Interview with Ahmed Jowa (R14), radio and TV presenter from Ta'aisha, Nyala, 2006.
4 Hubbania Hakkamah (R58) reciting at group interview with Hakkamat (G4), Nyala, 2006.
5 Group (G2, G3) and individual interviews, Nyala, 2006.

> Al-Hakkamah is the key to the tribe and holding her under control would imply that the regime has maintained control of the keys to the tribes and tribalism in Darfur ... Al-Hakkamat, the Nazir and the Dimingawi are the persons who have the power to influence all sectors of their communities. When the government restrained them, it would imply that they have maintained control over the whole tribe and al-Hakkamat would not dare to speak out against them.[6]

The government have consistently and obstinately attempted every access point to the tribal community, and blatantly manipulated their gatekeepers. Whole tribes have publicly pledged their political support to the ruling party (NCP/NIF) and tribal chiefs have either been coerced into compliance or replaced by subservient cadre. Having succeeded in getting al-Hakkamat publicly aligned with them, the government carried on with planning and executing measures to effectively appropriate their identity, both as individual actors and as a tribal institution, in order to enhance government war mobilisation campaigns and to promote advocacy projects like the CAP. This latter project was planned by the government to transform the Sudanese people to fit the NIF-conceived Islamic model. It was also meant to influence the Sudanese to be a society loyal to the ruling National Congress Party (NCP) and their institutions into government-sponsored and controlled organisations.

THE ORGANISATION OF AL-HAKKAMAT

In 2003, for the second time, al-Hakkamat became a target for the NIF government, as in 1991 when they were recruited into the PIM by the then riverine governor of Greater Darfur, al-Tayyib Sikha. By this time, Darfur was already split into three regions (North, South and West) in 1994. The revival of this old utilitarian initiative was indeed sponsored by government authorities in South Darfur, the region most densely populated by Baggara, under the auspices of another riverine politician, Atta al-Mannan, the governor of South Darfur (2002–6). The expressed intention was to strengthen the drive to challenge the mounting activities of the newly emerged insurgents against the government.[7]

Since then, al-Hakkamat and al-Sheikhat have been assembled together in Nyala town in what is called the Union of Hakkamat and Sheikhat (UHS), despite apparent discrepancies in the roles of the two personalities. The Ministry of Culture and Information of South Darfur was commissioned to supervise and look after them. Apparently, gathering al-Hakkamat and al-Sheikhat in one assembly was intended to synthesise and reap the maximum benefits from them both.[8] Both constitute prominent actors in their tribes and although al-Sheikhat do not compose as al-Hakkamat do, they are recognised as skilful and expert in other areas of community activism, such as cooking, and mobilising and organising women on various social occasions, including receiving and hosting

[6] Interviews with a journalist (R43) from Ta'aisha, Nyala, 2006.
[7] Group (G2, G3, G4) and individual interviews, Nyala, 2006.
[8] Ibid.

officials. These are the services that the government authorities often need, and tend to welcome free of charge.

It was thought that several factors were behind the formation of the UHS. For instance, the chairperson of the regional legislative committee of South Darfur at the time of this research argued that recent growing sociopolitical changes in the town have necessitated the authorities to stipulate that public activities should be executed through formally organised bodies. It follows that performing singing parties and/or any other public gathering in the neighbourhood would not be allowed without prior permission from the authorities. In the past, al-Hakkamah used to have personal autonomy and freedom in organising public celebrations within her neighbourhood. Now they have to abide by these regulations.[9]

Moreover, in order to exercise control over al-Hakkamat and guide their influence, the MCI required al-Hakkamat who moved from the village to settle in Nyala to affiliate to the UHS if they wanted to perform in public, in the neighbourhood or at government public events. This was articulated by a disaffected Hakkamah who reported that unless you were a member of the UHS you would not be allowed to participate in any official event, as was the case before:

> Before forming this organisation, you had your own freedom of choice and if you heard any interesting news, you could call your women [chorus] and do things on your own right. Now you must join the Union, otherwise, you will have no acceptance, although you could affiliate to the folkloric dancing and singing team of your tribe; as all tribes have this kind of group where al-Hakkamat play a leading role.[10]

Most of al-Hakkamat in Nyala town therefore have no option but to join and become entirely accountable to the UHS and associated government institutions. The number of al-Hakkamat and the Sheikhat recruited to the UHS through the PIM was found to be 150, which comprised almost all those already resident in Nyala and some recent arrivals from rural areas. Coercing al-Hakkamat into the UHS has generated an unfavourable impact on their agency and power relationships; one Hakkamah complained, saying that in her village the role of al-Hakkamah was highly cemented by the Ageed system and she had full freedom of choice in where, when and how she sang and carried out other activities. Now, others apply tight control over her, as she must seek permission and abide by regulations if she chooses to perform.[11]

Even though this development appears to have been resented by many Hakkamat, as it strips them of personal liberty, especially with regard to the autonomy and independence that they used to exercise and enjoy, it was nevertheless welcomed by some Hakkamat; as pointed out by one Hakkamah:

> Now it is better than the past, because, in the past, we could spark off conflict; as everyone could speak out their own ideas. Now, we are controlled and have

[9] Interview with the chairperson of the Regional Legislative Committee of South Darfur (R17), from Hubbania, Nyala, 2006.

[10] Interview with Salami Hakkamah (R51), Nyala, 2006.

[11] Ibid.

> limits; you cannot insult and cannot praise in your own right; we just talk about the government and about Allah and the prophet sayings. But in the past we were not good with Allah, nor were we good with people. Now I have less freedom, but it is better, because, in the past I was like a horse without *sareemah*,[12] and now I have found a *sareemah* that fits the size of my mouth; now the government knows me and the public know me, and I have prestige.[13]

Obviously, al-Hakkamat have become organised through an initiative that has been both male and government-led, with apparently very little initiative of their own. Nonetheless, they have been able to utilise the limits allowed by the power brokers in town, a context previously distant and alien to them. They might also have seen it expedient to go along with it, in order to maintain their engagement with unfolding situations, especially local inter-tribal and ethnic conflicts, not to mention the government's civil wars.

REMODELLING THE INSTITUTION OF AL-HAKKAMAH

Arguably, despite the continual migration of rural people into Nyala, the number of locally 'baptised' Hakkamat who left their villages and settled there was relatively small, compared to the large Baggara population in Nyala and its outskirts. This small presence of purebred Hakkamat implied that the government might not be able to use them to accomplish their desired outreach at the town boundaries, let alone in distant villages.

To remedy this deficiency, the government authorities attempted some actions that included disregarding the conventional initiation and inauguration processes of al-Hakkamat and their creation as originally in a village-based setting. They called for tribeswomen in Nyala who could sing and/or compose to join the procession as Hakkamat. This approach encouraged many Baggara women to carry their tribes' flags and arrogate for themselves the ability to perform the role of al-Hakkamat and thus to further the government's interests, despite the fact that they lacked the poetic and other unique skills that are characteristic of al-Hakkamat.

The posturing of those women might have been encouraged by their own ambitions and the convenience of the incentives and rewards that the government sometimes offer to al-Hakkamat. The following statement stands as a typical confession made by town-based Hakkamat:

> My tribe did not identify me as Hakkamah, because I have just recently become Hakkamah in Nyala ... If any woman composed nicely and in meaningful words and recorded them the radio and/or the television, people would identify her as Hakkamah ... In Nyala, we were introduced to the media by the chairperson of the UHS, and thereafter considered Hakkamat.[14]

Noticeably, most of the membership of the UHS are surrogate Hakkamat (the newly emerging town Hakkamat). The attitudes and manners of these

[12] The buckled straps around a horse's head that help you control its movements.

[13] Interview with Misseriya Hakkamah (R71), Nyala, 2006.

[14] Interviews with Ta'aishi Hakkamah (R50), Nyala, 2006.

Hakkamat have often clashed with those of the tribal village community, as a result of them either being constructed outside the village boundaries or having moved to the town long ago.[15] It was alleged that only four of the Hakkamat in the UHS were genuine, whilst the rest were dismissed as merely fraudulent Hakkamat, who carried the label but could not embrace its authenticity. They recited the songs and poems of other recognised Hakkamat, rather than trying to show themselves as artistic composers.[16]

This government approach of encouraging women to become fraudulent and surrogate Hakkamat and forcing their communities' approval constitutes part of their strategy to influence and monitor tribal communities, especially those residing on the outskirts of the town.

On the other hand, they extended the label 'al-Hakkamah' to encompass women singers of other tribes, a cultural interference that violates what some tribes might perceive as their unique cultural trait and legacy. For instance, they assigned the label 'Hakkamat' to women from African tribes, who might assume recognised positions in their communities but were neither culturally called 'Hakkamat', nor were their roles relevant to those of al-Hakkamat of Darfuri Arab society.[17]

The case of a woman who joined the UHS as Hakkamah, and who belonged to Forogay, a tribe affiliated to South Sudan, testifies to this. She explained that in South Sudan they have no horses or horsemen, and have no culture of praising or glorifying hunters, inciting fighters and/or celebrating the men's heroism. They only sing on happy occasions, for merriment. In the UHS, she was identified as al-Hakkamah and the voice of her tribe, and was required to embrace this identity at government public events, similar to the Baggara Hakkamat.[18]

Adopting the label 'Hakkamah' across the tribal spectrum in South Darfur, also confirms the observation that the label has become socially a well-recognised symbol of female authority, influence and agency, not only among Darfuri Arab society but across the diverse cultures of Darfur and Sudan. This is not say that Darfuri people do not normally differentiate between the original meaning and the extended use of the label to describe, by default, any woman with excellence and uniqueness of talents, skills, attitudes, or appearance. Yet they also comprehend the opportunistic usage that the regime has tried to normalise.

In addition, the authorities have also created a new type of Hakkamat – Hakkamat-at-Turath, or Hakkamat of folklore. This type of Hakkamat is presumably skilful in organising the Baggara folkloric arts, especially during parades and exhibitions. Their identification was perhaps fostered by the annual folklore exhibition that the national government organises in Khartoum, in which all regions take part and show their folklore arts. The Darfur region used to be represented by a group of women and

[15] Group and individual interviews (G1, G2, G3), Nyala, 2006.
[16] Group interviews with Hakkamat (G4), Nyala, 2006.
[17] This is a contentious issue, as African tribes also have singing women performers who may pledge similar, albeit non-identical, roles to their tribes, but go by other labels and titles.
[18] Interview with Hakkamah from Forogay tribe (R27), Nyala, 2006.

men with expertise in folklore, who usually demonstrated samples from different parts of the region. This type of Hakkamat could be a positive addition to the arts and development of folklore in Darfur. Nonetheless, they could not receive the attention required to boost their abilities, and their movements have so far been confined to the activities performed within UHS premises.[19]

On the other hand, women of many tribes joined the UHS as Sheikhat; meanwhile, others joined as both Hakkamah and Sheikhat. It was not unusual, however, for a woman to assume the two identities simultaneously. Five members of the UHS claimed to have both identities and claimed that al-Hakkamah could also, functionally, be Sheikha. Obviously, it is of no major concern for the governing authorities to differentiate between who is what, so long as their monopoly over both characters has been secured.

Given the lack of rural-based women's organisations in the towns of Darfur, and despite the political drive behind its formation, the UHS could have served as a platform for serving the welfare of immigrant rural women and facilitating their adaptation to challenges in the urban context, thereby defying the stereotyped perceptions and expectations of women and their subordination. But, it is also believable that apart from mobilising women to serve government interests, the UHS has no vision concerning women and women's issues. It has made no effort to transform itself into a civil society organisation advocating for the rights of women and/or human rights; it remains strictly a government-driven and guided body.

ISLAMIC IDEOLOGICAL GUIDANCE (INDOCTRINATION)

Soon after they seized power in 1989, the NIF government began to propagate their Islamic ideology and policies among the public. They identified women as a potential locus for ideological intervention and a symbol of identity politics and targeted them with policies designed to cast them in the NIF Islamists' doctrinal model. Prominent as they are among women, al-Hakkamat became subject to indoctrination to cast them into an NIF-projected image of ideal *Muslim* women. They received intensive religious teaching and preaching through literacy sessions, meetings, conferences, workshops, etc.

The instruction put extra emphasis on the position of women under Islamic shari'a,[20] and advised that al-Hakkamat must abstain from inciting conflict, which is, according to the shari'a, deemed temptation and sedition and therefore strictly forbidden. These sessions were seen as theoretically the most useful initiative that the government offered al-Hakkamat

[19] Group and individual interviews, Nyala, 2006.

[20] For instance, under shari'a wives can be beaten, females inherit half as much as their brothers, wives should be subservient to their husbands and do not possess the same rights of divorce, female rulers are frowned upon, women are deemed lacking in faith and intelligence, raping female captives is permissible, etc.

as they were meant to reduce their harmful influence in inciting conflicts. Al-Hakkamat in particular, appeared to have appreciated these efforts, which enabled them at least to write and read their names. They have learned some of the Quran, and how to pray and perform religious rituals, e.g. bathe a corpse at burial and other religious matters that they were unaware of.[21] One Hakkamah described her experience and expressed her appreciation to President Omar al-Bashir upon his visit to Nyala, by the following recitation:[22]

English
Peace be upon you, *Takbeer, Tahleel.*
Peace be upon you, Omar al-Bashir.
Oh, this is you, the autumn of the flood,[23] which raised the orphans.
He who rules by shari'a and holds at bay its detractors.
I've recited the poem and apologise that I am illiterate.
Thanks to Omar al-Bashir and his delegation.
He opened a door for me to combat illiteracy that we now study in the evening.
We represent the heritage, as in erecting *al-shibriyah*[24]
Who meets her in the morning realises her aspiration.
Who meets her in the evening, the kids of the organisation will draw her portrait.

Transliteration
salām ʿalayk, takbīr, tahlīl.
salām ʿalayk, yā Omer al-Bashir.
da ʾinta al-kharīf ʾabū nīl al-rabbā al-ʾattāmā.
al-ḥākim bey-l-sharīʿa wa kaffā ẓullāmā.
gaddamtā al-gasīda wa baʿtazir ʾumiyyia.
mashkūr Omer al-Bashir wā al-wafd al-murāfiq layyā
fatah layyā bāb, lī maḥwa-l-ʾummiyya, nagrā maʿ al-ʿuṣriyyā
namaththil al-turāth al-kawwāʿan al-shibriyyā.
al-gābalhā maʿ al-ṣabāḥ, ʾajabat al-ʾumniyyā.
al-gābalha maʿ al-ʿashiyyā, rasamūhā ʾawlād al-jamʿiyyā.
(H/S. R4, G4, Nyala, 2006).

This orientation was further harnessed by sponsoring some Hakkamat to perform the Hajj rite in Makka. The Hajj, together with the subjects discussed at the literacy sessions, reinforced the belief of al-Hakkamat in the regime's pursuits as legitimate and based on Islamic doctrine. Therefore, they felt obliged to uphold and comply with the NIF's policies, as they were geared towards building an Islamic state and fostering an Islamic society. Furthermore, al-Hakkamat were requested to direct their compositions and influence to serving the NIF's advocacy campaign and that of its successor, the NCP, as a divine obligation. It seems only inevitable that al-Hakkamat's conformity with these religious messages figured quite prominently in their songs and recitations, as could be observed in the following recitation:[25]

[21] Group and individual interviews, Nyala, 2006.
[22] Recitation of Salami Hakkamah (R4) at group interview with Hakkamat (G4), Nyala, 2006.
[23] i.e. the rainy season.
[24] al-Shibriyah is a carriage for nomad women, hoisted on the back of a camel for moving around.
[25] Interview with Hubbania Hakkamah (R32), Nyala, 2006.

English
Saying, 'In the name of Allah, the Beneficent, the Merciful'.
Expels Satan and restores faith.
At the Religious Affairs Office, I have insightful holy scholars.
I got holy religious scholars who are well versed in the Quran.
The officials of the Comprehensive Advocacy believe in Allah, the sole Subduer.
They worship and fast.
The religious scholar opens his book.
In the big mosque, 'Allah say this, the prophet says that …'
Oh, my dear Hakkamat.
I withdrew my forces from singing.[26]
As I would like to join *al-khalwa*, to differentiate between *halal* and *haram*.[27]

Transliteration
gawlit bismi-llāhī al-rahmāni-l-rahīm.
hī bitrudd al-shayṭān wa bi-tanazzil al-ʾīmān.
fī maktab al-shuʾūn al-dīnīyyā ʿindī fugarā ʿullām.
ʿindī fugara ḥāmlīn shihādāt al-qurān.
nās al-daʿwā al-shāmlah mityyaqqinīn bay ʾallah al-wāḥid al-dayyān.
māskīn al-ʿibādāh wa-l-ṣiyyām.
al-ʿālim farrā kitābā.
fi al-masjid al-kabīr, ʾallah gāl dā, al-rasūl gāl.
hey yā ḥakkāmātī
min al-ghunā saḥab quwwātī
dāyrā ʾandas fī al-khalwā ʿashān ʾafruz al-ḥalāl min al-ḥarām.
(H. R32, Nyala, 2006).

It was generally noticed by the locals that before the 1990s the expressions that al-Hakkamat used in their songs, poems and speeches were grounded almost entirely in words that celebrated the surrounding habitat and the culture of the rural settings, and were completely devoid of any religious idioms or articulations. Following the religious tuition, al-Hakkamat's diction and expressions have noticeably included some religious idiom and overtones. Local people also portray how the government's religious slogans (e.g. *Takbeer*; *Tahleel*; *bil-jalalah wa al-takbeer*; *Allahu Akbar, Allahu Akbar*)[28] have crept into al-Hakkamat's poetic diction because of this oriented induction. Now, al-Hakkamat have switched their focus to praising the president (and his associates), leaving out some substantial themes of their own culture that used to dominate in the village setting, such as glorifying generous members and prominent leaders of their tribes.

Alongside the regularised literacy sessions, the government also organised one-day meetings for more than thirty Hakkamat with government officials: most were actually visitors from Khartoum.[29] The meetings were led by a senior judge accompanied by other judges, holy men and high-ranking military cadre, to explore al-Hakkamat's role – their activities and capabilities, methods of influence, and how they exercise agency.[30]

[26] i.e. I gave up singing.
[27] i.e. the permitted and the forbidden, in Islam.
[28] People shout and exclaim, 'Allahu Akbar, Allahu Akbar', i.e. 'Allah is great; Allah is great', at rallies in order to express Islamic solidarity and loyalty.
[29] Group interview with Hakkamat (G4), Nyala, 2006.
[30] Ibid.

Apparently, this kind of assembly was meant to fulfil multidimensional objectives for the ruling and governing elites. It would enable them to review the experience of al-Hakkamat, their dynamics and effectiveness, as this could help them analyse, comprehend and explore their methods of exercising influence. It might subsequently enable the projection of further ways to exploit al-Hakkamat's qualities to the full, for promoting the government's counter-insurgency campaigns in Darfur.

The presence of riverine governing elites in the complete absence of al-Hakkamat's formal and informal local gatekeepers, for instance, the MCI of South Darfur and the tribal authorities, was indeed suspicious, especially if we realise that this happened shortly after the eruption of the Darfuri insurgency in March 2003. Besides, the involvement of judges with al-Hakkamat might well suggest that the judiciary in Sudan had been one of the government's political and executive institutions and was complicit in promoting violence and wars. It was not an independent and impartial institution as constitutionally it should have been.

Further indoctrination of women was pursued when a dress code was imposed in 1991 on all adult females – students, government employees and petty traders, e.g. tea sellers, who were required to wear a characteristic hijab in public places. This was instantly interpreted by Sudanese women activists as intended to seclude women and restrict their freedom of movement, and was therefore strongly denied and resisted (Hale 1992). Al-Hakkamat were also required to comply with the code should they aspire to exercise their agency and perform in public.

The change in the style of their dress struck at the heart of the folklore art, as could be noticed in some popular Baggara dances, such as *Iraij* or *al-Gidairee. Al-Gidairee* dance usually involves a woman dancing like *gimriyah* (a dove) and landing slowly on the floor with a 'kareer' sound (*Kur, kur, kur*), resembling that of a dove, whilst moving her head to both right and left and letting her hair fall on her shoulders. Her male partner hits the ground with his feet making a lovely sound (*takah, takah, takah*), and symmetric sequences of steps in tune with the dancing movements of the woman.

This woman dancer used to be al-Hakkamah. Wearing the hijab has reduced the meaning and the quality of the dance, and impeded the dancers' movements.[31] The entire value of *al-Gidairee* dance has been distorted; for instance, the tossing of a woman's hair over the shoulder or the forehead of the man during dancing was impeded. The *shabbaal*[32] is a gesture of admiration made by a woman for her dancing partner. It has now become impossible with the hijab, which replaced the *mukashkash*[33] that women used to wear on these occasions. This change has forced people to abstain from performing many folk dances, and reduced the scope of innocent enjoyment and entertainment in rural societies. Some

[31] Interview with Ahmed Jowa (R14), radio and TV presenter from Ta'aisha, Nyala, 2006.

[32] Interview with Ahmed Jowa, Nyala, 2006. *Shabbaal* also involves a soft touch of the forehead of a dancing man by the hair or head of his woman partner in the dance.

[33] A *mukashkash* is a dress like that of a ballerina.

of the dances have even disappeared entirely as a result of the regime enacting of the Public Order Act, which has banned men and women from dancing together.[34] The Act outlaws all types of mixing between women and men, allegedly to prevent the possibility that it will lead to adultery.

Al-Hakkamat's extensive exposure to religious orientation and preaching did not resolve the many problems they encountered in Nyala, especially with regard to their deteriorated welfare. Nonetheless, al-Hakkamat have appeared to be keen to be seen as loyal and compliant with the government's aspirations and to show that they have transformed into the Islamic model recommended by the NIF. This attitude was partially communicated through the appeal made by one al-Hakkamah to President al-Bashir's second wife when she visited Nyala. She requested the president's wife to fulfil her aspiration to perform the Hajj ritual. Acting generously, the wife sponsored the Hajj, not only for al-Hakkamah who presented the appeal, but for twenty-four more Hakkamat. Below is the recitation al-Hakkamah delivered:[35]

English
Oh, my mouth was set free as speech needs a key.
Omer Hassan al-Bashir is like Jebel Marrah that is seen from far away.
Al-Zubair Mohamed Salih, the flooding autumn that pleased the farmers.
Al-Tayeb Ibrahim, the Governor of Darfur states.
As pure as the certified gold of Bani Shangol.
I will wear you on the congregation day over there.
Hey, my rulers, the least I want is to issue me a certificate.[36]
For I would like to visit Saudi Arabia out there.[37]

Transliteration
wey khashmī ʾinfakkā, lil-ḥadīth muftahā.
Omer Hassan al-Bashir, jabal marrā al-min baʿīd birāʾā.
al-Zubair Mohamed Salih, al-kharīf al-dalaj, al-baṣat al-zurāʿā.
al-Tayeb Ibrahim, ḥākim wilāyāt Dārfawr.
al-ṣāfī dahab banī shangūl.
balbasak bagābil bayk yawm al-ziḥām hināk.
hayā yā ḥukāmī, bal-ʾabkhas dāyrah taṭalliʿū layyā shihādah.
ʿashān ʾazūr al-saʿūdī hināk.
(H. R32, Nyala, 2006).

Considering al-Hakkamat's protest and resentment about being unemployed, this could have been an opportunity to raise their demands: perhaps the president's wife could have helped.

In general terms, through Islamic indoctrination, al-Hakkamat's identity, both as individual actors and as an institution of traditional authority and influence, has been recast to fit the Islamic female model of the NIF and to serve the declared Islamic project of the ruling elites. Al-Hakkamat were dissociated from the folkloric heritage and culture of Baggara society, which habitually enriches people's lives with a sense of beauty

[34] Ibid.
[35] Interview with Hubbania Hakkamah (R32), Nyala, 2006.
[36] i.e. a visa.
[37] Muslims perform Hajj in Saudi Arabia where the Muslim sacred sites are located.

and joy. The Islamic project was indeed incompatible with the Baggara community's culture and social values, which accord women a favourable place and space to exercise their choices and influence that of their folks. In effect, the power with which al-Hakkamat are entrusted to observe and preserve the cultural boundaries of their societies has diminished.

THE MILITARISATION OF AL-HAKKAMAT

The most significant measure pursued by the NIF regime in co-opting al-Hakkamat was organised military training and al-Hakkamat's subsequent informal incorporation into the military. The training was carried out within and outside Darfur region. Having completed the training, most of al-Hakkamat were offered military identities and rank titles, for instance, the chairwoman of the UHS was offered the rank of *naqeeb* (captain).[38]

Four Hakkamat proudly declared that they were trained several times by different military and paramilitary bodies, such as the Popular Defence Forces (PDF), the Popular Police Forces (PPF), and al-Salaam Forces (ASF). Their training with the PDF lasted for almost nine months and involved shooting, assembling and disassembling of weapons, standard military drills and manoeuvres, etc. Thereafter, they were annexed to the PPF for almost seven years and were given several identity cards,[39] including those of the NCP and the UHS.[40]

The militarisation of al-Hakkamat was clearly phenomenal, as almost all Hakkamat, in Nyala in particular, were trained and attached to the military.[41] It was pursued following the introduction of compulsory military conscription in 1990, and was managed and executed by the PDF. It was enforced on all female employees in the public sector as a condition of remaining in the job, and on job seekers as a condition of employment.[42] The policy was carried out in Darfur with special vigour and coercion, compelling many female employees to refuse to receive the training; they were subsequently expelled from office. All female government employees had to submit to conscription, and Al-Hakkamat were no different.[43]

Receiving military training therefore, raised the expectations of all Hakkamat that they would be employed instantly with regular salaries,

38 Group and individual interviews, Nyala, 2006.

39 One Hakkamah showed me her Popular Police Card issued on 30 May 2003. It shows her blood group and her rank title of Areef, corporal. There was no expiry date shown on the card. The photo shows her wearing a scarf and tobe. The ID card was signed by the Commander General of the Popular Police Force. On the back of the card was written: 'The holder of this card has full authority as that of a policeman based on the 1992 Police legislation on arresting, searching and initial interrogation and seizure of stolen and suspect goods'.

40 Interview with Hakkamat (G4), Nyala, 2006.

41 Interview with Dr Mahmoud Adam Daoud (R47), a university lecturer and folk expert from Fur, Nyala, 2006.

42 My personal working experience in Darfur for over 10 years.

43 Interview with the chairperson of the Regional Legislative Committee of South Darfur, from Hubbania (R17), Nyala, 2006.

as pledged by their recruiters. Some al-Hakkamat were appointed as office caretakers at the brigades' headquarters and made to wear the uniform. Others were attached to specific brigades and became identified with them, e.g. 'al-Hakkamah of the Sixth Infantry Brigade'. Three were appointed as 'Hakkamat of the Moral Orientation Unit'[44] of the military in Nyala, and offered the titles of 'private' and 'corporal' (*areef*).[45] Meanwhile, three powerful Hakkamat were ranked as captains (*naqeeb*) and were used to escort the troops to Raja[46] during the civil war in the south, where they were pushed on the battlefield to sing to hearten the soldiers to fight with courage and vigour.[47] Nevertheless, given their large number, and perhaps due to the lack of a plan and/or any sincere intention to fulfil the pledge of the authorities to offer them jobs, the rest of them were disappointed, as expressed by four of them, who claimed that they have never benefited from the training.[48]

Among these Hakkamat, a Misseriya Hakkamah testified that she could not find work as *Farrashah* (caretaker) in the government offices, even though she joined the PDF in 1996 and completed the military training stipulated as a condition for getting a job. She joined the UHS and was required to attend and register at the PDF every Saturday.[49]

Noticeably though, female civil servants who received military training in Darfur were not offered military titles or uniform, or attached to the military, as was the case with al-Hakkamat. Paradoxically though, some Hakkamat who received military training were denied employment, while female employees who refused the training were discharged from work. This inconsistency in policy implementation might well indicate an patriarchal Islamist approach that not only frequently discriminates against (working) women, but also forces them into submission in order to keep their jobs.

Apparently, this experience was disheartening and disempowering for al-Hakkamat, as their songs lost their appeal for the audience. On a different note though, for many people, the militarisation of al-Hakkamat was contentious, especially with regard to the low fitness requirement for women applicants to the army or the police. Most of al-Hakkamat were advanced in age and seemingly unable to tolerate the physical strenuousness associated with military training, let alone be considered as potential fighters on the battlefield.

Some views suggested that although military training teaches and instils discipline, by subjecting women, al-Hakkamat in particular, to such

[44] Equivalent to a psychological operations department in modern armies.

[45] Interview with al-Hakkamat and Sheikhat (G3), Nyala, 2006.

[46] A district located in Western Bahr al Ghazal state at the border with South Darfur where the last battle was fought between the SPLA and the Sudanese government. It is now on the western front of the border between Sudan and South Sudan. Following this battle, the peace process was enhanced and progressively enforced by the international community, leading eventually to the signing of the CPA between the SPLA and the Sudanese government in 2005.

[47] Interviews with a government employee from Fur (R41), Nyala 2006.

[48] Ibid.

[49] Ibid.

training, and their subsequent engagement with the PDF, the *Inghaz*[50] regime has weakened women's positive attitudes to peace. Women have become transformed into aggressive and violent actors, inciting war and advocating for conflict, in a way that contradicts the commonly held claim that it is not in women's nature to fight and kill.[51]

Aggressive attitudes in women in society ought to be censured and dismissed, and women should be guided and encouraged to advocate for peace, love and unity. It is only fair to emphasise that the state government has moral obligations to direct and enable al-Hakkamat to uphold and promote the values of peaceful coexistence and social cohesion, and to disengage from campaigns involving fighting, killing and polarising people. Apparently, the military training was meant to incorporate the belligerent voice of al-Hakkamat into the military, whereas the real need was for all to work for peace. On the other hand, the governing elites never take into account the risks their strategies impose on their subjects, as manifested by the great loss of Baggara recruits in the wars (as acknowledged by al-Hakkamat), alongside other disastrous outcomes endured by the entire Darfuri society.

Paradoxically though, whilst military training was offered to women who might not actually need it, those who tended to need it most were denied the opportunity. These were the vulnerable rural women who have become the direct victims of war atrocities and who needed to learn skills necessary to protect themselves and their dependents. Given the precarious context in Darfur, it was felt that if the government was genuine about empowering women, then they should offer all rural women training in the use of firearms, not just a select few![52]

Nonetheless, whilst the militarisation of al-Hakkamat was dismissed locally and widely as no more than exploitation, manipulation and ethnic polarisation in pursuance of divide-and-rule politics, it was generally perceived by al-Hakkamat, in addition to a minority of the general population, as a useful experience that enabled them to act as community police and enhance their self-defence skills and application. Some have pledged to carry guns if circumstances call for it.

From a feminist point of view, the militarisation of women is a representation of women's empowerment and equal rights. This discourse is however perceived from two different perspectives on empowerment: feminist antimilitarists reject militarisation on the basis that it is associated with the culture of masculine violence, and that its social, political and economic outcomes inevitably lead to women's oppression. Military culture therefore conflicts with women's culture and feminist goals, and obstructs justice and peace. On the other hand, the feminist egalitarian militarists perceive military service as part of women's rights and responsibilities, and part of their rights of full citizenship. Yet they

[50] Group and individual interviews, Nyala, 2006. Inghaz (translating as the Salvation Government) is the recognised name of the first NIF government after they seized power in a coup d'état in 1989.

[51] Group and individual interviews, Nyala, 2006.

[52] Group and individual interviews, Nyala, 2006.

emphasise the fact that for a long time women have been engaged with military assignments without being acknowledged and/or fairly rewarded (Feinman, 2000, p. 1).

Al-Hakkamat's engagement with the military appears to occur against the backdrop of the central principles of the two feminist approaches to women and militarism: both participating in the culture of violence that resulted in mass killings and inhumane atrocities committed by both the military and militia horsemen in Darfur, especially against women; and, on the other hand, not being formally incorporated in the ranks and/or decently rewarded but instead being manipulated and exploited to the maximum.

The purpose of al-Hakkamat's militarisation could equally be understood as partially intended to replicate the bond that al-Hakkamat had maintained with the Ageed organisation and its horsemen; it was presumably a form of compensation designed to sustain their connection to yet another parallel institution of authority, in this case the armed forces. But the Ageed organisation has a moral obligation to respect, empower and protect al-Hakkamat and enhance their role, any time and everywhere within the tribe's territories, while the military has failed to formulate any term of reference that could emphasise respect and protection for al-Hakkamat. The military co-option of al-Hakkamat was therefore not pursued to advance the patriotic goals of equal citizenship and equal rights for women and their protection; rather, it was used simply as a vehicle to exploit al-Hakkamat and perpetuate violence and aggression against women.

CONCLUSION

It is more than just conceivable that the government has relied on al-Hakkamat of the Baggara communities of South Darfur to further their policy and war campaigns. The Baggara constitute the backdrop of the human resource that the politics of ethnic and racial interpretation of wars appeal to; and there would be no better actors or campaigners to champion this objective than al-Hakkamat. Hence, they were encouraged to persuade their communities to align against the government's political rivals in South Sudan and in Darfur and to advocate its Islamic project, the Comprehensive Advocacy Project, which was designed to cast the Sudanese people into the National Islamic Front (NIF)-conceived Islamic model.

The process of empowering al-Hakkamat's agency to undertake these roles was launched by extensively engaging with them in programmes disseminated by government-owned TV and radio. The radio was used more often because it was more popular in rural areas. Communicating with those communities through familiar and appealing voices is indeed crucial to earning their sympathy and commitment. Featuring al-Hakkamat on the radio and TV certainly appeased the tribesmen, the youth in particular, and encouraged them to join the government's campaigns in droves, whereas al-Hakkamat were held in high esteem.

The government then expanded the measures that served the dual objective of appropriating al-Hakkamat into a government-sponsored body and manipulating their influence, and garnering the greatest support from Arab tribes in Darfur, especially the Baggara. These measures included arrangements such as their assemblage together with women representatives in the traditional leadership structures of the African tribes, al-Sheikhat, into the Union of al-Hakkamat and al-Sheikhat (UHS) in Nyala town.

Driven by the need for more Hakkamat, the ruling elites demonstrated a disrespectful attitude towards local cultural values when they granted the title 'al-Hakkamah' to any woman aspiring to the role of leadership, regardless of whether they showed the culturally agreed qualities required for al-Hakkamat. They also expanded the title to cover women outside Baggara cultural boundaries. This intervention was detrimental to the institution of al-Hakkamah, and the appropriated Hakkamat could only earn their tribes' disaffection.

The religious teaching and preaching designed for al-Hakkamat have served well in reshaping the poetic expressions of al-Hakkamat, which came out loaded with religious passion and diction, especially the NIF slogans, e.g. *tahleel*, *takbeer*, etc. The hijab that is enforced on them has ostensibly confirmed their affiliation to the NIF/NCP, but it has also stripped them of much of the elegant Baggara storytelling and performance arts (for instance, dancing movements that display the neck), forcing rural communities to relinquish many of them. Yet the military training has been the most significant reinforcement of al-Hakkamat's belligerent voice on violence and ethnic polarisation. Noticeably, al-Hakkamat's military training was not induced on the premise of gender equality and/or as part of the government's general compulsory conscription policy; rather, the training was used to empower their belligerent voice and to distort the prospects for peace. This was clear, because most rural women, especially those most vulnerable to attacks and those who had been victims of war atrocities, were entirely excluded. The militarisation of al-Hakkamat, therefore, tends to be a racial and discriminatory procedure used by the government to consolidate their engagement with Arab tribes against Africans and to use Arab women as impetus in perpetrating abuses against Africans, especially African women. This has been revealed in the gender-based violence and war atrocities committed against African women during the course of the conflict in Darfur since 2003.

7

New Duties and Obligations

As outlined earlier, the recent history of Sudan has been plagued with wars and armed struggle. The civil wars were caused mainly by discontent with the domestic politics pursued by the riverine ruling and governing elites who have been unable to design and execute a national programme that could address the problems of the whole country. Instead, they have concentrated power, economic and political resources in the hands of a few groups that are limited socially, racially and geographically, and deprived the vast majority in the remote regions.

In efforts to win the support of the Arabs as a racial group, the government interpreted the causes and consequences of these conflicts in entirely discriminating racial terms. They dismissed insurgent movements as motivated primarily by racial hatred saying that their intention was to exterminate and/or dominate the Arabs. This interpretation was used to urge and mobilise racial and religious consciousness, which are powerful instruments in appealing to the respective people. Arab tribes and ethnic groups were presumed to take the matter in their hands and fight on behalf of the government to challenge these regional movements. Besides, their confronting one another could divert their attention from challenging the government's discriminatory domestic politics to which these regions have been treated: the politics that constituted the prime cause of such violent confrontations.

Al-Hakkamat have been part and parcel of the government mobilisation to serve these bloody confrontations and to maintain a momentum for their escalation. Thus, having been coached, goaded and co-opted into the government's domain of politics on a racial basis, al-Hakkamat, whether willingly or grudgingly, have had to undertake certain duties and obligations that included, among many others, mobilising for war in South Sudan and against the Darfur insurgency, escorting the army, providing sustenance (food rations), recruiting women and engaging with officials and public events. These matters are discussed in detail in the following sections.

MOBILISATION FOR CIVIL WAR IN SOUTH SUDAN

As already affirmed, since 1991 al-Hakkamat have been identified as a crucial element in the military strategy to defeat the insurgencies and to secure political support for the NIF regime. The riverine ruling elites have been using them extensively since then to mobilise and recruit the youth, on a racial and religious basis, to join their allegedly Jihad campaign against the non-Muslim southern SPLA of the former South Sudan region (now the independent State of South Sudan), and on a racial basis, against indigenous African-led insurgents in Darfur, the Nuba Mountains and the Blue Nile.

The dramatic and relentless wars that this NIF regime has either escalated and/or initiated since 1989 have demoralised the fighting spirit of the army regulars as a result of the death toll and the injuries many of them have sustained. The general instability and lack of future prospect for ending them and allowing the soldiers to settle down with their families were a major concern for the soldiers. Finding ways to rebuild the morale of combatants, especially those from the Baggara tribes in South Darfur who actually constituted most of the fighters was of stategic importance to the government. The authorities started organising extensive public singing parties in Nyala where the most reputable and popular Hakkamat were brought to perform by singing and praising the army. The poetic diction and quality of the articulation of al-Hakkamat were manifested in celebrating the bravery of the *mujahidin*[1] and the martyrs. Their performance and speech enabled the recruitment of thousands of people into the PDF, especially the youngsters from Baggara tribes. The outcome proved their considerable influence on the youth and their unrivalled impact on military mobilisation, as clearly attested to by a journalist from Baggara:

> I have witnessed two battles and al-Hakkamat of the Rezeiqat of Ed Diein province were inciting their men to go to the south and to bring wealth, cows and weapons. This was an overt truth that cannot be denied. When the train comes to collect the youth from South Darfur to join the war in the south, the boys used to run away and hide, refusing to join the Popular Defence Force or the army forces. Surprisingly, their mothers, among them were Hakkamat, used to come out and sing encouraging them to go and eventually they go.[2]

General observations suggest that considerable numbers of the young Baggara men in Darfur rural areas have dropped out of education beyond primary school. This was corroborated by the findings of research conducted by Alex Cobham, which reveals that in 1993, the average literacy rate in Darfur was estimated at 44.4 per cent, 63.2 per cent for males and 24.0 per cent for females. In 2002, the average literacy was estimated at 38.6 per cent for males and 37.4 per cent for females, which indicates a 37.0 per cent decline in the males' literacy (Cobham, 2005).This retrogression re-echoes the trend of ruling elites' policy of keeping Darfur as a reservoir of army recruits.[3] Most of the Baggara youth have therefore joined either the tribes'

[1] Muslim fighters in the cause of Islam.
[2] Interview with a Ta'aishi journalist (R43), Nyala, 2006.
[3] The Sudanese army during the first civil war was predominantly Darfuris in its rank and file but exclusively riverain in the officer ranks (Harir, 1994, p. 155).

militias or the state army forces (as soldiers or paramilitary militia men) as the only source of subsistence available to them.

Obviously, al-Hakkamat's importance in mobilisation lies by and large in their ability to recreate in the army the same enthusiasm that they normally arouse in their own tribe/village audience. When they addressed the army soldiers, who share a similar cultural background to Baggara people, individually and collectively, the soldiers would be captivated by al-Hakkamat's voice and expression, which embody the faith in the tribe and other cultural motivations that al-Hakkamat can emphasise and solicit. This time al-Hakkamat were guiding them to an ally, the government. By virtue of their loyalty to al-Hakkamat, the soldiers would submit, obediently, to their will.

In line with this, accounts of a prominent Baggari man suggest that in the midst of the battlefield, al-Hakkamat's would dramatically visualise in the souls and minds of soldiers and combatants from Baggara Arab communities. They would often remind themselves of al-Hakkamah by saying, 'Hey, remember al-Hakkamah!' The man recounted that one of his friends was fighting in the civil war in South Sudan together with a colleague who was recognised as close kin to the famous late Ta'aisha Hakkamah, Bit Hassaan. During the fight, a kinsman of this Hakkamah often stood with an artillery gun (*doshka*), shooting, cheering them up and reminding them of Bit Hassaan. This often stirred up the soldiers' fighting spirit and spurred those lurking in trenches to carry on with the attack. This is because, as he explained, they were sure that their news would swiftly reach al-Hakkamah Bit Hassaan, and they would end up either celebrated as heroes, or publicised as cowards.[4]

Al-Hakkamat are never reluctant to acknowledge their contribution to such violence. On the contrary, they are ostentatious about their involvement; for instance, they admitted their proactive participation in the mobilisation campaign for the civil war in South Sudan against John Garang, the late SPLA/SPLM leader. Some of their recitations to that effect included the following:[5]

English
Tell him, the panic of women is little, mine is massive.
Soldiers changed tyres and fuelled up.
Loaded the canon gun and donned the G3 rifles.
The ram lambs of sacrifice who donate their souls.
These are the men of women who uphold their reputation; and return victorious.

Transliteration
gūl-lah, "hamm al-ʿawīn shiyyā, wa ʾannā hammī katīr".
ad-daysh ghayyaran ʿajalāt wa kabban banzīn.
shaḥanū al-mudfaʿ, ʾitwashshḥū al-jīm.
kubāsh ḍaḥiyyāh bi-l-rūḥ mutbariʿīn.
dawl rijāl ʿawīn, shāylīn l-simʿah, jaw fāyzīn.
(H. R20, G4, Nyala, 2006).

4 Interview with Ahmed Jowa (R14), radio and TV presenter from Ta'aisha, Nyala, 2006.

5 Recitation of Hubbania Hakkamah (R20) at group interview with Hakkamat (G4), Nyala, 2006.

Another Hakkamah has admitted her participation in encouraging men to join the army. She escorted the army when leaving to the south[6] and performed the following recitation:

English
Oh, soldiers! I miss you so dearly.
I wish to see the day you got into tanks, armed with bombs.
I would love to see the force ready for tomorrow.
Oh, soldiers, when will your month[7] come?
I'm so pleased with the soldiers.
They shouted *al-jalalah*,[8] and got armed.
Their speech provokes the horseman;
And embarrasses the coward.
I would like to go to the soldiers and sing for them overnight.
Oh, speeches that I am giving are plenty, not few.
Those who take part in the holy war, volunteering their lives, are sheep of sacrifice.
They will deliver victory, a hundred per cent!

Transliteration
garmānah laykū, yā al-ʿasākir.
yawm rikibtu ad-dabbābāt, silāḥku qanābil.
badūr ʾashūf al-qūwah lay wakit-hā yawman bākir.
al-dayyāshā mitayn shaharkū yagābil.
mabṣūṭā min rijāl al-daysh.
humm shālū al-jalālah, wey al-bijaynāh.
ḥadīthum lil-fāris bihīnah.
wā lil-baṭal biḥayyirah.
marādī namshī lil-jaysh naḥayyī layyā laylah.
wal-ḥadīth al-bagūlah katīr, mā shīya.
al-jiḥād mutbarriʿ bay ʿumrah, kabish ḍahiyyah.
jāyybīn al-naṣur miyyah fī al-miyyah.
(H. R32, Nyala, 2006).

Whilst al-Hakkamat's effort in mobilisation was distinctly useful for the government, it was detrimental to the Baggara community: whereas hundreds of men often responded to their appeal and join the fight, only twenty or thirty would come back alive. Ironically although al-Hakkamat are aware of the fatal consequences of their mobilisation for the sons of the Baggara tribes, which they have acknowledged in their recitations, they appear to encourage it remorselessly; as indicated in the recitation of a reputable Hakkamah below:[9]

English
The bridgers of the gap.
Oh, Company Commander; whose shoulders are fully decorated with his men.
The day you discharged your ammunition, al-Hakkamah joyfully ululated.
Oh, the victorious soldiers, thanks to Allah, you've arrived safe.
You never panicked, you just said we are ready.
You picked up your kit and rode with Azrā'il.[10]

[6] Interview with Hubbania Hakkamah (R32), Nyala, 2006.
[7] i.e. time of battle.
[8] i.e. ready to engage.
[9] Recitation of Ta'aishi Hakkamah (R37) at group interview with Hakkamat (G4), Nyala, 2006.
[10] Even though it is not mentioned in the Quran, Azrā'il is the popular name given to the 'angel of death' which is actually mentioned in the Quran, the angel who takes the souls

Oh, the day you left in hundreds, only to return in fifties.[11]
You endured a night when you ate bullets and drank benzene.

Transliteration
saddādīn al-khānā.
qāyid al-sirriyā, bay rijālak katfak malānah.
yawm ṣaraftū al-jabakhānāh, al-ḥakkāmah zaghradat farḥānah.
ḥimdillah bil-salāmah yā al-jayyāsha yā fāyzīn.
yawm mā hammakū gultū ʾanīnā ḥāḍrīn.
laffaytū al-nimrah, rikibtū maʿ ʾisrāʾīl.
yawm mashaytū miyyah, gabbaltū layy khamsīn.
ʿindaku laylah bi-tāklū raṣāṣ wa-b-tashrabū banzīn.
(H. R37, G4, Nyala, 2006).

Though al-Hakkamah, in her song above, is overwhelmed by joy seeing the combatants holding and firing weapons, a blur of grief and tears of sorrow seem to have permeated that joy when the harsh reality of sorrow unfolds. However, even if they have to lose all their fighters, it is incumbent on them to egg the fighters on for the honour of defending what they perceive as a legitimate cause. They glorify the state of violence, but they are also aware that many would die along the way and in this case, it appears only a few have returned (counted as fifty).

The observation of al-Hakkamat and their communities of such a massive loss of the lives of Baggara youth in this war is supported by the figures reported in the 'Black Book', which shows the number of martyrs from the civil war in South Sudan (Table 2.1). Those coming from South Darfur appear to represent the highest number among the three regions of Darfur and the rest of Sudan. In addition, as the Baggara population constitutes the largest single block of South Darfur population, these figures also suggest that the greatest number of recruits to the army from South Darfur have actually come from the Baggara ethnicity. Accordingly it would not falsify the truth to claim that most of the martyrs came from Baggara society.

MOBILISATION AGAINST DARFUR INSURGENCY

We have indicated in the previous section how the ruling elites expected al-Hakkamat to use racial and religious themes to demonise the armed insurgency in the 'Christian' south and mobilise warriors in the north against them, especially from Western Sudan. There was no way, however, that the NIF regime could invoke the same holy war agenda in Darfur, because the Darfuri insurgents are all Muslim; some of them had even subscribed to the same Islamist ideology as the NIF government. But they could still use racial ideology to equally devastating effect by conceptualising the conflict as a war of the (African) Zurga against the Arabs – a polarising discourse adopted by the pro-Arab

(contd) of all creatures. The figurative expression in the song simply means, 'riding with death', i.e. ready to sacrifice your lives.

[11] i.e. most died in battle.

Islamist government. By resorting to the racial tune, the government featured al-Hakkamat in the media and other public forums and gatherings on the premise that their appeal would be promptly responded to by the youth.

Nevertheless, it has been noticed that despite their active involvement at the inception of the campaign against the Darfuri insurgents, al-Hakkamat became less responsive to the government's anti-insurgents call against them. In a clear and striking manner, they refrained from using the inflammatory language that they used during the civil war in South Sudan. For instance, although they would describe the southern Sudanese as 'slaves' who ought to be conquered and subdued, their approach to Darfur has been different. They have reproached the Darfuris generally for waging war against the state. They might have opted for this line of argument just to go along with the government political discourse, on the one hand, and on the other to maintain some courtesy to the social ties that connect them with the societies to which the insurgents belong.

They labelled Darfuris as 'sons of the land' and demanded that they lay down arms and seek dialogue and negotiations to settle their differences, as it was shameful to fight one another. Although they entreated the insurgents to come to the table and submit to the logic of reason, they dared not mention the role played by the other party to the conflict, the government, as indicated in the recitation below:[12]

English
Shame on you, sons of the region, to revolt.
You've revolted,[13] forming your own forces.
When we asked and investigated, we were told they are native sons of the land.
Darfur turned into summer;[14] it needs magnanimity.
Life in this world is delusive; its sweetness is but incomplete!
He who enters the jungle[15] will only kill a brother, uncle and a cousin.
He strikes his neighbour and becomes stained with his blood.
Oh, people, repent! The house of darkness boasts with his mother.[16]

Transliteration
ḥarām ʿalayku ʿiyyāl al-balad titmarradū.
ʾal-shāyylīn al-silāḥ ʿamaltū laykū quwwā.
yawm saʾalnā wa ʾistafsarnā gālū laynā ʿiyyāl al-balad juwwā.
dārfawr ṣayyfat dāyraḥ marūwā.
al-dunniya gharrārah ḥilūwwahā mā b-intammā
al-khashshā al-ghābah baktul ʾakhū, baktul ʾammah, baktul wa-l-ḍamah.
ḍarab jārah wa-gamma milakhbaṭ bey-dammah.
yā nās ʾarjaʿū tūbū bayt al-ẓallām bitnabbar bi-ʾammah.
(H. R37, G4, Nyala, 2006).

Though scolding the Darfuri insurgents rather mildly has become a characteristic of al-Hakkamat's compositions, it is just a way of reinforcing the government's allegations and its mainstream of racial

[12] Recitation of Ta'aishi Hakkamah (R37) at group interview with Hakamat (G4), Nyala, 2006.
[13] i.e. taken up arms.
[14] i.e. it went through hard times.
[15] i.e. as an insurgent.
[16] i.e. when his mind is obstructed, evil prevails.

polarisation. Their ultimate goal, however, has been to demand that they submit to the calls for dialogue and reconciliation; as echoed in this recitation:[17]

English
Men of Darfur who invented schisms and horror!
Before the war in Darfur, we – both the Arab and Fur.
No one else ever tasted our nice coexistence:
We have our customs and traditions.
Those connect with these and these connect with those.
Those go to these and these come to those.
We have the hoe and we have the plough.
We have the farms and we have the gardens.
We have the male and female camels.
We have the cow and the ox.
And Allah complemented it for us with oil.
We don't differentiate between Arab and Fur.
Arms down! I don't want anyone to kill anyone else anymore.

Transliteration
yā rijāl dārfawr al-ʿamaltū al-bidaʿ wa-l-hawl.
ʾaniḥnā gabl al-ḥarib fī dārfawr, ʾanihnā al-ʿarab wa al-fawr.
ḥāltnā mā ḍāg-hā zawl.
ʾindanā ʿādāt wa taqālīd.
dawl yawāṣlū dawl, wā dawl yawāṣlū dawl.
wa dawl yamshū lay dawl, wa dawl yajū lay dawl.
ʿindannā al-jarrāyyah wa ʿindannā al-ṭurriyyah.
wa ʿindannā al-mazāriʿ, wa ʿindannā al-janāyyin.
wa ʿindannā al-nāgah wa al-jamal.
wa ʿindannā al-bagarah wa-l-tawr.
wa rabbī tammāhā laynā bi-l-bitrawl.
mā ʿindannā fariz bayn al-ʿarab wa al-fawr.
ʾarḍan silāḥ, ʾannā mā dāyyrah zawl yaktul zawl.
(H. R31, Nyala, 2006).

The imagery used tends to signify the subsistence tools of both parties to multiple conflicts: the hoe and the plough referring respectively to Fur farmers and Baggara Arab agro-pastoral farmers; and camels and oxen to Abbala and Baggara Arabs. The general import of the song is to remind them all of the past, often peaceful times they now wish to revive. In a different but not unrelated tone, another Hakkamah composed a verse that blames all the rebels equally and reminds them of the inhumane acts they have inflicted on people:[18]

English:
Peace be upon you, *Tora Bora*.[19]
Peace be upon you, Janjawiid.
Peace be upon you, Justice and Equality.[20]
Peace be upon you, Beshmirga.[21]
Wars are destructive; they destroyed the whole Sudan.
Wars are destructive; they killed our men.

[17] Interview with Hakkamah from Rezeiqat Mahriyah/Hemdaniya (R31), Nyala, 2006.
[18] Interview with Misseriya Hakkamah (R71), Nyala, 2006.
[19] i.e. nickname for the rebels.
[20] i.e. JEM, the rebel movement.
[21] Another reference to rebels.

Wars are destructive; they turned our women widows.
And displaced our kids.
Oh, they razed down *al-khalawi* and overwhelmed our minds.
Common brothers; oh, common old men,
Set your hearts in quiet mood.
Stay at home for us.
Don't cause us wars.
Don't block the roads.[22]
If you meet a brother in the meadows, don't fight him as you do the Jews.
Anything God brought unto us would heal with time (a reminder!)

Transliteration
al-salāmu 'alaykum yā ṭurrā bawrā.
al-salāmu 'alaykum yā jānjawīd.
al-salāmu 'alaykum yā 'adl wā musāwāh.
al-salāmu 'alaykum yā bāshmirgā.
al-ḥurūb damār, dammaran laynā al-Sūdān 'āmm.
al-ḥurūb damār katalan laynā al-rijāl.
al-ḥurūb damār 'armalan laynā al-niswān.
wey, sharradan laynā al-'iyyāl.
wey, tashtashan laynā al-khalāwī, shālan laynā al-bāl.
ta'ālū yā 'akhwān; way; ta'ālū yā al-rijāl al-kubār.
khuttu laynā al-gulūb.
'ag'udū laynā fawq al-biyūt
wa mā tasabbibū laynā al-ḥūrūb.
wa mā tamsikū laynā al-ṭurūg.
'akhuku kan ligitū fawg al-khalā, mā tajāhdū mujāhadat al-yahūd.
'ayyi shay' rabbannā jābah, bi zamānah bi-fūt.
(H/S. R71, Nyala, 2006).

The political rhetoric of the government's politics and views against the international aid providers and workers who have responded to the humanitarian appeals to help the victims of war in Darfur also found its way in al-Hakkamat expressions. Their dynamic presence in the scene was shown through the recitation below:[23]

English
Oh Darfur, peace be upon you.
I've a word to say to you; please do think of it carefully.
Darfur has gone astray; bring it back.
Let it calm down; unite your word.
It contains criminals who might destroy the land.
By *jalalah*[24] and *takbeer*,[25] we protect Darfur
Lest non-Muslims get in.[26]

Transliteration
salāmu 'alayk yā Dārfawr.
'indī kilmah bagūlha, 'a'glawhā.
Dārfawr kānat ṣāyha; Dārfawr gabilūha.
'agaw'du tiḥit; kilmitkū waḥḥidūhā.
fīhā majārmah, lil-balad bikharbūhah.
bil-jalāhah wal-takbīr Dārfawr bi-naḥmūhah.

22 i.e. by laying an ambush.
23 Interview with Hubbania Hakkamah (R32), Nyala, 2006.
24 Jalla jalalah is a religious expression meaning 'may His glory be exalted', and is said repeatedly in supplication.
25 A religious expression meaning 'God is great'.
26 i.e. aid organisations and intervention from the international community.

min al-kuffār mā yadkhulūhah.
(H. R32, Nyala, 2006).

In 2012, the government planned for an extensive youth recruitment-ment campaign amongst the Arabs in Darfur against the insurgents who were still active in Darfur. Their plan involved using al-Hakkamat to mobilise Arab communities in South and West Darfur. Subsequently, the governing authority of Nyala organised a tour for a group of powerful Hakkamat from South Darfur region to *Dar* Masalit, the region of West Darfur that has been in violent armed conflict since 1996 between the Masalit and the newly dispersed Chadian Arabs in the region. Some of the most renowned and influential Hakkamat, e.g. al-Batail, Maryam al-Gheerah and another Hakkamah nicknamed al-Computer were among the delegates. Their mission was to mobilise the Arab community and they were therefore made to deliver public speeches and perform songs and recitations urging the audience to respond to the government's appeal. Their visit was said to have made significant impact, as hundreds from the Arab ethnicity attended their performances (Zakariya, 2012). This visit and similar others echoed the earlier tours of al-Hakkamat in Darfur when they were used for the first time by the Darfur governor in 1992, in the campaign to confiscate illicit weapons from people in rural areas that were used by groups of bandits to attack travellers.

ESCORTING THE ARMY

During conflicts and disputes between tribes, al-Hakkamat reportedly escorted the horsemen and become complicit in raiding villages to loot them or, allegedly, in pursuit of thieves and/or repelling attacking aggressors. In such situations, al-Hakkamah might be armed, riding a horse and partaking in the shooting. During these adventures she might be killed or taken captive.[27] In 2006, Hakkamah and a group of horsemen, out looting, burning and killing people in a Fur village in South Darfur, were captured by government authorities. She was prosecuted and sentenced to death.[28]

Two other Hakkamat were also arrested around the village of Giraida, South Darfur, whilst escorting thousands of Janjawiid troops who had stolen over six hundred cattle and killed thirty people from Umm Balola village on Friday, 27 January 2006 and eleven more from Ibdoos village on the following day.[29] South Darfur court records in Nyala show that during 2002 and 2003, several cases of Hakkamat involved in violent incidents and raids were brought before the courts, and the accused were all prosecuted (see Table 7.1).

[27] Group and individual interviews, Nyala, 2006.
[28] Interviews, Nyala, 2006. Also appears in Nyala Court documents, 2006.
[29] *The News* [online], available at: <www.sudaneseonline.com/anews2006/jan28 48927> [accessed 29 January 2006].

Table 7.1 Hakkamat tried at Nyala Court, South Darfur (2002–3)

Court case number and trial date	*Name of accused*	*Legal codes of prosecution*	*Remarks*
No.: 66/2002 Date: 27 July 2002	Mariam Adam Azrag Age: 30 years Tribe: Sa'ada Village: Jabra District: Mirshing	26/42/21/175/ 69/68/130 21: criminal complicity 26/42: possession of weapons and arms 175: armed robbery 69: nuisance and threatening the peace 168: participation in violent conflict 130: homicide Sentenced to death	The claimant was Ahmad Ali Osman from Fur tribe who lives in Jabra village, on the outskirts of Mirshing district. Fur and Sa'ada had resided in the village for a long time. An unknown group of people stole 65 cows from Hajj Osman Dorain from Sa'ada (Arab) and Fur people were accused. Sons and kin of Dorain went out for *Faza'* on Thursday raiding and burning Jabra village, and killing its people. Fourteen were arrested including Hakkamah, Mariam Azrag, nicknamed Mariam Zakheerah (literally translated as 'munitions'), who was on horseback trilling and inciting the horsemen.
No.: 26/2002 Date: 10 March 2002	Fatumah Musa Abdel-Rahim Age: 25 years Tribe: Sa'ada Village: Kajikaji District: Kass	168/130/107 168: armed conflict 130: homicide 107: concealing crime	No detailed information was found.
No.: 5/2003 Date: 30 December 2002	Fatma al-Doom Adam Age: 18 years Village: Singita District: Kass	21/42/175/139/130. 21: criminal complicity 42: possession of weapons 175: armed robbery 139: causing severe harm 130: homicide	Al-Hakkamah accompanied the horsemen from various Arab groups (the majority from Ta'alba and Tergam) raiding the Singita village of Fur, killing forty-one and burning the entire village. She incited her attacking companions by ululating. Thirty-eight of her companions were sentenced to death by hanging.

(*Source*: Nyala Police Court Records, as accessed June 2006)

Al-Hakkamat's engagement in violence and aggression and their conduct received inconsistent assessment from the authorities, however. Those who escorted tribal militias in raiding and looting were charged with complicity and prosecuted as criminals, whereas those who escorted the pro-government militias and army forces inciting them to commit similar acts were endorsed by the authorities. The latter constituted the genuine fulfilment by al-Hakkamat of their obligations, especially with regard to promoting the government's position in the war, and were therefore endorsed and blessed.

Speaking, singing and composing as the basic components of al-Hakkamat's performance have become cemented by the dynamic of conflict incidents in Darfur and al-Hakkamat's proactive engagement in them, especially when escorting militias and/or soldiers. Their poetic and singing presentations have steadily become a ceremonial farewell feature in the departure of army troops to the battlefields in the south.[30] Four prestigious Hakkamat unveiled the fact that many Hakkamat have actually escorted army commanders and troops to points outside the perimeter of Nyala, either to bid farewell to departing army forces, or to receive combatants returning from the battlefield and to celebrate their victory and heroism.

Many Hakkamat took an active part in the reception and hosting of groups of soldiers, PDF and PPF, when they returned from fighting against the Bolad insurgency. Their reception was organised under the shadows of huge trees in a place called Sineetah, near Nyala town. Al-Hakkamat donated two cows and spent a couple of days in the village, helping the men to cook. They also went to Raja to congratulate the army brigadier general on his victory over the SPLA. They travelled in two military aircraft to see the dead of the enemy, the SPLA. When they came back, they went to the general's house and organised a party where they sang in celebration of his heroism.[31] At this occasion one Hakkamah delivered the following recitation:[32]

English
You who plugs the pits of shame with the palms of your hand.
You, the horseman who offers dinner to birds,[33] my wish is to sing for you.
Gallantry and generosity are kin[34] to you.
He is a strong male; he's worth of nobility as a gift.
The day the horses race for him,[35] the horseman longingly kills, like a lion.

Transliteration
saddād nugār al-ʾayb bay kufāf ʾīdayk.
al-fāris al-bi-ghadī al-ṭayr, marādī ʾaghanī layk.
al-rajālah wa al-jūd nisbah layk.
dā ḍakar miʿaytib, al-ḥasab layyā hadiyyāh.
yawm al-khayl ʾiṭṭāradan layyā, al-fāris baktul garīb lī-shawk dūdan layyah.
(H. R32, Nyala, 2006).

30 Group and individual interviews, Nyala, 2006.
31 Interview with Hakkamat (G4), Nyala, 2006.
32 Interview with Hubbania Hakkamah (R32), Nyala, 2006.
33 i.e. kills the enemy, leaving their corpses as nourishment for birds.
34 i.e. belong.
35 i.e. the enemy chases him.

Four other Hakkamat also accompanied the army to Torit, further south, during the civil war. They departed from Nyala in military aircraft and were joined by a large number of army forces and high-ranking officers of the Popular Police Forces (PPF). The latter has recently become in charge of al-Hakkamat. Upon arrival, some Hakkamat recited in praise of the army. Below is an example:[36]

English
The forces marched out and the mother of two feet[37] was hovering over.
The hawk pointed at al-Hakkamah and said: 'I don't want lean bodies,
I'd like to have the obese whose fat leaks.'
The Moral Orientation instructed the brigade (to fulfil the hawk's desire).
Oh, don't bother.
The 'army of the west'[38] kick their enemy as though they play volleyball.

Transliteration
al-quwwah maragat wa ʾamm gadamayn ḥāyymā.
kilding shāwar al-ḥakkāmah gāl layhā al-bāṭil mānī dāyrah.
ʾannā badūr al-samīn abū dihnan sāylah.
al-tawjīh al-maʿnawī wajjah al-sirayyāt.
jaysh al-gharbiyyah mā tasāʾlah.
bilʿabu bil-ʿadu kūrā ṭāyrah.
(H. R32, Nyala, 2006).

Another Hakkamah reaffirmed that when the fighters came back to the airport, she praised the commander of the army forces by composing and reciting:[39]

English
Oh, Commander Hafiz, the lion of the meadow.
You've inherited generosity and open-handedly from your mother and father.
You are but the one-week moon that sparkles up in the sky.
The autumn, which fills up the streams.
Oh, tonight my conscience is so pleased.

Transliteration
Janābū Ḥāfiẓ ʾasad al-gardūd.
al-karam wa-l-jūd, shiltahum min ummak wa ʾabūk
ʾintā gamar al-sabūʿ al-fawg al-samā mawjūd
al-kharīf al-malā al-rihūd
al-laylah al-ḍamīr mabṣūṭ
(H. R51, Nyala, 2006).

Escorting fighters to the battlefield seems to be the greatest honour, and a platform for the pinnacle manifestation of al-Hakkamat's agency and power. The accounts of most of the renowned Hakkamat testified to their participation, in one way or another, in the Raja battle and others. The chairperson of the Union of Art and Folklore (UAF) in South Darfur told me that forty Hakkamat took part in this final battle

[36] Interview with Hubbania Hakkamah (R32), Nyala, 2006.
[37] i.e. the hawk.
[38] Army stationed in Darfur.
[39] Interview with Salami Hakkamah (R51), Nyala, 2006.

and all documented their experience with recitations like those cited above.[40]

Paradoxically, by escorting the army al-Hakkamat breached the 1991 Public Order Act that was introduced by the Islamist NIF government. The Act plainly curtails women's freedom of movement and provides their travel be escorted by a male blood relative[41] (Burr and Collins, 1999). This restriction on women is, indeed, guided by the Quran, which urges women to 'remain in your houses' and never come out unless it is absolutely necessary (Abdalla, 1987, p. 341). The clear prejudice of the authorities in the discriminatory exemption of al-Hakkamat from such a condition lies within the general premise that the governing and the ruling elites can simply override shari'a law and norms when they collide with the fulfilment of their own vested interests.

Furthermore, during an investigation of human rights abuses in Darfur by Amnesty International in 2003, female victims in Deisa village said, 'Arab women were accompanying the attackers singing songs in praise of the government and encouraging the attackers'. The Darfuri refugees called al-Hakkamat the Janjawiid women. Several testimonies have also signalled the part that al-Hakkamat played in communicating information to their leaders during the attacks and their direct involvement in looting the villages. Victims have also accused al-Hakkamat of verbally harassing and insulting them (Amnesty International, 2004b).

This profile of al-Hakkamat's engagement in violence and atrocities perpetrated against women of other ethnicities demonstrates their ethnic zealotry and rather blind loyalty. Thus prompted, they condoned and encouraged acts of gender-based violence against others just because they did not share the same ethnicity, race and/or political ideology. Al-Hakkamat, submissively or otherwise, have ironically allowed the ruling elites to earn their allegiance and moral commitment and to reinforce this sinister aspect of their spirit. They have exercised no self-restraint or self-censorship to limit the harmful impact of their engagement with the government. It was obvious that this would lead to the destruction of social coexistence in the Darfur community, destruction that would most severely affect women – the human group with which they ought to share sympathy and empathy.

Al-Hakkamat's involvement with armed forces does not seem to be a novelty among rural African women, however. Spirit mediums in Zimbabwe also escorted rebels in support of their nationalist struggle to liberate their land from the invading whites. They accompanied them to show them inlets and outlets of forests and woods and to advise and protect them from natural hazards and from the enemy. The struggle was worthy of the sacrifice of their own lives, young as well as old. But al-Hakkamat's involvement in these wars falls short of being patriotic as they were not standing in confrontation against the invaders of their land. Besides, the situation created also posed the same risk to them as to their communities. Al-Hakkamat have only been used and abused for evil

[40] Interview with Ali Noah Nyala, 2009.

[41] Mahram, in Islamic culture/jurisprudence.

purposes by the government and the Hakkamat institution itself, with no ethical restraint whatsoever.

PROVIDING FOOD

As soon as they became militarised, al-Hakkamat were requested to enhance the government's logistical war campaigns by contributing to *Zad al-Mujahid*[42] for the Jihad campaign that was launched by the NIF government in 1991.[43] Ever since, the practice has been an enforced customary contribution on the community to aid the government of Sudan in mobilising resources, especially food rations and fodder for the horses and camels of the fighters, i.e. the militias. For instance, al-Hakkamat supplied sustenance to government combatants – army soldiers and horsemen who fought in Raja and other battlefields. These fighters were recruited from other Darfur areas and often encamped in Nyala on their way to the battlefield.

The food contribution was identified to include ingredients such as *kisra*,[44] dried vegetables, *damsoro*,[45] grains, millet, tea, etc. Sometimes the PPF would provide al-Hakkamat and al-Sheikhat with ingredients such as flour for making *kisra*. The PDF imposed compulsory donations on the community and each *harah* (neighbourhood) was instructed to offer a sack of grain. Al-Hakkamat and al-Sheikhat were tasked by the authorities with raising these quantities.[46]

Al-Hakkamat and al-Sheikhat were also made responsible for supplying rations, food and accommodation for the horsemen (who were often invited from rural areas to formal occasions in Nyala), and for their horses, too. Many Hakkamat and Sheikhat confirmed that they often resorted to peer groups for collecting money and food items, and might organise joint cooking in the UHS office even though some would prefer to work from home. Five Hakkamat revealed that in 2006 alone they repeatedly received horsemen in Nyala. Despite the fact that al-Hakkamat were always keen to make contributions to the army, these revelations suggest that they were actually unhappy with at least some of the added roles that they are now required to undertake.

On the other hand, the MCI, al-Hakkamat's main guardian, frequently seemed not to have been fully engaged in the politics surrounding the relationship between those institutions of power and al-Hakkamat. Besides, some officers tended to be indignant at the obligations on al-Hakkamat's shoulders. Al-Hakkamat have, notwithstanding, carried on fufilling these obligations despite their awareness that the degree to which they were required to meet the government demands has not been well defined, as could be gleaned from the following revelation from al-Hakkamah:

[42] i.e. Muslim fighters' food rations.
[43] Group (G1, G2, G4) and individual interviews, Nyala, 2006.
[44] i.e. dried pancakes.
[45] A famous local recipe in Darfur using dry ground dura or millet thick pancakes mixed with groundnuts, salt and sugar; a small portion of it can make a whole meal, to which you only need to add water.
[46] Group interview with Hakkamat and Sheikhat (G3), Nyala, 2006.

> We are the people who offer help any time; if there are wounded, we will attend to them; if there was an occasion and people asked us to cook, we would cook for them; we have become part of the government. Wherever the government want us to go, we will go and will not argue with them; we are at their disposal. If they ask us to vote for them, we will do and if they ask us to side with the government we will. We will do everything for our government.[47]

Apparently, this uncompromising loyalty that al-Hakkamat pledged to the government constitutes a crossroads in perceptions of al-Hakkamat and their relationships with other people in the region, especially the government's opponents and those ethnicities that the government discriminated against on racial grounds. The government must have realised that this Samaritan soul of al-Hakkamat was worth optimal exploitation; as such exploitation is indeed, advantageous to their current and future plans. Al-Hakkamat have also reacted positively and consciously in good faith, proving their integrity and allegiance. This affectional relationship with the government has paved the way for Hakkamat to situate themselves firmly within formal political institutions, the military in particular. They have learned to manoeuvre political acts and succeed in conducting politics at a pace and scope that other Darfuri women, especially educated urban politicians, have been unable to accomplish.

MOBILISING WOMEN

The role of al-Hakkamat in mobilisation for government is not merely confined to military recruiting and associated war activities, but extends to other activities, such as election campaign and help in soliciting votes. It has been al-Hakkamat's duty, together with al-Sheikhat, to mobilise women and appeal for them to show up during elections and when officials pay visits to rural villages and Baggara camps. Women would often respond more readily to such appeals from Hakkamat than to a summons from any city-based women's organisation established and led by educated women, such as the Sudanese Women's Union,[48] the women's wing of the NIF government which has branches in rural areas.

Three Hakkamat have thus claimed that, since the 1990s, they have been contributing, through the PIM, to election campaigns organised by the government and have been able to sway the political opinion of people in rural areas to the government's advantage, especially during the presidential elections in 1999. Thus, it could be suggested quite credibly that al-Hakkamat's position and value in their own settings are so embedded that they have almost monopolised the *informal* status of gatekeepers, not only as far as women are concerned but in the entire rural community. This of course dwarfs any leverage that outsider government-sponsored women's organisations could dream of exerting. Government officials have invariably found them irreplaceable in achieving successful campaigns and have hence become considerably reliant on them.

[47] Interview with Misseriya Hakkamah (R71), Nyala, 2006.
[48] Group (G3, G4) and individual interviews, Nyala, 2006.

Al-Hakkamat's efficiency in mobilising people for the government's particular interests and the respect rendered to their appeals have unfolded significantly during campaigns that the ruling elites have been launching since the early 1990s to influence the huge presence of rural-based Baggara society in Nyala. Al-Hakkamat were further used to mobilising women in Nyala and the surrounding villages when their influence proved to override that of local women's organisations. This was relevant in September 2005, when the governor of South Darfur demanded both the Youth Union and UHS to call for a public meeting for all women in Nyala. His intention was to explore women's potential to mend the social fabric that was torn apart by the vicious war. Within two days, al-Hakkamat succeeded in mustering more than three thousand women, thus revealing their enormous capacity and influence in mobilising women.[49]

On the other hand, ordinary women in Darfur face many challenges that macerate their capacity for participation in the public domain, and restrain their development. Meeting senior government officials and influential figures, such as the governor, could have served as a valuable opportunity for them to raise concerns about their perceived needs in education, health and sustainable livelihoods. Yet neither the women nor al-Hakkamat were able to voice such concerns or make their voice heard before the governor.

Besides, although al-Hakkamat tend to share such concerns with women, they have not endeavoured to address them through speech, composing and/or symbolic protesting. Their obvious concern, in the town, is now to comply with the government: as articulated by al-Hakkamah, 'We will do everything for our government'. It follows that al-Hakkamat in town may not have been as forthcoming and positively vocal about the wellbeing of their own gender and community as they were about standing for positions dictated by the government, with whom they now have developed a strong patron–client relationship. This relationship seems to have shifted the focus of al-Hakkamat from serving society at large and/or becoming advocates for women's rights, to following their own personal interests.

ENGAGING WITH OFFICIAL EVENTS

The obligations of al-Hakkamat included attending government public and official events, where they composed and recited in praise of prominent officials and cooked and organised receptions in coordination with al-Sheikhat. They also participated in other social ceremonies organised by the authorities, such as mass circumcision and national celebrations, such as Eid or the Birthday of the Prophet Mohamed.[50] It has become

[49] Interview with a government employee from Fur (R41), Nyala, 2006.

[50] Group interviews with Hakkamat (G4), Nyala, 2006. The NIF government has been organising mass circumcision ceremonies for boys in attempt to garner social back up to sustain their power.

quite noticeable in Nyala that al-Hakkamat usually take the lead at these public occasions, which are organised in open public yards.

At these occasions, the presence of al-Hakkamat has often served to create a persuasive image of popular support for the regime as their presence often encouraged large groups of audiences, particularly from the Baggara communities, to attend. Also by singing, they have tried to raise the profile of government public figures whose prestige has suffered, creating an image that has seemed more acceptable to the audience. In these undertakings, al-Hakkamat were usually accompanied by Sheikhat who would carry the special flag of their respective neighbourhoods and *Dallookah*.[51] Normally, a group of young girls from the neighbourhood would accompany al-Sheikha as a chorus, singing and dancing at the reception.[52] Below is an example of Hakkamah praising al-Tayeb Sikhah, then governor of the state of Darfur:[53]

English
Peace be upon you, the Governor of the region.
You who fought bullet firing[54] and sitting at the bar.[55]
You took care of the widow and the orphan, from the very beginning.
But your Sheikha is aggrieved; your Hakkamah's freedom is suppressed.
Your Sheikha is lifting up the flag; she welcomes the visitor without knowing.[56]
Your Hakkamah has a role – she elevates some and degrades some.
She elevates the horseman who has a poisonous canine and a spiked blood-covered spear.
The day the calamity struck, he boasted of the females of his tribe.[57]

Transliteration
salām ʿalayk yā ʾintā wālī al-wilāyyah.
al-ḥārabta, ḍarabta al-raṣṣāṣah wa jalsat al-ʾandāyyah.
naẓarta lil-ʾarmal wā al-ʾatīm fī ʾawwal al-bidāyyah.
lākin shaykhtak maẓlūmah, wā ḥakkāmtak ḥurriyyat-hā maktūmah.
shaykhtak rāfaʿah al-ʿalam; gābalat al-zāyir ghayr mā yaʿlam.
ḥakkāmtak layha dawr; rafʿat zawl, wā ramat zawl.
rafaʿat al-fāris abū faṭran bay simmah, wā abū kawkāban bay dammah.
yawm jāt al-ḥārrah, ʾitnabr bay gabīlat banat ʿammah.
(H. R4, G4, Nyala, 2006).

Mostly self-explanatory like this one, their poems are intended to raise the profile of the regime, the governing elites and the officials among Baggara communities, not only in Darfur but across all Sudan. Al-Hakkamat were summoned several times to Khartoum to sing at conferences organised by the federal authorities. This new representation of al-Hakkamat reinforces the general perception that they have become transformed into a political icon associated with the state's national institutions of power, a state of prestige that has paradoxically weakened their

51 A drum made locally from wood, mud and leather, and normally played only by women.
52 Group (G2, G3, G4) and individual interviews, Nyala, 2006.
53 Recitation of Salami Hakkamah (R4) at group interview with al-Hakkamat, Nyala, 2006.
54 i.e armed robbery.
55 i.e. drinking alcohol.
56 i.e. prepares for their visit.
57 i.e. swore to fight head on.

local worth and social significance.[58] The comments made below tend to reflect the general indignation felt by the Baggara people about the conduct of al-Hakkamat:

> By taking her away from the tribe and the village and away from speaking out about the beauty of nature and the values of generosity and open-handedness, the regime has killed the nice picture that al-Hakkamah was recognised by. She has now become seen just as a *political* person who plays a political game in favour of the state.[59]

Having heard such a reaction and other similar ones, it was unsurprising that al-Hakkamat who were recruited and used by the government in town have been virtually isolated from their local and rural constituency, as they have now lost a large portion of their genuine rural audience and old loyal supporters. For tribes that have had Hakkamat speaking on their behalf for as long as they could remember, their town-based Hakkamat have ironically now become entangled in an unenviable situation of extolling the virtues of the ruling NCP/NIF and governing elites, to whom many if not all of their tribal affiliates might actually be opposed.[60] Inevitably, such a trend will undermine the credibility of the purebred authentic Hakkamat.

Furthermore, those Hakkamat have lost the sympathy of rural-based women who contributed significantly to their creation and development. It is for this reason alone that they now appear to have lost connection with the values and the presumed authenticity of al-Hakkamah as an institution. Pointing at such engagement of the town-based Hakkamat, a Rezeiqi university graduate disapprovingly argued:

> This is just a government's discourse which we don't care about. As a tribe, we no longer care about this Hakkamah, because we normally care about encouraging the horseman, glorifying and singing for the generous man and for the genuine fighter who protects us, protects our heritage, our wealth and our land. But, this Hakkamah sings for the state, which does not concern us as a tribe and therefore, she finds herself isolated. The government just used her to promote their campaign and to show their ability in influencing people, but they do not care about the wellbeing of the community and how they survive.[61]

As the comments highlight, the co-option of al-Hakkamat, and the utilitarian contributions they have made to the aggression and ethnic wars of the ruling and governing elites, did not bring dividends to the Baggara communities in Darfur, either in social services or in terms of economic aid. Inversely, they have begun to suffer the repercussions of violence and degraded welfare, both at individual and community levels. In the end, the ruling elites have perpetuated the vulnerability of not only the vast majority of the African ethnicities in Darfur, but more severely of the Baggara community as well.

[58] Group and individual interviewes, Nyala, 2006.
[59] Interview with Mohamed Salih (R12), radio and TV presenter from Shoba tribe, Nyala, 2006.
[60] The vast majority of the Baggara belong to the Ansar (Partisans) Sect and therefore stand in opposition to the NIF-led government, at least politically.
[61] Interviews with a Rezeiqi government employee (R5), Nyala, 2006.

CONCLUSION

Having been co-opted and appropriated to serve the government politics and policies, al-Hakkamat became engaged in organised duties and obligations that transformed them into actors with an obsession for establishing their status within the government domain and to earn the officials' sympathy and admiration. Through the process, they have become trapped in a complex political setting that has forced them, consciously or unconsciously, to overlook the values, ethics and issues of concern for the village and tribe. They ventured into adopting a fairly new language in order to fit with urban politics and politicians.

Their new context in the town has hampered and stilted their spontaneity and imagination. Noteably, it has influenced a change in the conventional diction of their poetry and reduced its authenticity. The newly engineered style has marred their speech and compositions with lifeless imagination, and diction overloaded with Islamic NCP/NIF slogans and flattery of people just because of their status as officials or politicians, rather than their qualities or recognised achievements.

In addition, by attending to these duties, a more belligerent voice of al-Hakkamat and their warmongering status has become reinforced and heightened. Their reputation and agency have in turn suffered tremendously in the eyes of their tribespeople. They have become identified as mere government instruments with little independence to resist temptation and/or to develop and impose their own perception, the agency for which they were so well recognised back in the village or camp.

On the other hand, inability and indifference have unfolded in al-Hakkamat's attitudes to women's concerns and rights, as throughout their recent political incarnation they have stood little chance of promoting the rights of women. Their disengagement from the issue of rights has tended to cast a shadow on their prospects for becoming advocates for peace and/or human rights in Darfur and in Sudan at large. Considering the status quo, transforming them into a positive voice seems to be more of wishful than a probable objective. This, however, should not detract from their agency to influence positive discourse when the right motivations have developed and the environment has become conducive.

8

Roles in Peace and Reconciliation

Investigating violent armed conflict and wars in Sudan has revealed that rural women, Darfuris in particular, were most affected; women became vulnerable victims of the atrocities of war, including gender-based violence that left women at the head of 70 per cent of households (El Hassan, 2008). This bitter experience undoubtedly makes them the most aspirant gender to stop war in favour of reconciliation and peace. Al-Hakkamat's tremendous contribution to inciting conflict, making war and creating dire situations that primarily affect women presupposes a pivotal need for their engagement in reconciliation and peace processes. However, they have been ordinarily dissociated from peace initiatives attempted in Darfur as we now going to explain.

WOMEN AND AL-HAKKAMAT IN PEACE AND RECONCILIATION

The people of Darfur, according to the prevailing culture in most African societies, have their own historical indigenous mechanisms for conflict resolution and resettlement of disputes locally referred to as *Ajaweed* (single: *Ajwadi*), which functions as a native arbitration court/council dealing with individual and tribal conflict. It is one of the lasting cultures that still prevails in Darfur.

The *Ajaweed* comprises a voluntary group of wise elderly men who are skilful, knowledgeable and well versed in various aspects of the society. They use their lifelong expertise and persuasive abilities to advocate instantly and to impartially resolve conflicts between tribes or among individuals that are brought to their attention. The council runs its activities through a meeting board called *judiyah* (traditional mediation). In their arbitrations, the *judiyah* is guided by the local customs and norms, known as ʾaʿrāf (conventions), or *rākūbah* (shelter). These conventions and customs have the Canon of *Dali* (*Qanoon Dali*) or *Dali* Code as a common legislative reference adopted during the Fur sultanate in which local customs are incorporated with the Islamic shari'a commandments (Mohamed and Badri, 2005, p. 52; Kamal El-Din, 2007, pp. 93–4).

During the colonial period (1921–33), the government introduced the so-called 'government-sponsored *judiyah*' as part of the newly introduced native administration system in which the Nazir, the Omda and the Sheikh were included as members. Despite this interference, by and large the *Ajaweed* retained its structure and mechanism, as the governmental presence was only nominal. It carried on in that manner until the 1970s when the *judiyah* was weakened; it has ever since become ineffective in addressing conflicts between tribes and ethnic groups (Mohamed and Badri, 2005, p. 53).

No matter what skills, experience or knowledge they possess, Darfuri rural women, including al-Hakkamat, are neither formally included in the *judiyah* or the *Ajaweed* forum, nor are they represented in government formal reconciliation initiatives. Though women were empowered and represented at the highest echelon of the Fur sultanate, the nature of the *judiyah* contrasts with the mainstream of the sultanate, which treated women respectfully and promoted their position in social and political domains. The reasons for this institutional failure are the obligations shouldered on women, who are farmers and hard workers, which make them unable to show up or uninterested; and the attitudes of men, who might think that women are not good at conversing with them on serious issues.

Women are thus forced to isolate themselves, thereby confirming the prevailing patriarchal attitudes about their communication skills. They are perceived, by default, to be incapable of participation by virtue of the gender division of labour and the notion that public decision making is a private man's domain and business. Besides, there are still some men who believe that these native male-led institutions do actually solicit women's opinions from within the private domain and take them on board. In the Nuba Mountains, for instance, another conflict zone in Sudan, the Sheikhat, who are recognised as powerful and charismatic, have been able, after an initial rejection, to force their membership in the *Ajaweed* councils and participate in resolving disputes between tribes. Sometimes they organise meetings in their own houses to settle family disputes (Rahama and Elhussein, 2005, p. 105).

Among the vast majority of rural women in Darfur, however, al-Hakkamat are recognised to have undertaken only a marginal, yet a symbolic, role in supporting resolution conferences; perhaps in keeping with typical perceptions of women as attached to the domestic services of venue organisation and hospitality. On a few occasions, Hakkamat were invited to celebrate agreements reached and to give encouraging speeches to embolden attendees' resolve and commitment to the deals. Arguably, there is more substantive value to the presence of al-Hakkamat. They were considered informal guarantors of the outcomes of the *judiyah*, as the conflicting parties who might refrain from adhering to the terms agreed could instantly be slandered by these Hakkamat. In a reconciliation conference held to resolve a conflict between the Daju and Bani Helba and the surrounding tribes in al-Hijair al-Abyad in 2005, one Hakkamah from the Hubbania addressed the audience in what seemed to be an expression of the government's view:[1]

English
Peace be upon you, brothers.
I've come to you from Buram;[2] You who are feuding among yourselves.
You'd better sharpen your long spears and wear your spiritual charms.
Beware the enemy lurking there will come to you.

Transliteration
al-salāmū ʿalaykū yā ʾikhwān
anā jītkū min Burām, yā l-bi-tanghashshū fī baʿaḍkū
ʾintū sinnū shalakū, wa ʾalbasū warakū
fī gabīlah ʿadū baʿīd hināk tarā bi-talḥakū
(H. R32, Nyala, 2006).

She warned them of the threat looming from the south (the then South Sudan SPLA) and encouraged them to put aside their internal petty disputes in favour of the looming threat.

In other dispute settlement events, the organisers asked al-Hakkamat to address the opening of the conference proceedings, where they appealed to the assembly to maintain unity and solidarity and cheered the anticipated reconciliation. This approach was adopted in the conferences held to resolve disputes between Hubbania and Fellata in 2004, and between Birgid, Daju and Misseriya in March 2006 in the village of Nittaigah in South Darfur. In the latter conference, the Misseriya Ageed invited ten Hakkamat. At the onset of the conference, they recited and sang for the participants, urging them to discuss peacefully and reconcile.[3] The following is a typical recitation of Hakkamah on such occasions:

English
If water becomes turbid, it will be filtered.
The *Misseri* rode the blue-eyed broad-chested male, holding a loaded gun.
The Birgidawi said, 'O look brother, he was enticing us'.
The Dijawi said, 'Oh, we will not host you, never again'.
Tell them my companions, 'Oh, dear, why did you destroy your land and cause your heart to pang'.

Transliteration
al-mī kān ʿikir bi-l-ṣaffā.
al-misīrī rikib l-ḍakar ʾabb ʿaynan zargā,ʾabū tiris, ʾabū lūzāt, al-khāttī l-jabakhānah.
wa-l-birgidāwī gāl battān ʾikhwānī dā fawgnā khassāh.
wa-l-dīgāwī dā battan maʿānā hinā dā mā bi-tindassā.
gūl layhum siyyād l-rafag, mālkū kharabtū baladkū, wa galbukū khaffā.
(H. R32, Nyala, 2006).

This Hakkamah claimed that following her keynote recitation, the leaders vowed not to cause anybody any more grief as a result of losing beloved ones in fighting. An excited man stood up and swore the oath of divorce: 'By divorce, we will not let the enemy come between us anymore';

[1] Interview with Hubbania Hakkamah (R32), Nyala, 2006.
[2] District in South Darfur, which is the main centre of Bani Helba tribe.
[3] Recited by a Hubbania Hakkamah (R32), Nyala, 2006.

a solemn pledge that will not only bind this man to realising peace, but also hold others to account for any failure to realise the substance of such undertaking.

Al-Hakkamat have thus proved their ability to communicate objectively with people and influence their actions, and many of the agreements were significantly abided by because of people's respect for and fear of al-Hakkamat.

WHY EXCLUDED FROM PEACE PLATFORMS?

It is noticeable that in any reconciliation forum within and between tribes in Darfur, the participation of women, be they urban or rural, educated or illiterate, is limited or only shows instances of window-dressing representation. This deliberate omission, especially as far as al-Hakkamat are concerned, appears to be justified by some actors on the grounds that women are ill prepared for these particular tasks. Some have suggested that al-Hakkamat lack negotiating skills and the knowledge necessary for participation. They attributed their difficiency to the pattern of gender division of labour and the stereotyped socio-cultural segregation between public and private domains that identifies women's activities as indoors and men's as outdoors.[4] This perception reverberates apologetically in the accounts of the chairperson of the Regional Legal Committee of the NCP in South Darfur. From his position, he can exercise tremendous influence on decisions and policies on women in the state based on the following personal perspective:

> Men are the gender responsible for managing problems because they are the ones who either attack or be attacked; but women are seldom attacked or become attackers. Even if they were attacked or being attackers, it is customarily in our communities that the role of women is usually confined in space and type; because they are less educated and therefore they participate less. No doubt ... if they acquired some kind of education, there would be no barrier for them to be part of these councils or committees. At present, their involvement is nil.[5]

His statement suggests that he tends to overlook the socio-economic and environmental context of Darfur, which can hardly be said to reflect the concept of private woman and public man. On the contrary, gender division of labour in rural areas generally seems to identify Darfuri rural women as the main economic producers and social actors (see Musa, 2002, pp. 78–94). His point of view is therefore inconsistent with both the historical and contemporary social and economic frameworks and the dynamics that connect the vast majority of Darfuri women with society.

Moreover, a lack of education does not necessarily mean a lack of skills, knowledge and/or ability to make insightful judgements, choose and influence appropriate courses of action and/or participate in public

[4] Interviews, Nyala, 2006. Also, on public and private see Rosaldo, 1993, pp. 18–42).
[5] Interview with the chairperson of the Legal Committee of the Regional Council of South Darfur region (R17), Nyala, 2006.

matters. By virtue of high illiteracy in the Darfur rural areas, most of the *Ajaweed* are illiterate, but well versed in community matters and with substantial experience through exposure and learning. The emergence of illiterate women as Hakkamat with solemn social and political weight in rural societies constitutes conclusive evidence to refute such an assumption. Yet it was still unsurprising to hear such views from a devoted Islamist politician and a member of the NCP.

Paradoxically though, this informant does not refrain from using al-Hakkamat to serve objects he agrees with; as in his verbatim description below:

> Al-Hakkamah are among the natural leaders of the community, especially in instances that require enthusiasm where they are needed most. Their speech would incite men to go at top speed and be fierce in fighting. They strive to maintain good virtues of generosity, courage and nobility and vigilant care and therefore, they have received a great response and interaction from the community. They can produce good things for the society or evil things that bring calamity to the society.[6]

He acknowledges al-Hakkamat's power and agency in facilitating good or evil outcomes in the service of their community's welfare, but denies them the right to participate in those conferences where these very outcomes are forged. Thus, he admits their worth in one respect based on their *ability* and denies them any worth in another based on *lack of ability*.

Moreover, interesting reasoning for excluding al-Hakkamat from reconciliation conferences or processes is formulated by three prominent Baggara leaders who are often involved in these discussions. They say that the negotiations are usually conducted through a process of give and take in which *strong* and provocative language is often used that may easily derail the reconciliation objective. As al-Hakkamat are indeed quite passionate, it is feared that their response might evoke negative reactions among the conflicting parties and thus solidify positions that are actually required to soften in order to bridge the differences.

Besides, in conflicts that were partially triggered or escalated by Hakkamat, al-Hakkamat's very presence at these meetings might weigh heavily in the negotiations and discussions. A prominent Hakkamah shared this perception and offered her own explanation by saying, 'Because al-Hakkamat do not agree on compromises and insist on revenge, they might incite new war if they attended the discussions'.[7] Hubbania tribes subsequently chose this position to reach outcomes that could be communicated to people to solicit their acceptance, even though there were always those who found it hard to overcome the bitterness of the incidents and reconcile.[8] Such negative expectations of al-Hakkamat's reaction was the implicit justification behind excluding them from reconciliation conferences held to resolve the conflict between Salamat and Ta'aisha tribes in 1979/80.

[6] Interview with the chairperson of the legal committee of the regional council of South Darfur region (R17), Nyala, 2006.
[7] Interviews with Hakkamah from Rezeiqat Mahriyah/Hemdaniya (R31), Nyala, 2006.
[8] Interview with Omda from Hubbania (R18), Nyala, 2006.

In addition, some regular resource persons for the reconciliation conferences argued that government-sponsored reconciliation conferences usually followed a conventional pattern in addressing these conflicts by focusing primarily on the statistics of casualties and the assets damaged and/or destroyed. The focus was therefore often geared towards financial compensation for the assets lost and blood money. The underlying causes of these conflicts were never being properly addressed.[9]

Consistent with these views, the role played by al-Hakkamat in conflict was either obscured, or only mentioned obliquely. When it was mentioned, some 'silly bureaucrats' simply suggested that these Hakkamat must be put on trial. But these alien and naive ideas were simply met with scornful laughter from both sides to the conflict.[10] Apparently, this ignorance on the part of executive participants about local culture and knowledge underpins the recurrent failure of most of the government-sponsored and/or government-led resolution attempts. The lack of knowledge about rural women and gender power relations in these societies further explains the failure to take on board the experience of women, their capacities and their interests, and to listen to their voice. Knowledge of gender power relations and the position of women in Darfur society constitutes a substantial asset for achieving lasting peace.

On the other hand, excluding women from the negotiating table, except in a token fashion, is a rife practice for the Sudanese government, and was pointedly exercised in the peace negotiations pursued by the state's institutions that led to the signing of the CPA (the Comprehensive Peace Agreement, started in 2001 and signed on 9 January 2005) and the DPA (Darfur Peace Agreement, on 5 May 2006) to reconcile the civil wars in South Sudan and Darfur, respectively. In the CPA negotiations, women were not engaged effectively. They were only annexed to the delegations at short notice and were therefore unable to consult among themselves and/or organise their agendas and arguments. Their inadequate numbers further obstructed their full engagement in political debate with the well-seasoned but gender-prejudiced politicians who dominated the negotiation processes. Indeed, they were only required to uphold and advocate their party's position and not to voice their own concerns (Itto, 2006, p. 58).

Nevertheless, the determination of southern Sudanese women to make their voice heard and to influence the negotiation outcomes induced them to pass written recommendations under the doors of the closed negotiation rooms. They also organised protests to raise issues that they believed to have been overlooked or poorly considered, e.g. disability and gender (Mathiang, 2008, p. 17). Obviously, the organisers and the political actors of both parties failed to abide by UN Resolution 1325, which urges all actors to consolidate women's participation in the prevention and resolution of conflicts and incorporate a gender perspective in all peace processes.

The experience of the state actors with regard to women's participation in peace processes was reproduced in the DPA negotiations in Abuja,

[9] Interviews, Nyala, 2006.

[10] Email communication with Ali Jammaa, 2009.

Nigeria. Darfuri women were only involved in the seventh round of the negotiations, in December 2005, as a result of pressure from international mediators. They took part as gender consultants, however, not as negotiators, and they left before the concluding session.[11] Even though those women represented a spectrum of diverse tribes and ethnic groups, they appeared to belong mainly to the urban and civil society organisations of educated city women. As such, the concerns and views of rural women might not have been solicited and/or represented. Ironically, al-Hakkamat, the most influential rural women who were directly involved, positively or negatively, in the conflict under discussion, were neither consulted, nor were they physically involved. The disengagement of women from conflict resolution processes, was addressed in the DPA document, which emphasised women's inclusion in all decision-making institutions. The practice that followed has still provided no meaningful inclusion of women in negotiations, and their engagement in peace processes has continued to be minor and ineffective.

This exclusion therefore is not the result of women's lack of experience and skill in conducting negotiations; rather, it is down to a historically patriarchal culture that prevails in both North and South Sudan, as also in Africa at large. It excludes women from public decision making and perpetuates their position in the private domain. This is despite United Nations Resolution 1325 (2000) and the advocacy of international human rights organisations for gender mainstreaming in peace and reconciliation processes. Both traditional and governmental institutions have thus allied in blocking women's voices, lessening and overlooking their skills and experiences and perpetuating their subordination.

AL-HAKKAMAT'S ABSENCE AND IMPLICATIONS FOR PEACEBUILDING

The limited or non-participation of al-Hakkamat in reconciliation forums has had unhelpful outcomes. Their absence tends to make them unaware of the issues discussed and how they are resolved. They often receive confusing information from secondary sources that is not fully consonant with what the meetings have discussed, agreed on and decreed. Subsequently, if they are not satisfied with what they hear, they may undermine the authenticity of the process, including the agreement itself.[12]

In addition, they may choose to influence the negotiations by passing erroneous information to the *Ajaweed* council and/or the Ageed if he is present, which may confuse and obstruct the entire proceedings and induce continuation of the conflict. The cases of the conflict of Bani Helba and Mahriyah in 1976 and between Salamat and Ta'aisha in 1980 stand as distinct proof of this. In the first, al-Hakkamat encouraged and

[11] Those twenty women succeeded in highlighting the perceived needs of women, especially with regard to peace, resettlement and reconciliation, and advocated for gender-sensitive discourse to be mainstreamed in the final Accord (DPA document).
[12] Group and individual interviews, Nyala, 2006.

incited their tribesmen to reject the peace deal, which was reached under government coercion:[13]

English
The Government was emboldening the parties to reconcile.
But the Hilbawi rode on his horse, marching,
Carrying his long spear that stabs really sharply.
It bisects the back and smashes the ribs.

Transliteration
al-ḥukūmāh biṭṭariḍ.
wa-l-hilbāwī shaddā mārig.
markunday 'umm ṭa'anan bārid.
bi-tafṣil l-ḍahar, wa bi-takassir l-tawārib.

The point was emphasised quite distinctly by a teacher, who said:

> Yes, their absence has negative consequences because women are left to continue reciting their songs and they are not committed to the resolutions as they are often not part of the discussions. Their songs lead the youth to raid and take revenge. Most of these conflicts were influenced by this situation that al-Hakkamat were not involved in the reconciliation achieved.[14]

The reconciliation agreement between the Salamat and Ta'aisha tribes in 1980 was forced by the government on the two reluctant parties and it was promptly violated; many think that this was because it was rejected by al-Hakkamat, whose opinion very rapidly triggered the resumption of hostilities. When the government attempted a second round of reconciliation talks, government authorities in Nyala censured al-Hakkamat and ordered them, rather less insightfully, not to sing publicly or interfere in any other way; and, in the words of one informant, they 'put them under control'.[15] The outcome of these talks fared no better than the first; in a counter move, al-Hakkamat crafted their own method of hitting back – they recorded their songs and recitations on cassette tapes and circulated them in rural areas where they would have the most effect.[16] Al-Hakkamat thus realised and exercised their agency and authority to reach out to an audience far wider and more effectively than if they had sung in the public forums where the negotiations took place.

AL-HAKKAMAT AND PEACE ADVOCACY

Despite the notable structural absence of rural women from the men-led local and regional conflict prevention and resolution initiatives, rural women from parts of Sudan that have experienced violent armed conflict and wars have exercised influence in making peace and developed a sound expertise in building and maintaining peace at grassroots level.

[13] Interviews with a teacher and folk researcher from Bani Helba (R22), 2006.
[14] Ibid.
[15] i.e. al-Hakkamat were ordered to stay at home. Group and individual interviews, Nyala, 2006.
[16] Ibid.

Photo 8.1 Six Baggari Hakkamat performing at a peace festival, 23 December 2014 (*Source*: Ministry of Culture and Information, al-Fashir. Photograph taken at a folkloric music festival in al-Fashir, North Darfur, 23 December 2014)

For instance, in the region of South Sudan women's contributions range from encouraging male relatives to refrain from fighting by singing for peace, intermarrying across adversarial parties or pursuing dangerous missions across conflict zones. Women can deploy intimidating measures, such as threatening to desist from conjugal commitments and to appear naked (a curse in most Sudanese customary beliefs). They have mediated in resolving inter-ethnic conflict through reconciliatory forums, and people-to-people processes. The latter was recognised for facilitating reconciliation accords at the grassroots, e.g. the Wunlit Covenant between the Nuer and the Dinka, and the Lilir Covenant between Nuer groups. Most striking was the initiative of the wife of a Dinka chief who persuaded her husband, despite comprehending the associated lethal risks, to lead a peace mission to the Nuer Land (Itto, 2006, pp. 57–8).

Similarly, there have been worthwhile instances of al-Hakkamat pursuing peace and reconciliation on their own volition and on their own terms. These vary from their mediation to subside and resolve disputes among women and families, e.g. between husbands and wives, to positively interfering in serious conflicts between tribes. One of these instances points to the failure of repetitive reconciliation attempts to stop the conflict between the Rezeiqat Mahriyah and Bani Helba in 1976. Alarmed by the volatile situation, two Hakkamat from the tribes came together and decided to stop the conflict once and for all. They invited the Nazir of Bani Helba, all the Sheikhs, Omad and the Augada of both tribes, to a place called Bala Furash. At the assembly, al-Hakkamat appealed to the congregated men to make a solemn vow that they would submit to the mind of al-Hakkamat when they unveiled it. Reluctantly, but well-disposed to al-Hakkamat's wishes, they swore the oath; as they believed the attitudes of the two Hakkamat to be mutually beneficial. The two Hakkamat then asked them to give up fighting immediately and reconcile by letting bygones be bygones. According to the narrative, all the attendees honoured their oath and became reconciled, leading to a relatively long-lasting peace resettlement.[17]

Similarly, an armed conflict erupted long ago between Khuzam and Rezeiqat when a camel of Awlad Rashid, a clan of the Rezeiqat, encroached on the farm of the Nazir of Khuzam and caused severe damage to the crop. The Khuzam demanded the camel in compensation for the damage, but the Rezeiqat refused, leading to violence between them, in which kin from neighbouring Chad were involved. Fed up with killing and aggression, al-Hakkamah decided to cut down the dispute, and so she killed the camel, the source of the trouble, and soon the war stopped![18]

Though modest and simple, these are meaningful examples, which reveal the practical experiences of al-Hakkamat in using their influence to handle disputes and convince people to accept their choices in achieving conducive and relatively sustainable peace and reconciliation. They also indicate that al-Hakkamat have demonstrated not only the potential, but also the actual agency to transform into reliable mediators who can rival the traditional *Ajaweed* and the stereotyped government-led platforms, and, perhaps, surpass them in practical terms. Noticeably though, the conflicts that stirred those Hakkamat into action were actually fought among and between Arab tribes who more or less share an understanding of, and respect for, al-Hakkamat. Therefore, they submitted to the choices they made, even when they belonged to opposite sides. As this trend has succeeded in extinguishing the fire of war among Arab tribes, it could also be strengthened and utilised as an effective mechanism for peace resettlement and reconciliation of all tribes across the board in Darfur.

Obviously, these animated interventions of al-Hakkamat show that al-Hakkamat's peace-promoting spirit and the positive voice can sometimes override their recognisably agitating spirit, and they could be the female force to reckon with. Conflict resolution and peacebuilding institutions should take on board these experiences, and incorporate and mainstream them within their 'best practice methodology' for gender-sensitive conflict resolution. This is because sustainable reconciliation and peace resettlement cannot be accomplished in Darfur and Sudan at large, unless the positive and the negative voices of al-Hakkamat and the other women are substantially taken account of.

This is despite the fact that the association with government suggests that they can only adopt a peaceful voice when it turns to mirror the government's wishes, even if their intentions do not entirely coincide. To this end, following both the Nefasha CPA in 2005 and the Darfur Peace Agreement (DPA) in May 2006,[19] al-Hakkamat were involved in

[17] Interview with Salami Hakkamah (R51), Nyala, 2006.

[18] Group and individual interviews, Nyala, 2006.

[19] The first of these agreements ended Africa's longest civil war in the then South Sudan, now independent South Sudan and the second was signed in Abuja in 2006

advocacy for peace and social reintegration. They gathered at the public yard – *Sāhat al-Mawlid* (the Prophet's Birthday Yard) – in Nyala town, composing songs rather prosaically, performing dances and delivering speeches that were recorded and broadcast live by local radio and TV.[20]

The way they delivered their peace appeal to the public was seen as lackadaisical and uninspiring to their audience, who might have aspired to see their authentic local tribe-based Hakkamat, rather than the town Hakkamat who were keen to act in tune with the government's intentions. For instance, in their songs, the SPLA leader, the late John Garang, whom they have invariably portrayed as a slave and *kafir* in the past, has suddenly become a darling cousin who shares the concern for peace:[21]

English
Hi John Garang; the hero!
I come to you as a cousin.
To adorn your hands with rings.

Transliteration
hey yā John Garang, al-baṭal.
ʾana jītak ka-bit-ʿamm.
ʿashān ʾamlā ʾīdayk bil-khatam.

This change in al-Hakkamat's attitudes and performance was attributed to the suffering and grief that emanated from their personal experience of losing dear ones, which have left al-Hakkamat as traumatised as other bereaved women in Darfur. One of these Hakkamat expressed her distress by saying:

> We are only for peace; we call the people in rural areas that we are for peace and we call for them to join us and be compassionate because we are the losers. We are the ones who are killed; the orphans are our children and the widowed are us and those who get burned are us, too. If some people from the opposition group were killed, our tears would run and if someone from the citizens were killed, we would cry and so if our soldiers were killed. Now, no one should die in this conflict; as those who died were all our sons ... who were educated, graduate youngsters and army officers brought here to die. This should not have happened and we don't want it to happen again.[22]

Learning from such a bitter personal experience, al-Hakkamat seem to have developed a perception against war in Darfur and to have become less readily mobilisable or mobilising. They have begun moderately to resist the government's attempts to push their hostility against Darfuri insurgencies, as the accounts of Hakkamah appear to suggest:

> At the moment, this opposition and rebel groups are our sons; they are not outsiders. If al-Hakkamah said, 'come on government shoot the opposition, you the *Janjawiid* shoot the opposition', this would be an enticement that we wouldn't accept as also we wouldn't accept to say to the opposition shoot those people, because they are all our sons.[23]

(contd) to settle the armed conflict in Darfur.
20 Group and individual interviews, Nyala, 2006.
21 Interviews with a politician and government employee from Fur (R28), Nyala, 2006.
22 Interview with Hakkama from Rezeiqat Mahriyah/Hemdaniya (R31), Nyala, 2006.
23 Ibid.

The precarious security situation in Darfur particularly when the government's rhetoric was also conciliatory, obliged them to voice their concerns against wars and advocate for peace through the means that were available to them. Below are some examples of anti-conflict and pro-peace recitations delivered by some Hakkamat during various conflict events in Darfur. One Hakkamah appealed against war and its disastrous consequences and called for peace:[24]

English
War is destruction; it is loss for the country.
It killed the male of cows and the mature ox.
And killed the Omda and orphaned his kids.
And killed the *Shartai* and destroyed his homeland.
I aspire for reconciliation; as it helps building the country.
We hope for peace with *jalalah* and *takbeer*:
Allahu Akbar, Allahu Akbar (God is Great)!

Transliteration
al-ḥarb damār, lil-balad khasārah.
kattal faḥal al-bagar al-tilib ʾabū ḥaddārah.
wā kattal al-ʿumdah wa ʾattam ʿiyyālah.
wa kattal al-shartāyy wa kharrab dārah.
ʾatmannā al-ṣuluḥ lil-balad ʿamārah.
natmannā al-salām bil-jallālah wa al-takbīr.
(H. R4, G4, Nyala, 2006).

Another Hakkamah emphasised that Sudan is overwhelmed with wars and violence and she therefore called for all people of Sudan to appeal for peace:[25]

English
Peace be upon all of you, men of Sudan.
Peace be upon you; peace is welcome and peace is indeed welcome.
He who approaches us with peace, we let them in.
I want peace everywhere and I want peace prevailing all over Sudan.
West Sudan aspires for peace and so does East Sudan.
South Sudan aspires for peace and north Sudan aspires for peace, too.
Inside Darfur too, I want peace!
Hey; you, the militias who climb up the mountains, I call for peace,
To the armed bandits in caves and *Wadis*, I appeal for peace.
I want a well-managed peace with discipline and respect,
I want consolidated security, so we can rebuild the wrecked,
I want serious peace, peace with no winding and twirling.

Transliteration
salām ʿalaykū yā rijāl al-Sūdān jumlah
wa ʿalaykum al-salām, marḥab bi-l-salām, wa marḥabāb al-salām
al-jāyyīnā bi-l-salām, bi-nafaḍḍilah gudām
ʾanā dāyrā al-salām fī kul makān, wa dāyrah al-salām yaʿumm l-Sūdān
gharb l-Sūdān dāyr l-salām wa sharg l-Sūdān dāyr l-salām
wa janūb l-Sūdān dāyr l-salām, wa shamāl l-Sūdān dāyr l-salām
wa juwwah dārfawr kamān dāyrah al-salām
yall-malāyish al-ṭalʿah fawg al-jibāl, ʾanā banādī b-l-salām

[24] Recited by Salami Hakkamah (R4) at group interview with Hakkamat (G4), Nyala, 2006.
[25] Interview with Hakkamah from, Rezeiqat Mahriyah/Hemdaniya (R31), Nyala, 2006.

wa l-nahab l-musallaḥ fī al-karkar wa al-khīrān, ʾanā banādī b-l-salām
ʾanā dāyrah salām bay ʾadab wa ʾiḥtirām
ʾanā dāyrah al-ʾamn yakūn mustatib, wa naʿammir l-kharbān
ʾanā dāyrah salām tamām, mā fīhu laff wā-lā-dawarān
(H. R31, Nyala, 2006).

Similarly, there are Hakkamat who have reminded the people of Sudan of the terrible consequences of war and appealed to Darfuri warriors to reconcile so that everyone could farm and produce their own food and get rid of aid agencies:[26]

English
Peace be upon you, all Sudanese!
I am telling you something, I hope it won't bother you.
Oh! Just look and see what happened to Saddam!
Clear up your hearts and give up wars.
Oh, don't let awful things happen in our country again.
Al-jarrāyah and *al-kadankah*[27] have been here since the days of our ancestors.
Let the *khawwajas*[28] take their aid and leave us.

Transliteration
al-salāmu ʿalaykū, yā al-Sūdān ʿām.
ʾanā bawarīkū laykū kalām, kalāmī mā yabgā laykūm baṭṭāl.
wey key shūfū al-bigā fī Ṣaddām.
ṣaffū al-gulūb, wā khallū l-ḥurūb.
weyyā al-shayn fī baladnā mā yakūn mawjūd.
al-jarrāyah, al-kadankah min zaman al-jidūd.
al-khawājā bey ʾighāthtah khal yamrug yafūt.
(H. R71, Nyala, 2006).

Meanwhile, another Hakkamah appealed to the people of Darfur to seek negotiation and reconciliation and warned that Sudan has become a target for external forces:[29]

English
My advice to all men of Darfur.
Arab and Zurga, please, listen to me.
Sharati,[30] Nazirs, sultans and holy men who excel in religion,
Go back to the wisdom of our old ancestors.
Sit under trees,
Study your position whilst your mat was spread and your food tray was big.
The country has become a target.
I advise you, my men – don't be drowsy and inadvertent.
As your country was ruined whilst you were oblivious.

Transliteration
ʿindī waṣiyyāh li-rijāl Dārfawr biṣifah ʿāmah.
ʿarabī wā zurgāwi, tukūnū layya ṣāntīn.

[26] Interview with Misseriya Hakkamah (R71), Nyala, 2006.
[27] Al-jarrāyah (used on goz soils) and al-kadankah (used on clay soils) are types of hoes, the former symbolising the Baggara Arabs and the latter the African tribes.
[28] Europeans who deliver aid through INGOs.
[29] Recitation of Ta'aishi Hakkamah (R37) at group interview with Hakkamat (G4), Nyala, 2006.
[30] (Sing. *Shartai*): the title of the supreme tribal chief in the tribal administration hierarchy of indigenous Darfuri African tribes.

al-sharātī wa al-nuzẓār wal-salātīn wal-fugarā gāryyīn al-dīn.
ʿarjaʿū lay rāyy al-judūd al-gadīm.
ʾagʿudū fī guʿūr al-shadar.
ʾadursū rāykū, birishkū mafrūsh, wa al-gadaḥ al-kabīr.
al-balad fawg-ha ṭumūḥ.
bawaṣṣīkū yā rijālī mā tukūnū dāgsīn.
baladkū khirbat wa ʾintū ghaflānīn.
(H. R37, Nyala, 2006).

Another Hakkamah also appealed for peace but in the meantime, she proposed that as Darfuri people were responsible for the war, now they ought to contribute to peace:[31]

English
The war in Darfur is our own responsibility.
Come on, let us put our ideas together!
Let us be proactive.
Rehabilitate our *khalawi* and repair our schools.
Let our soldiers rest from carrying guns.
Our army officer takes the register, and meets his beloved.
We, the women, our hearts are miserable and our livers are burned.
Our hearts rejected the words of gloating, and caring for orphans
Saying, 'a young man orphaned his kids!'
Saying, 'a prominent person bundled his pots!'
A land with no youth is in ruins.
I advise you, men of Darfur, to speak with one voice.
Enough! Put away your G3 and AK47.
Let the tank rest from snoring.
Enough! Stop the running tears.
My horsemen, throw away your spears and knives.
Life is so productive, why destabilise it?
Let the vulnerable taste its sweetness.

Transliteration
ʾanīnā fī Dārfawr, al-ḥarib dī masʾūliyatnā.
nadaggig fikratnā.
narjaʿ nasawwī lay jiddattnā.
naʿammir khalāwīnā, naṣalliḥ madārisnā.
Jundīnā yanjammah min shayl ʾabū ḥammālah.
ẓābiṭnā yākhud tamāmah, yagābil ḥibānah.
ʾanīnā al-ʿayyīn, al-gulūb najḍānah wal-kubūd ḥargānah.
galibnā ʾabbā gawlit shamtānā, wa tarbiyyat ʾattāmā.
gawlat ṣabī ʾattam ʿiyyālah.
gawlat masʾūl ṭabagan gudḥānah.
dār balā shabāb kharbānah.
bawaṣī yā rijāl Dārfawr kilmitkū waḥidūhā.
ʾal-jīm wal-kilāsh kafākū tagilūhā.
ʾal-dabbābah min al-shakhīr rayyihūha.
ʾal-damʿah al-sāylah kafākū wagifūha.
al-ḥarbah wal-sikīn furāsī jaddiʿūha.
ʾal-dunnyā hiyya bikayriyyah mālkū jahjahtūha.
khallū l-miskīn yaḍūg ḥulūha.
(H. R58, Nyala, 2006).

[31] Recitation of Hubbania Hakkamah (R58) at group interview with Hakkamat (G4), Nyala, 2006.

When the DPA was signed in 2006, a famous Misseriya Hakkamah called on the fighters to hand over their weapons and submit to the peace agreement:[32]

English
Peace be upon you, guys, who left for the wilderness.
You're Sudanese, not outsiders.
Oh, in the wilderness there is hunger, there is thirst.
You abandoned your beds and lay in the damp.
Give up your weapons as our peace has been accomplished.
Give up your weapons as our peace has now prevailed.
Let's live in our country,
Oh, let's sit under our tree.
Oh, let's make our mind.
Who would deny us this?

Transliteration
al-salām ʿalaykū, yā al-rijāl al-shiltū laykū khalā.
ʾintū min al-Sūdān, mā jītūnā min barrā.
wayā al-khalā bay jūʿah, al-khalā bay ʿaṭashah.
khallaytū al-sarāyyir, ragadtū fawg al-nadā.
ʾajmaʿū al-silāḥ, ʾaniḥnā salāmnā tammā.
ʾajmaʿū al-silāḥ, ʾaniḥnā salāmnā ʿammā.
khallū naʿīsh fī waṭnā.
way nagʿadū fī shadratnā.
way nadaggigū fikratnā.
yātū al-bijī yasʾalnā.
(H. R71, Nyala, 2006)

These examples reveal that al-Hakkamat's interests have expanded beyond the limited boundaries of tribes and ethnic groups. They have manifested their ability to survive the blatant challenges they faced in the town environment where many now live. They have acquired new qualities, which enabled them to embrace the different social contexts they now associate with. The complex urbanisation processes they endured have persuaded them to perceive themselves, as one of the most powerful Hakkamat in Nyala expressed with pride, as 'national Hakkamat'. [33]

This change of perception, however, seems unlikely to effect abrupt change in the overriding role of al-Hakkamat as hawks, which they have been exercising, and that is also seen by others as an integral cause of the havoc that has been wreaked in Darfur. Rather than be solicited to normalise official calls for peace that they seldom believe in as a just endeavour and/or an objective that can be realised so soon, a real transformative impact might begin to impinge on events if their voices were truly empowered in order to cement a genuine call for peace and social reintegration. This is the only juncture that could transform them into real partners for peace and reconciliation.

Arguably, it was this underlying perception that drove the women consultants in the DPA negotiations in Abuja, 2006, to underscore the necessity of including both al-Hakkamat and Sheikhat in any peace resettlement negotiations and conflict resolution sought at local and national

[32] Interviews with Misseriya Hakkamah (R71), Nyala, 2006.
[33] Group interviews with Hakkamat (G4), Nyala, 2006.

levels. They should be deemed crucial actors in achieving real and sustainable peace, for they could be motivated and guided to direct their agency towards promoting forgiveness and healing among war victims and urging fighters, the Baggara in particular, for peace. Their proven ability to influence the war discourse within their societies, especially among the youth and the horsemen, presumes that if they converted into advocates for nonviolence, peacebuilding and social reintegration, they could make a significant difference in the life of people in Darfur. Emphasis was however, on the wisdom of focusing on those Hakkamat who have hitherto been residing in the village, the camp and the *murhal*, and who remain uncompromising, obstinate members faithful to the ethos of their societies (DPA document, 2006).

Nevertheless, the DPA recommendations and similar others that were delivered in the Doha peace agreement, which followed the failure of DPA, were not implemented and/or reviewed to assess progress and figure out the exact problem. At the regional level, in September 2012, a workshop was organised in Nyala to identify effective ways to promote the role of al-Hakkamat in the media. Nonetheless, al-Hakkamat have remained isolated and their positive voice disguised; they were not incorporated in peace discussions, as recommended, nor were they involved in the implementation of the peace accords.

On the other hand, from their experience with the government, al-Hakkamat understand that they were not always included in the activities that they believe they should have been part of; especially peace advocacy. Having been suspicious of government motives, some Hakkamat have developed resilient attitudes on their own volition and attempted to engage in peacebuilding and reconciliation. One Hakkamah claimed that they 'have converted from sedition to wisdom' (*taḥawwalnā min al-fitnā 'ila-l-ḥikmah*) (ibid.).

Apparently, this resilience drew the attention of the MCI in Darfur, and instigated them to organise a folklore festival in 2014 in al-Fashir, again, to promote peace through folklore. At this festival, al-Hakkamat from South Darfur were featured quite powerfully through songs, and dancing performances. Apparently, apart from entertaining some officials, the NCP seemed to have wanted to reach out to the Arab community in al-Fashir, especially the youth. However, the event was like a formal celebration that had no effects beyond the temporal and spatial boundaries of the invitees who were mostly NCP affiliates. This is largely attributed to the nature of the demographic context of al-Fashir, which suggests that the Baggara population who can grasp and respond to the message of the Hakkamat are quite few. Besides, at the time of the festival, many tribes were involved in aggression and violence, especially those of south Darfur. If the government had been serious about peace advocacy, the right place for this event would have been the villages where al-Hakkamat could make a positive impact.

CONCLUSION

The near-universal stereotypical portrayal of women as passive victims tends to emphasise the negative perception of women as generally weak, incapable of pursuing effective measures to preserve their rights and lives, and always in need of men's protection, especially in armed conflict situations. This patriarchally based conception has disguised and underrated women's experience and skills in creating and maintaining peace in society and overshadowed their ability to engage in active peace advocacy. Darfuri women also share with African women generally the same estrangement from participation in reconciliation and peace resettlement, despite their recognised position in the social and political domains.

Al-Hakkamat have been used as warmongers by local and national power brokers to promote the elites' vested interests. In keeping with the trend of undermining women's voices, al-Hakkamat's voluntary contribution to reconciliation was literally blocked, rather than engaging them in peace initiatives that could have enlightened them and helped to develop their skills in negotiation and reconciliation. This appears to be a deliberate intent to gain their acquiescence in what the power brokers set out for them. Their vehement involvement in times of war has thus heightened their belligerent voice and enabled it to thrive at a time when the quest for peace has become a paramount concern.

Apparently, such an exploitative trend has reinforced a belief among al-Hakkamat that their combative voice is legitimate and patriotic, by virtue of their allegedly serving an Islamic government and a divine objective. Al-Hakkamat's disengagement from peace processes therefore would often prompt them and their war partner, the Ageed, to keep their authority and influence intact when exercising choices that in many cases were incompatible with resettlement agreements, hence perpetuating animosities and violence.

Nevertheless, there have been some Hakkamat who have urged conflicting parties to exercise restraint and to reconcile through negotiations. Those self-censoring Hakkamat could be a significant voice in healing, reconciliation, social reintegration and peacebuilding. Counting on al-Hakkamat's voice to galvanise people into action could make a difference to the quest for peace in Darfur; every effort is still needed to cement the call for peace, especially on the part of women who have been the most affected by the atrocities of armed conflict.

Hope lies in transforming al-Hakkamat into peace advocates and empowering them to take the lead in calling for an end to war and violence. This mission is not out of the question, especially if we review their trajectory and experiences in adapting to the social, political and environmental challenges that they have encountered in the town where they have now settled, as mentioned earlier and as we are going to review next.

9

Urban Identity and Social Change

The previous discussion pointed to al-Hakkamat's ability to exercise agency and influence in all the settings in which they are involved. Their emigration from the village to settle in Nyala town suggests that they have become associated with different social and political settings, where they have encountered fortuitous or planned events that have functioned as turning points in the journey of their development. This new context has necessitated readjustment and the development of their personal identity to meet the challenges encountered. Some of the critical incidents and the way they have impacted on al-Hakkamat are explored here.

IDENTITY AND CHANGE

Identity, community, territory and culture are not natural, static and/or taken-for-granted orders, but are discursively and historically constructed through certain modes of power relations and resistance of the subjects to change or form their identity (Gupta and Ferguson, 1997, p. 18). Resistance in this respect is a form of power that 'categorises the individual, marks him by his own individuality, attaches him to his own identity … a form of power which makes individuals subjects'.[1] Identities are thus dynamic processes that are changing throughout the course of personal development when people remodel characters and reposition their identities to suit changing and challenging circumstances.

In the town of Nyala, al-Hakkamat encountered multifaceted forces that challenged their rurally acquired skills. These mainly comprised government influence and urbanisation processes. In adapting to these challenges, we must bear in mind that institutions and interest groups usually seek to forge solidarity and political alliances with (utility) groups across new sections and territorial boundaries in order to fulfil their own objectives. Sometimes these processes involve methods that restrict the range of choices available to individuals, who will be required to command respect and obedience to the rules and/or to act in what

[1] There are two meanings of the word 'subject': 'subject to someone else by control and dependence, and tied to [one's] own identity by a conscience or self-knowledge' (Foucault, cited in Ferguson and Gupta, 1997, p. 18).

may look as against the norms.[2] The NCP/NIF government of Sudan has designed processes and measures to mould the identities of the followers and to ensure a firm control over them so that they serve the regime's doctrine and interests. Al-Hakkamat are a living testimony of a utility group upon which the NCP exercised co-opting procedures that enabled the full manipulation of their identity and agency and directed them to serve the vested interests of the ruling elite.

Urbanisation and the movement of people outside their original social and geographical boundaries are also significant in identity change.[3] These elements tend to affect people's loyalty and commitment to the local norms, customs and patterns that they have normally associated with in their relatively homogeneous *native* communities and locales. In the new destinations, they may forge new relationships, adopt new perceptions and make new alliances that might bring new sources of meaning, e.g. gender and sex, place, etc., which may eventually become more influential in shaping people's perceptions and their transforming identities (Giddens, 2001).

Nonetheless, the dynamic of the processes that have engulfed al-Hakkamat suggests that agency is the ultimate driving force in reconstructing personal identity and enabling its engagement in social relations and activities. As one's ability to choose one's own identity is often defined by the freedom of action available to one, women often find it a bit harder than men do. This is because they are often faced with a set of patriarchal barriers that undermine their efforts and demoralise their aspirations to exercise agency and political influence. Autonomy and conscious agency are therefore crucial for women in making choices and formulating mechanisms for cementing relationships with others, individuals and/or institutions. Al-Hakkamat have experienced many changes to their personal identity and their relationships with others, as indicated below.

AL-HAKKAMAT AND CHANGE IN TOWN

The heyday of al-Hakkamat was when they were in the village, the camp or the *murhal* – their natural habitat, amid their tribes and clans. These are the places where they emerged and enjoyed tremendous prestige and an ardent following. In the town, they become engaged with the government and were introduced to the general public, a context of diverse tribal and ethnic groups. They were made to address these groups, on different occasions. Certainly, some might have liked them and others might have abhorred them, each for her/his own reasons.

Several programmes were designed for regional and national radio and television to enable their communication with a wider public. These included producing specific radio programmes, such as *Murḥākt-al-gawl*

[2] For more on urbanisation and change, see Giddens, 2001, pp. 570–98.

[3] For more on the images of immigration and ethnicity see Strauss (1991: 287–90), and on transformation of identity (pp. 313-338).

('the grinder of speech') and *al-Mughrāfah* ('the ladle/scoop', i.e. of wise sayings).[4] This way, al-Hakkamat became exposed to a large rural audience, both in the village and in the towns, especially from the Baggara and Abbala communities, not only in Darfur but across all Sudan, including those from the neighbouring Kordofan region. It was a critical approach in promoting al-Hakkamat's agency and transforming their identity from local and tribal into an institution that was guided by regional and national political concerns.

Furthermore, in the village, al-Hakkamat would put on their performance individually or perhaps in a group, supported by a group of female peers who were all affiliates of the same tribe. When they moved to town, they become connected with groups of Hakkamat of diverse tribes and ethnic origins and were obliged to assemble with others to serve social and political events, such as official receptions, *Zad al-Mujahid*, etc. This exposure to others has forced them to learn the necessity and also the diplomacy of coordinating and exchanging cordial overtures with parties they had never expected to communicate with.

The conventional autonomy of al-Hakkamat has become restricted in Nyala town as a result of being controlled by others, namely, government officials and the UHS, especially the chairperson. Indeed, it was the first time that al-Hakkamat had been chaired and supervised by a Hakkamah who might even be of a different tribe. Besides, every Hakkamah was required to seek permission and to abide by certain procedures if she desired to partake in public events, as appears in the following statement:

> Al-Hakkamah is an important person and has an important role. In the past her role was genuine and highly supported by the system of the Ageed and she had full freedom of choice in singing, doing, where and when and why... Now she has become controlled by others. She has to take permission and has to comply by the regulations to be able to compose.[5]

> We obey and follow the instructions of the chairperson of the Union, because, she is the one who goes to the government offices and we follow her like the 'blind in the parade' ... It is the first time for me to be chaired by somebody else.[6]

Al-Hakkamat's proclaimed loyalty to the co-option processes that they were subject to was translated into actual support by their engaging in mobilisation for the government's wars against its rivals all over the country. Such a sincere contribution reads as if they have been completely recast as agents for inciting violence and aggression, and would not see peace as an alternative to the turmoil that has been going on for ages in Sudan, particularly in Darfur. Yet contrary to the government's expectations, al-Hakkamat appeared to have developed a negative perception of war. Apparently, the grief of losing a beloved person (husband, son or brother) has made them less willing to engage in the call for war, especially in the mobilisation against Darfuri insurgencies; and al-Hakkamat

[4] Group (G2, G3, G4, G5) and individual interviews, Nyala, 2006.
[5] Interviews with Salami Hakkamah (R51), Nyala, 2006.
[6] Interviews with Hakkamah from Rezeiqat Mahriyah/Hemdaniya (R31) Nyala, 2006.

have been outspoken in their refusal to advocate warmongering among 'sons of the land'.[7]

Whilst the changes outlined above have been perceived by many Baggara as favourable for al-Hakkamat, there have been some others that are less welcome. These include the presumption that al-Hakkamat have lost their conventional sources of income and become dependent on the handouts they receive in return for occasionally praising and serving the government and the officials. A marked change was also observed in the style of their poetic diction, which has allegedly declined in both strength and authenticity, compared to when they called on their village-based proficiency in spontaneous reaction and authentic production. In the village, they focused on the community's dearly held virtues: generosity, bravery, decency and the beauty of nature; as stated by a Baggara man:

> When al-Hakkamah describes a person as a formidable lion, 'dood' or like a jumping lion, it gives a meaning that has strength, symbol and sweetness, and she can attract the attention of the community to him and everyone will fancy him. But when she is asked to go on repeating, 'peace is good for you, peace is good for you', these are empty words that seldom show the nice, affectionate and the operative meanings that she normally reflects, by her own words and phrases, in celebrating things in the village that deeply touch people's feelings.[8]

This observation was also cited by al-Hakkamah who was still resided in the village and would come to Nyala town only occasionally. She outlined the difference between the village Hakkamat and those in the town by saying, 'But they do not compose on the cow like us, and the kind of poetry they compose is like what they compose in praising Omer al-Bashir'.[9] Another Hakkamah also agreed, saying that 'When I arrived in Nyala, I heard women singing in Katim but I could not understand what they were saying'.[10] Many people subsequently agreed that al-Hakkamat in the town have proved to lack the skills of innovative composing and performing, and many of them were observed to have continued using the old recitations as templates, with just minor changes to match the names of the officials. Their production has thus become less genuine and more spurious; as was borne out in the following articulation:

> Before moving to the town, they used to react to matters in their village environment through spontaneous composing without imposition and/or dictation by others. But when you are dictated or forced to speak out about things that do not make any sense to you, you will forfeit the authenticity and honesty of what you are saying. This led to them losing the spontaneous spirit of folklore that forms the basis of their role as Hakkamat.[11]

Many people were therefore convinced that the complexity of the social and political context in Nyala is the main force behind the erosion

[7] Interview with Hakkamat (G4), Nyala, 2006.
[8] Interview with Ahmed Jowa (R14), radio and TV presenter from Ta'aisha, Nyala, 2006.
[9] Interview with a village-based Hakkamah from Hubbania (R19), Nyala, 30 May 2006
[10] Interview with Salami Hakkamah (R62), Nyala, 30 May 2006.
[11] Interview with Dr Mahmoud Adam Daoud (R47), a university lecturer and folk expert from Fur, Nyala, 2006.

of the very essence of al-Hakkamat's identity, i.e. their creative poetry and authentic performance. Moreover, having been nominated in the village, al-Hakkamat are usually supported financially and morally by their communities to enable them to undertake their obligations. But the Inghaz regime adopted an approach that encouraged and urged women to arrogate the identity of Hakkamat to the public and to come out in droves to receive visitors and officials by singing. These women were not adequately rewarded but occasionally received some money and sugar. More often than not, they were compelled to go chasing after officials in order to be paid gratuities and to hold them to account for the promises of rewards they had made prior to the events.

Having seen their esteemed Hakkamat turned into street performers and buskers, both tribesmen and tribeswomen have become discontented with al-Hakkamat's disgraceful behaviours and practices. They have earned an indignity they had never experienced from the village audience. The following remark is a typical point of view:

> This is a new thing and a tremendous change of what was usually known about al-Hakkamat. In the past, they represented certain values; they sang about the value of man for the community and for herself. Now, it has become a paid job ... In the town, they have formed a Union that has assembled all al-Hakkamat. They do many paid-for-things, and, therefore, they lost their value and originality and have become *maṣnaʿjiyyah*[12] and their agency and influence have declined.[13]

Furthermore, the welfare of al-Hakkamat has been tremendously compromised by the respective authorities and officials; as declared by a dismayed Hakkamah:

> We just attended workshops. We were invited to many other workshops in al-Fashir this year (2006) and they offered us bus tickets. I said to them that I could only go, if you granted us aeroplane tickets, otherwise I would not risk my life by using other means of transport; as you know pretty well, there is no security along the route to al-Fashir.[14]

These trivial incentives encouraged many women in the town, who lacked the necessary talent and skills, to masquerade as Hakkamat by holding the flag of the tribe and wandering around government offices looking for handouts. For those who know al-Hakkamat, these behaviours are at odds with those of the genuine and dignified Hakkamat in rural areas. Those fake and opportunist Hakkamat are currently at the forefront of those with whom the government have forged alliances, even though these officials comprehend quite well that they fall short in both talent and tribal endorsement.

The phenomenon of the arrogated Hakkamat in Nyala town was felt to have inflicted a serious affront to the real Hakkamat, for the fake Hakkamat lack any real support from the respective communities and have no connection with the inspirational setting of the village, which

[12] Maṣnaʿjiyya are manufacturers.
[13] Interview with Ahmed Jowa, Nyala, 2006.
[14] Interview with Hakkamah from Rezeiqat Mahriyah/Hemdaniya (R31), Nyala, 2006.

normally gives them an enthusiastic ovation. Their approach was to appeal for support, and the response was often determined by the personal disposition of the governing elites and authorities, as exemplified by their appeal to the president's wife to go to the Hajj.

On the other hand, the tribes that once had Hakkamat speaking on their behalf have now encountered a situation whereby some of their affiliated Hakkamat are extolling the virtues of political parties, the ruling NCP and governing elites, who are strongly opposed in many rural communities. These attitudes have undermined the credibility of Hakkamat, even the truly creative ones who had paid dearly by forfeiting their village-based audience, especially the female community and the spontaneously organised platforms where they used to express themselves freely, honestly and joyfully.

The Baggara people, who came from rural areas and settled in Nyala town, were also still observing the manifestations of al-Hakkamat, and watching with loathing and indignation, the transformation that they had gone through. This was agitatedly expressed by one of the Baggara men who said that what al-Hakkamat have been talking about is not relevant to the discourse of the Baggara tribes which centres around glorifying and celebrating generosity, bravery and valiantly behaving men who take care of the tribe and rise to the challenge of protecting their people and their wealth. In their eyes, al-Hakkamat in town appeared to allow themselves to be exploited by the authorities without recompense, thus ending up not only less considered by their own community but also debased by the state authorities.[15]

As a result of the issues and audience in Nyala being so different from those in the village, the role of al-Hakkamat and their songs have much less strength and influence in town than they had in the village. In contrast, al-Hakkamat in rural areas remained authentic in attending to their roles in maintaining the norms, and observing the attributes of their identity and agency and their social and political significance.[16] This could simply be attributed to the society in the town being tribally and ethnically diverse, with the result that some might believe in al-Hakkamat and some might not. In addition, al-Hakkamat might influence some people, mainly from their own tribe, but might not influence affiliates of other tribes, especially if those tribes were in dispute with each other. All the changes that al-Hakkamat have experienced are summarised in Table 9.1.

Noticeably though, apart from al-Hakkamat in Nyala town, those who still move with the *murhal* and/or stay in the village or the camp constitute the majority of al-Hakkamat in Darfur. They are not militarised or being incorporated in the government's social and military projects. Obviously, the farther al-Hakkamat are from the focus of the government, the more independent they would remain, and the more they could maintain the local characteristics of their identity.

There is no doubt that al-Hakkamat's emigration to Nyala has enabled them to develop relationships with diverse social and political modalities

[15] Interviews with a Rezeiqi government employee (R5), Nyala, 2006.
[16] Ibid.

Table 9.1 The effects of government liaison with al-Hakkamat

Attributes of al-Hakkamat	*Before (rural)*	*After (urban)*
Identity	Rural: Village and tribal-oriented, only locally recognised	Urban, town-oriented, more ethnically tolerant, regionally and nationally recognised.
Personal movement/ mobility	Restricted within geographical and social boundaries of the tribes and Nyala Town.	Access to the whole country.
Association with military system	Alliance with the tribe's system of defence, the Ageed, the horsemen and the youth of the tribe. Involvement in locally motivated wars between tribes and ethnic groups.	Alliance with the government, military institutes, government authorities, officials, soldiers, and militias of diverse Arab tribes. Involvement in regionally and nationally motivated wars between ethnic groups and insurgents' wars against the state government.
Organisation	Acting individually and/or engaged with groups from the same tribe.	Acting in groups of diverse tribes and ethnicities through the UHS; solidarity and networking with other NGOs, have their own office to coordinate their activities.
Connection with Sheikhat	Independent of the Sheikhat and might voluntarily collaborate.	Have been assembled in a single organisation (the UHS) and are obliged to collaborate in serving the public events.
Target audience/ public	The tribespeople – the Ageed, leaders and notables, horsemen, youth, women and children.	All Arab tribes and horsemen within and outside Darfur boundaries and the state army forces and pro-army militias.
Public avenues and means of communication	Village-based activities and events, e.g. *Faza'*, *nafir*, raids, dance parties, social occasions, the market, etc.	Town-based public platforms, official receptions and farewell parties, radio and TV, religious festivals, workshops, etc.
Discourse of al-Hakkamat	Mobilising the tribe's horsemen and the youth for tribal-based interests; escorting fighters to the battlefields; safeguarding the culture through indoctrination, socialisation and setting arbitrations against the offenders.	Mobilising formal army forces and tribal militias for state-sponsored wars; escorting army troops to the battlefields; advocating government's policies and campaigns.

Attributes of al-Hakkamat	*Before (rural)*	*After (urban)*
Poetic diction and issues addressed	Focusing primarily on the tribe's prominent people – the generous, the well-behaved, the brave horsemen and the tribe's leaders; praising the good people whom they know quite well. The tribes' ethics and virtues are their main concern.	Praising government institutes: the army, police, PP, PDF, etc., governing elites and officials, the politicians about whom, apart from their names and positions, they know very little.
Aspirations	Respect, recognition, solidarity, praise and simple gifts, such as tea, sugar and money.	Employment, salaries, sugar, Hajj and others.
Accountability	To the tribe's community and the Ageed organisation	To government authority, the police and formal and informal military institutes.
Source of power	Their unique qualities, societal norms and values, community support, the Ageed organisation and the whole tribe.	Their agency and ethnic identity and their engagement with the government.

(*Source*: Author)

and structures, which they have never previously anticipated. They have developed an awareness of issues such as diversity, national wars, mass mobilisation, peace, coordination, organisation, ammunition, etc., and also perceptions about other people. They have become more acquainted with the urban environment, where they now move freely and confidently. They should not be blamed for the roles they have been undertaking, if these roles were interpreted as a diligent attempt by al-Hakkamat to maintain an active exercise of their agency and identity in a context where they might otherwise have ended up as lost and/or forgotten women.

Besides, the influence that changing circumstances and events in the town have had on al-Hakkamat's perceptions, which has affected the reconstruction of their identities, is an important and breathtaking experience in the trajectory of their adaptation, though it has been perceived by some as against the norm and, perhaps as a 'violation of identity'. It is therefore unsurprising that the changes in al-Hakkamat's behaviour and attitude and their implications for al-Hakkamat's talents have astounded their pristine rural audience, who might have aspired to see their Hakkamat performing on town platforms but in the character of their village stereotypes. This shows that some attributes/aspects of identity are sensitive to change, and that the ability to make choices is crucial in this process. This is largely influenced by prevailing power relationships, but individual agency, rather than that of the group, is the ultimate guidance for the person to make choices.

The trajectory that al-Hakkamat have followed in the town clearly mirrors the concept of human agency that characterises individuals and groups as 'autonomous, purposive actors, capable of choice' (Lister, 1997, p. 36). The actions and choices of these actors certainly express their own purpose and needs, and frame a process of self-development that is 'of concretely becoming the person one chooses to be' (Gould, 1988, p. 47). It is a mutually exclusive process that comprehends engagement in collective activities both to meet common goals and individuals' own interests. The outcomes are presumed to broaden the range of actions, social interactions and relationships that have the potential to maintain a steady flow of animated activities and the sustainable development of capacities. If those other people who moved into the town called into question al-Hakkamat's integrity, perhaps they reflect on similar attempts and changes they have made on their own journey. But whilst legitimising their own readjustments, as a coping strategy when faced with a challenging new environment, paradoxically they disapprove of al-Hakkamat's adjustments – perhaps just because they are women!

AL-HAKKAMAT VERSUS FEMALE SPIRIT MEDIUMS IN ZIMBABWE

Al-Hakkamat's authority and social worth could be compared with those of female spirit mediums, which stand as an intriguing example of women's influence on social and political matters in Southern Rhodesia, now Zimbabwe. This is despite the genuine disparity between the basis for the emergence of each, and their approach to exercising authority. Through mediumship, women assumed a most interesting and ambiguous role in the precolonial period (Cheater, 1986, p. 68). Like al-Hakkamat, the mediums were also an institutionalised leadership position for women, which was grounded in the traditional authority and leadership system in some ancient African societies. The emergence of al-Hakkamat is governed by their initial demonstration of the relevant skills and talents, and their ability to exercise and nurture them through a complex social process and for a long period of time.

A significant difference is that spirit mediumship is a religious-based construction of authority and a process that is established in a belief in mediums chosen by the spiritual powers of deceased people to act on their behalf. It is defined as 'a form of possession in which the person is conceived as serving an intermediary between spirits and men'. It serves as a communication media between the supernatural/God and a particular community, through conscious actions and words that can be translated into specific meanings and messages. Spirit mediumship should not be confused with spirit possession, which is a form of trance in which behaviour and actions of a person are interpreted as evidence that a spirit normally external to him controls his behaviour (Firth, 1959, p. 141). Spirit mediumship is thus conscious acting by the mediums, whereas spirit possession is a state of unconscious acting.

The persons chosen to be mediums often exhibit recurrent symptoms such as headaches, low appetite and frequent bouts of sickness, also well versed in the territory's affairs (Butcher, 1980, pp. 47–8). Whilst the spirits are predominantly male, the gender of the person undertaking the roles of mediums who pass the spirits' messages to people is indeed irrelevant. As such, there are more women assuming the roles of male spirits than men taking on the roles of female spirits (Firth, 1959, p. 141).

There are many justifications for awarding such an advantageous role to women, such as women being denied official responsibility in the conventional religious system. Spirit mediumship serves as a compensatory way for them to exercise power and authority that cannot be contested, being endorsed by the same religious methodology (ibid., p. 144). But, the religious administration is not the only system that bans women from office; rather, it is a custom that women have either no or limited access to political office. Besides, as women in the vast majority of Africa are traditionally presumed to be obedient to men, the mediums have the chance to redress this position, at least for themselves, by their ability to earn society's respect and more access to free movement than ordinary women. Mediums were able to reap a substantial fortune, particularly in contexts such as Nkore in East Africa where women, apart from witches and princesses, have no right to inherit property and are seen as inferior (Berger, 1976, p. 173).

Religious obligations in traditional belief systems have therefore conferred on women who resisted the female stereotype an opening to the distinguished status of exercising power and authority based on the same religious doctrine (Cheater, 1986, p. 69). Hence despite the different sources of their power, both al-Hakkamat and the mediums stand as a significant challenge to the dominant ideology of patriarchy, gender discrimination and female subordination.

In precolonial Africa, spirit mediums were of significant importance in the governing system, which consisted mainly of kings, chiefs and village heads. In Zimbabwe, for instance, there were two dominant political structures, demonstrated by the two kingdoms of Ndebele and (Ma)Shona. The Shona kingdom was run through a decentralised political framework and composed of relatively autonomous chiefdoms. The chiefdoms were managed by chiefs together with democratic councils of notable men who provided political guidance and spirit mediums who provided spiritual governance (Chigwata, 2015, p. 445). As in Darfur, this traditional system of authority has largely survived and continues to operate in parallel to the state's formal structures of governance, exercising power over people and land.

There is an embedded belief in the mediums in Shona society, as being spiritually assigned to oversee and protect the land from adversaries and intruders. They are thought to be connected with the spirits of prominent deceased people who assumed ruling positions within the territory. These spirits are subsequently recognised as the 'land owners', or 'territorial spirits', locally called *mhondoro* (a maneless lion). It is believed that after the burial ceremony, the spirit of the deceased wanders in the forests for a minimum of five years. Then it comes back to take on a person as a host, through whom it communicates with people and exercises full command over the chiefdom. People show their respect for the mediums by removing their hats and shoes; men clap and women ululate (Butcher, 1980, pp. 47–8).

We understand that al-Hakkamat are present in each clan, and there could be more than one Hakkamah, as it is all subject to the women's talents and aspirations. The culture of spirit mediumship in Zimbabwe suggests that sometimes there may be more than one medium who claims to be possessed by the same spirit. Yet Nehanda is the only spirit that has two traditions and, thence, two legitimate mediums that are independent of each other, even though sometimes they might get in competition with each other. One is in the Mazoe region and the other in Dande. Charwe was the medium of the Mazoe Nehanda. With the exception of Nehanda, all other *mhondoro* can have only one legitimate medium at any one time (Lan, 1985, p. 105).

Support and advice from these spirits are usually sought in times of crises, such as shortage of rain, and attacks by pests and disease. The possessed mediums can always show the people what faults they have committed against the territory and how to amend them and get rid of the calamity (Butcher, 1980, p. 49). In attending to their divine responsibilities for preserving their lands, these tribal-territorial mediums have played significant roles in mobilising Zimbabwean people against British colonials – Zimbabwe's invaders from the 1890s until independence in 1979.

When the British captured Zimbabwe in the late 1880s, a convention of resistance was soon built among the public, especially the mediums. The mounting discontent burst in 1896, the first rebellion of Shona people against the new colonial state. Among the representatives of the territorial spirits, Sharwe, the female Nehanda who was the most prominent medium in Shona land, was at the heart of the revolt. She was said to have acted as a powerful commander, together with her male partner, the Chaminuka. The revolt was fiercely terminated in mid-1897, and Sharwe Nehanda was arrested and sentenced to death in 1898 (Butcher, 1980, p. 48; Cheater, 1986, p. 68 and Lan, 1985, p. 17).

Sharwe's name, her sincerity, dedication and resolve against the colonials have not just become a pleasant historical relic, but have remained a perpetual source of emotional recovery and a legacy of sacrifice, dignity and pride for her society. Whilst awaiting her prosecution, her belief in independence never diminished, as expressed in her prophecy that 'my bones will rise' to triumph over the colonialists. Recognising this patriotic dedication, and in order to perpetuate the tradition of resistance, two of the early operational zones of ZANU (Zimbabwe African National Union) in the northeast, were named Nehanda and Chaminuka (Lan, 1985, p. 17).

The violent prosecution of Sharwe could not stop the wave of resistance, however. Rather, it fortified nationwide resolve and determination to resist, especially in Shona society. With the resurrection of a new medium for Chaminuka, the precarious situation burst out again in 1903, following an increase in the hut tax. The medium launched a new rally against the colonials but without success (Butcher, 1980, p. 51).

The nationalist movement arose in the 1950s, launching a successful public mobilisation against the colonial government. To counteract the movement, like the government's approach in Sudan, the colonial government employed the divide-and-rule approach, to polarise the society and weaken its solidarity. They reinstated the chiefs, who hitherto ignored by the British rulers, and empowered them using salaries, access to officials, etc. (ibid., p. 27). For people thirsty for authority and prestige, there can be no more privileges they could aspire to, and inevitably, they would be ready to perpetrate whatever it takes to maintain such a franchise.

The chiefs then acted against the African National Congress Party (NCP), founded in 1957, and compelled the leaders to change the party's name frequently in order to avoid political harassment until it split into two factions: The Zimbabwe African People's Union (ZAPU) and the Zimbabwe African National Union (ZANU). When the white-led Rhodesian Front Party assumed power, a National Council of Chiefs was introduced, whereby the chiefs become entirely subservient to the colonials. In 1965, the chiefs upheld the Unilateral Declaration of Independence (UDI), which was strongly rejected by the nationalists as it ensured a firm grasp of power in the hands of the whites for years ahead (ibid., pp. 28–9; Lan, 1985, p. 147). For that reason, Rhodesia could not achieve independence in the mid-1960s as most of the Britain's former African colonies did and the struggle continued.

Amid the rising precariousness of the situation, in 1971 the leaders of ZANU launched a guerrilla attack, the first since the 1896 rebellion event, on the Rhodesian state, to mark the inception of the guerrilla war in Rhodesia. During the struggle, the relationship between ZANU guerrillas and peasants' religious leaders – spirit mediums and female mediums in particular – was significant in helping the guerrillas to achieve victory. It started in 1971 when the guerrillas were desperate for the support of and cooperation with Dande society and the peasants, Shona in particular; for they were the most frustrated by the past events.

The rebel leaders resorted to the mediums because of their authority and the allegiance owed to them by the peasantry. Subsequently, appealing to territorial spirits and the mediums of tribes drove more citizens to join in (Butcher, 1980, p. 52; Lan, 1985, p. 134). It was of utter importance that the leaders were not guided to the mediums by a belief in the myth and/or an intention to mobilise people on notions of tribalism and tribal division, but because by then the mediums symbolised national identity, not a limited ethnic identity, as al-Hakkamat did.

In forging such alliances, the guerrillas met with the mediums and lived with them in their villages. One of these mediums was an old female spirit medium Nehanda, a medium of the *mhondoro* spirits who are recognised to have the power of rain and the power of war. She was said never to have bathed and ate only once or twice a week; she hated everything about Europeans. More precisely, she was described as:

> A small woman, very thin and very old, with white hair and skin that was exceedingly black. She was dressed in a piece of black cloth that was wrapped around her body and she wore bangles. Some of them gold, on her wrists, and other ornaments around her neck. Her skin was dry and cracked with age, and dung was regularly rubbed on to protect it from the sun. (Commander Mayor Urimbo, cited in Lan, 1985, p. 147)

Despite the advanced age of the Nehanda medium and her deteriorated health, she enthusiastically pledged full support to help the leaders in their quest to liberate Zimbabwe. Urimbo acknowledged her contribution, saying that she 'was doing her command work, directing us in Zimbabwe'; also another leader emphasised that 'she led us in the war of liberation' (cited in Lan, 1985, p. 16). She provided them with directions, routes, advice on where to sleep and hide weapons, foods to avoid and other ritual prohibitions to help the fighters live safely and win the fight. She supplied them with protective medicines and cures and alerted them to warning signs of the enemy approaching. Together with other mediums, she led a communal mobilisation among the villagers urging them to join the guerrillas in order to rid Zimbabwe of the Europeans.

When she died in mid-1973, her body was buried with ceremonial rituals like 'a chief, on a wooden platform sunk in the earth surrounded by a hut built and thatched in a single day' (ibid.). In the aftermath of the war, Urimbo, who was then the National Political Commissar of ZANU/PF and a member of parliament, told the end of Nehanda's story: 'Her house ... is still there. Fire comes and goes but it will never burn. When we crossed into Zimbabwe, we put our weapons there and praised the ancestors and said: We are going to liberate Zimbabwe' (ibid.).

However, since the first rebellion in 1896, the colonials have become acquainted with the significance of the mediums in people's beliefs. When they realised the connection between the mediums and the guerrillas in the 1960s, they followed suit by recruiting and using spurious mediums to counteract the guerrillas' intensified attacks. This looks similar to the approach of the Sudanese authorities in recruiting faked Hakkamat and using them in war campaigns, even those who had no relevance to the institution of Hakkamah. The white-led Zimbabwean government broadcasted from aeroplanes, recordings that were falsely attributed to mediums condemning the guerrillas and urging people to side with the government. They dispersed leaflets with similar messages over the operational zone (ibid., p. 18).

As the experience in Darfur suggests, employing traditional means in wartime can only solidify the stubborn fighting, aggression and violence on both sides. The mediums proved their sympathy and unconditional support for the people of the whole country. They never weakened or fell behind during the long trajectory of struggle, full of grievances and sacrifices, and it took the movement fourteen years following the UDI before they achieved independence in 1979.

Despite the different objectives and motives, al-Hakkamat's contribution in arousing ethnic affection among the Baggara youth and horsemen and mobilising them for the wars in Sudan resembles that of the mediums, which inspired masses of Shona people to join from rural areas in support of the guerrilla movement (ibid.). On the other hand, the mediums are territory-specific foundations, both in issues and in space. Their engagement with leaders and in conventions outside their territories constituted a significant development and was a break from the Shona tradition and their conventional loyalty to their own chiefs. Yet the mediums have developed a positive attitude, which shows an insightful perception and apparent flexibility in engaging in patriotic concerns. Obviously, the mediums comprehend that sometimes the focus becomes serving the national boundaries in the best interests of all the citizens, not only Shona tribal territory.

Whether al-Hakkamat have the potential to adopt similar perceptions to those of the mediums and change into agents serving the best interest of all the citizens in Darfur and Sudan at large is partly subject to political developments in Darfur and war methodology in Sudan. However it depends in the first place, on al-Hakkamat's vision of their future and the future of the country.

CONCLUSION

For various reasons, considerable numbers of al-Hakkamat have emigrated from their villages and settled in Nyala town, in a context with entirely different characteristics from their homogeneous rural village habitat. This movement has entailed considerable adjustments to enable them to cope with the dynamic challenges in the town, where they have had to navigate their way cautiously but firmly. They have engaged in continuous negotiations with the social and political forces of the urban environment, which have enabled them to transform their skills and expand relationships with government civil and military institutions. They have been able to build more confidence and reach out well beyond their conventional sphere of influence. By internalising and managing their multiple social and ethnic identities, they have established their own space and status as prominent female actors, especially within government institutions, where rules and actors change constantly.

Their engagement with social and political actors, including government institutions, in such an urban environment has necessitated their compliance with the rules, customs and discourses pertaining to these structures. Their accountability, in turn, has largely shifted from the exclusive village/camp and tribal society to rest with wider groups of Arab ethnicity in Darfur and beyond but more authentically with the government, their new masters. Observably though, whilst some of the readjustment measures they pursued were certainly required and beneficial to their position and personal development, many others were quite detrimental to their own communities, let alone the whole of Sudanese society, as evident, for instance by the huge numbers of youngsters who died in the wars they promoted.

The character of al-Hakkamat could be equated with the female mediums of Shona society in Zimbabwe. Both constitute significant positions of women as 'territorial agents' in the African traditional system of authority that survived colonial and postcolonial anti-women patriarchal forces. They showed uncompromised ability to exercise influence in the social and political domains of their societies. Shona female mediums, in particular, were able to transcend ethnic and tribal boundaries by joining the liberation struggle and offering great sacrifices to redeem Zimbabwe from the invaders. The alliance they built with the liberation movement in Zimbabwe constitutes a manifestation of the voice of wisdom that they embraced and confidently exercised, responding to the urge for unity in order to achieve a patriotic goal for the whole society, and not just for their own ethnic band.

Contrary to this epic, al-Hakkamat have been unable to craft a similar path and/or to develop a patriotic vision and personality that could transcend their limited ethnic boundaries and reach out to others in order to foster peace and coexistence in society. Had the emigrant Hakkamat developed a propensity and a vision for peace, the outcomes could have been quite different from the tribulation that has been produced.

10

Conclusion

Engaging al-Hakkamat Baggara women of Darfur in Sudan's civil wars has been instrumental, yet it needs to be seen in the context of armed conflict between tribes and ethnic groups in Darfur and the wider context of power and struggle in rural Africa more generally. This contesting against the central government has not been stimulated primarily by reasons of differences in culture, identity or religion, although along the way these have become rallying points. There is a lot of evidence to indicate that these conflicts have been induced by the struggle of people to secure livelihoods and political power within a context overwhelmed by conflicting and tense power relations. This context has been instigated by the state's administrative approach in managing tribal and ethnic groups in rural areas, where most of the population are in pastoralist and agropastoralist communities. Since the annexation of the Darfur sultanate into the condominium rule of Sudan in 1917, the state's rulers have consistently demonstrated an inability to manage fairly the affairs of these communities, which had been well organised and effectively managed in the past.

COLONIALISM AND POSTCOLONIALISM

As we have seen, to understand al-Hakkamat role it is of paramount importance to comprehend the history and administrative system of the Darfur sultanate (1445–1916) and how it succeeded in maintaining a relatively stable environment and coexistence among diverse tribes and ethnic groups. During the sultanate, tribes were administered through specifically allocated specific homelands, the *Dars*, where most of the tribes were allocated *Dars* and tribal chiefs entrusted with considerable autonomy and leverage to administer their own people and the land on behalf of the sultan. Yet these *Dars* were well connected to the central power of the sultanate and under its close supervision. In the aftermath of the sultanate conquest, first by the Anglo-Turkish (1874–81) and then by the condominium (1917–56) administrations, the sultan was killed and the sultanate hierarchy of satellite authorities (*Sharati*, Nuzzar, Omad, etc.) were weakened. The *Dars* and tribal authorities were left disconnected and detached administrative units deprived of a close patron who could earn or enforce their allegiance to the principles of the state and who would also come to their rescue if help was needed.

Following 1956, the national postcolonial regimes have been unable to modernise or energise the *Dar* system and the tribal administration, but renamed them the 'native administration'. Still isolated and neglected, they were transformed into mere security units to maintain law and order in the best interest of the ruling elites. Tribes were left to take the entire responsibility for responding to the needs of their people in maintaining security and peace, rather than the respective governmental institutions.

In 1970 the *Dars* and tribal administration, that is, the native administration, was specifically targeted, not by reform, however, but by 'deform'. This was when the tribes' ownership over their *Dars* was threatened by the Unregistered Lands Act (ULA) (1970), followed by the disempowerment of tribal authority by the dissolution of the native administration in 1971. This was enacted without review and/or consultation with the real stakeholders. These policies were enacted at a critical time for the rural Darfuri people who were still suffering the repercussions of the economic crises that had hit the country since the late 1960s, combined with a deterioration of natural resources caused by the Sahelian drought. The latter resulted in the emigration of huge populations, who sought residence in the *Dars* of the less affected tribes. These policies together with the enactment of the Local Government Act, which stipulated the election of the councillors, have stimulated an outbreak of violent conflicts over the country's meagre natural resources. Conflict over the power of administering the *Dars*, which have now become accessible for outsiders was, according to the stated policy, even more vicious. The need for solidarity started to grow progressively among the *Dars'* owners and soon developed into a forceful defence to block the ambitious outsiders and set a clear demarcation to affirm and maintain the tribes' rights over the *Dars*, regardless of the government's will.

This situation has heightened the feeling of 'us', leaving a little room for 'them', and subsequently resulted in tribes become agitated on the slightest provocation. Even when the *Dar* system was loosely reinstated by the democratic regime in 1986, it is doubtful that this was meant to reform the system and/or deliver services to the inhabitants. As history shows, it was used to serve the elites' interests in election campaigns whilst the conflict continued unabatedly. Hence, the failure of the postcolonial state to integrate tribes and ethnic groups socially, economically and politically into the dynamics of nation state building and/or to maintain law and order have reinforced the value of the *Dar* and its status as the tribe's own sanctuary where tribal sovereignty trumps national fealties.

Tribes have thus projected themselves as autonomous entities, at the extreme end, and seen their *Dars* as mini-states capable of bestowing on them what a nation state normally confers on its citizenry. Whilst this understanding enables them to preserve their socio-cultural privacy qualities and value systems, it also makes them less respectful of the rule of law, if this clashed with their perceived interests. In this context, they often fall back on their own conventional tribal defensive mechanisms, for instance, the Ageed of the Baggara communities in which al-Hakkamat constitute integral and crucial partners.

The engagement of al-Hakkamat in this troubled environment is but an intrinsic moral commitment, purposely constructed to serve their communities in both peaceful and turbulent times. Similar to the female spirit mediums of Zimbabwe, al-Hakkamat also serve as 'territorial agents', maintaining the socio-cultural boundaries of their tribes. They strive to ingrain and safeguard their tribes' moral values and standards and to hold their communities accountable. The position of al-Hakkamat is reinforced by the belief in the tribes' autonomy and authority over their *Dars*, and therefore al-Hakkamat instil in the tribespeople the value of 'rise and sacrifice' for the sake of the tribe's dignity and existence.

Al-Hakkamat are therefore well prepared to move to extremes in honing the ethnic consciousness of their people to pursue, or pre-empt, aggression when they suspect that the values and existence of their tribes under threat. This is when they become fully integrated with the Ageed military organisation. Nevertheless, they would often act independently as an ethnic voice that could influence men to opt for war, sometimes even without the Ageed*'s* consent. Hence, by serving both a peaceful and a combative role, al-Hakkamat seem to have the pragmatic power and agency to influence any situation. That is perhaps why they were described by many members of their society as 'a double-edged sword' that can help, but can also hurt.

Al-Hakkamat's status was not new to Darfuri women, however, nor was it exceptional. It is an extension of the gender-friendly power relations that seem to have prevailed during the Fur sultanate, where women were equal with men in obtaining material resources, such as land, had social and economic autonomy and their general political participation was obvious. Women, both young and old, were among the leading figures in the sultanate and their views were often required, solicited on serious political issues and respected. It was clear that their influence in the last days of the sultanate was the trigger that prevented the sultan's retreat and thus led to the immediate demise of the sultanate. That was when the sister of Sultan Ali Dinar, *iiya basi Mayram* Taja, incited him to fight the British, otherwise she would take his place because he would not be a man! Unable to endure the humiliation if he were to act otherwise he confronted the invaders unprepared, only to see himself killed and his sultanate terminated thereafter. The royal women's agency appears to have acted as a decisive stimulus even when the outcome was inevitably going to be catastrophic.

This and other experiences of exercising power and authority by Darfuri women remain historical incidents affecting royal female figures but they equally allude to, and symbolise, the sultanate's gender policy that appears to have consolidated the position of women in general. Such favourable gender relationships in Darfur, compared to other parts of northern Sudan, seem to have influenced the general position of Darfuri women, as manifested in the roles and experiences of al-Sheikhat and al-Hakkamat.

Al-Hakkamat's political participation was also evident during the reign of Sultan Ali Dinar, as witnessed by the testimony of al-Hakkamah Safiyaat, a singer at the sultan's court, whereby she communicated the arrival of British troops to the sultan in a most eloquent recitation. But their involvement in ethnic mobilisation seems to have been quite rare, perhaps because widespread tribal conflicts were also quite rare at the time. Besides, the sultanate had a strong grip in maintaining law and order and containing conflict before it escalated into stages that might invoke al-Hakkamat. But minor incidents saw them mocking men and inciting them to fight.

In the aftermath of the British invasion, al-Hakkamat appeared less victimised than other public female actors in Darfur, especially recognised royal figures. For instance, the unique titles of the royal women, e.g. *iiya basi* and *Mayram*, were removed from the administrative structure along with their entitlements of power and prestige (although Darfur society continues to used them out of courtesy and deference but divested of their power and status). This was indeed common practice for British colonials in African societies, such as the Ibo community in Nigeria, as shown in this book, where the female historical icons were stripped of their power and status whereas those of the males were preserved.

The annexation of Darfur to the state of Sudan in 1917 brought no advantage to the Darfuris; rather, the successive colonial rulers and subsequent national administrations continued their utilitarian approach to the administration of tribes. They instituted the marginalisation and isolation of the region from the state organisational strategies and development processes. The rural areas suffered severe negligence and deterioration of the social service and livelihood infrastructure, which became either virtually non-existent or much diminished. In effect, rural people were left to rely on their own primordial welfare and decision-making frameworks to address their perceived needs and redress the implications of the elites' policies of neglect. The traditional frameworks are governed by local customs, power relationships, solidarity and casual arrangements, such as the *Faza'* and *nafir*.

Women, in particular, were forced by such circumstances to continue to associate with subsistence farming and animal husbandry, more than men, who either migrated to work in the irrigated mechanised agricultural enterprises along the River Nile or joined the army to fight in the civil war in Southern Sudan. Meanwhile, huge numbers immigrated across borders. This deteriorating social and economic contexts offered women more responsibilities but also an extra economic space, which in many ways have paradoxically influenced local norms and customary laws to their advantage. Arguably it also served as a conducive environment for al-Hakkamat, especially given their extra leverage and abilities. It has eventually enabled the revitalisation and reformulation of the culture of al-Hakkamah, both as an institution and as an actor, within the social organisation of the conventional authority and leadership of the Baggara communities so that it cannot be dispensed with or overlooked.

The combination of the natural crises, economic pitfalls and the continued neopatrimonial domestic politics in Darfur has exacerbated rural people's suffering and increased their vulnerability to the lack of sustainable livelihoods. Again, those people found no outlet but to resort to their primordial means to secure access to the deteriorated resources for survival. As it was a matter of life or death for them, the once negotiable inter-relationships turned into hostility, tension, and readiness for confrontation. In minding their obligations, al-Hakkamat reappeared on the scene with a powerful voice to embolden their people to stay put in fighting their adversaries. This was the time when al-Hakkamat were needed most to shelter their tribes and exposing others, often displaying a hawkish and warmongering drive. They forged a strong liaison with their wartime counterpart, the Ageed organisation, where they perform mutually integrated roles: al-Hakkamat mobilising the community for war and the Ageed planning and executing the war: a relationship of common purpose uniting these two organisations.

Al-Hakkamat's manifestations in these turbulent times as 'territorial agents' have proved the worth of their social and political roles, such that they function as an SOS voice for the vulnerable, particularly women and children. Such undertakings appear to be structural obligations and pre-emptive procedures that strike a balance in the gender division of labour in the social organisation of the Baggara tribes. Al-Hakkamat espouse belligerence to ensure that men can ward off danger. Their communities therefore feel grateful for their contributions, and some described them as 'the shadow of a big tree for the whole tribe', even though their detractors perceive them 'as evil as a Devil'. It is indeed reasonable to conclude that al-Hakkamat's formidable agency and influence have transcended the publicised stereotype of rural women, in Sudan and in African at large, as merely passive victims. When their interventions appear to cross the line they can still be justified as a coping strategy to avoid the dehumanising and withering effects of defeat that they now observe happening to other Darfuri rural women, including gender-based violence, especially rape.

AL-HAKKAMAT MOBILISATION IN THE CIVIL WARS

Until early 1990, the institution of al-Hakkamat seems to have operated in a largely local tribal sphere in promoting their tribes' special interests but also helping riverine political parties in election campaigns. From 1986 to 1990, the government of Sudan pursued regional geopolitical politics and domestic policies that allowed Chadian and Libyan opposition groups to use Darfur as a rear base for launching military attacks against their governments and allowed Arab immigrants who fled from Chad to have unrestricted access to resettle in Darfur. The activities of these groups turned Darfur into a marketplace for ammunitions and weaponry smuggled from these turbulent countries, which made it quite easy for small arms to fall into the hands of individuals and tribes. When the NIF government launched a disarmament campaign in Darfur in 1991, al-Hakkamat contributed significantly in encouraging rural populations to hand in their weapons, marking the inception of their association with government authority and the state ruling and governing elites.

The racial discrimination and neopatrimonial political approach of the riverine governing elites were clearly manifested by the introduction of the *emara* policy in 1995, which granted more than 60 per cent of *Dar* Masalit to the Chadian Arabs. This discriminatory policy against the indigenous locals to the advantage of immigrant Arabs, was combined with the political attitudes that turned Darfur into the scapegoat of the geopolitics of the riverine ruling elites. This difficult situation has generated overwhelming grievances that prompted the most affected indigenous African groups, particularly from the Fur and Masalit tribes, to initially organise as peaceful activists before being forced into an armed struggle, after their concerns and demands were rejected. They were labelled criminals and their movements interpreted as ethnic, racial and/or religious insurrections. The deliberate misinterpretation by the government of political movements in Sudan, a well-established practice of the riverine elites, enabled them to mobilise Darfuri Arab society to bolster the declared pan-Arabism advocacy and Islamism ideology adopted by the NIF regime.

This commenced by interpreting Bolad's insurgency (1991/2) as an anti-Islamic and anti-Arab attack by the African Fur. The civil war in Southern Sudan since mid-1992 was also considered a holy war, and last but not least, the Darfuri insurgency, which emerged in 2003, was propagandised as anti-Arab. These portrayals were convincing enough for most of the Darfuri Arab tribes to fight alongside the government. Apparently, these are the main pillars of the divide-and-rule strategy projected by the elites, which embrace the consequential idea that 'the end justifies the means'. They can serve dual agendas: ethnicity based on race can be used to incite tribes and ethnic groups to confront one another, and on the other hand, mobilisation of ethnic consciousness in a multi-ethnic society can serve as an effective instrument for the state to challenge and confront regional political movements and rival groups. Again, this can leave these polar groups embroiled with each other in diversionary pursuits and local confrontations.

This ethnicised and racialised context was a favourable environment for al-Hakkamat whose social identity was symbolic in the war strategy of the ruling elites. This is because from their position as an Arab tribal institution, they could be counted on to authentically serve the objectives meted out by the ethnic interpretation of conflict and ethnic polarisation in Darfur and throughout Sudan. Thus, it was expedient for the government authorities to incorporate and operationalise al-Hakkamat's symbolic meaning and turn the direction of their positive contribution to the government campaign into a combative role against the insurgencies. Al-Hakkamat were then recruited and incorporated within the premise of the domestic politics, assimilating tribes and ethnic groups in Darfur and their conventional institutions. Their roles were reformulated and their institution reconstructed to match the government's demands. They have been transformed into loyal partners incorporated in the mobilisation strategy of the state's military apparatus. Their agency and influence have been reinforced but manipulated in the government's favour.

Al-Hakkamat have sincerely carried out their obligations to the satisfaction of their masters who were now the riverine ruling elite, not the tribal leaders, as used to be the case. Their dedication has also contributed significantly to turning Darfur into a clearly polarised society of Africans *vis-à-vis* Arabs, where the government consistently stood in support of the Arabs, whether locals or immigrants. Al-Hakkamat also reinforced the de facto perception of Darfur as a reservoir of military recruits for the civil wars in Sudan. These elements have collectively turned Darfur into a place overwhelmed with the precarious security situation, violent conflicts and aggression, as almost all tribes became involved in violent conflicts with each other.

Ironically, al-Hakkamat, both in the village and in the town, had no advantageous position over other women as far as the government services and support were concerned. Nevertheless, they could not champion the cause of gender development and/or address the rural women's perceived needs, especially the destitute and the vulnerable women in the conflict zones. Instead, they allowed the power brokers to use them to inflict suffering on those women and subject them to more inhumane atrocities, which al-Hakkamat strive strenuously to avoid happening in their own communities.

Besides, their significant contribution to the mobilisation of recruits has caused huge loss of life, primarily among the Baggara society. By upholding the racial notions of the ruling elites on the causes of war, al-Hakkamat tended unconsciously to solidify the government position in manipulating Darfuri Arab tribes. This position was discouraging tribes from revolting against the central government, either on their own and/or by joining the Darfuri insurgents, even though they were no less marginalised than those they were fighting. Instead, those Darfuri Arabs either fought each other and/or joined the government forces to fight the rebels who were protesting the deteriorating situation in the region, which troubled both Africans and Arabs. This position of the Arab tribes might equally encourage and cement al-Hakkamat's position of engaging with the government, which could in turn weaken their prospect of becoming advocates for peace and reconciliation.

Nevertheless, al-Hakkamat's position is quite comprehensible given their obligations to back their kinfolk, especially during conflicts, whether victims or perpetrators, driven by their own cause or mobilised by the state for similar impulses. This is al-Hakkamat's moral obligation, which has added to the emerging cleavage in social relationships between ethnic groups in Darfur. On the other hand, al-Hakkamat cannot be blamed on ethical grounds for their conduct given the lack of any positive influence or guidance to emphasise the need for a peaceful resolution of disputes. Besides, most of al-Hakkamat's compositions show that they subscribe to the ideals of their tribes and ethnic groups more than they do to other codes of conduct that might be imposed on them. In their conduct, they were authentically expressing the social values attached to the institution of al-Hakkamah, and in fulfilling their obligations, they always go as far as their agency can take them.

AL-HAKKAMAT IN PEACE AND RECONCILATION

The situation in Darfur demands that all local and regional actors and power brokers come on board in the quest for reconciliation and peace. As al-Hakkamat have been in the forefront of the conduct of confrontation, it is their duty to take an active part in repairing damaged relationships in as much as this might also preserve the dignity and honour of their tribes, whose cause they have been elevating all along.

However, the pressing approaches and efforts of the ruling and governing elites and local power brokers in using the belligerent voice of al-hakkamat and maintaining them as hawks of conflict have hampered their transformation into potential doves of peace. This has clearly unfolded in the approaches to conflict resolution and reconciliation attempted at local, regional and national levels, from which rural women in general, and al-Hakkamat in particular, have been excluded. The government's failure to see al-Hakkamat, which was so successful as an agent in the conflict, being useful in making peace contracts, contradicted its recognition of al-Hakkamat's influence. Obviously, their project was not to devalue the agency of al-Hakkamat, but to institutionalise and sustain their belligerent voice and to disempower their positive attitude to solving social problems.

This exclusion is certainly detrimental both to the women and al-Hakkamat let alone the whole society of Darfur. Al-Hakkamat, who are usually well versed in the social context of their tribes, have now become less aware of the processes of negotiation and reconciliation. This lack of awareness has often made it their safest bet to see it as a moral duty to uphold their tribe's dignity and integrity by resuming the war. Notwithstanding this stalemate, in the narratives presented in this book, al-Hakkamat have also proved through their independent initiatives that they can be effective in mediating for reconciliation, and successful in creating a conducive environment for peace resettlement and sustainable reconciliation – situations in which women feel secure and al-Hakkamat need not call for war.

We have seen that some Hakkamat have maintained autonomy in making choices that appeared to have defied the will of power brokers; for example when they started, in 2003, appealing in a fraternal spirit of solidarity to the 'sons of Darfur' to stop the war, and avoided mobilising people against one another. Such positivity, no matter how late or minor, also enhances the urge for peace that al-Hakkamat could have fulfilled rather more effectively if they had they been brought on board the peace processes. If this positive spirit of al-Hakkamat towards peace was nurtured and promoted, the UHS could turn into a civil society organisation mandated with peace advocacy, gender development, and women's rights in rural areas. It might also be a leading organisation for pivoting the attitudes of Baggara rural societies towards reconciliation and peacebuilding.

On the other hand, we have also seen how the government has used al-Hakkamat to play an instrumental part in the country's war and violence campaigns whilst ignoring their basic needs for a decent living. This is a result of the adverse impact for al-Hakkamat of moving outside their natural tribal habitat in the countryside, which caused them to lose their previously guaranteed sources of income. Besides this, they witnessed a decline in the authenticity of their poetic product, as their people repeatedly remarked. Although these Hakkamat might have developed some resilient outlets, they nevertheless put their values and prestige to the test, and ended up provoking their 'primordial' communities and earning far less genuine recognition.

AGENCY OF AL-HAKKAMAT BAGGARA WOMEN

Both in the village and town contexts, al-Hakkamat have proved themselves as powerful female political actors in a context overwhelmed by war and violence. The recently emerged actors in the town constitute some of the causes and the products of the sociopolitical changes experienced in Darfur in the last three decades. Their relationship with government authorities has transformed them into a force to count on in most if not all of government wars fought in Sudan since 1991. Their belligerent voice and influence have been dramatically empowered, to surpass that of other tribal institutions and/or women's organisations. In this respect alone, they constitute a critical component in the map of violent armed conflict between tribes and ethnic groups in Darfur, as well as of military strategies in Sudan in which Darfuri people took part as active militants, either in the army and/or in pro-government militias.

Like most women, al-Hakkamat emerged out of a context characterised by historical and contemporary patriarchal gender frameworks that often isolated women from public decision making and dictated their subordination. Al-Hakkamat represent a case of women's power and agency against the patriarchy and the complexity of gender-subordinating forces that normally preclude the females' liberty and thriving, especially in rural areas where women lack access to social services and development initiatives. They have exercised their agency and established themselves as 'territorial female agents', earning their communities' acceptance, respect and support. Since the NIF seized authority in 1989, however, the local qualities and ownership of al-Hakkamah as an institution have become subject to manipulation by the ruling and governing elites. This interference has further situated them as important agents in all the wars fought in Sudan, whether locally stimulated between tribes in Darfur, or by the government against their rival insurgents in the country.

We have also seen how the powerful agency of al-Hakkamat has contributed to escalating and/or igniting violence in order to fend off threats against women and tribal territories. This proactive involvement of al-Hakkamat in conflict suggests that despite the stereotyped identity of women and the nature of gender division of labour that often defines the conduct of women and limits their space, women can exercise other more emancipating forms of social identities, e.g. tribal and ethnic. Al-Hakkamat have embraced these identities and invested in the roles legitimised for them by society, thereby exercising the roles of either hawks or doves, as dictated by the social and political environment.

When the women's abilities earn social and political worth, it becomes irrational and socially detrimental to ignore them and/or deny their importance. This implies the necessity for peacebuilding actors to work towards exploring and promoting indigenous frameworks and approaches to conflict management and reconciliation, and building local capacity. Most significant is to review the characteristics of gendered power relations in society and take on board positive values and customs in conflict analysis and resolution as guiding principles in order to ensure women's involvement in reconciliation and peacebuilding processes.

Illiterate rural women have thus proved their ability to gain a prominent status in the domain of public politics, and become equal partners with men through a complex process of self-construction and social recognition. They have established themselves within the stereotyped conventional structures of contemporary Africa, which are usually designed to elevate men and disregard women. In many African settings, rural women in similar positions of authority and influence in the system of traditional authority and leadership have almost vanished, including the powerful female spirit mediums in Zimbabwe.

On the whole, through the narrative presented in this book, al-Hakkamat reveal themselves as a vivid testimony to women's agency and power in rural Darfur. No matter what restrictive circumstances they have faced, they have exercised their own choices by speaking out and performing, with very little censorship other than what their own choices have dictated. When they moved outside their tribal sanctuaries, they also succeeded, by and large, in maintaining their self-esteem whilst navigating through the thorny town environment.

In the fluid and precarious political context in Darfur and Sudan in general, al-Hakkamat's future seems uncertain, however. Their status might drop because of the increased downturn of rural values and influence but they might still continue to exercise agency in the social domain. The prospect of maintaining the same influence and values might also intertwine with the general status of rural women in Darfur in future, especially considering the increasing numbers of females now pursuing higher education. These young females might establish connections with human rights and women's rights institutions and promote sustainable development in their communities. The outcome of interacting with these institutions would certainly redefine most of their relationships and interactions – within and beyond Darfur's borders (as indicated in the network of al-Hakkamat, Figure 0.1).

Appendix: Darfur Chronology, 1445–2017

Note: This chronology has been constructed from sources including O'Fahey and Tubiana (2007); Daly, 2007; the following online sources, all accessed March 2017: <www.aljazeera.com/news/africa/2007/02/200852517257257723>, <www.bbc.co.uk/news/world-africa-14095300>, <https://en.wikipedia.org/wiki/War_in_Darfur>, <https://enoughproject.org/blog/darfur-conflict-timeline>, <https://www.hrw.org/legacy/features/darfur/fiveyearson/timeline.html>, <https://www.reuters.com/article/sudan-darfur-idAFLAE55791520110505>, <www.bbc.co.uk/news/world-africa-14095300>, <http://crawfurd.dk/africa/sudan_timeline.htm>, <https://www.cia.gov/library/publications/the-world-factbook/geos/su.html>, <www.security-councilreport.org/chronology/sudan-darfur.php?page=2>.

1445–1874	The Darfur sultanate was established at its birthplace in Jebel Marrah before it extended to the east during the reign of Suleiman Solung, the Arab who ruled the sultanate during the years c.1660–c.1680, and was considered the founder of the Keira Dynasty
1874–81	The Turco-Egyptian administration after the demise of the sultanate in the Manawashi Battle, 1874
1881–98	The Sudanese Mohamed Ahmed al-Mahdi led an Islamic-inspired revolution against Turco-Egyptian rule in Sudan, establishing the Mahdiyya rule. It incorporated Darfur from 1882
1898–1955	Joint Anglo-Egyptian rule in Sudan, known as the condominium
1898–1916	Sultan Ali Dinar fled to Darfur after the defeat of the Mahdiyya at the Battle of Omdurman in 1898 and revived the sultanate
1917	Sultan Ali Dinar was defeated in 1916 by the Anglo-Egyptian Conquest and Darfur was officially annexed to Sudan in January 1917
1922	Indirect rule over Darfur was confirmed and consolidated
1956	Sudan became an independent country on 1 January, with the civil war in the south starting only weeks earlier
1958	A military coup led by General Abboud took over from the first democratic rule (1956–8)
1963, December	The Darfur Development Front, representing Darfuri political activism, was founded by a young Darfuri politician, Ahmed Ibrahim Diraige, and Ali al-Haj, the Muslim Brother and later secretary general of the Popular Congress Party, which was established and led in 1999 by the late Hassan al-Turabi after the infamous split in the ruling Muslim Brotherhood

1964–9	The second democratic regime was brought in by the October Revolution, 1964
1969–85	Nimeiri's military regime
1970	The Unregistered Lands Act (ULA)
1971	Abolition of the Native Administration and the beginning of the end of indirect rule over Darfur
1972	The Addis Ababa Accord ended the first round of the country's long civil war in the south, which established the Southern Sudan Autonomous Region. It was abolished in 1983 after Sudan decreed Islamic shari'a as law in Sudan
1976	Armed conflict between Bani Halba and Rezeiqat Mahriyah tribes
1979	Armed conflict between Salamat and Ta'aisha tribes
1980	Nimeiri's regime introduced the Regionalism Policy, which led to the appointment of Diraige, from the Fur tribe, after a popular protest by Darfuris rejecting the appointment of a non-Darfuri as governor
1983	Resumption of civil war in South Sudan, led by John Garang's Sudan People's Liberation Army/Movement (SPLA/SPLM)
1984–5	Famine struck Darfur, documented by Alex de Waal in his book, *Famine That Kills* (1985)
1985, April	Nimeiri's regime was overthrown by a popular revolution, the April/*Rajab* Revolution
1985–6	A transitional military government took power and allowed democratic elections to take place, handing power to a civilian administration
1986–9	The third democratic regime was led by al-Sadiq al-Mahdi, the leader of the Umma Party and Imam of the Ansar sect
1987–9	Armed conflict in Darfur between Fur and an alliance of twenty-seven Arab tribes
1989, 30 June	The National Islamic Front (NIF) overthrew democratic rule in a *coup d'état* and established a religious dictatorship that was led by Omar al-Bashir but masterminded and dominated in the first ten years by Hassan al-Turabi
1991	The NIF transformed the Civil War in South Sudan into a Holy War
1991	Regularisation of the Popular Defence Forces (PDF).
1991/92	The Darfuri Bolad's incursion into Darfur, then an affiliate of the SPLM/A. Bolad was defeated in January 1992, captured and killed
1994	Following the administrative redivision of Sudan into states (*wilayaat*), Darfur was divided into three states: North, South and West.
1999	Upsurge in tribal fighting (Masalit and Arab tribes since 1996) as well as armed banditry especially in North Darfur
2003, February	The Sudan Liberation Army/Movement (SLA/M) announces its launch followed shortly after by the Justice and Equality Movement (JEM)

2004, September	Negotiations started in Abuja between Darfuri rebels and the Sudanese government US Secretary of State, Colin Powell, described Darfur atrocities as genocide
2005	The Comprehensive Peace Agreement (CPA) was signed between John Garang's SPLA/SPLM and the Sudanese government
2005, May	The Darfur Peace Agreement (DPA) was signed between Sudanese government and SLA/M (Mini Minawi), but SLA/M (Abdulwahid Nur) and JEM declined
2007, July	The United Nations Security Council authorised a 26,000-strong force for Darfur peace keeping role. Sudan cooperated with this hybrid mission called the United Nations African Union Mission in Darfur (UNAMID)
2008, May	Khalil Ibrahim's JEM mounted a surprise raid on Omdurman, Khartoum's twin city across the Nile
2009, March	The International Criminal Court (ICC) in The Hague issued an arrest warrant for President al-Bashir for war crimes and crimes against humanity in Darfur
	Following the ICC indictment of the Sudanese president, the government expelled 13 NGOs providing humanitarian assistance in Darfur, including Médicins Sans Frontières, MSF (Doctors Without Borders), the International Rescue Committee (IRC), Britain's Oxfam and US-based CARE
2010, April	President Bashir won presidential elections that were boycotted by most opposition parties and were described as rigged
2011, May	Darfur was divided again into five states, by adding two more to its three existing ones: Central Darfur and Eastern Darfur, with Zalingei and Ed Diein as capitals respectively
2011, July	South Sudan became independent after an overwhelming referendum result (January 2011) decreed secession A new Darfur peace agreement, the Doha Agreement based on the Doha Document for Peace in Darfur (DDPD) was signed by the Liberation and Justice Movement (LJM), led by Tijani Sese. The agreement provided for the appointment of a vice president from Darfur and the creation of the Darfur Regional Authority, an administrative structure above the level of states
2011, December	Government forces killed Khalil Ibrahim, founder of the Justice and Equality Movement (JEM)
2015, April	President Bashir was re-elected. Turnout was low and most opposition parties boycotted the elections The Battle of Gawz Dango between JEM and the Rapid Support Forces (RSF) militia in which the RSF surprised and decisively defeated JEM forces
June	UNAMID reported 'limited progress in the peace process' and a worsening security situation which led the United Nations Security Council (Resolution 2228) to renew its mandate for another year
13 July	The Doha Agreement officially came to an end

October	President Bashir launched a National Dialogue process to resolve issues of dissent and achieve unity among Sudanese but was widely boycotted by opposition parties and armed movements
2016	Widespread fighting was reported especially around Jebel Marrah between SLA-Abdulwahid and government forces and allied militias, leading to 'significant displacement of people'. Amnesty International reported in September that chemical weapons were used by government forces against Darfuri people in the area
2016, 11–13 April	The delayed Darfur Status Referendum, which was provided for in the 2006 Abuja Accord, took place. The ballot paper offered two options: either retain the status quo of five states or return Darfur to its pre-1994 status as one region. The former option won by nearly 98 per cent in what has also been described as rigged balloting
2017, April–May	The Sudan Liberation Army – Mini Minawi (SLA/MM) and the Sudan Liberation Army – Transitional Council (SLA/TC), on the one hand, and the Sudanese government forces spearheaded by the RSF militia, on the other, had clashed in battles that ended with a decisive defeat for the former groups
May	Almost two years after the 2015 National Dialogue, a government of National Accord, led by First Lieutenant General Bakri Hassan Saleh, was formed in May 2017, purportedly to realise the outcomes and recommendations of this national dialogue

Bibliography

PRIMARY SOURCES

1. Individual and group interviews with 72 persons in al-Fashir and Nyala.
   a. Group interview with 10 tribal leaders (G1), al-Fashir, March 2006.
   b. Group interview with 3 participants from Fur (G2), Nyala, April 2006.
   c. Group interview with 12 participants from Hakkamat and Sheikhat (G3), Nyala, 2006.
   d. Group interview with 12 Hakkamat (G4), Nyala, June 2006.
   e. Group interview with 5 participants from the Regional Council (G5), May 2006.
   f. Individual interviews with ten participants, al-Fashir, March 2006.
   g. Individual interviews with al-Hakkamat and others in Nyala (30).
2. Email communication with Ali Jammaa, a Baggari and former commissioner of South Kordofan Province who also worked in Darfur (2009).
3. Personal notes written by Ali Noah, a tribal leader from Hubbania and former chairperson of the Union of Art and Folklore, Nyala, 2006.

Secondary Sources

ENGLISH-LANGUAGE PRINTED SOURCES

Abdalla, A. H. 1987. Demographic and Socio-economic Factors Affecting the Participation of Family Labour in the *Rahad* Scheme. In: M. A. Mohamed-Salih and M. A. Mohamed-Salih, eds. *Family Life in Sudan*, Graduate College Publications No. 18. Khartoum: University of Khartoum, pp. 58–71.

Ali, M. 1996. *Ethnicity, Politics and Society in Northeast Africa: Conflict and Social Change.* Lanham, MD: University Press of America.

Allen, J. 1976. Aba Riots' or Igbo 'Women's War'? Ideology, Stratification and the Invisibility of Women. In: N. Hafkin and E. Bay, eds. *Women in Africa: Studies in Social and Economic Change.* Stanford, California: Stanford University Press, pp. 59–86.

Appiah, K. A. 1999. Ethnicity and Identity in Africa. An Interpretation. In: *Africana: The Encyclopaedia of the African and African-American Experience.* New York: Civitas Books.

Barth, F. 1969, reissued 1998. *Ethnic Groups and Boundaries: The Social Organization of Culture Difference.* London and Bergen-Oslo: George Allen & Unwin; Universitetsforlaget.

Bashar, Z. M. 2013. *Local Approaches of Conflict Resolution and Reconciliation in Darfur.* Germany: Lambert Academic Publishing.

Bayart, J. 1993. *The State in Africa: The Politics of the Belly.* London and New York: Longman.

Bechtold, P. K. 1991. More Turbulence in Sudan: A New Politics this Time. In: J. O. Voll, ed. *Sudan State and Society in Crisis.* Indiana: Indiana University Press, pp. 1–24.

Berger, I. 1976. Rebels or Status-Seekers? Women as Spirit Mediums in East Africa. In: N. Hafkin and E. Bay, eds. *Women in Africa: Studies in Social and Economic Change.* Stanford, California: Stanford University Press, pp. 157–82.

Berghe, P. L. 1967. *Race and Racism. A Comparative Perspective.* New York, London, Sydney: John Wiley & Sons.

—— 1975. Introduction. In: P. L. Berghe, ed. *Race and Ethnicity in Africa.* Nairobi: East African Publishing House, pp. viii–xxviii.

Browne, G. W. 1806 [1799]. *Travels in Egypt, Syria and Africa, from the Year 1792–1798* (2nd edn). London: T. Cadell and W. Davies.

Burr, M. J. and R. O. Collins. 1999. Africa's Thirty Years War: Libya, Chad and the Sudan, 1963–1993. Boulder, CO: Westview Press.

—— 2008. *Darfur: The Long History to Disaster* (2nd edn). Princeton, NJ: Markus Wiener Publishers.

Butcher, H. 1980. *Spirits and Power. An Analysis of Shona Cosmology.* Cape Town: Oxford University Press.

Caton, S. C. 1990. *Peaks of Yemen I Summon.* California: University of California Press.

Cheater, A. P. 1986. The Role and Position of Women in Pre-Colonial and Colonial Zimbabwe. *Zambezia*, 13 (2), 65–79.

Clapham, C., ed. 1982. *Private Patronage and Public Power: Political Clientelism in the Modern State.* London: Frances Pinter.

Cunnison, I. 1966. *Baggara Arabs. Power and the Lineage in a Sudanese Nomad Tribe.* Oxford: Clarendon Press. London: Hurst.

Dalal, F. 2002. *Race, Colour and the Processes of Racialization: New Perspectives from Group Analysis, Psychoanalysis and Sociology.* Boca Raton, FL: Brunner-Routledge.

Daly, M. W. 1993. Broken Bridge and Empty Basket: The Political and Economic Background of the Sudanese Civil War. In: M. W. Daly and A. A. Sikainga, eds. *Civil War in the Sudan.* London and New York: British Academic Press, pp. 1–26.

——2007. *Darfur's Sorrow: A History of Destruction and Genocide.* Cambridge: Cambridge University Press.

Davies, J. 2007. Cultural Diversity in the Sudan at Independence. *Sudan Studies*, no. 35 (July), 31–49.

De Waal, A. 1993. Some Comments on Militias in Contemporary Sudan. In: A. A. Daly, and A. A. Sikainga, eds.*Civil War in the Sudan.* London, New York: British Academic Press, pp. 142–56.

——2004. Tragedy in Darfur: On Understanding and Ending the Horror. *Boston Review*, 29 (5), 9.

—— 2005. *Famine That Kills: Darfur, Sudan* (2nd edn). New York, Oxford: Oxford University Press.

—— ed. 2007. *War in Darfur and the Search for Peace.* Harvard University, MA: Justice Africa.

Deng, F. 1987. Myth and Reality in Sudanese Identity. In: F. Deng, ed. *The*

Search for Peace and Unity in the Sudan. Washington DC: Wilson Center Press, pp. 59–77.

—— 1993. Hidden Agendas in the Peace Process. In: M. W. Daly and A. A. Sikainga, eds. *Civil War in the Sudan*. London; New York: British Academic Press, pp. 186–215.

Dodo, O. 2013. Traditional Leadership Systems and Gender Recognition: Zimbabwe. *International Journal of Gender and Women's Studies*, 1 (1), 29–44.

Economic Research Forum Central Bureau of Statistics. 2006. Sudan Household Health Survey. Khartoum, Sudan.

Egemi, O. 2012. Pastoralist Peoples, Their Institutions and Related Policies. Working Paper. Somerville, MA: Feinstein International Center.

El-Battahani, A. 2009. Ideological Expansionist Movements versus Historical Indigenous Rights in the Darfur Region of Sudan: From Actual Homicide to Potential Genocide. In: S. M. Hassan and C. E. Ray, eds. *Darfur and the Crisis of Governance in Sudan: A Critical Reader*. Netherlands: Cornell University Press and Prince Claus Fund Library, pp. 43–67.

El-Bushra, J. 2000. Transforming Conflict: Some Thoughts on a Gendered Understanding of Conflict Processes. In: S. Jacobs, R. Jacobson and J. Marchbank, eds. *States of Conflict: Gender, Violence and Resistance*. London and New York: Zed Books, pp. 66–86.

El Hassan, B. 2008. Securing Pastoralism in East and West Africa: Protecting and Promoting Livestock Mobility in Sudan. Khartoum: Report to SOS Sahel UK.

El Obeid, H. 2000. *Small Arms Survey in Darfur and Investigation of the Child Soldiers*. Khartoum: Charm.

Feinman, I. R. 2000. *Citizenship Rites: Feminist Soldiers and Feminist Antimilitarists*. New York and London: New York University Press.

Firth, R. 1958. *Human Types: An Introduction to Social Anthropology*. New York, Toronto, London: New English Library.

Flint, J. 2007. Darfur's Armed Movements. In: A. de Waal, ed. *War in Darfur and the Search for Peace*. Harvard University, MA: Justice Africa, pp. 140–72.

Flint, J. and de Waal, A. 2005. *Darfur: A Short History of a Long War*. London: Zed in Association with International African Institute.

Francis, D. 2008. Understanding the Context of Peace and Conflict in Africa. In: D. Francis, ed. *Peace and Conflict in Africa*. London and New York: Zed Books, pp. 3–16.

Fruzzetti, L. and A. Ostor. 1990. *Culture and Change along the Blue Nile*. Boulder, CO: Westview Press.

Fukui, K. and J. Markakis. 1994. Introduction. In: K. Fukui and J. Markakis, eds. *Ethnicity and Conflict in the Horn of Africa*. London, Athens: James Currey and Ohio University, pp. 1–14.

Giddens, A. 2001. *Sociology* (4th edn). Cambridge: Polity.

Gould, C. C. 1988. *Rethinking Democracy: Freedom and Social Cooperation in Politics, Economy and Society*. Cambridge: Cambridge University Press.

Grawert, E. 1998. *Making a Living in Rural Sudan: The Case of Kutum, Darfur*. London: Macmillan.

Gupta, A. and J. Ferguson 1997. Beyond 'Culture': Space, Identity and the Politics of Difference. In: Gupta, A. and J. Ferguson, eds. *Culture, Power, Place: Explorations in Critical Anthropology*. Durham, NC and London: Duke University Press, pp. 1–32.

Haaland, G. 1972. Nomadism as an Economic Career among the Sedentaries in the Sudan Savannah Belt. In: I. Cunnison and W. James, eds. *Essays in Sudan Ethnography*. London: Hurst, pp. 149–72.

Haggar, A. 2007. The Origins and Organisation of the Jananjawiid in Darfur. In: A. de Waal, ed. *War in Darfur and the Search for Peace*. Harvard University, MA: Justice Africa, pp. 113–39.

Hale, S. 1992. The Rise of Islam and Women of the National Islamic Front in Sudan. *Review of African Political Economy* (ROAPE), 54, 27–41.

Hamza, M. N. 1986. Fur Customary Land Tenure in Southern Darfur. Manuscript, Customary Law Project, University of Khartoum.

Hans, W. 1961. *A Dictionary of Modern Written Arabic*. Sydney, Australia: Allen & Unwin.

Harir, S. 1983. Old-Timers and New-Comers; Politics and Ethnicity in a Sudanese Community. *Occasional Papers*, No. 29. Bergen: Lilian Barber Press.

—— 1994. 'Arab Belt' versus 'African Belt': Ethno-Political Conflict in *Dar* Fur and the Regional Cultural Factors. In: S. Harir and T. Tvedt, eds. *Short-cut to Decay: The Case of the Sudan*. Uppsala: Nordiska Afrikainstitutet, pp. 144–86.

Harir, S. and T. Tvedt. 1994. Foreword. In: S. Harir and T. Tvedt, eds. *Short-cut to Decay: The Case of the Sudan*. Uppsala: Nordiska Afrikainstitutet, pp. 5–10.

Hassan, S. M. and C. E. Ray, 2006. Introduction: Critically Reading Darfur and the Crisis of Governance in Sudan. In: S. M. Hassan and C. E. Ray, eds. *Darfur and the Crisis of Governance in Sudan: A Critical Reader*. Ithaca, New York: Cornell University Press, pp. 15–28.

Hughes, E. C. 1984. *The Sociological Eye: Selected Papers*. New Brunswick, NJ: Transaction Books.

Ibrahim, A. A. 1985. Regional Inequalities and Underdevelopment in Western Sudan. PhD, Sussex University, UK.

Jenkins, R. 1997. *Rethinking Ethnicity: Arguments and Explorations*. London, Thousand Oaks and New Delhi: Sage Publications.

Kamal El-Din, A. 2007. Islam and Islamism in Darfur. In: A. de Waal, ed. *War in Darfur and the Search for Peace*. Harvard University, MA: Justice Africa, pp. 92–112.

Kapteijns, L. 1985. *Mahdist Faith and Sudanic Tradition: The History of the Masalit Sultanate, 1870–1930*. London, Boston: KPI.

Khalid, M. 2009. Darfur: A Problem within a Wider Problem. In: S. M. Hassan and C. E. Ray (eds), *Darfur and the Crisis of Governance in Sudan: A Critical Reader*. Netherlands: Cornell University Press and Prince Claus Fund Library, pp. 35–42.

Kurita, Y. 1994. The Social Bases of Regional Movements in Sudan, 1960s–1980s. In: K. Fukui and J. Markakis, eds. *Ethnicity and Conflict in the Horn of Africa*. London, Athens: James Currey and Ohio University, pp. 202–16.

Kursany, I. 1984. The Dynamics and Limits of Private Capitalist Development in Sudanese Agriculture. *Development and Peace*, 5, 183–99.

Lampen, G. D. 1933. The Baggara Tribes of Darfur. *Sudan Notes and Records*, 16 (11), pp. 97–118.

Lan, D. 1985. *Guns and Rain: Guerrillas and Spirit Mediums in Zimbabwe*. Northwestern University: Melville J. Herskovits Library of African Studies.

Lister, R. 1997. *Citizenship: Feminist Perspectives*. New York: Macmillan.

Mathiang, T. 2008. Women's Participation in Peace Negotiations in Sudan. In: C. Hendricks and M. Chivasa, eds. *Women and Peacebuilding in Africa*. Workshop Report, 24–5 November. Pretoria: Institute for Security Studies, p. 17.

Medard, J. 1982. The Underdeveloped State in Tropical Africa: Political Clientelism or Neo-patrimonialism? In: C. Clapham, ed. *Private Patronage and Public Power; Political Clientelism in the Modern State*. London: Frances Pinter, pp. 177–92.

Mohamed, A. E. 2003a. Women and Conflict in Darfur. *Review of Political Economy* (ROAPE), 1 (119), 2–3, 479–81.

—— (2009) *Darfur from Insecurity to Social Peace* (in Arabic) (2nd edn), Institute of Public Administration and Federalism, University of Khartoum, Khartoum, Sudan.

Mohamed, A. E. and B. Y. Badri. 2005. A Case Study of the Darfur Region. In *Inter-communal Conflict in Sudan: Causes, Resolution Mechanisms and Transformation.* Building Peace through Diversity Series. Ahfad University for Women, Omdurman.

Mohamed Salih, M. A. 1990. Government Policy and Options in Pastoral Development in the Sudan. *Nomadic Peoples*, 25 (27), 65–78.

Mohamed Salih, M. A. and S. Harir. 1994. Tribal Militias: The Genesis of National Disintegration. In: S. Harir and T. Tvedt, eds. *Short-cut to Decay: The Case of the Sudan*. Uppsala: Nordiska Afrikainstitutet, pp. 186–203.

Morton, J. F. 1992. Tribal Administration or No Administration: The Choice in Western Sudan. *Sudan Studies*, 11, 26–47.

Musa, S. M. E. 2002. Feeder Roads and Food Security, Darfur, Sudan. In: P. Fernando and G. Porter, eds. *Balancing the Load. Women, Gender and Transport*. London and New York: Zed Books, pp. 78–94.

Nagel, J. 1998. Constructing Ethnicity: Creating and Recreating Ethnic Identity and Culture. In M. Hughey, ed., *New Tribalism: The Resurgence of Race and Ethnicity*. New York University Press, pp. 237–72.

Natsios, A. S. 2012. *Sudan, South Sudan, and Darfur: What Everyone Needs to Know*. New York: Oxford University Press.

Niblock, T. 1987. *Class and Power in Sudan: The Dynamics of Sudanese Politics, 1898–1985*. London: Macmillan.

O'Brien, J. 1979. *The Political Economy of Development and Underdevelopment: An Introduction*. Khartoum: Khartoum University Press.

O'Barr, J. 1984. Women in Politics and Policy. In: M. J. Hay and S. Stichter, eds. *African Women South of the Sahara*. London and New York: Longman, pp. 140–55.

O'Fahey, R. S. 1980. *State and Society in Dar Fur*. London: Hurst.

—— 2008. *The Darfur Sultanate: A History*. London: Hurst.

O'Fahey, R. S. and M. I. Abu Salim. 1983. *Land in Darfur: Charters and Related Documents from the Dar Fur Sultanate*. Cambridge: Cambridge University Press.

O'Fahey, R. S. and J. L. Spaulding. 1974. *Kingdoms of the Sudan*. London: Methuen.

Okonjo, K. 1976. The Dual-sex Political System in Operation: Igbo Women and Community Politics in Midwestern Nigeria'. In: N. J. Hafkin and E. G. Bay (eds) *Women in Africa. Studies in Social and Economic Change*. Stanford, CA: Stanford University Press, pp. 45–58.

O'Neill, N. and O'Brien, J. 1988. *Economy and Class in Sudan*. Aldershot: Avebury.

Prunier, G. 2007. *Darfur: The Ambiguous Genocide*. London: Hurst.

Rahama, A. A. and D. M. Elhussein. 2005. A Case Study of the Nuba Mountains. In *Inter-communal Conflict in Sudan. Causes, Resolution Mechanisms and Transformation*. Building Peace through Diversity Series. Ahfad

University for Women, Omdurman.
Rex, J. 1986. *Race and Ethnicity.* Milton Keynes: Open University Press.
Richardson, J and J. Lambert. 1985. *The Sociology of Race.* Lancashire: Causeway Press.
Rosaldo, M. Z. 1993. Women, Culture, and Society: A Theoretical Overview. In: M. Z. Rosaldo and L. Lamphere, eds. *Woman, Culture and Society.* Stanford, CA: Stanford University Press.
Runger, M. 1987. *Land Law and Land Use Control in Western Sudan.* London, Atlantic Highlands: Ithaca Press, pp. 49–51.
Scherrer, C. 1999. Towards a Comprehensive Analysis of Ethnicity and Mass Violence: Types, Dynamics, Characteristics and Trends. In: H. Wiberg and C. Scherrer, eds. *Ethnicity and Intra-State Conflict.* Abingdon: Ashgate, pp. 52–88.
Schwartz, T. 1976. Introduction. In T. Schwartz, ed. *Socialization as Cultural Communication: Development of a Theme in the Work of Margret Mead.* Oakland, CA: University of California Press, pp. i–vii.
Shaddaad, M. Z. 1987. Some Recent Trends. In: F. Deng, ed. *The Search for Peace and Unity in the Sudan.* Washington DC: Wilson Centre Press, pp. 29–35.
Sharkey, H. 2003. *Living with Colonialism:Nationalism and Culture in the Anglo-Egyptian Sudan.* Berkeley, Los Angeles, London: University of California Press.
Sikainga, A. A. 1993. Northern Sudanese Political Parties and the Civil War. In: M. W. Daly and A. A. Sikainga, eds. *Civil War in the Sudan.* London and New York: British Academic Press, pp. 78–96.
Slatin Pasha, S. 1930. *Fire and Sword in the Sudan, 1879–1895* (2nd edn). London: Edward Arnold.
Smith, A. 1981. *The Ethnic Revival.* Cambridge: Cambridge University Press.
Strauss, A. 1991. *Creating Sociological Awareness: Collective Images and Symbolic Representations.* New Brunswick, London: Transaction Publishers.
Sudanese Strategic Report. 1998. Centre for Strategic Studies. Khartoum, Sudan.
—— 2000. Centre for Strategic Studies. Khartoum, Sudan.
Svoboda, T. 1985. *Cleaned the Crocodile's Teeth: Nuer Song.* New York: Greenfield Review Press.
Tanner, V. 2005. Rule of Lawlessness: Roots and Repercussions of the Darfur Crisis. Interagency Paper, January.
Theobald, A. B. 1965. *Ali Dinar: Last Sultan of Darfur, 1898–1916.* London: Longman.
Thomson, A. 2004. *An Introduction to African Politics* (2nd edn). London and New York: Routledge.
Toubia, N. and A. Rahman, eds. 2000. *Female Genital Mutilation: A Guide to Laws and Policies Worldwide.* London: Zed Books.
Vail, L. 1989. Introduction: Ethnicity in Southern African History. In: I. Vail, ed. *The Creation of Tribalism in Southern Africa.* London: James Currey, pp. 1–20.
Verney, P., D. Johnson, W. James, M. A. Mohamed Salih, S. M. Kuol and A. Hassan. 1995. *Sudan: Conflict and Minorities.* Minority Rights Group, International Report.
Wipper, A. 1984. Women's Voluntary Associations. In M. J. Hay and S. Stichter, eds. *African Women South of the Sahara.* London, New York: Longman, pp. 69–86.

Yongo-Bure, B. 2009. Marginalization and War: From the South to Darfur. In S. M. Hassan and C. E. Ray, eds. *Darfur and the Crisis of Governance in Sudan: A Critical Reader*. Netherlands: Cornell University Press and Prince Claus Fund Library, pp. 68–83.

English-language online

Althaus, F. A. 1997. Female Circumcision: Rite of Passage or Violation? *International Perspectives on Sexual and Reproductive Health: A Journal of Peer-Reviewed Research*, 23 (3), Guttmacher Institute. Available at: <https://www.guttmacher.org/journals/ipsrh/1997/09/female-circumcision-rite-passage-or-violation-rights> [accessed 2 February 2017].

Amnesty International. 2004a. Sudan: 'Too Many People Killed for No Reason'. Available at: <https://www.amnesty.org.uk/press-releases/sudan-too-many-people-being-killed-no-reason> [accessed 7 February 2004].

—— 2004b. Sudan, Darfur Rape as a Weapon of War: Sexual Violence and its Consequences. Available at: <https://www.amnesty.org/en/documents/AFR54/076/2004/en/> [accessed 20 May 2013].

Chigwata, T. C. 2015. Decentralization in Africa and the Resilience of Traditional Authorities: Evaluating Zimbabwe's Track Record. *Regional and Federal Studies*, 25 (5), 439–53. Available at: <http://dx.doi.org/10.1080/13597566.2015.1121873> [accessed 31 October 2016].

Cobham, A. 2005. Causes of Conflict in Sudan: Testing the Omar. Working Paper Number 121. Available at: <www3.qeh.ox.ac.uk/pdf/qehwp/qehwps121.pdf> [accessed 20 July 2011].

Darfur Information Centre. 2015. Darfur Population. Available at: <www.darfurinfo.org/dialup/mainFrameset-4.htm> [accessed 20 June 2016].

Darfur Peace Agreement (DPA), Government of Sudan (GOS) and Sudan People's Liberation Army/Movement (SLA-Minawi) 2006, 5 May. Signed in Abuja, Nigeria. Avaialble at: <http://www.un.org/zh/focus/southernsudan/pdf/dpa.pdf> [accessed June 2009].

DRCD (Darfur Relief and Documentation Centre). 2010. Fifth Population and Housing Census in Sudan – An Incomplete Exercise. Geneva (Switzerland). Available at: <www.pambazuka.net/images/articles/470/Sudan.pdf> [accessed 14 April 2011].

Firth, R. 1959. Problem and Assumption in an Anthropological Study of Religion. *Journal of the Royal Anthropological Institute of Great Britain and Ireland*, 89 (2), 129–48. Available at: <www.jstor.org/stable/2844265> [accessed 12 December 2016].

Itto, A. 2006. Guest at the Table? The Role of Women in Peace Processes. Peace by Piece: Addressing Sudan's Conflicts. Accord issue 18, 56–9. Pact Sudan/Alex Dianga Available at: <www.c-r.org/downloads/Accord18_19Guestsatthetable_2006_ENG.pdf> [accessed 18 February 2017].

Morton, J. F. 1996. Land Resources in Darfur Region, Sudan: Prisoners' Dilemma or Chaos Outcome? *Journal of Development Studies*, 33 (1), 63–80. London: Frank Cass. Available at: <https://papers.ssrn.com/sol3/papers2.cfm?abstract_id=2157607> [accessed 8 October 2016].

Morton, J. 2011. How to Govern Darfur. Available at: <www.jfmorton.co.uk/pdfs/How%20to%20Govern%20Darfur.pdf> [accessed 19 September 2016].

Nolen, Stephanie, 2005. A Year after Kabila Declaration on Darfur: 200,000 Deaths. *The Globe and Mail*. Available at: <https://www.sudantribune.com/spip.php?article8625> [accessed May 2015].

O'Fahey, R. S. and Tubiana, J. 2007. Darfur: Historical and Contemporary

Aspects. Available at: <https://org.uib.no/smi/darfur/A%20DARFUR%20WHOS%20WHO3.pdf> [accessed 5 March 2017].

Pedersen, Thomas T., Transliteration of Arabic. Available at <https://transliteration.eki.ee/pdf/Arabic_2.2.pdf> [accessed March 2008].

Pugalenthi, P. and D. Livingstone. 1995. Cardonolides (Heart Poisons) in the Painted Grasshopper Poecilocerus Pictus P. Available at: <www.jstor.org/stable/25010156?seq=1#page_scan_tab_contents> [accessed 15 September 2011].

Seekers of Truth and Justice, 2000. *The Black Book: Imbalance of Power and Wealth in Sudan.* Available at: <www.sudanjem.org/sudan-alt/english/books/blackbook_part1/book_part1.asp.htm> [accessed 24 December 2010].

Smith, C. 2014. What Makes us Generous. Available at: <https://generosityresearch.nd.edu/new/48736-what-makes-us-generous> [accessed 13 February 2016].

UN Report. 2004. Report of the International Commission of Inquiry on Darfur to the United Nations Secretary-General, Pursuant to Security Council Resolution 1564 of 18 September 2004. Available at: <http://www.un.org/zh/focus/southernsudan/pdf/dpa.pdf> [accessed June 2010].

UNDP. 2017. About Sudan. Available at: <www.sd.undp.org/content/sudan/en/home/countryinfo.html> [accessed 20 February 2017].

Arabic printed sources

Abdel-Jaleel, M. A. 2003. ʾanmāṭ wa ʾitijāhat al-hijrah fī Dārfawr wa ʿalāqatuha bil-tanmiyyah (Types and Trends of Migration in Darfur and their Connection with Development). In: A. E. Mohamed, M. A. Abdel-Jaleel, S. Ombadda and M. E. Saif, eds. al-tanmiyyah miftāḥ salām dārfawr. Sudan: Centre for Peace Studies, Juba University and Friedrich Ebert Foundation, pp. 162–222.

Ahmed, N, E. R. 1998. ʾAsbāb al-nizāʿāt al-qabaliyyah al-taqlīdiyyāh wa al-mustaḥdathāh fī al-Sūdān. (Causes of Traditional and Modern Tribal Conflicts in Sudan). In: A. E. Mohamed and, E. I. Wadi, eds. *ruʾā ḥawl al-nizāʿāt al-qabaliyyah fī al-Sūdān.* Khartoum: Institute of Afro-Asian Studies, Khartoum University, pp. 139–60.

Al-Gaddaal, M. S. 2002. *Tārīkh al-Sūdān al-ḥadīth*, 1820–1955 (The Modern History of Sudan, 1820–1955). Markaz Abdalkarīm Marghanī (Abdalkarīm Marghanī Centre).

Al-Tunisi, M. O. 1965. *tashḥīdh al-ʾazhān fī sīrat bilād al-ʿarab wa-l-Sūdān* (Entertaining the Intellect with Stories from the History of the Lands of the Arabs and the Blacks) (Sudan). Cairo: al-Dār al-Maṣriyyah Publishing Company.

Bashar, Z. M. 2003. ʾāliyāt taḥqīq l-taʿāyush al-silmī wasaṭ al-majmūʿāt al-qabaliyyah fī Dārfawr: dirāsat ḥālat muʾtamarāt al-ṣulḥ al-qabalī (Mechanisms for Attaining Peace among Tribal Communities in Darfur). Unpublished MA dissertation. Institute of African Studies, University of Khartoum.

Bilal, A. A. 2003. niẓām al-ḥukm wa namaṭ al-tanmiyyah fī al-Sūdān:al-ʾikhḍāʿ bayn al-markaz wa al-ʾaṭrāf (System of Governance and the Patterns of Development in the Sudan: Control between the Centre and Peripheries). In: A. E. Mohamed, M. A. Abdel-jaleel, S. Ombaddah and M. E. Saif, eds. *al-tanmiyyah miftāḥ salām Dārfawr.* Sudan: Centre for Peace Studies, Juba University and Friedrich Ebert Foundation, pp. 131–49.

Fadul, H. I. 1998. *ruʾā ḥawl al-nizāʿāt al-qabaliyyah fī al-Sūdān* (Insights on Tribal Conflicts in Sudan). Khartoum: Institute of Afro-Asian Studies, Khartoum University, pp. 227–42.

Haggar, A. A. 2003. *al-bu'd al-siyāsī li-l-ṣirā' al-qabalī fī Dārfawr* (The Political Dimension of the Tribal Conflict in Darfur). Sudan: Sudan Mint Company, pp. 211–36.
Ibrahim, A. A. 2007. 'aṣīl l-mārkisiyyah: al-nahḍah wa-l-muqāwamah fī masīrat al-ḥizb l-shuyū'ī l-Sūdānī (Originality of Marxism: Renaissance and Resistance in the History of the Sudanese Communist Party). Dār al-'amīn lil-'anashr wa al-tawzī' (al-'amīn for Publishing and Distribution).
Idrees, N. M. 2001. tajribat al-jam'iyyah l-Sūdāniyyah li-l-tanmiyyah. (The Experiment of the Sudanese Association for Development). In: Sudan Studies Centre Forum, al-mar'ah wa-l-'ibdā' fī al-Sūdān (Women and Creativity in Sudan), pp. 245–75.
Khair, M. A. 2001. 'amal l-mar'ah 'adat taḥawwul 'amm 'istighlāl. (Women's Work: Is it a Tool for Change or Exploitation?). In: Sudan Studies Centre Forum, al-mar'ah wa-l-'ibdā' fī al-Sūdān (Women and Creativity in Sudan), pp. 90–124.
Manzool, A. M. 1998. al-qabīlaha wa-l-qabaliyyah wa-l-ṣirā' fī l-sūḍān: 'ishkāliyāt al-mafāhīm wa l-siyāsāt (Tribe and Tribalism and Conflict in Sudan: the challenges of concepts and policies). In: A. E. Mohamed and E. I. Wadi, eds. ru'ā ḥawl al-nizā'āt al-qabaliyyah fī al-Sūdān. Khartoum: Institute of Afro-Asian Studies, Khartoum University, pp. 139–60, 71–98.
Masajid, A. A. 1995. 'al-'idārah al-'ahliyyah fī l-Sūdān. ḥālat qabīlat al-rizaygāt (Native Administration in Sudan: The Case of al-Rezeiqat Tribe). Unpublished BA Dissertation. Sudan: Department of Economics, Faculty of Economics and Social Studies, University of Khartoum.
Mohamed, A. E. 1998. al-taghyīr fī al-mujtama' wa 'atharahu fī al-ṣirā' al-qabalī fī al-Sūdān: bi-'ishārah khāṣah 'ilā Dārfawr (Societal Change and its Impact on Tribal Conflict in Sudan: the Case of Darfur), in A. E. Mohamed and E. I. Wadi, eds, ru'ā ḥawl al-nizā'āt al-qabaliyyah fī al-Sūdān (Insights on Tribal Conflicts in Sudan). Khartoum: Institute of Afro-Asian Studies, Khartoum University, pp. 33–69.
—— 2003b. Naḥwa tajāwuz ḥālat al-'iḥtirāb fī Dārfur: al-madkhal al-tanmawī (Overcoming the State of War in Darfur: The Development Approach). In: A. E. Mohamed, M. A. Abdel-jaleel, S. Ombaddah and M. E. Saif, eds. 'al-tanmiyyah miftāḥ al-salām fī Dārfawr' (Development is the Key to Peace in Darfur). Sudan: Centre for Peace Studies, Juba University and Friedrich Ebert Foundation, pp. 21–75.
—— 1998. al-taghayyur fī al-mujtama' wa 'atharuhu 'alā l-ṣirā' al-qabalī fī al-Sūdān: bi-'ishārah khāṣah li-'iqlīm Dārfawr. (Change in Society and its Impact on Tribal conflict in Sudan: with a Specific Reference to the Region of Darfur). In A. E. Mohamed and E. I. Wadi, eds. Khartoum: Institute of Afro-Asian Studies, Khartoum University. pp. 33–69.
Mohamed. A. E. and E. I. Wadi, eds. 1998. ru'ā ḥawl al-nizā'āt al-qabaliyyah fī al-Sūdān (Insights on Tribal Conflicts in Sudan). Khartoum: Institute of Afro-Asian Studies, Khartoum University.
Mohamed, F. E. 1982. 'al-turāth al-sha'abī lī qabīlat al-ta'āyshah (Folklore of Ta'aisha Tribe). Silsilat Dirasat fi El-Turath El-Sudni (Sudanese Folkloric Studies Series), 29. Khartoum: Department of Folklore, Institute of Afro-Asian Studies, Khartoum University.
Mohammed, Y. A. 2003. Dārfur, al-malāmiḥ al-ṭabī'iyyah wa muqawwimāt al-tanmiyyah (Darfur's Physical Features and the Foundations for Development). In: A. E. Mohamed, M. A. Abdel-Jaleel, S. Ombaddah and M. E. Saif, eds. al-tanmiyyah miftāḥ salām Dārfawr. Sudan: Centre for Peace Studies,

Juba University and Friedrich Ebert Foundation, pp. 207–22.
Mukhtar, E. A. 1998. ḥawl l-nizāʿ al-qabalī fī dāfūr: ʾasbābuhu wa muʾtamarāt faḍḍ al-nizāʿāt wa ʾālīyāt tanfīdh al-qarārāt (On the Tribal Conflict in Darfur: its Causes, Conflict Resolution Conferences and the Mechanisms for the Implementation of Resolutions). In: A. E. Mohamed and, E. I. Wadi, eds. ruʾā ḥawl al-nizāʿāt al-qabaliyyah fī al-Sūdān. Khartoum: Institute of Afro-Asian Studies, Khartoum University, pp. 257–306.
Musa, A. M. 2009. Dārfur min ʾazmat dawlah ilā ṣirāʿ al-quwwā ʾal-ʿuẓmā. (Darfur from the State Crisis to the Competition of Great Powers). Arab Scientific Publishers and Aljazeera Studies Centre.
Ombaddah, S. 2003. muʾashirāt al-ghubn al-tanmawī fī al-rīf al-Sūdānī (Indicators of Development Grievances in Rural Sudan). In: S. Ombaddah and M. E. Saif, eds. al-tanmiyyah miftāḥ salām Dārfawr. Sudan: Centre for Peace Studies, Juba University and Friedrich Ebert Foundation, pp. 76–130.
Salih, E. M. M. 1998. ʻmusabbibāt al-ṣirāʿ al-qabalī fī al-Sūdān (Causes of Tribal Conflict in Sudan)'. In: A. E. Mohamed and, E. I. Wadi, eds. ruʾā ḥawl al-nizāʿāt al-qabaliyyah fī al-Sūdān. Khartoum: Institute of Afro-Asian Studies, Khartoum University, pp. 99–138.
Shuqayr, N. 1981. tārīkh al-Sūdān (The History of Sudan). Beirut: *Dar* al-Jeel.
Takana, Y. 1997a. Taqrīr ʾan al-ṣirāʿ al-qabalī bi-Dārfur (A Report on Tribal Conflict in Darfur). Unpublished report.
Takana. Y. S. 1997b. Tadahwur al-mawārid al-ṭabīʿiyyah wa ʾatharuh ʿalā al-nashāṭ al-raʿawī bi-Dārfur – taqrīr li-lajnat ḥimāyat al-bīʾah (The Decline of Natural Resources and its Impact on Pastoralism in Darfur). Khartoum: A Report to the Environment Protection Group.
Takana. Y. S. 1998. al-ʾāthār al-mutaratibbah ʿalā ẓāhirat al-ṣirāʿ al-qabalī bi Dārfawr (The implications of the phenomenon of tribal conflict in Darfur(. In: A. E. Mohamed and E. I. Wadi, eds. ruʾā ḥawl al-nizāʿāt al-qabaliyyah fī al-Sūdān. Khartoum: Institute of Afro-Asian Studies, Khartoum University, pp. 195–226.

Arabic online

Al-Asbat, O. 2014. al-ḥakkāmāt lisān ḥāl al-qabīlah wa mustawdaʿ tārīkhih wa turāthihā ('Famous among Tribes of Western Sudan: al-Hakkamat, the Spokespersons of their Tribes and the Repository of their Heritage and History'). Available at: <http://sudanvoices.com/?p=8487> [accessed 22 May 2015].
Zakariya, M. 2012. gharb Dārfur... al-ḥakkāmāt, al-ʾintiqāl min al-fitnah ilā al-ḥikmah (West Darfur … al-Hakkamat and their transition from sedition to wisdom). Available at: <www.sudaress.com/alintibaha/14002> [accessed 21 April 2012].

Index

A'aiyasha Al-Austowania, Hakkamah 88, 89
Abbala, nomadic Arabs 10, 14, 17, 18, 21, 28, 30, 31, 33, 35, 36, 40, 45, 65, 73, 76, 81, 82, 103, 111, 137, 169
Abboud, General Ibrahim 98
Abd ad-Dayyem, of the Nawaahya clan 37
Abdalla, A. H. 143
Abdel-Jaleel, M. A. 17, 28
abductees 91, 92, 104, 112
abeed (transl abīd) 15, 82, 83, 102
abid, *see* abeed
Ab-Karank 80, 81
Abu-Darag 35
Abuja 39, 155, 159, 164, 182
Abu Salim, M. I. 20
abuses, *see under* human rights
Abu Tamūnga 76
Abyei 35
access, to Dar 37, to education 15, 96, land 36 n.7, 79, to political office 16, to production resources, 20, 21, 29, 32, 33, 44, 102, 117, 176
activism 1, 99, 102, 113, 117, 179
activist(s) 1, 2, 43, 104, 124
actor(s) 5–8 *passim*, 19, 66, 84, 90, 106, 108, 117, 125, 128, 129, 149, 153, 155, 165, 175, 177
Adam, Fatma al-Doom 140
Addis Ababa Accord 180
administering (see, *Dar* administration)
administration and Ethnicity in Darfur 19–26 *passim*, tribal administration 3, 18 n.7, 116, 162 n.30, 183
administrative tool 20, elected councils 23, flexible 18, legacy 22, micro states 29, 38–40 *passim*, 71, 78, 79, new framework 25, 28, states 10, structures 19, tribes 12
Adult Literacy Campaign (ALC) 105
advocacy 7, 54, formative CAP 106, 117, gender mainstreaming 156, al-Hakkamat and peace 158–65, 166, 172, NIF's 122, 123, 129, for nonviolence 165, peace 84, for rights and justice 45, for women's rights 146, peace for 149, 166, 188; advocates 106; advocating, al-Hakkamah 80, 102, for conflict 128, 173, UHS 121, *see also under* CAP
Africans, indigenous 14, 15, 17, 28–9, 34, 37, 41, 45, 72, 82, 82 n.35, 83 n.36, 93, 102, 104, 130, 188
African tribes 18, 56, 103, 120, 162
Ageed 7, and *Khail*-Hakkamat 52, 53, 61, 62, 66, military organisation 68–72, 77, 84, 94, 110, 118, 129, 152, 156, 166, 169, 173, 174
Ageed al-Augada (also Ageed al-Shooshah) 52, 69, 70–1, 84
agency 4–8, al-Hakkamat's agency and power 46, 129, 142, 169, al-Hakkamat's 46, 47, 49, 52, 54, 64–6, 68, 72, 73, 88, 90, 111, 112, 114, 118, 120, 123, 124, 129, 142, 149, 154, 158, 159, 165, 167–9, 171, 172, 174, 177, Human agency 90, 174, women's agency 8, 64, 184, 191, women's agency, power and resolve 64

agents 34, 94, 177, 191, of aggression 5, 169, territorial 79, 181, 184, 186, 190
agreement(s) 31, CPA, DPA 39, 104, 155, 157, 159, 164, 165, land policies and peace 38–9, 153, 166, reconciliation 37 n.9
agriculture 11, 23, 33, mechanised 1 n.2, 28, 32, 185, subsistence 23, 185
agro-pastoral 10, 17–18, 137, agro-pastoralists 21, 28, 76
Ahmed, N. E. R. 35, 36, 82
Ajaweed 38, 150–1, 154, 156, 159 Ajwadi 150
Ali, M. 20
Ali al-Haj, the Muslim Brother 179
Ali Dinar, Sultan 9, 30, 34, 86
Ali Noah 107
Aljazeera 28
Allen, J. 63
Althaus, F. A. 53
al-Tunisi, M. O. 5 n.6; p87
America 116, American-led 116
Amir 24–5
Amnesty International 83, 104, 143
ancestor(s) 15, 20, 23, 34, 107, 162, 179, common 12, 14
Anglo-Egyptian 6, condominium 9, 15, 19, 20, *see also* condominium
animal Husbandry 11, 18, 185
Anlu 63–4 *passim*
Appiah, K. A. 13
Arabian Peninsula 10
Arabised 16
Arabism 16, 102, pan- 16, 29, 187
Arab(s) 5–6, 12, 12 n.2, 15, 17, 28–9, 30–4 *passim*, 35–7, 37 n.9, 38, 41, 45, 72, Abbala 30, 40, affiliates 10, Baggara 8, 21, Chadian 25, 35, 36, 37, 45, 81–2, 139, 187, congregation 40, horsemen 43, landless 24–6, and Masalit 81–3, 93, 103–4, 131, militia(s) 3, 42, 101, 102, 104, 114, Misseriya 35, non- 15, 102, race and ethnicity 14–18, against Zurga 135, 137, 139, 162, 188
arbitration(s) 39, 47, 61, 62, 71, 75, council 61
ARCC (Arms Repossession and Confiscation Campaign) 105
Ardaybah, al-Rahad 57, 58
armed Struggle 2, 25, 27, 29, 99, 102–3, 131, 187
arrangements 79, 130, 185, administrative 21, military 68, traditional 32
al-Asbat, O. 65
association, with government 159, 187, with military 67, 173, with violations 94
Atbara River 35
atheism 97, atheists 102
atrocities 5, 44, 44 n.16, 65, 93–4, 101, 104, 128–9, 143, 150, 166, 188
AU (African Union) 2
audience 48, 55, 106, 116, 127, 133, 139, 147, 148, 152, 158, 160, 169, 171–4
Augada, *see* Ageed
authentic 4, 68, 172, authentic Hakkamat 148, 160, 170–2, authentic performance 171, authentic production 170, tribe-based Hakkamat 160
authority 4, African women of 64, of al-Hakkamat 66, 81, 84, 88, 120, 125, 158, 166, 175, of arbitration 47, 60–4, 67, 71–2, centralised 19–23 *passim*, 25, 28, charismatic 73, divine 20, moral 38, native 37, 41, sign of 52, 53, of spirit mediums 175–81, state 34, traditional/tribal 18, 22, 23, 28, 29, 30, 32, 39, 46, 66, 100, 175
autonomous 19, 90, 175, 176, 183
awareness 53, 144, 174, 189
Awlad Rashid 159
Azrag, Mariam Adam, Hakkamah 140
Azzah Gaidoom, Hakkamah 106

Badri, B. Y. 150–1
Baggara 4 n.5, 8, 14, 17–21 *passim*, 30–7 *passim*, 40, 44–7 *passim*, 54, 56, 60–2, 66, 68, 69, 72, 73, 84, 88, 93, 95, 101–5 *passim*, 108–14 *passim*, 116–17, 119, 120, 124–6, 128–37 *passim*, 145–8, 154, 162, 165, 169, 170, 172, 186, 81, 83, Baggari 47, 61, 74, 111, 133
Bahr el Ghazal 4 n.5, 127 n.46
Bala Furash, a place 158
ballot Paper 182
banditry 24, 105, 109
bandits 42, 139, 161

Bani Helba 17, 18, 31, 32, 34–6 *passim*, 43, 47, 61, 62, 70, 72–8 *passim*, 92, 94, 103, 108, 152, 156–8 *passim*
Bani Shangol, a place 125
Baraka, Mohamed al Amin Salih 37
Baramkah 7
Barth, F. 13, 19
Bashar, Z. M. 3, 35, 37, 72
al-Bashir, President Omer Hassan 2, 36, 82, 83, 105, 107, 108, 122, 125, 170
al-Batail, Hakkamah 139
battle(s), also battlefield(s) 1, 3, 43, 60, 82, 91–3, 106–8 *passim*, 127, 127 n.46, 132, 133, 135, 141, 144, 173, escorting to 142
Beja 10, 35, 99
Belal Nagur, Sheikh 85
belligerence 72, 186, belligerency 41, belligerent voice 95, 111, 128, 130, 149, 166, 189, 190, *see also under* voices(s)
Berger, I. 176
Berghe, P. L. 12, 14
Beshmirga 137
Bilal, A. A. 17
Birgidawi 152
Bit Hassaan, Hakkamah 81, 88, 89, 90, 133
blood 83, blood-based 14, group 126 n.39, money 155, relationship 18, relative 143
Bolad, Daud Yahya Ibrahim 43, 93, 101–4 *passim*, and al-Hakkamat advocacy 106–8, 112, 113, 115, 141, 187
Borday 52
Border Guards 36
Borno, a tribe 17
al-Boshan 50, 52
boy(s) 48, 51, 58, 132, 146 n.50
boycott(ing) 60, 61, 63, 64
British 24, 53 n.29, 59, 86, 177–8, 184–5
Browne, G. W. 30
Buram 106, 107, 109, 111, 152
Burr, M. J. 10, 25, 101, 103, 143
Bushara, Major General Ibrahim 103
Butcher, H. 20, 176, 184
Cadal, a dance 51
camel herders 17, 21, 77, *see also* Abbala
campaign(s) 31, 43, 88, 91, 93, 101, 105, 106, 113–15, 117, 122, 124, 128–30 *passim*, 132, 133, 136, 139, 144–6 *passim*, 148, 172, campaigners 105, 129
camp(s), village(s) 8, 48, 54, 66, 87, 94, 145, 165, 168, 172, 180
CAP (Comprehensive Advocacy Project) 106, 117, 129
captive(s) 91, 92, 121 n.20, 139
Caton, S. C. XV, XVI
celebration(s) 7, 48, 52, 57, 60, 91, 105, 107, 118, 141, 146, 165
ceremonial 19, 141
ceremony(ies) 18, 52, 53, 58, 60, 93, 146, 176
charisma(tic) 49, 54, 69, 73, 81, 151
Cheater, A. P. 175, 176
Chief(s) 7, 18–20, 24, 52, 68, 69, 70, 82, 84, 93, 158, 162
chiefdoms 19, 117, 176, 177
Chigwata, T. C. 176
chivalry 47, 56
circumcision 49, 53 n.29, 58–9, 146, 146 n.50, *see also* FGM
class(es), clientele 96, privileged 97, urban middle and working 98
clientelism *see* patron(s)
clients 3, 41, 100
coalition 36, 41, 42, 98
Cobham, Alex 132
coercion 126, 157, coerced 117, coercing 118
Collins, R. O. 10, 25, 101–3, 143, 184
colonial(s) 4, 6, 9, 13, 15, 20, 22, 28, 63, 64, 96, 97, 98, 100, 151, 184, 201
colonialists 63
combatants 28, 43, 44, 45, 68, 95, 106, 113, 114, 115, 127, 132, 133, 135, 141, 144
combative role 184, 188
commissioner 84, 85
common ancestor 12–14, 31, 47
community(ies) 3, 5, 6, 7, 13, 20, 23, 25, 27, 30, 31, 33, 36–7 *passim*, 39, 47–9 *passim*, 56 n.36, 59, 61, 64, 65, 68, 69, 73, 78, 83, 88, 91, 95, 97, 111, 117, 120, 129, 130, 133, 135,

139, 143, 145, 147, 148, 167, 168, 169, 171–2, 180, 182, 184, 186, 188, 190, community-centred 49
al-Computer, a Hakkamah 139
CONCORDIS 33
Condominium Administration 9, 15, 20, 22, 86, 96, 98, *see also* Anglo-Egyptian
conflict 1, 2, 25, history of 30–1, root causes 31–44, 40, 44, 68, 72, 73, 78, 81, 84, 88, 103, 113, 160
conflict resolution(s) 3, 6, 21, 30, 32, 38, 69, 85, 112, 150, 151, 155, 156–7, 159, 164, 189, 191
Congo, the Democratic Republic of 10
conquest 6, 20, 22, 182
co-option 40, 100, 105, 115, 126, 129, 131, 148, 149, 168, 169, *see also under* al-Hakkama(h/t)
council(s) 7, 22, 23, 35, 62, 64, 69, 71, 78, 79, 151, 153, 154, 156, 176, 182, 183, 190
councillor 34, 35, 79
counter-insurgency 3, 43, 101, 104, 124
coup d'état 98, 104, 128, 180
cowardice 60, 61
CPA Comprehensive Peace Agreement (CPA) 39, 127, 155, 159
CPAF (Creative Popular Arts Festival) 105
Cunnison, I. 88

Dabaka, Issa, Nazir of Bani Helba 77
Dabanga 86
al-Dabe, a dance 52
al Dabi, General Mohamed Ahmad 36, 82
Dahab al-Madīnāh 92
Daju 9, 17, 151–2, Dijawi 152
Dali Code 150
Dallookah 147
Daly, M. W. 24, 97, 103
Dambare 20
Damsoro 144
Dancer(s) 50, 76, 77, 124
Daoud, Mahmoud Adam 126, 170
Dar(s) (also Dār) 1, 4, 5, 9, 11, 12, 17–22, 24–30, 29–31, 32–8, 41, 43–5, 53, 55, 57, 60, 69–71, 73–5, 77, 79, 81–3, 85, 86, 93, 101, 106–10, 117, 118, 121, 125–7, 132, 135–40, 142–4, 152–4, 157, 160–3, 179–82, 185–7, 189, 191, 192, *Dar* Aba Diima 19, 63, 122, 183, *Dar* Abbo Uumo 19, *Dar* al-Takanawi 19, *Dar* Bakhota 38
Dar administeration 3, 19–21, 29, 68,
Darb l-Marʿūb 62
Darfur 9, 25, 26, 31, 40, 43, 68, 72, 103, 109, 126, 132, 155, 173, 179, 183–92
Darfur Information Centre 21
Davies, J. 21
death toll 2, 110, 132
decision-making 68, 71, 156, 185
defence institution(s) 2, 3, 36, 45, 52, 68, 69, 173
Deisa, village 183, 43
demeaning 61, 63, 76, 85
democracy 40, 98
Democratic Unionist Party (DUP) 25, 41, 97
demographic 40, 165
demonise 7, 135
Deng, F. 14, 16
development 1, 5, 13, 26, 32, 39, 45–7 *passim*, 69, 82, 87, 99, 118, 121, 146, 148, 167, 175, 178, 179, 186–92 *passim*, 201, sustainable 175, 192
devolution 19
differentiation 13–15, 17, 19, 41, 44, 54
Diid koor (war songs) 88
Dijawi, *see* Daju
Dimingawi 18, 18 n.7, 117
Diraige, Ahmed Ibrahim 25, 40
dispute(s) 3, 6, 16, 20, 21, 30, 32, 34, 35, 38, 39, 45, 52, 68, 69, 72, 73, 74, 75, 79, 80, 84, 110, 139, 150–2, 158, 159
divide-and-destroy 3
divide-and-rule 40, 45, 101, 103, 128, 178, 186
divorce 77 n.24, 121 n.20, 88, 152
Dodo, O. 23, 69
Doha Peace Agreement 39, 165
domain(s) 6, 13, 16, 40, 97, 151, 166, private 151, 153, 156, public 5, 5 n.6, 14, 66, 146, 191
domestic politics 12, 15, 17, 40, 41, 44, 96, 99, 101–3, 113–15, 131
double-edged sword 94, 95, 184
DPA (Darfur Peace Agreement) 39, 104, 155, 156, 159, 164–5

DRCD (Darfur Relief and Documentation Centre) 12
drought 25, 27, 31, 32, 74, 79
DUP (Democratic Unionist Party) 25, 41, 97

ears, cut off 92–5
Eastern Sudan 10, 12, 35, 39, 99
Eastern Sudan Peace Agreement 39
education 15, 18, 26, 32, 39, 47, 58, 70, 132, 146, 153
egalitarian 128
Egemi, O. 33, 39
Eid 7, 48, 57, 80, 146
El-Battahani, A. 2, 3, 4, 40
elections 24, 25, 39–41, 45, 97, 145
El Hassan, B. 34, 35, 150
Elhussein, D.M. 38, 151
El Obeid, H. 45
emancipation, of women 90
Emara(t) policy 25, 26, 29, 36, 81, 187
embargo 116
emigration 31, 32, 167, 172
emirates (*see*, *Emarat*)
employment 16, 17, 96, 126, 127, 174
empowerment 128–30 *passim*, empowered 151, 164, empowering 87, 128, 129, 166
environment 16, 51, 72, 101, 149, 164, 174, 175, 177, environmental 2, 6, 24, 32, 44, 153, 166
escorting fighters 81, 131, 134, 139, 127, 141, 143, 173
estate (see, *hakura*)
estates of privilege 20
ethics 49, 90, 149, 174, ethical 68, 73, 144
Ethiopia 10
ethnicity(ies) 12, 16, 17, 34, 135, 139, 143, 145, 148, 173, 180, 187, administration and 22–6, 40, 41, 72, 76, 82, 94, concept of 12–21, ethnic group(s) 2, 3, 9, 10, 13–18 *passim*, 20, 25, 34, 35, 39, 41, 72, 82, 85, 96, 99, 104, 151, 156, 164, 168, 173, 182–3, 187–8, 189, 190, interpreting armed struggle in 102–4, ethnic rapprochement 40, ethnicisation 16, 40, ethnicising 40
exclusion 4, 16, 101, 102, 156, 189
existential resource 37
exploit(ation) 4, 14, 100, 102, 128, 145, (-ative) 166, (-ed) 28, 129, (-ing) 19, 41

al-Fadl, Mohamed, Governor of West Darfur 25
Fadul, H. I. 36
failure 23, 71, 80, 94, 151, 153, 183, 189 of DPA 165, of reconciliation 4, 155, 158
famine 24, 27, 41
al-Fashir 2, 8, 24, 36, 53, 65, 86, 102, 104, 105, 158, 165, 171
favouritism 15, 40, 41, 97
Faza' 7, 23, 49, 60, 62, 69, 140, 173, 185
Feinman, I. R. 129
Fellata 17, 35 n.6, 72, 152
female(s) 4, 6, 20–1, 46–8, 49, 50, 56 n.36, 58, 66, 85, 87, 104, 120, 121 n.20, 124, 132, 143, 147, 159, 169, 172, 184, 185, 190–2, civil servants 126–7, Islamic model 125–6
female spirit mediums 4, 175–80, 184, 191
female title(s) 6, *iiya basi* 5, 86, 87, *iiya Kuuri* 87, Queen Mother 5, 87, *see also* Mayram
feminist 128, 129
Ferguson, J. 167
festival(s) 53, 80, 105, 158, 165, 173
FGM (Female Genital Mutilation) 53 n.29, 59
Firth, R. 13, 175, 176
Flint, J. 25, 36, 37, 40, 42, 43, 82, 101, 103, 105
flag, of Sudan 52, 107, of tribe 52, 119, 147, 171
folklore(ic) 53, 105, 106, 118, 120, 121, 125, 124, 142, 165, 158, 170
Forogay, a tribe 120
Foucault, M. 167
framework(s) 2, 3, 6, 12, 13, 22, 25, 60, 61, 68–9, 71, 79, 115, 153, 176, 185, 190, 191
Francis, D. 100
fraudulent, census 12, Hakkamat 120
freedom 118, 119, 124, 143, 147, 169, of speech 90
Fruzzetti, L. 14
Fukui, K. 13
fuqara 21

Fur, a tribe 5, 9, 11, 17, 18, 20, 21, 22, 24, 25, 28, 30–7 *passim*, 40–1 *passim*, 43, 47, 53, 56, 72, 90–1 *passim*, 94, 101–3, 137, 139, 140, 150, 151, 184, 187
fursan 69, 103

Gadarif 28, 35
Garang, John, the SPLA/M Leader 108, 133, 160, 194, 195
gatekeepers 117, 124, 145
al-Gaydoomah, a dance 50
General Union of Nuba Mountains 99
gender 4, 15, 146, 153, 155, 168, 176, 184, 190, analysis 6, -based violence 2, 104, 130, 143, 186, constraints 90, consultants, 156, 156 n.11, development and 5, 188, 190, discrimination 87, 176, division of labour 5, 151, 153, 186, 191, equality 130, gendered 48, mainstreaming 156, perspective 155, policy 184, power relationships 4, 6, 46, 47, 48, 87, 155, 184, 191, -prejudiced 155, recognition 58, -sensitive 59, 156, 159, -subordinating 66, 190
al-Geneina 24, 33, 35, 105
generosity 49, 56, 57, 66, 141, 142, 148, 154, 170, 172
genocide 2, 102
geography, of Darfur 9–12
geopolitics 31, 35, 45, 101, 187
gharaabah 14
al-Gidairee, a dance 51, 124
Giddens, A. 168
Gimir, a tribe 17, 24, 32, 35
Giraida, a village 139
girl(s) 47, 48, 49, 51, 58, 59, 62, 80, 89, 104, 147
Gordon Memorial College 15
Gould, C. C. 175
governing elites (also ruling elites) 1, 3, 12, 14–16, 19, 25–9 *passim*, 28, 40, 41, 46, 97, 99–104 *passim*, 115–16, 121, 124, 128, 139, 143, 147–8, 172, 174, 187, 189, 191
grassroots 101, 157, 158
gratuity(ies) 57, 84, 91, 171
'grinder of speech' 115, 169
guardian(s) 59, 144
guidance 6, 36, 38, 121, 174, 176
Gupta, A. 167

Haaland, G. 18, 20
Habboba 87
Hadaleel, a tribe 93
Hadday 50 n.13
Haggar, A. 25, 32, 35–8, 42, 43, 82, 103
Hajj, a ritual 122, 125, 172, 174
al-Hakkama(h/t) 4–6, 8, 34, 40, 45, 46–66, 70–4, arrogated 91, 171, civil wars and 132–45, composition(s) 9, 48, 72, 122, 149, contribution(s) 6, 40, 49, 91, 108, 115, 133, 144, 148, 169, co-option of 115–29, exclusion of 156–7, and government 105–14, influence 4, 6, 47, 50, 63, 65, 71, 74–85, 92, 109, 112, 113, 117, 119–20, 122–6, 132, 146, 153–7, 159, 165, 171–4, 184, 186, 188–91, *al-Khail-* 48, 50, 52, 53, 54, 62–3, 71, 79, 80, *al-mada* 50, 52, 54, 78, mores of 72, nicknames 92, 139, 140, nomination of 52, 71, objectives, roles, attributes and relationships 7, and peace 150–6, 157–65, projection of 48–50, recognition of 50, 54, 66, 88, 92, 95, 109, 174, 189, remodelling of 115, 119–21, representation(s) 111, 114, 147, social and political significance of 46–8, 70, 114, 148, 172, 175, social recognition of 50, 191, *al-Soja* (*al-Boshan*) 50, 50 n.13, 52, surrogate 119, 120, as territorial agents 79, 181, 184, 186, in town 119, 168–75, 148, at-Turath 120, vis-à-vis spirit medium 175–80, *see also under* voices(s) and women
hakura (*hawakir*) 20, 21, 23, 34, 35, 37, 38, 87, 93 n.69, acknowledgement of 38
Hale, S. 124
Hamza, M. N. 23
Hans, W. 46
harah 144
ḥaras al-ḥudūd, *see* Border Guards
al-Harimah, a dance 50
Harir, S. 24, 32, 36, 40, 41–3 *passim*, 103, 132 n.3

Hassan, S. M. 13
Hegeir, Sheikh Ali Wad 85
hegemony, cultural 1, 96, 99, Islamic 98–9
Helbawi(yah) 56, 74, 75, 76, 77, 78, 83, 89, 157
heroism 66, 93–4 *passim*, 120, 141
al-Hijair al-Abyad 151
al-Hilu, Abdel Aziz Adam 107, 107 n.16
homeland(s) 9, 20, 24, 27, 33, 35, 37, 82, 106, 161, 182
horsemen(man) 7, 30, 43–4, 50 n.13, 52–4, 59, 60–1, 68–70, 71, 74, 76–8, 84, 91–4 *passim*, 102– 4, 107, 109–10, 116, 120, 129, 134, 139–40, 141, 144, 147–8, 163, 165, 173–4, 179
hostility(ies) 37, 44, 94, 102 n.6, 157, 160, 186
household(s) 49, 53, 86, 150
Hubbani(a) 35, 50, 52, 54, 55, 61, 72, 107, 109, 110, 112, 151, 152, 154
Hughes, E. C. 13
human rights 59, 83, 104, 121, 156, 192, abuses 2, 143, against Africans 130
humanitarian crises 2, 27, 31,
Hussain, a dance 52

Ibdoos, a village 139
Ibrahim, A. A. 103
Ibrahim, Lieutenant Colonel Abuelgasim 105
Id al-Goor village 79
Idd al-Fursan 62, 103
Idd al-Fursan Rural Council 62
identity(ies) 7, 8, 9, 13, 14, 16, 19, 34, 54, 55, 76, 113, 117, 120, 125, 126, 167–74, 178, 182, 187, politics 91, 115, 121, social 112, 191, stereotyped 191, *see also under* ethnicity, al-Hakkamat and women
ideology 13, 29, 42, 54, 87, 91, 98, 101, 106, 121, 135, 143, 176, 187
idiom 123
Igbo society 63, women 63, 63 n.69
iiya basi 5, 86, 87
iiya Kuuri 87
illiteracy 122, 154
illiterate 66, 122, 153, 154, 191
impunity 44, 104
incentive(s) 90, 105, 119, 171
inciting 34, 75, 81, 85, 104, 112, 120–2 *passim*, 128, 132, 140, 141, 150, 169, 185
independence 2, 15–17, 28, 59, 64, 96, 98, 100, 118, 177, 178, 179
indigenous 14, 17, 18, 26, 28, 34, 36, 37, 79, 82–3, 105, 132, 150, 162, 187
indirect rule 22
indoctrination 49, 121–6, 173, *see also* socialisation
inequalities 12, 27 n.19, 99, 114
influence, *see under* al-Hakkamat
institution(s) 2, 6, 16, 22, 24, 33, 39, 40, 46, 52, 54, 57, 59, 64, 66, 71, 100, 101, 102, 104, 105, 111, 112, 114, 117, 118, 119–21, 124, 125, 129, 144–8 *passim*, 151, 155, 156, 159, 167–9 *passim*, 175, 179, 183, 186–92 *passim*
insurgency(ies) 1–3 *passim*, 7, 17, 27, 30, 31, 35, 43, 72, 93, 99, 101–4, 109, 114, 124, 131, 132, 135, 141, 160, 169, 187–8
insurgent(s) 1, 3, 12, 38, 93, 102–4 *passim*, 107, 109–10, 112, 117, 131, 132, 135–6, 139, 173, 188, 191
al-Iraij, a dance 50
al-Jilaihah, a dance 52
Islamism 16, 187
Islamist(s) 98, 101, 102, 103, 105–6, 121, 127, 135–6, 143, 154
al-Itaireenah, a dance 52
Itto, A. 88, 155, 158

Jallaba 31
jalsat inbisatah 115
Jamal Ragad, a dance 50
Jangal, a dance 82
Janjawiid 3, 24, 36, 36 n.8, 43–5, 65, 82–3 *passim*, 93, 101, 104, 137, 139, 143, 160, proclamation 83
Jebel Marrah 9, 11, 33, 35, 125
JEM (Justice and Equality Movement) 99, 101, 102, 103
Jihad 103, 106, 116, 132, 144
Jihadi war 88
Judiyah 38, 150, 151

Kajikaji, a village 140
Kaltoum Bit Gawindah, Hakkamah 110

Kamal el-Din, A. 46
Kanfus 86
Kapila, M. 2
Kapteijns, L. 5, 24
kasrat-qaid 90
Kassala 28, 35
Kassū, nickname of a Hakkamah 92
Katila, a town 35 n.6
al-Katim, a dance 50–2, 80, 170
Kebkabiya 27
Keira 9, 12 n.2
al-khail 50
Khair (Sikhah), al-Tayeb Ibrahim Mohamed 105, 125, 147
Khair Allah, E. D. 50 n.16
al-khalawi 84 n.40, 138, 163, al-khalwa 84, 123
Khalid, M. 1, 3
Khan 13 n.4
Khartoum 12, 24–6, 28, 41, 111, 120, 123, 147
khashum Bait 14, 49, 68, 79
Khuzam, a tribe 159
kingdom(s) 9, 11, 12 n.2, 19, 97, 176
Kirainik Mosque 82
Kom women of Cameroon 63
Kordofan 4, 10, 12, 35, 37, 39, 42, 43, 47, 88, 97, 102, 111, 169
Kurita, Y. 22, 99
Kushite kingdoms 12 n.2
KUSU (Khartoum University Student Union) 101
Kutum 34, 65

land 11, 19–22 *passim*, 25 n.18, 27, 64, 68–9, 75–7, 82, 83, 112, 136, 138, 143, 148, 152, 158, 163, 170, 172, 176, 177, 182, 184, conflict and 31–9, land grabbing 33, 36, landless 24, landowners 17, 26, 79, redistribution of 34, tenure 37, 38, tribal ownership 5 n.6, 34, 35, 79, 183, 191, *see also* law(s)
law(s) 32, 33, 37, 59, citizenship 37, communal 23, customary 23, 32, 185, land 31, 34, 183, and order 24, 30, 31, 42, 45, 68, 71, 102 n.6, 183, 185, *see also* ULA and *shari'a*
legislation 22, 31, 34–5, 36
Libya(n) 10, opposition 35, 45, 186
Lister, R. 90, 175
livelihood(s) 10, 12, 14, 17, 18, 21, 23, 26–8, 32, 27, 44, 45, 46, 48, 58, 60, 64, 108, 112, 146, 182, 185, sustainable 26, 29, 32, 146, 186
livestock 17, 21
Livingstone, D. 89 n.55
local conventions 21, 30–2 *passim*, 150
loyalty 12, 12 n.3, 14, 17, 25, 40, 41, 57, 71, 83–5 *passim*, 100, 105, 116, 123 n.28, 133, 143, 145, 168, 169, 180
lyrics 51

al-mada 48, 50, 78, *see also* al-Hakkamat
al-mada Hakkamat 54
Mahamid, a tribe 30, 35
al-Mahdi, Mohamed Ahmad 9
al-Mahdi, Sadiq 40
Mahdiya 9, 20, 85, 86 n.43
Mahriyah, a tribe 30, 34, 72–81, 82, 156, 158
Manzool, A. M. 12, 14
Marareet, a tribe 34
marginalisation 27 n.19, 102, 114, 185
Markakis, J. 13
Maryam al-Gheerah, Hakkamah 139
Masajid, A. A. 53 n.28
Masalit, a tribe 5 n.6, 17, 24 n.17, 24–6, 29, 33–8 *passim*, 37 n.9, 72, 81–4, 90, 139, 187, *see also Dar*
masarat, *see murhal (maraheel)*
Mathiang, T. 88, 155
Mayram 87, 93 n.69, 184–5
Ma'aliya, a tribe 35, 72, 84, 85
Medard, J. 100
mediation 2, 111, 150, 158, 189, mediated 4, 38–9, 158
mediators 156, 159
Meidob, a tribe 32
Mhondoro 176, 177, 178–9
militarisation, of society 31, 41–5, of al-Hakkamat 126–30, of women 128
military 15, 36 n.7, 42, 43, 44–5, 65, 82 n.34, 94, 98, 101–2, 104, 105–6, 115, 123, 126–9, 132, 141–2, 145, 172, 173–4, 180, 188, 184, 186, 188, 190, military organisation 67, 114, military training 115, 126–9, 130, *see also* Ageed Military Organisation

militia(s) 3, 28, 36, 39, 40, 42–5, 65, 82, 94, 101–2, 102–3 n.8, 104, 107–9 *passim*, 129, 133, 141, 144, 161, 173, 190, pro-government 28, 141, 173, 190
Misseriya, a tribe 35, 42, 102, 127, 152, 164, Humur 111, Zurug 111
Mikiri and Mitiri 63
Mohamed, A. E. 3, 4, 11, 21, 23, 24, 31, 33, 35, 36, 150, 151
Mohamed, F. E. 93 n.69
Mohamed Salih, M. A. 42, 102–3 n.8
Mohamed Tairab, Sultan 87
Morton, J. F. 15, 18, 20, 21, 22, 31
motivation(s) 81, 103, 133, 149
movement(s) 16, 30, 99, 102–9 *passim*, 131, 178–80
Muhammad al-Fadl, Sultan 31
Murahaliin 42, 102
Al-Murhakah 50 n.16, 75, *Murḥākt-al-gawl* 168, *Murhakt al-gol* 115
murhal (*maraheel*) 32, 33, 165, 168, 172,
Musa, A. M. 36, 40
Musa, S. M. E. 153
Musa Hilal 36, 38
mutilations 95
Muslim Brotherhood 17 n.6, 42 n.15

nafir 7, 173, 185
Nagel, J. 14
al-nahb al-musallah 105
Native Administration 6, 22–6 *passim*, 29, 32, 35, 39, 41, 68–9, 71, 78, 112, 151, 183
Natsios, A. S. 15
Nawaahya 37 n.10
Nazir (Nuzzar) 18, 24, 57, 61, 65, 70, 77, 90, 109–10, 112, 116, 117, 151, 158, 162, 182
NCP (National Congress Party) 4, 17 n.6, 42, 43, 59, 90, 117, 122, 126, 130, 153, 154, 165, 168, 172, 178
Ndebele, kingdoms of 176
negotiation(s) 2, 71, 82, 104, 111, 136, 153–7, 162, 164, 166,180, 189
negroid 103
neopatrimonialism 99–105, 115, 186, 187, patrimonialism/patrimony 100
NGOs, *see under* organisations
Niblock, T. 97, 99
nicknames, *see under* al-Hakkamat
NIF (National Islamic Front) 4, 17, 24, 25, 36, 40, 42, 59, 88, 91, 98, 99, 101, 103, 105–6 *passim*, 117, 121, 125, 126, 128, 132, 135, 143, 144, 145, 146 148, 168, 187, 190, *see also* NCP
Nigeria 63, 156, 185
Nile Valley 10, 21, 29, 39, 43, 185
Nimeiri 42, 78, 98
Nkore 176
Noah, Ali 107
Nolen, Stephanie 2
nomad(s/ic) 4 n.5, 10, 17, 18, 20, 21, 21 n.13, 32–3, 47–8, 66, 68, 74, 75, 77, 122 n.24
Nuba 83, *see also* abeed
Nuba Mountains 15, 16, 37–8 n.10, 88, 99, 102, 132, 151
Nubian(s) 10, 12 n.2
*Al-Nuggar*ah 51, 93 n.69
al-Nur, Abd al-Wahid Muhammad 101
nuzzar, *see* Nazir
Nyala 8, 23, 24, 62, 81, 89 n.57, 91, 105, 110, 115, 117–18 *passim*, 119, 121, 125–7 *passim*, 130, 132, 139–42 *passim*, 144, 146–7, 157, 160, 164, 165, 167, 169–73 *passim*
Nyala Court 139–40 *passim*
Nyika 20

oath of divorce 77, 152, *see also under* divorce
El Obeid, H. 45 n.17
obligation(s) 6, 47, 50, 54, 66–7, 68, 74, 91, 111, 131–48, 171, 186, 188, 189
Omda (Omad) 18, 37 n.10, 64, 82, 110, 151, 154, 158, 161, 182
Omodiya (Omodiyat) 37–8 n.10, 70
oppression 99, 102, 128
organisations, civil society 59, 121, 156, aid 24, 138 n.26, 162, conventional defence 3, NGOs 5, 8, 18, 33, 59, 173, women's 59, 121, 145–6, 190
Ostor, A. 14
ownership, land, *see under* land
Oxfam 5, 24
O'Barr, J. 64
O'Brien, J. 12
O'Fahey, R. S. 19–21, 31, 86
O'Neill, N. 12

pacification 111
Palace, royal 87 n.51, Sultan's 86
pan-Arab(ism/ist) 16, 26, 29, 45, 187
parade(s) 120, 169, tribal (Zaffa) 53, 53 n.28, 69, wedding 51
pastoral(ist/s) 10, 14, 17, 18, 21, 30, 32–3, 32 n.4, 35, 36, 39, 46, 66, 76–7, 111, 112, 182
patriarchal 127, 151, 156, 168, 176, 181, 190
patron(s) 22, 25, 40, 97, 100, 146, 187, patronage 26, 41, 100, patron-client 25, 26, 42, 97, 100, 146
PDF (Popular Defence Forces) 36, 42–3, 82, 108, 112, 126, 127, 132, 141, 144, 174
peace 2, 4–6, 33, 38–9, 71, 74, 82, 84, 102, 108, 116, 122, 128, 130, 137, 138, 140, 147, 149, 152, 153, 155–6, 169, 170, 174, 181, 183, 188, 189, advocacy 7, 84, 157–65, 190, agreements 31, 37 n.9, 38, 39, 104, 151, 153, 156, 157, 159 n.19, 164, 165, 166, and Hakkamat 150–3, 157, 190, negotiations 82, 155, 156 n.11, peacebuilding 33, 156, 159, 165, 166, 190, 191, resettlement 4, 6, 104, 159, 150, 164, 189
peer(s) 48, 58, 144, 169
Penal Code 59
peripheral regions 1, 96, 99, 114
phenomen(a/on) 30, 47, 72, 126, 171
philanthrop(y/ic) 49, 52, 60
PIM (Popular Information and Media) 105
platform(s) 48, 58, 60, 66, 121, 142, 153, 159, 172, 173, 174, 179
poet(s) 46, 47, 105
poetic 47, 52, 81, 85, 90, 94, 119, 130, 141, 190
poetic diction 66, 74, 123, 132
polarisation 38, 40, 45, 96, 99, 115, 128, 130, 137, 178, 187, polarised group 41, polarised society 188, *see also* social fragmentation
policies 1, 14–16 *passim*, 23, 28, 25, 26, 29, 31, 34, 36, 37, 38–9, 40, 44, 79, 82, 83, 96–9 *passim*, 102–3, 121–2, 126, 127, 129, 130, 132, 149, 153, 173, 183, 184, 185, 186, 187
politician(s) 8, 25, 37, 110, 117, 145, 149, 154, 155, 174
politics 12, 13, 15, 17, 40, 41, 44, 91, 96–7, 99, 100–04, 115–16, 121, 128, 129, 131, 138, 144, 145, 149, 186
population(s) 9, 12 n.1, 13, 16, 17, 26, 28, 32 n.3, 38 n.10, 51, 59, 82, 93 n.69, 115, 119, 128, 135, 165, 182, census 12, 13, 21 n.14, 28
power(s) 1, 4–8 *passim*, 21, 23, 24, 27, 27 n.19, 53–5, 60, 63, 64, 65, 70, 83, 88, 91, 96–100 *passim*, 103, 109, 116, 117, 121, 131, 147, 167, 174, 176, 178, 182, 184–5 *passim*, 190, 191, administrative 40, 183, brokers 85, 114, 119, 166, 188, 189, charismatic 54, discretionary 37, financial and judicial 22, personal 99, politics 100, postcolonial 4, 22–6, power devolution 19, pragmatic 184, precolonial 19–21, relationships 4, 6, 9, 14, 16, 31, 32, 44, 46, 47, 66, 87, 118, 155, 167, 174, 182, 184, 185, 191, sectarian 100, sharing 99, 114, spiritual 20, vacuum 28,
practitioners, folklore 105
preaching sessions 84
proclamation, *see under* Janjawiid
pro-government militias, *see under* militia(s)
propaganda 103, 104, 106, 112
provocat(ing/ion/ive) 2, 40, 51, 65, 72, 75, 81, 80, 87, 95, 105, 109, 110, 111, 134, 154, 183, 190
Prunier, G. 4, 11, 16,23, 36, 103
Pugalenthi, P. 89 n.55
punishment(s) 63–5, 61, punished 80
public and private domains, *see* domain(s)
Public Order Act 125, 143

Qanoon Dali 150
Queen Mother, *see* female title(s)
quest, for peace 4, 166, for aggression 74
quwaat al-Salaam, see Peace forces

race 12–14 *passim*, and ethnicity 14–19, and tribe
race-based 15
racial assimilation 96–113 *passim*, backgrounds 19, 104, basis, 131, 132, differences 28, differentiation 14, 15, 17, 19, 41, discrimination

9, 83, 96, 102, 187, eminence 16, hatred 94, 105, 131, ideology 135, notions 188, perceptions 3, 40, polarisation 45, 135–6, policies, prejudice 82, pretensions 4, religious consciousness 131 and, supremacy 34, terms 96, 114, 131, tune 136
racialised 34, 187
racism 1, 13, 14, 16, 31, 83
Rahama, A. A. 38, 151
Rahman, A. 59
raiding 41, 65, 69, 81, 84, 104, 139–41 *passim*
raids 62, 65, 91, 139, 173
Raja 141, 142, 144
al-Rājma, Hakkamah 92
rape 186, mass 2, 104
Rashaiyda, a tribe 35
recitation(s) 8, 48, 50, 54, 56, 61, 70, 80, 81, 86, 92, 105, 111, 112, 122, 125, 134, 136, 138, 139, 141, 147,152, 158, 161, 170, 185
reconciliation 2–4, 6, 36, 37 n.9, 38–9, 69, 75, 104, 108, 137, 150–9, 161, 163, 164–6, 188, 189, 190, 191
reconciliation conferences 3, 36, 36 n.7, 38, 151, 152, 154–5
referendum 10
reform 22, 29, 38, 39, 64, 100, 101, 183, 186
resolution(s), *see under* conflict resolution(s)
revenge 42 n.14, 50 n.16, 65, 76, 77, 80, 81, 93, 111, 154, 157
rewards 41, 50, 65, 91, 92, 94, 95, 97, 119, 129, 171
Rex, J. 14
Rezeiqat, a tribe 17, 31, 32, 34, 35, 37, 38, 41–3, 48, 53, 65, 72, 74–5, 81, 83, 84–5, 91, 94, 102–3 n.8, 110, 111, 132, 158, 159, Rezeiqi 94, 148
Richardson, J. 13 n.4
ridiculing 27, 61, 62, 63, 65, 85, 108
Rihaid al-Birdi 69, 79
Rosaldo, M. Z. 153
royal 5, women 6, 86, 87 n.51, 88, 184, 185, household 86
Runger, M. 23

Sa'ada 140
Sadiq al-Mahdi, Premier 40, 98
Safiyaat, royal court Hakkamah 86, 185
Sāhat al-Mawlid 160
al-Salaam Forces 36, 82, 126
Salamat, a tribe 34, 35, 54, 72, 78–81, 89, 154, 156–7, Salami 35, 54, 70 n.8, 80, 88, 90
Salih, General al-Zubair Mohamed, 105, 108, 125
Salih, E. M. M. 21, 32 n.4, 33
Sanjak, a dance 50, 52
Save the Children Sweden 59
Saylay, a village 86
Scherrer, C. 2 n.4, 13
Schwartz, T. 58
sectarian 25, 41, 45, 97, 100
security 2, 5, 15, 21, 23, 31, 36, 42, 45, 53, 70, 71, 83, 84, 105, 161, 183, 188
sedentary communities 5 n.6, 17, 18, 21, 28, 30, 31, 33, 35, 36, 48
sedition 93, 121, 165
Seekers of Truth and Justice 27 n.19, 43, 99
self-censorship 6, 61
settlement, in Darfur 17, 30, 32, 33, 35, 36, 37, 47, 76, 79, 102, 118, 119, 132, 166, 172, 180, 187, by confiscation 33
settlers 26, 79
Shabbaal 124 n.32
'shackle breaker' 90
Shaddaad, M. Z. 99
shame 61, 62, 113, 136, 141
shari'a 36 n.7, 53, 59, 91, 103, 121–2, 143, 180
Sharkey, H. 15, 16
Shartai (*Sharati*) 18, 18 n.7, 161, 162 n.30, 182
shartayas 19
al-Sheikhat 6, 56, 56 n.36, 71 n.9, 117–18, 121, 127 n.45, 130, 144–7, 151, 164, 173, 185
Shendi 16 n.5
al-Shibriyah 122
Shona 20, 176–8 *passim*, 180, 181
Showbash 50 n.12
Shuqayr, N. 20, 88
Sibdo, a village 53
Sikainga, A. A. 97
Singita, a village 140
'sitting on a man' 63–4, 63 n.69

Sixth Infantry Brigade 127
Slatin Pasha 85
SLM/A 99, 101–3
slogans 106, 123, 130, 149
Smith, A. 41
Smith, C. 56, 57
social acculturation 48–9
social ceremonies 146, *see also* circumcision
social change 18, 167–75, 177, 179, 181
social fragmentation 83
social harmony/cohesion 2, 5, 38, 79, 114, 128
social integration 22, 31, 160, 164–6 *passim*
social occasion(s) 48, 49, 65,70, 78, 117, 173
social organisation(s) 12, 18, 47, 66, 82, 186
social services 26, 29, 32, 148, 190
socialisation 13, 56–60, 66, and indoctrination 173
Socialist Party 97
society(ies) 1 n.2, 5, 6, 9, 12–18 *passim*, 20, 22, 25, 28, 29, 31, 40, 41, 46, 54, 58–64 *passim*, 66, 69, 71–2, 79, 81–4, 88, 90–1, 94, 96, 100–1, 104, 120, 122, 124–6 *passim*, 128, 135–6, 146, 150, 153–6 *passim*, 165, 172, 174–8 *passim*, 180–1, 184, 185, 187–91 *passim*
solo, performance 50 n.16, 52
songs 47–51 *passim*, 50 n.16, 58, 59, 61, 64, 72, 75, 77– 81 *passim*, 88, 106, 107, 109, 115, 120, 122, 123, 127, 135, 137, 139, 143, 157, 160, 165, 172
sovereign(ty) 20, 29, 37, 39, 47, 79, 111, 183
Spaulding, J. L. 21 n.13, 31
speech(es) 64, 66, 86, 88, 90, 107, 108, 110, 1111, 116, 123, 125, 132, 134, 139, 146, 149, 151, 154, 160, 169
spiritual charms 152,
spirit medium(s/ship) (also female spirit mediums) 4, 143, 175–80, 184, 191, spirit possession 175, territorial 176–7
spiritual authority 176, powers 20, 175, tribal-territorial mediums 177, worth 37
SPLA/M (Sudan People's Liberation Army) 39, 41, 42, 43, 88, 101, 103, 106, 107 n.16, 108, 127 n.46, 132, 133, 141, 152, 160
spokesperson(s) 7, 38, 65
staff-like stick 52, 53
stakeholders 4, 7, 183
status quo 19, 28, 149
stereotype(d/s) 6, 51, 121, 153, 159, 174, 176, 186, 191
Strauss, A. 168 n.3
subordination, female, 87, 176, women, 121, 156, 190
sub-Saharan 41
subsistence 133, 137, *see also under* livelihoods
Sudan Liberation Movement/Army (SLM/A), *see* SLM/A
Sudanese Women's Union 145
Sudanese Strategic Report 26–7
Sultanate(s) 5, 9–10 *passim*, 12 n.2, 16 n.5, 18 n.7, 19–24 *passim*, 24 n.17, 30–1 *passim*, 37, 56 n.36, 86 n.43, 86 n.46, 87, 150–1 *passim*, 182, 184, 185
sultan(s) 5, 20, 21, 24, 30, 31, 87, 162
sustainable resettlement 71
sustainable peace and reconciliation, *see under* peace
Suwaybah 57
Svoboda, T. 88
symbol(s/ic) 55, 56, 60, 61, 62, 66, 69, 70, 80, 81, 90–2 *passim*, 110, 110 n.23, 113, 120, 121, 146, 151, 162 n.27, 170, 178, 184, 187, 188
Symiayat, a tribe 34

taboo 90
Taja, Mayram 86, 87, *see also* female titles
*al-tajamu*ʿ al-ʿarabi, the Arab Congregation 40
Takana, Y. 18, 32 n.3, 39, 40
tangeet (see, *showbash*)
Tanner, V. 103
Ta'aisha, a tribe 17, 34–5, 69, 72, 78–81 *passim*, 80, 88–9, 93 n.69, 133, 154, 156–7, Ta'aishi 52, 57, 69, 79, 80, 89
Tergam, a tribe 35, 72, 140
territory(ies) 6, 9, 12, 19, 20, 39, 41, 47, 67, 111, 129, 167, 176–7, 180,

191, boundaries 67, 167
Thomson, A. 99, 100 n.9
throwing-spears 18 n.8
Tora Bora 65, 110, 137
Toubia, N. 59
traditional, arrangements 32, authority 4, 18, 23, 39, 63–4, 66, 69, 79, 125, 175, 176, 181, 191, belief systems 176, clients 41, frameworks 185 handicrafts 17, institutions 24, 40, 46, 156, leaders 22–4 *passim*, 32, 101, mediation 150, organisations 69, 130, 159, parties 25, 101, role 38, weapons 18 n.8, 18–19, 75,
transform(ation) 3, 19, 22, 29, 34, 35, 41, 45, 52, 64, 66, 83, 96, 98, 100, 102, 106, 111, 117, 121, 125, 128, 147, 149, 159, 164, 166, 168 n.3, 169, 172, 180, 183, 188, 189, 190
tribal, administration 3, 25, 70 n.7, 116, 183, affiliation 44, 45, authority 23, 29, 30, 44, 95, 100, 124, 182, 183, boundaries 46, 181, chief(s) 18 n.7, 68, 70, 82, 117, 182, community(ies) 23, 117, 120, conflict 34, 37 n.10, 38, 72, 81, 119, 150, 185, constituencies 19, 25, culture and norms 59, defensive mechanisms 184, disputes 34, 45, elites 39, endorsement 171, groups 2, 21, 26, 39, 111, 168, identity and culture 34, 76, 191, influence 39, institutions 33, 100, 111, 115, 117, 187, 190, land ownership 34, leaders 8, 21, 23, 24, 25, 38, 39, 41 n.13, 52, 65, 71, 93, 188, links 10, loyalty 17, militias 42–4, 101, 102, 141, 173, notables 40, objectives 24, organisation 20, parades 53 n.28, 69, polarisation 38, relations 103, sanctuaries 191setting 6, society 180, SOS call 61, sovereignty 29, 79, 183, support systems 24, territories 6, 9, 47, 180, 191,
tribalism 12, 14, 17, 41, 104, 117, 178
tribe's Military Commander 52 n.26, *see also* Ageed
triggers 3, 14, 103
Tubiana, J. 24
Turco-Egyptian(s) 9, 20, 22, 31, 85 n.42, 97 n.2, 98

UAF (Union of Art and Folklore) 142
UHS (Union of Hakkamat and Sheikhat) 117–21, 126, 127, 130, 144, 146, 169, 173, 190
ULA (Unregistered Lands Act) 22, 23, 34, 44, 79, 183
Um Jalul 35, 36
Um Keddada, a town 105
Umm Balola, village 139
Umm Digaynah, a dance 76
Umm Jekkay, a dance 50
UN Report 104
UNDP 10–11, 33
UNICEF 59
UNIFP 59
urban 6, 12, 17, 19, 21, 27, 53 n.29, 97 n.3, 98, 121, 145, 149, 153, 156, 167, 173–4, 180
urbanisation 39, 83, 164, 167–8
utilitarian 117, 148, 185

Vail, L. 13
Verney, P. *et al.*, 43
vested interests, 3, 96, 100, 103, 143, 166, 168, *see also* ruling elites
violation(s) 59, 60, 83, 94, 102 n.6, 110, 174
violators 60, 63, 67
violence 2, 5–6 *passim*, 30–1, 38, 44, 59, 65, 74–5, 81–2, 84, 99, 104, 114, 124, 128–9, 30, 133, 135, 141, 143, 148, 150, 159, 161, 165, 166, 169, 179, 186, 190, 191, *see also under* gender
voice(s), ethnic 41, 184, of female peers 58, government 115, al-Hakkamat's 95, 112, 114, 116, 120, 128, 129, 130, 133, 146, 149, 159, 164–5, 166, 184, 186, 189, 190, rights groups 45, 99, of spirit medium 181, of wife 85, women 6, 88, 155, 156, 166
voluntary group (*Ajaweed*) 150
vulnerability, of Baggara 148, of rural people 186
vulnerable, Darfur 28, 163, women 48, 51, 56, 128, 130, 150, 186, 188, victims 4, villages 41
de Waal, Alex 25, 36, 37, 40, 42, 43, 82 n.34, 101, 103, 105
warmongering 7, 149, 170, 186, warmongers 166

weapons 18, 19, 42, 55, 65, 71, 75, 77, 78, 102, 104, 105–6 *passim*, 126, 132, 135, 139–40 *passim*, 164, 179, 187
wedding(s) 7, 48–9, 51, 53, 60, 73, 78, 88, *see also under* celebrations
welfare/wellbeing 5, 45, 47, 66, 100, 121, 125, 146, 148, 154, 171, 185
widow(s) 76, 87 n.51, 138, 147, widowed 160
wilayat 24
Wipper, A. 63
wisdom 23, 46, 87, 87 n.51, 111, 162, 165, 181
Wolad Kawoon 79
women 4–7 *passim*, 8, 27, 45 n.17, 46–50, 51, 56 n.36, 58, 59, 61–6 *passim*, 69 n.3, 76, 82, 85–8, 89–91, 104, 112, 113, 117–18 *passim*, 119–21 *passim*, 124–9 *passim*, 131, 133, 138, 143, 145, 146, 148, 150–1, 153–6, 157–60, 163, 164, 168, 170, 171, 173, 174–5, 176–7, 181, 182, 184, 185–6, 188–91, activists 124, African 63, 64, 130, 143, 166, Arab 45, 130, 143, Baggara 88, 119, 182, 190, consultants 164, dress 91, 62 n.63, empowerment 128, freedom of movement 143, Fur 20, inclusion 156, influence 175, Janjawiid 143, lactating 112, and mobilisation 85–8, national dress 62, 88, oppression 128, ordinary 49, 88, 146, 176, passive victims 166, 186 political experience 6, protest 113, representation(s) 87, 128, 153, representatives 130, rights 59, 63, 63 n.69, 128, 146, 190, 192, rural 4, 5, 8, 49, 52, 64, 90, 121, 128, 130, 150, 148, 151, 153, 155–7, 186, 188, 189, 191, Salamat 89, singers 120, Southern Sudanese 155, Ta'aisha 89, tribeswomen 119, 171, *see also* al-Hakkamat

yards, dance 50, public 147, 160
Yongo-Bure, B. 1
youth and youngsters 7, 28, 43, 44, 46, 48–9 *passim*, 50 n.16, 51, 54, 58– 60 *passim*, 62, 66, 70, 76, 80, 85, 88–9 *passim*, 91–2 *passim*, 102, 106, 106–7 *passim*, 111, 129, 132, 135–6 *passim*, 139, 143, 146–7 *passim*, 157, 160, 163, 165, 173, 180, 184, 192
Youth Union 146

Zaghawa 10, 17, 18 n.10, 24, 32, 32 n.1, 34, 37, 38, 72
Zakariya, M. 139
Zalingi 105
Zantoot 69 n.3
ZANU (Zimbabwe African National Union) 178
ZAPU (Zimbabwe African People's Union) 178
Zarā'ib al-Hawā 32
Zarga, Hakkamah 77
Zayadiyya, a tribe 32
Zimbabwe 4, 69, 143, 175–81, 184, 191
zone(s), buffer 41, climatic 10, 11, 18, conflict 2, 109, 151, 158, 188, operational 177, 179
Zurga 14, 17, 135, 162

EASTERN AFRICAN STUDIES

These titles published in the United States and Canada by Ohio University Press

Revealing Prophets
Edited by DAVID M. ANDERSON & DOUGLAS H. JOHNSON

East African Expressions of Christianity
Edited by THOMAS SPEAR & ISARIA N. KIMAMBO

The Poor Are Not Us
Edited by DAVID M. ANDERSON & VIGDIS BROCH-DUE

Potent Brews
JUSTIN WILLIS

Swahili Origins
JAMES DE VERE ALLEN

Being Maasai
Edited by THOMAS SPEAR & RICHARD WALLER

Jua Kali Kenya
KENNETH KING

Control & Crisis in Colonial Kenya
BRUCE BERMAN

Unhappy Valley
Book One: State & Class
Book Two: Violence & Ethnicity
BRUCE BERMAN & JOHN LONSDALE

Mau Mau from Below
GREET KERSHAW

The Mau Mau War in Perspective
FRANK FUREDI

Squatters & the Roots of Mau Mau 1905-63
TABITHA KANOGO

Economic & Social Origins of Mau Mau 1945-53
DAVID W. THROUP

Multi-Party Politics in Kenya
DAVID W. THROUP & CHARLES HORNSBY

Empire State-Building
JOANNA LEWIS

Decolonization & Independence in Kenya 1940-93
Edited by B.A. OGOT & WILLIAM R. OCHIENG'

Eroding the Commons
DAVID ANDERSON

Penetration & Protest in Tanzania
ISARIA N. KIMAMBO

Custodians of the Land
Edited by GREGORY MADDOX, JAMES L. GIBLIN & ISARIA N. KIMAMBO

Education in the Development of Tanzania 1919-1990
LENE BUCHERT

The Second Economy in Tanzania
T.L. MALIYAMKONO & M.S.D. BAGACHWA

Ecology Control & Economic Development in East African History
HELGE KJEKSHUS

Siaya
DAVID WILLIAM COHEN & E.S. ATIENO ODHIAMBO

Uganda Now • Changing Uganda Developing Uganda • From Chaos to Order • Religion & Politics in East Africa
Edited by HOLGER BERNT HANSEN & MICHAEL TWADDLE

Kakungulu & the Creation of Uganda 1868-1928
MICHAEL TWADDLE

Controlling Anger
SUZETTE HEALD

Kampala Women Getting By
SANDRA WALLMAN

Political Power in Pre-Colonial Buganda
RICHARD J. REID

Alice Lakwena & the Holy Spirits
HEIKE BEHREND

Slaves, Spices & Ivory in Zanzibar
ABDUL SHERIFF

Zanzibar Under Colonial Rule
Edited by ABDUL SHERIFF & ED FERGUSON

The History & Conservation of Zanzibar Stone Town
Edited by ABDUL SHERIFF

Pastimes & Politics
LAURA FAIR

Ethnicity & Conflict in the Horn of Africa
Edited by KATSUYOSHI FUKUI & JOHN MARKAKIS

Conflict, Age & Power in North East Africa
Edited by EISEI KURIMOTO & SIMON SIMONSE

Property Rights & Political Development in Ethiopia & Eritrea
SANDRA FULLERTON JOIREMAN

Revolution & Religion in Ethiopia
ØYVIND M. EIDE

Brothers at War
TEKESTE NEGASH & KJETIL TRONVOLL

From Guerrillas to Government
DAVID POOL

Mau Mau & Nationhood
Edited by E.S. ATIENO ODHIAMBO & JOHN LONSDALE

A History of Modern Ethiopia, 1855-1991(2nd edn)
BAHRU ZEWDE

Pioneers of Change in Ethiopia
BAHRU ZEWDE

Remapping Ethiopia
Edited by W. JAMES, D. DONHAM, E. KURIMOTO & A. TRIULZI

Southern Marches of Imperial Ethiopia
Edited by DONALD L. DONHAM & WENDY JAMES

A Modern History of the Somali (4th edn)
I.M. LEWIS

Islands of Intensive Agriculture in East Africa
Edited by MATS WIDGREN & JOHN E.G. SUTTON

Leaf of Allah
EZEKIEL GEBISSA

Dhows & the Colonial Economy of Zanzibar 1860-1970
ERIK GILBERT

African Womanhood in Colonial Kenya
TABITHA KANOGO

African Underclass
ANDREW BURTON

In Search of a Nation
Edited by GREGORY H. MADDOX & JAMES L. GIBLIN

A History of the Excluded
JAMES L. GIBLIN

Black Poachers, White Hunters
EDWARD I. STEINHART

Ethnic Federalism
DAVID TURTON

Crisis & Decline in Bunyoro
SHANE DOYLE

Emancipation without Abolition in German East Africa
JAN-GEORG DEUTSCH

Women, Work & Domestic Virtue in Uganda 1900-2003
GRACE BANTEBYA KYOMUHENDO & MARJORIE KENISTON McINTOSH

Cultivating Success in Uganda
GRACE CARSWELL

War in Pre-Colonial Eastern Africa
RICHARD REID

Slavery in the Great Lakes Region of East Africa
Edited by HENRI MÉDARD & SHANE DOYLE

The Benefits of Famine
DAVID KEEN

www.ingramcontent.com/pod-product-compliance
Lightning Source LLC
Chambersburg PA
CBHW070801230426
43665CB00017B/2451
* 9 7 8 1 8 4 7 0 1 2 6 5 4 *